GARLAND MEDIEVAL BIBLIOGRAPHIES
VOL. 19

MUSIC AND POETRY IN THE MIDDLE AGES

GARLAND REFERENCE LIBRARY
OF THE HUMANITIES
VOL. 1102

GARLAND MEDIEVAL BIBLIOGRAPHIES

MUSIC AND POETRY IN THE MIDDLE AGES

A Guide to Research
on French and Occitan
Song, 1100–1400

Margaret L. Switten

GARLAND PUBLISHING, Inc.
New York & London / 1995

Library of Congress Cataloging-in-Publication Data

Switten, Margaret Louise.
  Music and poetry in the Middle Ages : a guide to
research on French and Occitan song, 1100–1400 / by
Margaret L. Switten.
      p.   cm. — (Garland medieval bibliographies ;
vol. 19) (Garland reference library of the humanities ;
vol. 1102)
    Includes discography (p.   ) and indexes.
    ISBN 0-8240-4797-4 (alk. paper)
    1. Songs, Old French—France—Bibliography.
2. Songs, Provençal—France—Bibliography.   3. Music—France—500–1400—Bibliography.   I. Title
II. Series.   III. Series: Garland reference library of the
humanities ; vol. 1102.
ML128.M3S9   1995
016.7824'3'0944—dc20   94-33935
                                                                CIP
                                                                MN

Printed on acid-free, 250-year-life paper
Manufactured in the United States of America

CONTENTS

ACKNOWLEDGEMENTS

This book originated in a Workshop and Institute on the Medieval Lyric, supported by the National Endowment for the Humanities and held at Mount Holyoke College in the summers of 1986 and 1987, of which I was director. My first expression of gratitude therefore goes to the NEH, to Mount Holyoke College, and to colleagues who participated in this venture, from whose expertise I drew great profit: Margaret Bent, All Souls College, Oxford University; Kevin Brownlee, University of Pennsylvania; Jacqueline Cerquiglini, Université de Genève; Howell Chickering, Amherst College; Robert Eisenstein, Director of the Five College Early Music Program; Paul Hillier, University of California, Davis; Louise Litterick, Mount Holyoke College; Stephen G. Nichols, The Johns Hopkins University; Nancy Regalado, New York University; Leo Treitler, The Graduate School and University Center of the City University of New York. My thanks go also to the participants in the Institute for numerous rewarding insights.

The help of the Mount Holyoke College Library has been central to the completion of the book and is here gratefully acknowledged. Anne C. Edmonds, College Librarian on the Katherine Johnson Hatcher Endowment until her retirement this spring, has always generously supported Medieval Lyric enterprises. Marilyn Dunn, Librarian for Public Services, and the Reference and Interlibrary Loan staffs have given unstintingly of their time, far beyond the call of duty, to track down necessary but sometimes quite arcane information. I express my appreciation to M. Alexandra Salinas, Kuang-tien Yao, Anne Drury, Kathleen Egan Norton, Bryan Goodwin, Susan Fliss, and Phyllis Joyce. I am grateful also for help received from the Werner Josten Library of Performing Arts, Smith College. Photographs of the medieval manuscripts reproduced here with appropriate permissions have been provided by the Bibliothèque Nationale in Paris, by the Biblioteca

Apostolica Vaticana in Rome, and by the Bibliothèque
Interuniversitaire, Section Médecine in Montpellier.
Special thanks are due the Bibliothèque Interuniver-
sitaire in Montpellier for expert photographic assitance.

   To Mount Holyoke College also, I express appreciation
for sabbatical leaves which have permitted work on the
book to progress toward completion.

   Several colleagues have generously responded to my
requests for information on matters large and small. It
is my pleasant duty here to thank Wulf Arlt, Musikwis-
senschaftliches Institut, Universität Basel; Charles
Atkinson, Ohio State University, for advice on subjects
theoretical; Rebecca Baltzer, University of Texas,
Austin, for sharing with me her work on 13th-century
motet manuscripts; Jacqueline Cerquiglini, who read parts
of my introduction and bibliography at an early stage;
Joel Cohen, The Boston Camerata; Eglal Doss-Quinby,
Smith College; Lawrence Earp, University of Wisconsin;
Mark Everist, King's College London; Christopher Page,
Sidney Sussex College, Cambridge University; Vincent
Pollina, Tufts University. I also express great
appreciation to Nancy Holden-Avard, Mount Holyoke
College, for a careful proofing of the manuscript.

   I owe my greatest debts to those friends and colleagues
who have sustained the work from the beginning. Howell
Chickering, Amherst College, who was co-editor of the
Medieval Lyric Anthologies, read the entire manuscript
more than once, returning the drafts each time with a
wealth of judicious commentary. As always, I relied on
his faithful friendship, on his critical acumen, and on
his editorial expertise. Robert Eisenstein generously and
always cheerfuly allowed me to profit from his knowledge
of Early Music and of computers. Claire Benoit, Secretary
of the Mount Holyoke College French Department and of the
Medieval Lyric Institute, brought to the typing and formatting of the book her considerable computer skills and
a sustaining willingness to accomplish the enormous labor
of putting the diverse elements together, without which
the book would never have been completed.

PREFACE

French was always the language of the chanson,
as Latin was of the Mass.
--Donald J. Grout and Claude Palisca,
A History of Western Music[1]

Associations between music and the medieval vernaculars that arose in the geographical area we now call
France produced some of the most important and influential art forms from the Middle Ages. These art forms have
been widely studied disjunctively, both in the sense of
scholarly scrutiny of discrete types and of scholarly
treatment of poetry or music. Less often have they benefitted from synthetic treatment. This *Guide to Research*
proceeds from the related notions that it is both timely
and important to look more closely at poetry and music
together, and that the multiple associations between music and the Occitan and French vernaculars offer a particularly rewarding field for interdisciplinary study.

FOCUS AND GOALS

The primary focus will be on secular songs. Research
in recent years has exploded old notions and sought new
understanding of the diversity and richness of Occitan
and French secular repertories. And, as John Stevens
pointed out in the introduction to his book *Words and
Music in the Middle Ages*, much work on *secular* melodic
traditions remains to be done, although he has, himself,
made a powerful contribution to our understanding of
these traditions.[2] The secular repertories that form the
subject of this *Guide* were not cultivated in isolation.
They entertained relationships with songs in other vernaculars and in Latin, and they proceeded from a culture
characterized by numerous intersections between sacred

and profane. The links between early troubadour songs and
the versus from Saint Martial of Limoges, or the artful
binding together of different languages in the 13th-
century motet come immediately to mind as two examples of
these features, among many others that could be cited.
Particularly from a musical perspective, borrowings
across linguistic boundaries and interchanges between
sacred and secular are common. But the complete song out-
put of the Middle Ages is enormous. Latin sacred song
alone could easily take up another guide more ample than
this one. In view of such wealth, limitations seemed necessary, without, to be sure, precluding all openings into
neighboring repertories, many of which the reader will
find in books listed in the bibliography. Moreover, serious study of text/music relations always has to contend
with linguistic features, and these features are not completely transferable from one language to another. Choosing to deal with two related medieval languages, Old Occitan and Old French, allows examination in depth of the
specificity of text/music combinations. In addition, this
choice makes feasible a chronological spread from the
12th to the 14th century. Tracing Occitan and French song
through three hundred years of innovation lays out a series of events not previously aligned chiefly on the basis of language. This approach cuts across both the development of Occitan and French poetry as such and the
development of musical styles, seeking to seize them at
successive points of intersection. It proposes a continuity but also significant breaks in the continuity, and
shifting perceptions of the weight given each partner can
be brought into sharp relief. In setting up these materials on Occitan and French song from the 12th to the 14th
century, I have adopted a generous definition of song:
all combinations of music and texts in the selected vernaculars have been deemed worthy of consideration whatever their medieval or modern generic designations. In
the same spirit, I have, though less often, used the
French word "chanson" in a general way to refer not only
to "chansons" *per se* but also to other types of song that
would not have been termed "chanson" in the Middle Ages.
Within the boundaries of scope and chronology chosen for
this *Guide,* I have cast as wide a net as possible to enable exploration of the stable yet changing associations

that the Occitan and French languages entertained with
music over the entire period of medieval song.
   Music and poetry are placed by our modern scholarly
gaze in uneasy relationship. What medieval practitioners
of the art of song joined at least initially as a matter
of course is disjoined by modern criticism. Relations between music and poetry do not constitute a discipline
with a distinguishing ideology and approaches sanctified
by use. There is even no satisfactory terminology to
speak of both at once. Instead music and poetry have been
fitted each with its own systems of analysis. But in the
critical climate of the late 20th century, interdisci-
plinarity is looked upon with increasing favor. And as
Steven Paul Scher has recently pointed out, musico-
literary study, though still in fervent need of expert
practitioners, has fared well: "during the last decade
or so, musico-literary study has become a respected and
increasingly popular field of interdisciplinary research".[3] It is the purpose of this *Guide* to encourage
interdisciplinary research on medieval music and vernacular poetry by delineating major problems, by providing
historical and theoretical perspectives, and by furnish-
ing tools to carry out such research, with emphasis on
recent critical studies, from 1980 to the present.

CHRONOLOGICAL OUTLINE OF THE SUBJECT

   French became the language of the *chanson* only because it took over that function from Old Occitan. The
earliest known creators of medieval vernacular song were
the troubadours who began to compose in southern France,
or Occitania, at the beginning of the 12th century. Their
language was not Old French but Old Occitan, or Old Provençal, or Limousin as some early grammatical treatises
referred to it. In the course of the 12th century, this
language attained great prestige; it was considered the
authoritative language of *chansons* by Raimon Vidal de
Besalú, writing around 1200, and it was called the mother
tongue of poets by Dante (*Purgatorio*, Canto xxvi). From
southern France, the cultivation of vernacular song
spread to other regions: Italy, Spain, Germany, and
especially France. But if the "French" *chanson* began in

Occitania, and if the Old French courtly lyric, or the *grand chant courtois*, derived most of its features from the Occitan *canso*, the cultivators of northern songs, or trouvères, soon distinguished themselves from their southern confrères by a broader range of themes and forms and a decreasing density of poetic expression. From a musical standpoint, the songs of both troubadours and trouvères were monophonic. There are fewer extant melodies for the troubadours as compared to the trouvères. The evidence we have suggests that the troubadours were more experimental in crafting melodic lines, while the trouvères tended to opt for the--by then--familiar patterns we associate with secular song in the vernacular. Clearly distinctions can and should be made between the repertories of early vernacular song. But for the purposes of organization and exposition, I shall here take troubadours and trouvères together as creators of an extensive collection of monophonic songs constituting a first stage in the development of the *chanson*, a stage that is at its height in the 12th and early 13th centuries, then fades and is displaced by other events as the 13th century draws to a close.

Whatever its beginnings, the future fortunes of the *chanson* were distinctively French. That this should have been the case is to be explained by the cultural and political dominance of northern France, while the south suffered the effects of the Albigensian crusade, and by the elaboration, especially in Paris, of the new musical styles we now globally term "polyphonic" (the term, at least in French usage, dates from the 19th century). Polyphonic music, simultaneously combining several melodic lines, was the music of the future, and the *chanson* as a musico-poetic entity could not have survived had it not been adapted to the new polyphonic styles. The process of adaptation is not entirely clear. It surely involved the taking over of secular texts, often related to various types of trouvère songs, into one of the new 13th-century polyphonic genres, the motet. The motet arose from the addition of words ("motetus" from the French "mot", "word") to the upper part(s) of what are known as discant sections, that is, measured or note-against-note sections, of a type of florid polyphonic composition cultivated at Notre Dame in Paris and called organum. The

lowest voice, called the tenor (because it "holds" the
piece together) continued, as in the organum, to sing a
Latin text drawn from the Chant. The words for the upper
voice(s) were not necessarily related to the piece to
which they had been added. Initially, the added words
would have been in Latin. But early on, vernacular texts
were adopted and adapted, so that, referring to mid 13th-
century developments, one may come to speak of a French
vernacular motet. Frequently when the motet has been
treated as a musical style, specific divisions on the
basis of language have not seemed necessary. Admittedly,
given the criss-crossing of languages in the polytextual
motet, for example, and the fact that musical styles are
not necessarily language specific, isolation of a French
vernacular motet is not always easily or cleanly accomplished. But focussing on the language has the virtue of
sharpening our understanding of the ways vernacular languages and early polyphonic music interacted, one of the
aims of this *Guide*, and of drawing attention to lines of
development this interaction engendered. The motet is
chiefly a northern French phenomenon. Although some Old
Occitan texts appeared in polytextual motets, Occitania
had no secular motet tradition of its own.[4]

By the middle of the 13th century, the polyphonic
motet was fast becoming the dominant musico-poetic
genre. Because its multi-form nature defied orderly description, the motet could indeed be taken as the genre
that typifies the century. Thirteenth-century songs do
not fall into neat categorizations. A trouvère monophonic tradition continued across the century, and because
trouvère songs circulated through the motet in various
guises, it is not always a simple matter to set the
boundaries between monophonic and polyphonic pieces.
Entirely characteristic of the porousness of generic
constructs is the behavior of refrains. These bits of
text, often with music, linked themselves to several
types of trouvère songs, notably dance songs whose structures they determined; showed up in motets; attached
themselves to a diversity of narrative or dramatic works.
The technique of inserting lyric pieces into narrative
was established in the early 13th century by Jean Renart
in his *Roman de la Rose*. The insertions into narrative
were for the most part monophonic, so far as can be

judged, because most of the manuscripts of 13th-century narrative do not have music. The insertions were refrains, dance songs, or troubadour/trouvère *chansons*. There were some polyphonic insertions in 13th-century works, such as the *Miracles de Notre Dame*, but polyphonic insertions would become the norm only in the 14th century. Many of these strands were drawn together in the works of Adam de la Halle. Adam was a key late 13th-century figure in the linking of the older styles of trouvères to the newer polyphonically-based styles. He composed a dramatic work with inserted refrains, monophonic *chansons*, motets, and the first examples of a new genre, the polyphonic rondeau. What chiefly characterizes the 13th-century songs in which Old French is used is experimentation, interaction, cross-fertilization and transformation of generic types. Consequently, I have taken as a second stage in the development of the French "chanson" (during which the term "chanson" itself cedes pride of place to other designations) precisely these 13th-century intersections, recognizing that separating them out from the continued cultivation of trouvère monophonic styles *per se* is an arbitrary, though I hope useful, operation.

During the late 13th and early 14th centuries, polyphonic secular song separated from the motet. Adopting the polyphonic textures newly elaborated through the motet and designated Ars nova (the "new art"), it metamorphosed into the *forme-fixe chanson*, whose main polyphonic types were the ballade and the rondeau. Guillaume de Machaut dominates the period, although specialists insist on the need for better assessment of Machaut's contemporaries. The *forme-fixe chansons* with their intricate formal designs characterize the 14th century and are still cultivated in the 15th, albeit with a return to greater simplicity. In the later part of the 14th century, the *chanson* was the locus of more and more sophisticated rhythmic elaborations, coupled with more independent melodic lines, culminating in what has been termed the Ars subtilior (the "more subtle art"). At century's end, the songs of Johannes Ciconia (c.1335 or 1370-1412) exploit the complexities of the most subtle art while also reflecting elements of Italian styles that anticipate the Renaissance. In the organization of this research guide,

the flowering of the fixed forms constitutes the third
stage of the French *chanson*. But another development is
traditionally assigned to the 14th century: the "definitive" separation of poetry and music, particularly with
Machaut's disciples. That separation was scarcely "definitive" because *chansons* with words and music continued
to be cultivated and already in the 13th century so important a poet as Rutebeuf composed no music. Machaut
himself composed a number of songs which, so far as we
can judge, were never intended to be sung. What seems to
be at stake here is a growing technical sophistication of
music, especially, but also of poetry, such that only
trained specialists could fully exploit the new resources
of either art. Poetry, as it were, set out on its own in
the hands of the great 14th-century masters, such as
Froissart or Deschamps. But in its theoretical under-
pinnings, poetry would long define itself as musical,
even when its greatest practitioners no longer composed
music. By the time of Ciconia, at the end of the century,
a strong tradition of French poetry had been established
in its own right, and musical techniques looking toward
Italy pointed away from the Middle Ages toward the
Renaissance and toward a new and different flowering of
the French *chanson*. Fittingly, then, our examination of
music and poetry in the Middle Ages ends there.

ORGANIZATION

The chronological framework I have just sketched out
will be used to structure presentation within the separate parts of this research guide. Arrangement of parts
for the *Guide* as a whole has been determined by its
overall aims. The goal of situating interdisciplinary
research on medieval song in larger historical and theoretical contexts will be pursued through the Introduction. Materials and tools of research will be furnished
by the Bibliography and Discography.

Introduction

Fundamental to interdisciplinary research is

disciplinary self-awareness. Disciplines set the research
agenda, determine the issues to be raised. The need to
cross disciplinary boundaries sharpens perception of the
boundaries themselves. But the increase in theoretical
sophistication in recent years has made it clear that
disciplinary boundaries are not immutable, that the disciplines through which we perceive our research subjects
are constructs of fallible human intelligence, and that
these constructs have a history. Taking cognizance of
this history has become a necessary part of modern research. "Interdisciplines" (if I may use that term) do
not have a history as such. But the way the two halves
of our subject, music and poetry, have been diversely
perceived and related does. Present ways of knowing are
dependent on past ways of understanding. What, for example, is the relationship between manuscripts and the objects they purport to represent, on the one hand, and between manuscripts and the modern editions that purport to
represent them on the other? In the Introduction to this
guide, I will address the issue of conceptual contexts
and briefly map out a history of the ways the combination
of poetry and music into medieval song have been perceived and understood, first in manuscripts and then
through printed books.

Not only questions of disciplinary "lenses" but also
issues of interpretation itself and how to go about it
have been raised by the development of critical theory in
the latter part of the 20th century. New approaches and
new methodologies force rethinking and reconceptualization of our knowledge of the Middle Ages and of our ways
of acquiring that knowledge. But new approaches cannot
merely displace previous ones. The invigorating thrust
of recent debates comes from the debates themselves, from
the interaction between theories about medieval studies
and practices of medievalists. I will consequently in the
Introduction also assess, in the light of changing critical orientations, the research agenda of the 1980s and
1990s that constitute the specific focus of the bibliography. I will seek to integrate theoretical approaches
and work on specific topics suggested by the research
itself: editing procedures; the intertwined issues of
rhythms and sounds; issues arising from work on style,
forms and structures, genre; new directions opened up by

new methodologies, including implications for research
of the historical performance movement.

Bibliography

The Bibliography has been organized with a view toward providing as complete reference as possible to research published since 1980 on the subject of the *Guide*,
with selected reference to basic tools of research, whatever their date of publication. The first four sections
of the Bibliography contain the tools of research and are
not annotated. The critical studies forming the final
sections of the Bibliography are annotated. The annota-
tions are descriptive; the intention is to give an idea
of contents rather than a complete summary or a critical
evaluation. Since the years 1974-1980 saw the appearance
of important bibliographies: Robert Taylor, *La Littérature occitane*; Andrew Hughes, *Medieval Music*; as well as
the monumental 20-volume *New Grove Dictionary of Music
and Musicians*, it seemed most efficient to provide a
thorough survey of critical and interpretive studies only
for the years following 1980. However, a few books deemed
essential to an understanding of the field have been included in the critical and interpretive studies even if
they pre-date 1980. In addition to the above mentioned
bibliographies, two other publications have influenced
the selection of works to be included in this Bibliography: Eglal Doss-Quinby, *The Lyrics of the Trouvères: A
Research Guide* (1970-1990) and Lawrence Earp, *Guillaume
de Machaut: A Guide to Research* (forthcoming). I have not
provided full coverage for Machaut, including only selected studies deemed important for our subject, or for
the trouvères. Further, I do not list reviews or short
notices, nor have I normally included unpublished dissertations. The principle adopted for my selection of critical and interpretive studies was a judgment that the
study could in some way illuminate text/music relationships. Choices were not restricted to articles or books
that focussed on both text and music; to the contrary,
studies of music alone or of text alone were brought
into the Bibliography if the treatment of text or music
seemed to offer the possibility of new interdisciplinary

insights. For the troubadours and trouvères, I have
emphasized studies of poets for whom we have music. The
Bibliography functions not only as a record of what has
been done but also as an invitation to do more and even
to do differently. Whether an article or a book can prove
enlightening to other scholars is always a subjective
call. By applying the most flexible kind of judgment, I
hope to have covered a full range of the topics that
have been explored and by the juxtaposition of these
topics, suggested new ones. In selecting the basic tools
of research listed in the initial sections of the Bibliography, I have given careful thought to the possible
needs of scholars in one discipline as they seek information about another. The list of journals searched, given
in the prefatory matter, can serve as an indication of
the most useful journals to consult. It has been my aim
to provide in this *Guide* a collection of information that
is wide-ranging but both compact and in itself accessible
to different disciplinary specialists.

I have followed the *Chicago Manual of Style* for all
entries. Several works by the same author are listed in
chronological order.

Discography

The Discography has been compiled with a view toward
including all recent recordings pertaining to Occitan
and French vernacular song. But because changing performance styles are an integral part of any research that
includes performance practice, some references to early
recordings have been included, and an effort has been
made to illustrate briefly performance styles going back
to the 1950's.

The Discography has been divided into sections following the chronological divisions adopted for the entire
Guide.

Within sections, recordings are presented alphabetically by title.

For each recording the following information is provided. (1) Title, ensemble and director (where there is
a director), performers, label (references are normally
made to names and numbers current in the US), and date.

(2) A list of composers and songs using Old French and Old Occitan. Constraints of space dictated the exclusion of songs in other languages; this has meant a very partial listing for some discs. Motets are listed if one voice is in the vernacular. I have made no attempt to regularize spellings for the Discography but tried to reproduce faithfully those of the recording. (3) Information about kinds of supporting materials provided with the recording (introductions, texts) in what languages, as well as indication of whether or not complete songs are performed (where that information is pertinent) and whether songs are performed with or without instruments. The goal has been to provide information useful to research. In some cases, performance styles are singled out for comment. Technical quality of the recording is not considered.

All items in both Bibliography and Discography have been personally examined, unless indication is given to the contrary.

Prefatory matter and Indexes

Abbreviations are used sparingly. A list of abbreviations is included with the prefatory matter. Manuscript *sigla* are also furnished but only for the manuscripts referred to in the *Guide*. The organization of the material has made it feasible to keep cross-referencing to a minimum. All internal references to Bibliography and Discography, including those in the indexes, are made by item number, preceded by the letter B for the Bibliography and the letter D for the Discography. The use of letters seemed useful, even though items are numbered consecutively throughout.

Two indexes have been provided. (1) An Index of Individual Poet/Composers, Medieval Theorists, Titles of Songs and Other Works includes all references from the Preface, Introduction, Bibliography, and Discography to medieval writers, composers, and their works. Songs in the Discography are fully indexed, except where performance is instrumental only. First lines are normally used as song titles; these lines have frequently been abbreviated. Polytextual motet titles show the first line of each text plus the tenor, separated by slashes. Spellings of names and titles indexed have been regularized only as necessary; to facilitate reference, it seemed useful to preserve as far as possible the appearance of names and titles as they occur in the Bibliography or the Discography. Cross-references are given for different spellings of medieval names.

(2) A General Index, also covering the Preface, Introduction, Bibliography, and Discography, includes all modern authors and editors, recording ensembles, directors of ensembles (but not individual performers), subjects, and medieval manuscripts mentioned in the *Guide*. Modern (Renaissance and after) titles have not been indexed.

Notes to the Preface

1. *A History of Western Music*, 4th edition (New York: Norton, 1988), 250.
2. B415, 6-7.
3. Steven Paul Scher, ed, *Music and Text. Critical Inquiries* (Cambridge: Cambridge University Press, 1991), xiv. Scher subscribes to the term "melopoetics" coined by Lawrence Kramer for the comparative discipline of "music-literary study," which as yet has no specific designation (xivn.2).
4. See Zaslaw (B785) for the single remaining Provençal motet. Everist (B672) provides the first full study of the vernacular motet, pointing out in his Preface that "the corpus of motets is the first in which vernacular poetry encounters polyphonic music" (xi). The importance of the encounter can hardly be overstated. Everist's description of origins is clear and useful. His consistent integration of poetry and music sheds new light on the nature of the motet. I regret the book appeared too late for me to include all of its findings in my review of research.

ABBREVIATIONS AND MANUSCRIPT *SIGLA*
USED IN THIS *GUIDE*

ABBREVIATIONS

B	Bibliography item in this *Guide*
BN	Bibliothèque Nationale, Paris
D	Discography item in this *Guide*
GRLMA	*Grundriss der romanischen Literaturen des Mittelalters* (B80)
IPC	In General Index cross-references, means Index of Individual Poet/Composers
New Grove	*The New Grove Dictionary of Music and Musicians* (B22)
PC	Pillet and Carstens. *Bibliographie* (B25) (Numbering of troubadour songs)
R	Spanke. *G. Raynauds Bibliographie* (B28) (Numbering of trouvère songs)
SATF	Société des Anciens Textes Français

TROUBADOUR MANUSCRIPTS

A	Rome, Biblioteca Vaticana, 5232
C	Paris, Bibliothèque Nationale, fr.856
G	Milan, Biblioteca Ambrosiana, R 71
M	Paris, Bibliothèque Nationale, fr.12474
N	New York, Pierpont Morgan Library, MS 819
R	Paris, Bibliothèque Nationale, fr.22543
U	Florence, Biblioteca Laurenziana, Plut.XLI, cod. 43
V	Venice, Biblioteca Marciana, app. cod. XI
W	Paris, Bibliothèque Nationale, fr.844 (Trouvère MS M)
X	Paris, Bibliothèque Nationale, fr.20050 (Trouvère MS U)
a^1	Modena, Biblioteca Estense, Campori, App. 426, 427, 494
e	Rome, Biblioteca Vaticana, Barb. 3965

TROUVÈRE MANUSCRIPTS

A	Arras, Bibliothèque Municipale, 657
E	Lost fragment from the Hague containing 3 *jeux-partis* with music
K	Paris, Bibliothèque de l'Arsenal, 5198
M	Paris, Bibliothèque Nationale, fr.844, Le Manuscrit du Roi (Troubadour MS W; Motet MS R)
O	Paris, Bibliothèque Nationale, fr.846, Le Chansonnier Cangé
T	Paris, Bibliothèque Nationale, fr.12615 (Motet MS N)
U	Paris, Bibliothèque Nationale, fr.20050, Le Chansonnier de Saint-Germain-des-Près (Troubadour MS X)
W(Pn)	Paris, Bibliothèque Nationale, fr.25566 (Pb)
a	Rome, Biblioteca Vaticana, Reg. 1490
b	Rome, Biblioteca Vaticana, Reg. 1522

THIRTEENTH-CENTURY MOTETS

Ba	Bamberg, Staatsbibliothek, Lit. 115 (olim Ed. IV. 6)
Cl	Paris, Bibliothèque Nationale, nouv. acq. fr.13521, "La Clayette"
Mo	Montpellier, Bibliothèque Interuniversitaire, Section Médecine, H 196
MüA	Munich, Bayerische Staatsbibliothek, Frag. mus. 4775 (gallo-rom. 42)
Tu	Torino, Biblioteca Reale, Vari 42
W2	Wolfenbüttel, Herzog August Bibliothek, Helmstedt 1099, Heinemman 1206

FOURTEENTH-CENTURY POLYPHONY

Roman de Fauvel

Fauv	Paris, Bibliothèque Nationale, fr.146

Guillaume de Machaut

A	Paris, Bibliothèque Nationale, fr.1584
B	Paris, Bibliothèque Nationale, fr.1585
C	Paris, Bibliothèque Nationale, fr.1586
E	Paris, Bibliothèque Nationale, fr.9221
F-G	Paris, Bibliothèque Nationale, fr.22545-6
Vg	Formerly in the possession of the Marquis de Vogüe. New York, Wildenstein Galleries, without shelfmark

Individual Sources

Ch	Chantilly, Musée Condé, 564 (olim 1047)
Iv	Ivrea, Biblioteca Capitolare, without shelfmark
Codex Reina	Paris, Bibliothèque Nationale, nouv. acq. fr.6771
OH	The Old Hall Manuscript. London, British Library, Add. MS 57950
Bologna Q 15	Bologna, Civico Museo Bibliografico-Musicale, MS Q 15
Trent 87-92	Trent, Museo Provinciale d'Arte, MSS 87-92
Trent 93	Trent, Biblioteca Capitolare, MS 93

JOURNALS AND PERIODICALS SEARCHED
FOR THE PERIOD 1980-1992

Acta Musicologica
Archiv für Musikwissenschaft
Basler Jahrbuch für historische Musikpraxis
Cahiers de civilisation médiévale (including the
     Bibliography issue)
Cultura Neolatina
Diapason (for the Discography)
Early Music
Early Music History
Fanfare (for the Discography)
French Forum
French Studies
Gramophone (for the Discography)
Journal of the American Musicological Society
Journal of Musicological Research
Journal of Musicology
Journal of the Royal Musical Association
Medioevo Romanzo
Medium Aevum
Le Moyen Age
Musica Disciplina
Music Analysis
Music and Letters
Neophilologus
Neuphilologische Mitteilungen
Nuova Rivista Musicale Italiana
Performance Practice Review
Plainsong and Medieval Music
Revue Belge de Musicologie
Revue de Musicologie
Revue des langues romanes
Rivista Italiana di Musicologia
Romance Philology
Romania
Romanic Review

Romanistische Zeitschrift für Literaturgeschichte/
    Cahiers d'Histoire des Littératures Romanes
Speculum
Studies in Music (University of Western Australia)
Studi Medievali
Zeitschrift für romanische Philologie

Encomia: Bibliographical Bulletin of the International
    Courtly Literature Society
International Medieval Bibliography
Modern Language Association International Bibliography
Répertoire international de littérature musicale (RILM)

Troubadour MS A. Biblioteca Vaticana, 5232, fol. 167v°, showing the *vida* - miniature - song configuration for the Comtessa de Dia, "Ab ioi et ab joven m'apais." In the margin, just barely visible, are instructions to the illustrator: "una dona que cante."

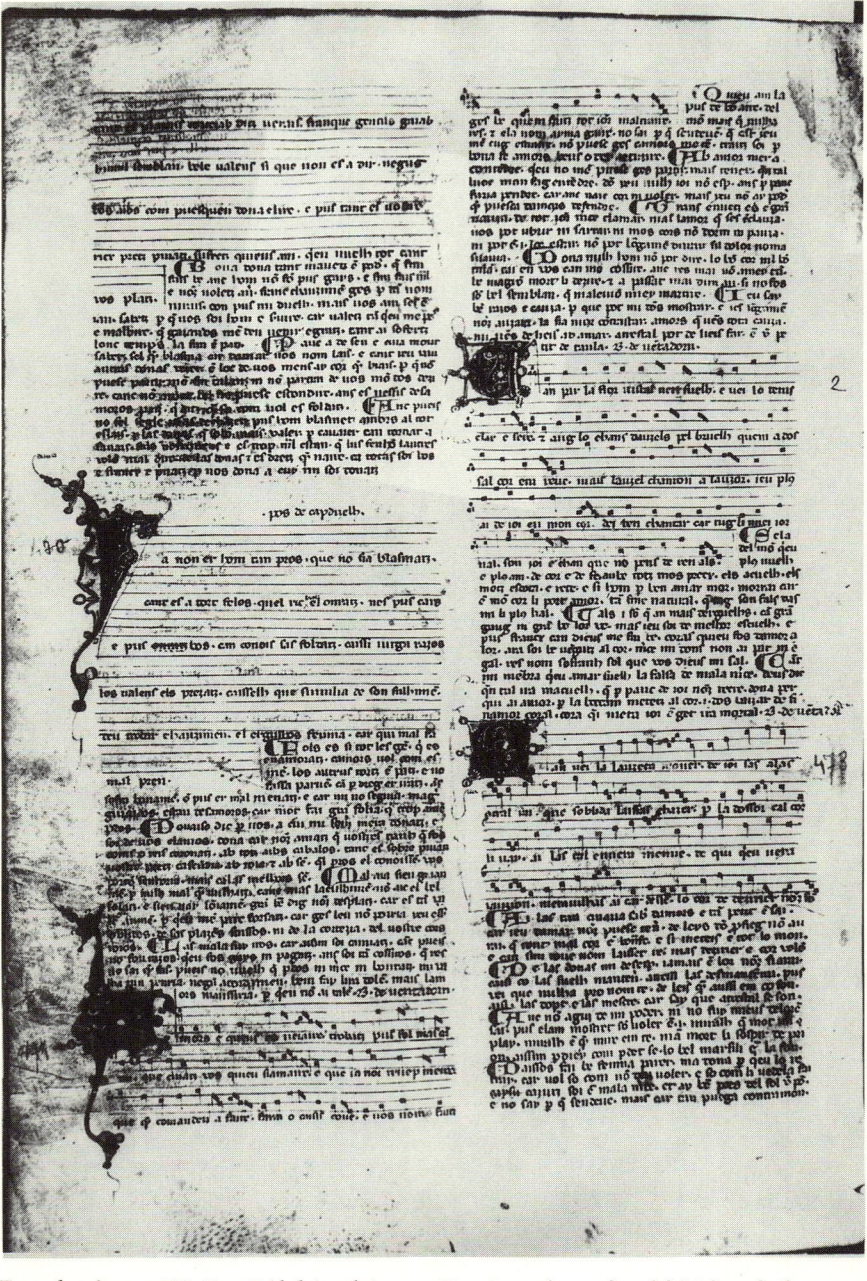

Troubadour MS R. Bibliothèque Nationale, fr.22543, fol. 56vº. Phot. Bibl. Nat. Paris.

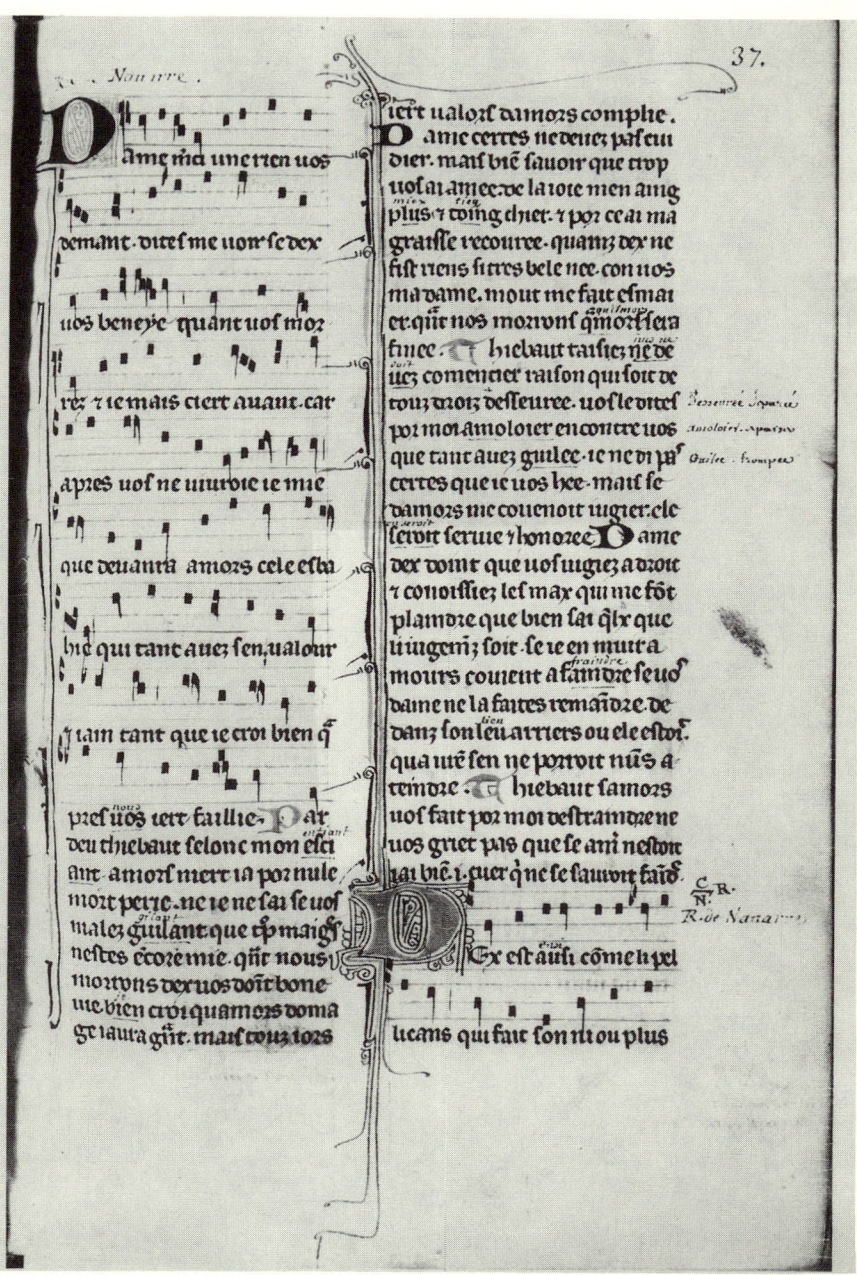

Trouvère MS O. Bibliothèque Nationale fr.846 (Le
Chansonnier Cangé), fol. 37 r°. Phot. Bibl. Nat. Paris.

Montpellier, Bibliothèque Interuniversitaire, Section
Médecine, H196, fol. 294 r°, motet "Or ne sai je/Puisque
d'amer/[Kyrie]L[eyson]."

Guillaume de Machaut, *Remede de Fortune*, Rondelet, "Dame mon coeur." Bibliothèque Nationale fr.1586, fol. 57r°. Triplum, Cantus, and Tenor. Phot. Bibl. Nat. Paris.

INTRODUCTION
A BACKGROUND TO RESEARCH

PART I
HISTORICAL PERSPECTIVES

Medieval song presents itself to our scholarly reflection only through written records: manuscripts that
have come down to us, reproductions and editions of these
manuscripts, with such further help as we can derive from
visual arts, contemporaneous descriptions in other works,
or documentary evidence. The song itself as a vocal phenomenon is irrecoverable. Yet we often behave as though
a written record--manuscript, score, or edition--
contained it entirely. The written records themselves
function within different conceptual frameworks. Manuscripts proceed from the scribe's or compiler's understanding of his task. Editions proceed from the ideological constructs within which the editor works. Scholarly
reflection brings its own interpretations of the records,
for scholars ask the questions their interests and critical orientations propose. Thus is set up a kind of dialogue between written records and scholarly reflection
that produces a continuously evolving understanding of
both. It is this dialogue that I will examine as a way of
situating contemporary research. I propose in the first
instance to map out a brief history, from the Middle Ages
to the early 20th century, of perceptions of music and
poetry in the repertories under consideration that undergird both the creation and the comprehension of the written records. This history of the subject will constitute
Part I of the Introduction. During the period beginning
around the middle of the 20th century, the rise of interpretation and critical theory transformed the scholarly
landscape. New emphasis on interpretation brought forward
new ways of interacting with written records. In Part II
of this introduction, I will focus on research agenda of

the 1980s and 1990s and the critical orientations from
which they proceed.

To set out the history of our subject, it is useful
to divide the written records into the conventional two
categories: manuscripts and books. A central marker thus
becomes the printing press, but the dividing line between
manuscript and book is neither sharp nor absolute. Although manuscripts are closer in time to medieval songs
and we consequently classify them as "sources," they are
in their own way already "editions." While the printing
press took its point of departure from the manuscripts,
it developed radically different relationships to the
works it made available, resulting in a new kind of textuality, unlike that of the manuscript. In examining the
transition from manuscripts to books, it becomes especially important to consider the intellectual contexts.
The way Renaissance scholars viewed the "Middle Ages"
which they, in fact, had newly invented, influenced the
use they made of manuscripts and the methods they began
to adopt to translate medieval textuality into books.
Renaissance views, in turn, are developed or displaced
by those of later scholars. To delineate these shifting
interpretational grids which are the very heart of the
dialogue I propose to examine, it will be convenient,
following the manuscript culture of the Middle Ages, to
periodize conventionally, using the Renaissance, the 17th
and 18th centuries, the 19th and early 20th centuries as
workable ideological units.

In the following discussion, and throughout the Introduction as the material warrants, I will adopt some
admittedly arbitrary divisions which I hope will serve to
clarify treatment of the issues. I will treat monophonic
repertories first and then polyphonic repertories, hoping
still to blur the too-rigid impression of chronology such
a tactic suggests by recalling the contemporaneousness
of many of the manuscripts containing the two repertories
and the number of intersections between them. Within
polyphonic repertories, it will often be useful to contrast schematically the 13th-century French motet and the
14th-century *forme-fixe chanson*, although the reality of
composition and transmission was surely far messier than

such schematic divisions suggest. Troubadour/trouvère song, vernacular motets, and *forme-fixe chansons* will thus often serve to represent in a compact way the stages of the French *chanson* outlined in the preface whose full unfolding is too complex to be adequately treated in an introductory essay.

MANUSCRIPTS

The main manuscript traditions for the repertories under consideration begin in the 13th century. Troubadour manuscripts, chronologically separated from the trouba-dours themselves, stretch from the mid-13th century into the 16th; but for the earliest songs in Old Occitan, we must reach back to one witness from the late 11th or early 12th century, to a manuscript from Saint Martial de Limoges. Trouvère sources, in contrast, are closer in time to the trouvères, and the sources stop in the 14th century, except if one includes Machaut whose manuscripts come from the 14th and early 15th centuries. Main manu-scripts for the French motet are concentrated in the 13th century. The later 14th-century polyphonic *chanson* survives in a diverse collection of manuscripts from the late 14th and early 15th centuries.

Besides simple chronology, several distinctions in manuscript tradition are pertinent to the diverse reper-tories: geographical, notational, and what might be called presentational, that is, page lay-out. For some repertories, it is important to distinguish North French, South French and Italian provenance. By notational dis-tinctions, I mean the presence or absence of any musical notation as well as the types of notation used in manu-scripts with music. Each of the repertories under consid-eration survives with different page lay-outs. In addi-tion, recent research has laid emphasis on the manuscript as a whole, including illumination. All of these factors will enter into the following discussion.

As I pointed out above, manuscripts do not simply bear transparent witness to a song's existence; they are already a kind of "edition": they provide perceptions of

that song shaped by attitudes governing the setting down
of the song in writing. One of the first things to strike
us as we open a manuscript is how the song looks, what we
could call its manuscript image. This image can propose
certain types of understanding. This is the first kind of
perception I shall address.

The earliest manuscript containing a song in Old
Occitan, words and music, is Bibliothèque Nationale,
fonds latin 1139 from Saint Martial of Limoges.[1] Dating
from around 1100, it is the only remaining witness to
Occitanian song at the time of its first flowering in
the works of William IX, Duke of Aquitaine (1071-1127).
Since the extant troubadour and trouvère chansonniers
(songbooks) do not appear before the 13th century, they
postdate the troubadours themselves by 150-200 years.
There are two noticeable differences between BN 1139 and
later chansonniers, and a number of essential similari-
ties. The first difference pertains to notation. In the
part of BN 1139 that interests us, we find a type of
musical notation, heightened neumes with no clef or
staff, which indicates pitch only with relative accuracy
and gives no indication of duration. In contrast, most
trouvère and troubadour manuscripts use square chant notation on a staff with clefs, permitting more accurate
indication of pitch (though not of duration). The second
difference concerns the notation of music for successive
stanzas. Normally, in the main troubadour and trouvère
manuscripts, only the first stanza has music; in the
earlier BN 1139, all stanzas have music. Although it
contains but a single example of a song completely in
Old Occitan, BN 1139 can open a tiny window on the manner
of repetition of a melody for successive stanzas of a
strophic song, and the kinds of musical adaptations to
specific textual features in different stanzas such repetition might bring.

These differences should not obscure important resem-
blances between the earlier and later manuscripts. Both
have two main features in common: the consistent coordination of a note or note group with a syllable and the
use of notation systems that provide no indication of
musical durations.[2] The syllable thus emerges as the main

unit of coordination, the basis of a tight visual linking
of words and music.[3] Further, in both BN 1139 and the
main troubadour/trouvère manuscripts, text lines and
stanzas may be marked off by such techniques as periods
or capital letters, but (with some exceptions, such as
troubadour MS G) lineation is not employed. The non-
notated stanzas in troubadour/trouvère manuscripts are
normally given as prose following the initial notated
strophe, with stanzas clearly demarcated. The song is
not visualized as a shape, as an abstract geometric
figure such as later would become the norm for poetry;
written practice reflects the successivity of an oral
presentation not the simultaneity of a visualized form
in space.

The fact that manuscripts present secular monophonic
repertories in this way is well known; the implications
of this perception, especially as it includes the early
Saint Martial manuscript, have not all been drawn. The
manuscript tradition reflects the emergence in Latin and
adoption in the vernacular of syllabic versification,
along with the intersection of music and the new versification. It invites the "reader" to follow the serial
progression of an *oral* performance; more than the eye,
the ear determines form. Further, the persistence of
non-mensural notation in later manuscripts may reveal a
perception of rhythmic properties according to which,
with the syllable as the basic unit, musical phrasings
and rhythms flow from text articulations. By the time
troubadour and trouvère songs came to be deposited in the
extant manuscripts, scribes had at their disposal a music
writing system that could indicate patterns of measured
duration. The fact that scribes did not, by and large,
use this system seems to indicate that they did not find
the system appropriate to the songs they were notating.[4]

A further characteristic of troubadour/trouvère manuscripts must be brought forward. The writing down of
troubadour/trouvère songs must be thought of as descriptive rather than prescriptive, as a way of recording and
thus preserving information about the song rather than as
a mandate to perform in a certain manner. If one considers the manuscripts not as a whole but individually, it

immediately becomes apparent that a single song can be preserved in as many different versions as there are manuscripts to preserve it. Versions show differences in specific readings, musical and textual, and in number as well as order of stanzas. Fluidity, "mouvance," to use Zumthor's term, rather than fixity, is inscribed in the manuscript image as a characteristic of the songs.

These, then, briefly sketched out, are the chief aspects of the manuscript image of troubadour/trouvère songs. Coordination between syllable and note or note-group plus the use of a notation system non-indicative of precise durations suggest an alliance between text and melody featuring the syllable as a basic unit, with flexible and not fixed rhythmic properties. For this repertory, it seems clear that communicating the text is of central importance, and melodies as presented in the manuscripts could respond to or reflect syntactical, formal, and expressive articulations of the text. This response is not pre-determined: variations in manuscript versions of both texts and melodies propose a concept of mobility that could operate on the level of performance or of writing: presumably neither performer nor scribe felt constrained to produce a song exactly as it might have been in a previous version deemed "authentic." However, the manuscript presentation, as I have briefly described it, does not capture important dimensions of the songs. In addition to the question of imprecise durations, such features as timbre, linguistic as well as musical, dynamics, or gesture, to mention only a few, are left out. Thus it is not the song itself that the manuscript offers to our contemplation. Rather do we have a medieval conceptualization of some of the song's central features and the consignment of that conceptualization to writing.

A simultaneous elaboration of new ideas of musical rhythm and of new ways of writing music took place at the end of the 12th and across the 13th centuries, for the most part in Paris. The salient feature of this fundamental shift was the idea that time and pitch could be synchronized, and that this synchronization could produce rhythmical patterns of long and short notes independent of any text.[5] It became possible to create accent by musical means alone. Notational methods necessary to record these new concepts were quickly found,[6] and the continuous refinement of both the concepts and the methods would occupy theorists and composers across the 13th and 14th centuries and beyond. Once music had an accentual system of its own, word-music relationships were thereby profoundly modified, and new linkages between music and text could be forged.

The new ways of notating music were linked to the development of polyphony. Throughout the 13th century, even as monophonic song reached its final flowering, vernacular poetry, especially in Old French, was being absorbed into polyphonic musical textures through the French motet. The polyphonic motet consisted of a tenor derived from chant which served as a basis for newly invented upper voice(s). The upper voices usually had different texts. Roughly speaking, one may say that originally texts were entirely in Latin; then vernacular texts were used in the upper voices with, still, a liturgical tenor; and finally all voices could be in the vernacular, with a tenor from secular song.[7] The term "motet" came from the French "mot," or its diminutive "motet," used to indicate a voice with words. From its inception in the 13th century to its relative decline in the 14th century, the French motet was the locus of numerous innovations, particularly emphasizing increasingly sophisticated rhythmic structures. The manuscript image of these new compositions became quite different from the image of monophonic song. It reflected a radically new conceptualization of music-text relationships, with ramifications stretching into the 15th century. Initially, certain types of polyphonic music, especially conductus, organum or clausula, were written in score, that is with parts horizontally superimposed and words below the lowest part as is usual in modern writing (see Fig. 1). But the motet in its most typical formulation was not written in score. Only with some difficulty did scribes arrive at a format suitable to the motet; the process took more than half a century.[8] Instead of being horizontally superimposed, the parts of the motet came to be juxtaposed in parallel columns, with one part, the tenor, below (Fig. 2), or covering two pages, with the tenor in a separate column (Fig. 3).

Figure 1: Polyphonic Piece in Score
(Montpellier, Bibl. Interuniv. Médecine,
H196, 22r°)

**Figure 2: 3-Part Motet in Parallel Columns
with tenor below** (Montpellier,
Bibl. Interuniv. Médecine, H196, 318r°)

Figure 3: 4-Part Motet in Parallel Columns across two pages (Montpellier, Bibl. Interuniv. Médecine,
H196, 44v°-45r°)

What are the implications of this manuscript image? In the first instance, the page layout could have responded to practical concerns. I have pointed out that the motet consisted of a fully texted upper part or parts built on a tenor. The upper parts were usually rhythmically more elaborate and notated syllabically. Thus there could occur a sharp incongruity between the length of the upper texted parts and the tenor. To assign equal space to the many notes of the upper parts and the fewer notes of the tenor could have been perceived as a waste of valuable parchment.[9] Further, it was important that the song be entirely contained on one page so that in performance all voices could move simultaneously from one page to the next. This need, too, influenced page layout.[10] But there was more than mere convenience involved in the elaboration of such a radically new design. The very possibility of conceiving such a manuscript image was dependent on being able to notate time coordinations, that is, rhythm, so that different melodic lines differently positioned on the page came out, in the end, together. However important the syllabification might have been in the upper voices, it was no longer the main criterion governing text-music relationships and the organization of the song. The main criteria had become musical: rhythmic (and "harmonic") ordering and coordinating of melodic lines.

This left the song free to exploit any number of juxtapositions. The upper voices could be newly composed or taken over from secular song; texts could be in different languages simultaneously: French, Latin, or Old Occitan could appear together in the same piece. The resulting composition was heterogeneous, so much so that it is almost impossible to arrive at a global definition encompassing all the characteristics of the genre--if, indeed the 13th-century motet can be termed a single genre. With this heterogeneity came a remarkable and seemingly undisciplined flowering of inventiveness, both musical and textual, growing out of the very possibility of confrontation and combination of apparently dissimilar and sometimes pre-existing elements. The manuscript image of the motet underscores both its heterogeneity and its polymorphous nature. The importance of spatial considerations in the song lay-out is demonstrated by the care with which the manuscripts were frequently prepared to receive the song. But the written vision of the motet is one of fragmentation; this contrasts sharply with the totalizing image of monophonic song. As the manuscripts present them, monophonic song and motet are two different types of song, simultaneously cultivated. The heterogeneity of the motet is not resolved on the written page; it awaits its resolution through performance. And the ways in which the fragmented piece might have been performed, heard, and understood, and by what public, still await satisfactory scholarly elucidation.

The motet became the main polyphonic genre of the 13th century. During the late 13th and early 14th centuries, the motet continued to serve as the locus for experiments in rhythmic notation. But the 14th century would see it yield popularity to a new *chanson*, the *forme-fixe chanson*; and as the motet returned to its Latin origins, vernacular song, having passed through the motet, flowered anew in this new *chanson*. The normal page lay-out for the polyphonic *forme-fixe chanson*, particularly the ballade and the rondeau, retained the separation of parts, yet reflected important stylistic changes, among them the virtual elimination of polytextuality by mid-century.[11] As for the motet, so for the *forme-fixe chanson*, hesitations, false starts, and incomplete understandings characterized the initial manuscript presentations. Adam de la Halle's polyphonic rondeaux, the first examples of this new genre, were still written in score format. Scribes had to learn to fashion for the new musical styles a page lay-out that would still permit simultaneous page turning. Lawrence Earp has seen evidence of initial scribal misunderstandings and eventual resolution of the problems in Machaut MS C.[12] Ballades and rondeaux had a single text, typically in a strophic form. A section of the text, the first stanza of the ballade, or the refrain of the rondeau, was underlaid to music in one of the voices: the "cantus." (It would be more accurate to say that the music was overlaid, since text was normally written first.) The other musical parts, bearing the designations tenor, contratenor, or triplum if there was a fourth part, were typically placed before or after the "cantus" on the page, the whole series of parts then following consecutively, copied one after the other. All parts except the cantus were textless or with simply an identifying piece of text. The remaining words in the song were not underlaid to music because the music already written down would be repeated for them; these words were frequently furnished in run-on lines. Thus while individual musical parts retained their independence, the song acquired a focal point: the single text underlaid to a core segment of music. Moreover, the tenor, which was the foundation of the motet, and there usually taken over from a pre-existing melody, was unmoored from previous connections and assimilated to the strophic form. This new structure then became the vehicle for increasingly complex and subtle rhythmic and melodic elaborations.

If it might seem that a single text would assure clearer written word/tone relationships, such is not necessarily the case. Even when the music for the ballade stanza or the rondeau refrain was "overlaid" accurately in the manuscript--and sometimes it was not--there remains the problem of coordinating subsequent portions of text from elsewhere on the page, not to mention the question of how textless parts were to be performed. Since in the *forme-fixe chanson*, the poetic text furnished the structural framework, correspondence generally obtained between poetic line and musical phrase; but within the phrase, when the music was at all ornate, manuscript layout does not always entirely clarify just where syllables should be placed with respect to the music. The fact that there is but one text means that a final coming together of verbal and musical sounds effects closure to mark off important structural units (in contrast to the polytextual motet where different texts, hence different verbal sounds, as well as overlapping phrases, may preclude such effects). But on the level of the individual phrase, music is represented in the *forme-fixe chanson* manuscripts as enjoying a certain freedom with respect to the text.

Thus the manuscript image of the *forme-fixe chanson* reflects a new conceptualization of song. The principle of juxtaposition of parts is held in common with the

motet. The strophic nature of the text, eliminating the
need to write out all repeated musical material, suggests
a resemblance to troubadour/trouvère song. But if this
resemblance forges a visual link with the earlier *chanson*, the limits of such resemblance are immediately apparent in the freer association of syllables and notes,
particularly in melismatic passages. The manner of embed-
ding the *forme-fixe chanson* in manuscripts responds to
new styles: it projects a looser hold of text on music in
detailed synchronizations of the texted part. The tight
adjustments of the troubadour/trouvère repertory are no
longer needed due to the ability to write down, unequivo-
cally, rhythmic intentions of the music. Yet the overall
structural base, as with the troubadour/trouvère repertory, remained the text. The perception of song that
emerges from the manuscripts thus joins a core text
acting as structural anchor to radically new flexibility
in the detailed elaboration of musical lines.

Our examination of manuscripts has thus revealed
three different conceptualizations. They characterize
different types of song, and one could apply to all our
repertories the argument Rebecca Baltzer has made for the
13th-century motet: "the achievement of a distinctive...
manuscript format was essential to the establishment--
and indeed to the definition--of the genre itself."[13]
First, we saw a firm coordination of music and text on
the level of the syllable, with music normally notated
non-mensurally. This concept was realized in the monophonic tradition and suggests a seamless union of melodic
motion with the natural idioms and poetic movements of
the vernacular language. But, leading to the second conceptualization, this coordination was radically transformed by the new methods of notating musical rhythms, of
controlling time musically, that accompanied the emergence of polyphonic music. Responding to more complex
sound systems, scribes developed formatting techniques
that projected independence of melodic lines, coordinated
in performance through rhythmic information furnished by
the notation. For the polytextual motet, although note/
syllable synchronization could pertain in the upper
voice(s), independent text lines (including the possibility of different languages) were the norm. Thus

coordination of the whole was effected through the music. Re-convergence on a single text characterized the more melodically elaborate *forme-fixe chanson* leading to a third conceptualization. Main structural outlines became again a function of music/text relationships; but the independence of melodic lines remained a central feature of the manuscript image, reflecting the continued exploitation of melodic and rhythmic complexities, coordinated still by the ever more precise calculations of musical durations. It must be pointed out that no more for polyphonic than for monophonic *chansons* do manuscripts capture all the dimensions of the song: timbre, dynamics, and the like, are left out. Even more obviously for polyphonic than for monophonic song, writing develops as a rationalization and a spatialization of sound. For music, it emphasizes those elements most amenable to mathematical analysis: pitch and rhythm. Manuscript images thus consistently offer to our contemplation medieval conceptualizations of some of the song's central features. These conceptualizations, in turn, imply different ways of "reading" and hence of understanding the songs. Monophonic song can be, so to speak, taken in at a glance; it is immediately available to the understanding through the image on the page. A polyphonic song cannot be similarly read at sight as a "complete piece." Its fragmentation on the page precludes immediate comprehension. Trained singers could doubtless sight read individual lines, and doubtless a trained musician comprehend the whole; but both of these possibilities presuppose an intellectual effort not required by monophonic songs. And, indeed, what degree of comprehension the listener achieves when hearing simultaneous rendition of *polytextual* motet parts has not, in the current state of research, been entirely elucidated. Possibly polytextual songs were only understood by an audience who either knew the words or had heard the texts singly before hearing them together.[14] The problem of comprehending different texts does not arise in the *forme-fixe chanson* having the configuration of a single texted cantus with other parts untexted. Different manuscript conceptualizations are thus characterized by sharp differences in "readability" or "comprehensibility." As we shall see, these features will determine the kinds of reception medieval songs will receive when manuscripts must be turned into books.

The manuscript image of the song includes not only the presentation of individual songs but the ordering of the entire codex. Ordering, so far as it is the result of conscious reflection and not haphazard collection, can indicate the use to which the manuscript is to be put and the audience to whom it is directed. Further, various types of decorations and illustrations both demarcate segments of manuscript contents and interpret those contents.

To the extent that ordering is the result of conscious reflection, it normally involves at least one of several methods of grouping: genre or form; author/composer; alphabetization; number of voices for polyphonic songs; language. Apart from these orderings, there are in the 14th century the manuscripts of Machaut, constituting an author corpus, the monumental *Roman de Fauvel*, technically a narrative and satirical work with lyric insertions, and the 13th and 14th century manuscripts of other romances with lyric insertions.

Groupings within troubadour and trouvère manuscripts are established chiefly on the basis of genre and author, infrequently alphabetization. If other materials, such as the motets in BN 844, are included, they have a separate section. Old Occitan sections in the northern manuscripts are separated out by language. The troubadour chansonnier R took a stab at chronology, presenting Marcabru, folio 5 r°, as "the first troubadour who ever was" and Guiraut Riquier last in the series of authors roughly grouped in early, middle or late generations. Trouvère manuscripts where author/composers are identified usually proceed hierarchically, opening with aristocratic names, not infrequently with that of Thibaut de Champagne, and proceeding down the social scale. Though motet manuscripts may contain some names, organization is normally based on musical criteria, specifically on number of voices, subdivided where necessary according to language. Alphabetical ordering is also found. Ascriptions occur in the later chansonniers, too, but as a general rule, they do not take precedence over musical criteria, such as the number of voices, or form, as a means of categorization.

Manuscript ordering techniques thus suggest several goals. The importance of genre or form is clear throughout, and ordering by genre can highlight newly emerging genres. To privilege the author/composer is to posit a creative principle centered on the individual, sometimes also to suggest a social hierarchy. The ordering of polyphonic songbooks seems to reflect the expertise needed for performance and practical matters of manuscript production. If polyphonic songs were to be performed by specially trained singers the number of voices and hence the number of singers needed is a useful piece of information. Grouping specific formats and languages together facilitates production of the book. In some of the later polyphonic chansonniers, there appear efforts to group songs by author/composer, complicated by the fact that in this repertory, unlike that of the troubadours and trouvères, author and composer are sometimes perceived as different individuals. All of the groupings in the vernacular songbooks differ from the liturgical ordering of sacred pieces according to function.

Iconographical programs, though certainly intended to embellish the manuscript, are not naively decorative, but often carry out ideological programs according to which a manuscript's contents are to be understood and interpreted. Almost all of the manuscripts employ decorated letters or illustrations to mark off sections, groups, individual songs and parts of songs, so that the use of the manuscript is facilitated: illumination classifies and orders. Where there are miniatures, historiated initials, or marginal illustrations, the link between decoration and interpretation becomes closer. By visualizing the contents, the illustrations can make a text easier to read and remember, gloss its meaning, or even subvert its intent. And, without necessarily drawing inspiration directly from the song's contents, illustrations can still set contexts and suggest relationships.

Both ordering and illustration, as well as the way in which the song is presented on the page, bring up the important question of who controls manuscript space and for

what purpose. This question raises complex and diverse
issues of manuscript production and ateliers as well as
geographical distribution. For the majority of troubadour
and trouvère manuscripts, it is all but impossible to
identify centers of production. Nor do we know how or
why the songs came to be deposited in the songbooks. We
can propose identification of different scribes and
scribal practices, usually separate for text and music;
we can surmise how scribes and/or compilers worked with
illustrators; we can date and localize with some assur-
ance. It seems evident that these manuscripts were lay
productions destined for lay audiences, and the 150 to
200-year gap between troubadours and their manuscripts is
due in part to the Church's monopoly on writing. Although
refinement of our knowledge of these matters and of their
implications remains a goal of scholarship, certitude
will probably always elude us. Motet manuscripts, in contrast, constitute a more centralized corpus in that the
main sources are Parisian, and book production in Paris
in the 13th century is sufficiently well documented to
allow for identification of ateliers.[15] For Machaut, the
problems are specific to the organization of an author
corpus.[16] Later chansonniers, which again grow out of
the courts, are more elusive. Like the troubadour
chansonniers, these sources are not entirely French in
origin, and the number of manuscripts from outside what
is now France attests to the dissemination of the French
chanson.

    The question of who controls manuscript space and for
what purpose brings me to the last issue I wish to raise
regarding manuscripts. I have so far mainly discussed the
manuscript contexts in which songs are embedded, and I
have argued that the placing of songs in contexts reflects both how the song is understood and its intended
use. Now I would like to relate manuscript presentation
to geographical provenance to propose links between geog-
raphy and ideology, taking my specific examples from the
troubadour tradition. In contrast to trouvère sources
which come from northern France, troubadour manuscripts
come also from southern France and, above all, from
Italy. Moreover, it is a remarkable characteristic of the
southern manuscripts that frequently texts appear not

only without music but even without staves on which the
music could be notated. Two exceptions, MS G from northern Italy and MS R from southern France, do have music
for substantial sections: in G this is the initial *canso*
section. But these remain exceptions among southern
sources, whereas northern manuscripts almost always have
music. When other idosyncratic features of troubadour
manuscripts are taken into consideration, the *vidas* (little biographies) and *razos* (short commentaries), the oc-
casional inclusion of grammar treatises,[17] there emerges
a conceptualization of the song as a literary work emanating from an identifiable *persona*. The emphasis on lit-
erariness separates southern from northern presentations
of troubadour song and particularly distinguishes the
Italian manuscripts.

Let us take as an example the troubadour manuscript
A. This manuscript originated in all likelihood in the
area around Venice in the late 13th or very early 14th
century. Its scribe may have been from Occitania, working
in Italy. It contains a section of *cansos,* followed by a
section of *tensos* and *coblas,* then a final section of
sirventes. The *cansos* open with the songs of Peire
d'Alvernhe and proceed mostly by author. There are 44
miniatures and 52 *vidas*. There are no staves, consequently no music.

In the *canso* section of the manuscript, song texts
are attached to a composing persona, defined by a *vida*
and an author portrait or miniature. The portrait usually
visualizes biographical information in the *vida,* specifically with respect to social class or professional activity. Exceptionally--this is the only case among Occitan manuscripts--written instructions to the illuminator
can still be seen in the manuscript margins. Although no
actual music is present in the manuscript, a performing
context is created by instructions to the illuminator
such as "a master who is singing." The performer is inserted into a social context according to his class and
sometimes professional identification: troubadour or
jongleur. The iconographic program of this manuscript,
linked to the *vidas,* stresses the truth, the authenticity, the "realness" of the song and of the emotions it

deploys by ascribing them to a "real" individual. Moreover, because the manuscript is produced at a time when
troubadours no longer ply their trade, it conjures up a
vision of the past, a vivid recollection of the art of a
bygone epoch. Troubadour manuscript A serves to illustrate two important features that would have influential
ramifications: 1) clear prioritizing of the poetic persona particularly with respect to the *canso*; 2) the kind
of reception troubadour songs received in Italy.

With regard to the first feature, I must immediately
emphasize, lest the portrait of Italian manuscripts seem
overdrawn, that the technique of creating an illusion of
a poetic persona through "author portraits" is by no
means exclusive to Italian manuscripts. Northern manuscripts, too, as I suggested above, include author portraits. But southern and particularly Italian manuscripts have more complete portrait programs, reinforced
by the *vidas* and *razos* which do not appear in northern
sources.[18] The illusion of poetic persona is thus more
fully exploited in Italian manuscripts and more consistently linked to the *vidas*.

However, the portrait-*vida-razo* complex is but one
way of attaching songs to a specific poet. The mere act
of ascribing songs to individual poets and of grouping
songs by authors so identified is in itself a powerfully
suggestive procedure. Rather than projecting the illusion
of a "real" creative personality whose emotions govern
the song (the source of the emotions being given often in
the *razos*), the grouping of songs of a single author/
composer suggests the concept of an author corpus. The
idea of author corpus appears in southern sources, but
it will receive its fullest development in the north.
The early 14th-century troubadour manuscript R (from
southern France) contains a veritable Guiraut Riquier
"songbook" with each song carefully labeled and dated as
if by the composer himself.[19] The late 13th-century
northern manuscript, BN 25566, is our earliest surviving
collection focussed on one composer: Adam de la Halle.
His manuscript contains not only monophonic but also
polyphonic *chansons* (the first known polyphonic rondeaux
and a few motets). Since early motets were produced

anonymously, the Adam de la Halle collection brings
secular polyphonic music into the orbit of a composing
persona for the first time. But the main medieval illustration of the concept of an author corpus for the repertories here under consideration is furnished in the 14th
century by Machaut: a series of manuscripts contain his
works exclusively. This phenomenon will not be repeated
during the Middle Ages for music; but for the French
poetry that during the 14th century separated itself out
from music to engage upon a new and independent path, the
author corpus will become a typical mode of presentation
and preservation of a lyric poet's works.

However, it is not so much the later and more complete author compilations that persisted to color modern
imaginations but rather the troubadour persona as it
passed through Italy. And this brings me to the second
feature underscored by Manuscript A. The reception of
troubadour song in Italy had a far-reaching effect not
only on the interpretation of the troubadours by modern
critics but also on the way medieval song during and
after the Renaissance was absorbed into scholarly thinking. We have seen in A, along with the importance placed
on historicizing individual troubadours, a marked emphasis on text which transforms singing into a metaphor and
opens the way to annex the lyric to philological studies.
The circumstances which produced texts without melodies,
or even space for melodies, in Italian manuscripts particularly, but also in southern French manuscripts, have
never been fully elucidated. Clarification of some of
these circumstances might come from a closer study of
contemporaneous Italian tastes and interests. Was the
clear difference between northern manuscripts, where
music is usually included (for troubadours as well as
trouvères), and southern manuscripts, where it is usually
excluded due to a more textually oriented Italian lyric
perception? However that question is answered, what seems
clear is that the troubadour lyric was received in Italy
as a text rather than as a song, and it was received as
a text emanating from a powerful creative personality.
The strongest influence on interpretation of troubadour--
and indeed all monophonic--songs came from Dante. Dante
speaks of music as well as poetry, to be sure; but, as we

shall see in Part II, the music is largely absorbed into the text. The poem has the aura of a song (and is so designated in the *De vulgari eloquentia*) without being attached to any actual melody. Arguably then, the elements of what would later become the myth of the troubadour are first assembled in Italy. And it is Italy that will continue to cultivate troubadour songs. While monophonic trouvère manuscript production virtually ceased in France in the 14th century as trouvères were absorbed into polyphonic song, and while southern French manuscript production likewise came to a halt, in Italy troubadour manuscripts were copied into the 16th century under the impetus of Dante and the Italian humanists. This Italian activity would provide a link between the manuscripts of the Middle Ages and the newly invented printing press.

The manuscript images and traditions that I have briefly described here determined the attitudes and approaches taken up by later scholars. On the one hand, we find a monophonic tradition easily assimilated by non-specialists. On the other, we see a polyphonic tradition, more and more complex, with a notation system eventually becoming more intricate than any subsequent musical sign systems before the 20th century, available only to the initiated. After the wholesale rejection of the Middle Ages by the Renaissance, the former would survive transformed, particularly in Italy, and with particular emphasis on troubadours, becoming the stuff of which legends are made. The latter, for a very long time, would not be understood at all.

BOOKS

The Renaissance and the Advent of Printing

It is commonplace of criticism to view the printing press as a mark of modernity, contrasted to the manuscript. It is equally commonplace to soften the contrast immediately by insisting on the slowness of the transformation. But if transformations were not instantaneous,

the invention of the printing press nevertheless reshaped
approaches to medieval lyric. And the attempts made from
the Renaissance to the early 20th century to confront
manuscripts and eventually arrange their contents for
printed books raise most of the issues that face modern
researchers.

In her important work on early printing,[20] Elizabeth
Eisenstein singles out a number of features characterizing what she terms the initial shift to printing. The
most important features for our purposes are those clus-
tered about the notions of standardization, permanency,
reproducibility and identity, which lead to other concepts such as authenticity, originality, authorial prop-
erty rights, and, indeed, to a transformed concept of
author. Important also is the development of historicism
grounded in permanency. By providing fixed spatio-
temporal reference points, permanency permitted recognition of progressive change, and this is linked by
Eisenstein to the Renaissance ability to view the past
from a fixed distance, separating it off from the present.[21] And finally, the printing press was as much a
technological and commercial revolution as an intellectual one. Differing technologies of music and text printing plus the commercial tendency toward specialization
all contributed to modern attitudes toward medieval
song, particularly the separation of music and poetry.

Standardization is, in a way, the key revolution-
izing concept. In its wake and by opposition, it brings
the concepts of the variant (which presupposes a standard
from which one can "vary") and the scribal copy regarded
as decay. Related to it is the normalization of language
and spelling.[22] With print comes the notion not only that
a text can have a fixed identity but that such fixed
identity should be as "correct" or as "authentic" as
possible. The medieval poet/composer and scribe possessed no such standards of stabilization. They may have
thought of composing as a way to attain fame, of writing
as preservation of their work; they may have had notions
of correctness; but attributing to a song a fixed, invio-
lable, "authentic" identity seems to have been foreign to
their concerns, although one must make distinctions of

era and approach. Arguably, medieval scribe/editors attempted to capture in writing features of a song still tied to performance traditions that, in some cases at least, were contemporaneous. From the Renaissance, links of writing to performance ceased to have the same importance; scrutiny of the written manuscripts became the focus of scholarly activity. Consequently the movement from script to print, to use H.J. Chaytor's term,[23] involved not just a translation from one kind of writing to another, but a clash between new and old conceptualizations and a new emphasis on writing that is sometimes spoken of as "reification," that is, turning the recorded work into an immutable object then to be revered as such. These features will become increasingly apparent as we follow the story of turning manuscripts into books.

But important as standardization *per se* would become, historicism had an initially stronger impact on Renaissance attitudes toward medieval song because it determined the conceptual framework within which Renaissance scholars worked. Initially, these scholars worked on manuscripts. Trouvère monophonic songs were no longer copied, but manuscripts remained the chief repositories of polyphonic song throughout the 16th century. And troubadour texts, without music, continued to be copied and commented on, especially in Italy, as we have seen. But even as they commented on manuscripts, Renaissance humanists brought to the medieval period new critical perspectives engendered by historicist methods. Not only did these methods shape perceptions of the medieval text as part of a past detached from the present, they also and perhaps more importantly led to the elaboration of a concept of the "Middle Ages" as a period of decay linking an idealized past, Classical Antiquity, to a present renewed by contact with that past. The most evident result of that periodization was the rejection of medieval artifacts into Gothic darkness. For music and poetry, the effects were devastating. The musical theorist Tinctoris, writing in 1477 (in the *Preface* of his *Liber de arte contrapuncti*), decisively repudiated medieval polyphony by asserting that no piece of music composed more than 40 years ago (that is, before about 1435) is worth hearing, whereas beginning with Dunstable, Binchois, and

Dufay, and continuing with Ockeghem or Busnoys, there are compositions of such beauty as to be suitable not only for men and heroes but also for the immortal Gods.[24] In his rhetorical treatise, *Défense et illustration de la langue française*, 1549, intended to show how French poetry can attain excellence through imitation of classical and Italian forms, the French Renaissance poet Joachim Du Bellay scornfully cast aside "toutes ces vieilles poësies Francoyses . . . comme rondeaux, ballades, vyrelaiz, chants royaulz, chansons, et autres telles episseries, qui corrompent le goust de nostre Langue. . . ."[25] Though contested as soon as they appeared, Du Bellay's ideas reflected perceptions of medieval song that stubbornly persisted. The pejorative value assigned to medieval music and poetry colored Renaissance approaches to medieval song and influenced scholarly thinking well into the modern period.

But pejorative value was not uniformly assigned to all our repertories, due to the way Renaissance revival of Antiquity played itself out. The admiration of the ancients that characterized Du Bellay's thinking became a dominant theme of discussion and debate throughout the Renaissance and the Early Modern periods. Were the Ancients better than the Moderns? The Middle Ages, since it was only a bridge, was largely left out of the debate. However, appreciation of medieval song was indirectly affected because the revival of interest in ancient poetry brought rejection of polyphonic music while allowing the assignment of some value to monophonic music. The study of classical song was forcibly text-based because almost no music survives. But the remaining evidence demonstrated that ancient music was exclusively monophonic. This opened the way to a linking of medieval monophonic songs to the songs of antiquity. Troubadours were the chief beneficiaries. While polyphonic repertories were marginalized since they could not in any way reflect antiquity, troubadour songs, because they were clearly monophonic, already text-based in the Italian tradition, admired by Dante and absorbed into humanist thinking, came to enjoy continuous cultivation, though not, as we shall see, continuously positive evaluation.

Indeed, the attention given to the troubadours provided some of the first efforts (all failed) at modern
text editing. These efforts grew out of the study of language from a historicizing perspective. To be sure, critical views on medieval poetry in the vernacular and
curiosity about language can already be found in the 13th
and 14th centuries. From that time came major vernacular
treatises: Raimon Vidal de Besalú, *Razos de trobar*
(c.1200); Eustache Deschamps, *L'Art de dictier* (1392);
the *Leys d'amors* (c.1356); and particularly Dante's *De
vulgari eloquentia* (c.1305).[26] And the antiquarian spirit
reflected in troubadour manuscripts is a historicizing
perception, conjuring up the image of poet/composers long
dead. So the attitudes we might now characterize as philological, historical, archeological were diffusely represented in medieval approaches to troubadour song. But in
the Renaissance, these attitudes would take on more precise characteristics. The Italian humanist Pietro Bembo
(1470-1547) investigated troubadour poems, collating and
annotating manuscripts as though dealing with works of
antiquity, in order better to trace the origin of Tuscan
in the context of the Renaissance "questione della
lingua." Bembo seems to have envisaged the publication
of "edited" texts, but this project, even though it was
revived by other Italian scholars, was never carried
out.[27] Italian scholarship, however, figured importantly
in subsequent approaches to troubadour song. One of the
more curious immediate responses came from a somewhat ec-
centric individual born in St.-Remy-de-Provence in 1507
named Jean de Nostre-Dame, brother of the astrologer
Nostradamus. In 1575, he published his *Vies des plus
célèbres et anciens poètes provençaux qui ont fleury du
temps des Comtes de Provence*. This work treats the *vidas*
largely as fact and thrusts them forward, rather than
the poems, as representations of troubadour art. Although
by its fanciful character the *Vies* eventually provoked
far stronger blame than praise, it was a long time before
the book could be entirely discredited, and in the mean-
time Jean de Nostre-Dame had set in place an important
segment of the troubadour myth.[28]

Although there was a historicizing element in the
Vies, the most influential historical approaches come

from northern France. To characterize them, we must take another look at the thorny notion of historicism. Viewed in one way, as we have seen, historicizing methods resulted in the detachment and devaluation of the medieval past. Viewed in another way, however, historicism led to the recuperation of works from that past, not as artifacts having value in themselves but as windows on a past which, though detached, still intrigued the present. This kind of historicism undergirds the work coming from northern France, centered on French works. In 1560, the *Recherches de la France* by Etienne Pasquier began to appear. These were researches on various aspects of French language, literature and especially culture; they would pass through several expanded reprintings. In 1581, Claude Fauchet published what could be called the first history of medieval French literature: *Recueil de l'origine de la langue et poésie françoise, ryme et romans*. Both Fauchet and Pasquier were essentially historians. Both scholars were concerned with cultural features, particularly with the exploits of chivalric heroes and their attendant feasts and ceremonies. Both thought of literature as real-life documentation which could help understand the past. They refer to trouvères along with troubadours and entertain a confusion between *roman* and song that would persist for some time, appearing in such later treatises on the *roman*, for example, as those by P.D. Huet, *Traité de l'origine des romans* (1670), and A.P. Jacquin, *Entretiens sur les romans* (1755). But as we shall see, it was through the historical, or historicizing approaches laid out by Pasquier and Fauchet that the path to editions led.[29]

Before pursuing the story of editions, it will be useful to consider briefly the question of how technologies of music printing and monopolies exercised by music printers influenced the contents of editions of medieval song. The Renaissance witnessed a considerable development in the use of printing for music.[30] Although, as I have pointed out, much polyphonic music was still deposited in manuscripts through the 16th century, the first publisher of polyphony was an Italian named Petrucci who worked from about 1500 to about 1520. He was the first to use movable type, a method that made possible wide

dissemination of printed polyphonic music. Greater commercial success was probably realized by the French
printer Pierre Attaingnant, a specialist in the French
chanson, whose first anthology appeared in 1527-8. After
Attaingnant, Parisian publishing saw the rise of Adrian
LeRoy and Robert Ballard. Ballard was attached to the
court which enabled him to obtain in 1553 from Henry II
the charge of "seul imprimeur de la musique de la chambre, chapelle et menus plaisirs du roi" for their enterprise.[31] This exclusive monopoly for music printing had
immediate impact on at least one fledgling effort to
print music and texts together. The first edition of
Ronsard's *Amours* by *La veuve* Maurice de la Porte (1552)
contained music, placed at the end with an *avertissement*
by her son, Ambroise de la Porte, promising its continued publication: "Ayant recouvré le livre des Amours du
Seigner P. de Ronsard, & le cinquiesme de ses Odes, avec
aultres siens opuscules: Et puis apres entendu que pour
ton plaisir & entier contentement il a daigné prendre la
peine de les mesurer sur la lyre (ce que n'avions encore
apperceu avoir esté faict de tous ceux qui se sont exer-
cités en tel genre d'escrire), suyvant son entreprise
avec le vouloir que j'ay de luy satisfaire & pour l'amour
de toy Lecteur: J'ai faict imprimer, & mettre à la fin
de ce present livre, la Musique, sus laquelle tu pourras
chanter une bonne partie du contenu en iceluy: te
promectant à l'advenir de continuer ceste maniere de
faire (en ce qui s'imprimera de la composition dudict
Ronsard) si je congnoy qu'elle te soit aggreable."[32]
Despite the success of his enterprise, however,[33] the
editor was obliged to renege on his promise, largely
because the monopoly accorded to LeRoy and Ballard made
it impossible for anyone else to print music. This
monopoly would remain in force for over two centuries
and, by forcing a separation between text and music publishing, would influence medieval lyric for longer than
that. The first editions of *chansons* chiefly adopted the
format of partbook, that is, a book supplying only a single vocal part and not the complete music. But the earliest examples of printed vocal music in score, with parts
for all voices written on staves one above the other,
date from the 16th century; and by the 17th century score
format had become the norm. This norm made the parallel

or sequential page lay-out of parts for polyphonic music
in medieval manuscripts, described above, seem altogether
alien. Not only was medieval polyphony in itself devalued; its page layout was perceived as irrational and
incomprehensible compared to printing in score.

The Eighteenth Century

Although medieval themes and forms permeated 17th-
century literature, and although many medieval works were
known, and scholars such as DuCange or Mabillon turned
their considerable talents toward the exploration of the
Middle Ages, the dominant thrust throughout the century
was still toward Antiquity, and the medieval period was
largely characterized as barbarous. This characterization would not soon change. However, during the 18th
century a more thorough and systematic approach to the
Middle Ages would bring the period to the forefront of
scholarly attention, and to this development we now turn.

The chief agent of this new orientation was the
Académie des Inscriptions, and the most important
scholarly figure in 18th-century historical medievalism
was Jean-Baptiste de la Curne de Sainte-Palaye, member
of the Académie from 1724 and four times its director.[34]
The Académie Royale des Inscriptions et Belles-Lettres,
founded by Colbert in 1663 to work on inscriptions and
medals for the glory of Louis XIV, was reoriented in the
early 18th century toward the study of national history.
This reorientation made it a central forum for the discussion of medieval subjects, since, in its view, as in
the view of Renaissance literary historians mentioned
above, medieval texts and medieval vernacular languages
offered primary evidence about national cultural history.
Linguistics and history were linked; and from this link-
age will arise the debate over the priority of troubadours vs. trouvères, which is not an artistic debate but
a debate of crucial concern for national identity. The
use of literary texts as sources of history is related to
the larger Enlightenment view of history as culture, as
well as to basic tenets of the Quarrel of the Ancients
and the Moderns.[35] Members of the Académie, pursuing

national cultural history, adopted positions more favorable to the Middle Ages than those of many *philosophes*, for whom there lay between antiquity and the modern period only long centuries of ignorance and barbarism.[36] Yet, while devoting themselves to study of the Middle Ages, the scholars of the Académie were generally unable to appreciate the esthetic values of the works they so patiently exhumed. Despite the fact that they began to establish modern methods of textual criticism, their focus was not so much on the texts themselves--even less the music--than on the "historical" information the texts could yield; and largely for this reason, a lack of appreciation of medieval song persisted alongside a great interest in learning more about it. Eighteenth-century scholars neither brought medieval song into print nor shaped an esthetic vision that allowed the song to be understood as art, but they laid the foundations for all that was to come.

Sainte-Palaye realized that his approach was neither entirely new nor radically innovative. In a paper read to the Académie des Inscriptions in 1743,[37] he referred to scholars like Fauchet who had already preceded him. What distinguished his work, however, was a ferocious attachment to sources. Much of his career was devoted to ferreting out and obtaining copies of manuscripts. No prior lists were available to him; the great 19th-century compendia did not yet exist. He visited Italy twice to consult manuscripts in Italian libraries. For medieval poetry, we can observe that he knew all the major troubadour manuscripts and obtained copies of 21 of them (ignoring or omitting, however, troubadour songs in northern 'French MSS); that he provided the earliest more or less complete list of troubadours; that he copied one Machaut manuscript, which also contained poems of Eustache Deschamps, whose importance he was the first to recognize; and that, in conjunction with his work on Froissart for the history of chivalry, he read to the Académie in 1738 a "Notice des poésies de Froissart."[38]

Beside the *Mémoires sur l'ancienne chevalerie*, his most important undertaking was the *Histoire littéraire des troubadours*, a three-volume work, finally published

in 1774 not by Sainte-Palaye himself but by the Abbé
Millot. This work demonstrates simultaneously the great
strengths as well as the weaknesses of Sainte-Palaye's
approach. The collection of materials that went into the
production of this work can only be termed stupendous,
and it nourished scholarly research throughout the 19th
century. The work itself was, when it appeared, a major
disappointment. Troubadours are presented one after the
other, with a short "notice" for each poet, together with
some prose quotations in French from several poems. No
original language appeared in the book (a feature that
would partly inspire Raynouard's 19th-century title
"Choix de poésies *originales* . . ."). The "notices"
provide some useful remarks on previous scholarship. The
whole work is the first to sort out troubadours from a
motley collection of trouvères and *romanciers* in order
to consider them as an entity. Yet, in the way they are
treated, the troubadours might as well be *romanciers*.
Quotations from their works are largely intended to iso-
late passages useful for historical study. The notion
that these works could, as poetry and music, have intrin-
sic value was foreign to Sainte-Palaye's thinking. Thus,
while he rendered enormous service to the study of medieval poetry, he maintained toward that poetry an exclusively textual and, from an esthetic point of view, a
generally pejorative stance, no different from other Enlightenment views stemming from Renaissance periodizations. Information about text sources had been greatly
increased; but the perception of text divorced from music
--to which the troubadour manuscript tradition as it came
through Italy lent credence--was now more firmly anchored
in scholarly procedures.

Part of the difficulty Sainte-Palaye and others faced
in their researches on medieval song was the resistance
of 18th-century public taste to such scholarship. There
was, in contrast, an enormous public appetite for chivalric romances--real or imagined, authentic or fanciful;
and through the vulgarisation of medieval subjects, a
public for the fruits of scholarship would eventually be
created.[39] Sainte-Palaye participated in this popularizing of medieval works by his publication of *Aucassin et
Nicolette* in modern French (subtitled *Les Amours du bon*

vieux temps), but not as extensively as his friend, the
Comte de Tressan. Tressan was at the forefront of a movement that can best be described as pseudo-medievalism,
one of whose effects would be the creation of a new literary genre, the "genre troubadour."[40] Pseudo-medievalism
was to become perhaps an even more important factor in
the perception of music than in the popularizing view of
poetry.

In Sainte-Palaye's system, there was no room for
music. He knew of its existence: in transcribing a
Machaut manuscript, he left a place for it; and although
in 1773 he copied the so-called La Clayette Manuscript,
an important 13th-century motet source, without including
or even mentioning the music, he may well have known
there was music, because a letter describing the manuscript addressed to one of his collaborators spoke of
"chansons notées."[41] Sainte-Palaye's attitude was understandable within the conceptual framework of his time,
inherited from the Renaissance. Beyond the general concept of the Middle Ages as barbarous, the study of medieval secular music continued to suffer from the repudia-
tion of the very idea of polyphony in favor of a Greek
monophonic concept; and even actual medieval monophonic
music (as distinct from texts), which in theory conformed
to the Greek concept, was often dismissed as merely a
kind of odd-sounding plain chant.[42] As we shall see, the
translation of medieval secular song into something the
public could presumably enjoy would usually quite deform
its nature. Nevertheless, despite the handicaps from
which it suffered, a surprising amount of medieval secular music was known and discussed by Sainte-Palaye's
friends. More importantly, the 18th century saw the first
general histories of music and the rise of musical
historiography.

If the title of being the first history of music in
France could be bestowed on the curious *Histoire de la
musique et de ses effets depuis son origine jusques à
présent* by Pierre Bourdelet, published in 1715 under the
name of his nephew Jacques Bonnet, more extensive work
was carried out by scholars associated in one way or
another with Sainte-Palaye and his circle. Thus the Abbé

Jean Lebeuf read papers for the Académie, published in the *Mémoires*; and, writing with the Comte de Caylus in 1746 and 1747, he called attention to the works of Machaut. Both men were primarily interested in presenting facts of an historical nature, but both mention music in their descriptions of manuscripts, although some of Lebeuf's remarks were scarcely flattering--the "chants profanes," in his view, "n'étaient guère mélodieux," or again, the "chansons françaises" found in Parisian manuscripts "n'étaient que comme du chant grégorien."[43] Lebeuf recognized the evident contemporaneous appreciation of these songs, but it passed his understanding: "Les oreilles de ces temps-là y étaient apparemment accoutumées, et ces airs leur paraissaient beaux."[44] Both Lebeuf and Caylus reveal a major obstacle to the understanding of medieval polyphony: the notation. Caylus merely expresses puzzlement and calls for help.[45] He is not impressed either by Machaut's poetry, which he calls "lâche" and badly written.[46] Lebeuf is more sophisticated in his awareness of different kinds of musical notation; he describes how different parts are laid out on the page, expressing some surprise that words appear under one part only in some pieces.[47] But he is unable to proceed beyond description to understanding.

The first complete edition of the works of a trouvère including, at the end, nine melodies, appeared in Paris in 1742: Levesque de la Ravallière's *Les Poésies du roy de Navarre avec des notes et un glossaire françois*. This was a landmark work. It is possible that publication was facilitated by public interest in the story of Thibaut de Champagne and Blanche de Castille to which La Ravallière gave a certain prominence by attempting to refute it, but which lent to the "edition" an air of "romance." Whatever the deficiences of La Ravallière's work, he was the first to try to justify music as an integral part of medieval song, although he conceded that the melodies might appear insipid to ears accustomed to the operas of Lully and Rameau.[48]

Toward the end of the 18th century, several works appeared which took account of the medieval period and marked a considerable advance in musical historiography:

almost simultaneously, in England, John Hawkins published his *General History of the Science and Practice of Music* (5 vols) in 1776 and Charles Burney the first volume of his four-volume *A General History of Music* (1776-89); in France, Jean-Benjamin de La Borde published an *Essai sur la musique ancienne et moderne* in 1780; and in Germany J.N. Forkel's *Allgemeine Geschichte der Musik* appeared in 1788 and 1801 (it was never completed). All of these historians drew on the work of Sainte-Palaye, Lebeuf, and La Ravallière. A brief look at two of them, La Borde and Burney, will serve to illustrate their perceptions of medieval secular song.

La Borde's *Essai* was chiefly important for its ample and universalizing treatment of songs from all over the world. Book IV (of the six books of the *Essai*) is entitled "Des Chansons." Some 250 pages of this book are devoted to French song from the 12th-14th centuries. Book IV is followed by a musical collection, a "Choix de chansons mises à quatre parties." Book I of the *Essai* contains introductory matter, and there is appended to Book VI a brief essay by the Abbé Rive rectifying what he contends are grievous errors made by Lebeuf and Caylus in their work on Machaut. La Borde's work forms a somewhat disorganized but for his time useful compendium of materials. He claims he is not writing a history but presenting for others' use the fruits of some thirty years of collecting. A brief perusal of some of his tangled narrations makes one rather glad he did not write a history. Participating in what had been and would be an ongoing discussion about which came first, troubadours or trouvères, La Borde recognizes neither the primacy nor the value of the troubadours; his focus is exclusively on trouvères. He begins with a discussion of romance languages, after which he provides the first anthology of 12th- and 13th-century trouvère texts, in a format similar to Sainte-Palaye's troubadour history, except that La Borde's extracts, in some cases entire poems, are in Old French with modern translations. The songs of the Châtelain de Coucy form a separate section, and only in that section are melodies given for four songs attributed to the Châtelain.[49] Otherwise, there are no musical examples in the discussion, and no reference is made to the existence of music in the table of manuscripts drawn up for the *Essai*. La Borde's evaluation of the material he has so laboriously collected does not entice one to carry his researches further: "Le grand défaut de ces chansons est leur monotonie insupportable. . . ."[50] A listing of 14th- and 15th-century poets then concludes La Borde's treatment of French *chansons*. For Machaut, there is only a brief reference to the essay by the Abbé Rive appended to Book VI.

The surprising feature of La Borde's *Essai* is the heavy emphasis on languages and texts, and the sparse treatment of music. La Borde seems almost as puzzled by medieval music as his historian colleagues. From his introductory remarks about notation,[51] it seems clear that he has some concept of note forms, some idea of their development, but no sense of how notation systems might have worked. It also seems evident that motet page lay-out remained something of a mystery for him.[52] For La Borde, notation only becomes legible in the 16th century. Therefore when he transcribes medieval song, he has no compunction about "improving" it. For the Châtelain de Coucy, La Borde gives first a supposedly diplomatic edition of the melodies along with, however, added tempo markings such as "très lent," followed by a somewhat arbitrary transcription into modern rhythmic notation. The "Choix de chansons mises à quatre parties" at the end of Book IV includes in its motley collection two monophonic songs attributed to Raoul de Soissons or Richard Coeur de Lyon (this collection is as much pseudo-medieval as truly medieval), to which are added three parts, doubtless of La Borde's fabrication, in order to make the songs more palatable to his public: "Nous avons préféré de les [all types of songs] arranger à quatre parties, plutôt que de les donner simplement avec une basse, parce que cette manière d'exécuter des airs nous a paru délicieuse. . . ."[53] Knowledgeable appreciation of medieval song is still a long way off.

The *History* of Charles Burney is much more methodical than La Borde's *Essai*: it is, indeed, a history. Burney sees music as innocent luxury and entertainment; his outlook is primarily modernist. Book II of the

History is devoted to medieval music, sacred and secular,
with secular song described in a long chapter entitled
"Of the Origin of Modern Languages, to which written
Melody and Harmony were first applied; and general state
of Music till the Invention of Printing about the year
1450." The way Burney divides his material in Book II
reveals some perceptive observations. In the first instance, music (mostly sacred) is separated into periods
before and after the "Formation of the Time Table," that
is, the invention of rhythmic notation. Rhythmic notation
freed music to develop (i.e. make progress) on its own;
before this invention, it had been a slave to language:
"The discovery which was . . . made in the invention of
characters for time . . . constitutes the true area of
musical independence; for till then, if melody subsisted,
it was entirely subservient to all syllabic laws."[54] Control of rhythm makes modern music superior to ancient
music. Then to proceed, Burney adopts a division into
pre- and post-printing. The chief effect of printing was
to "increase musical production."[55] The press did not
relieve all difficulties of notation, as Burney explains:
". . . the perusal of old music, after it is found, is
attended with much more trouble than literary works of
equal antiquity: for being published and preserved in
single parts, these parts must previously be put into
such a state, that the eye may compare their several
relations at one glance; or, to use the language of
Musicians, they must be *scored*, before their beauties or
defects can be discovered, and this, from the difficulty
of obsolete notation, and the want of *bars*, is rendered
a very slow process."[56]

Given his clearly modernist leanings, one would not
expect Burney to have a more favorable view of medieval
song than his contemporaries. He did not find medieval
music entertaining. Indeed, his work on the Middle Ages
is flawed by a monumental lack of interest. He opens his
discussion with the following pronouncement: "If it be
true that the progress of music in every country depends
on the degrees of civilization and culture of other arts
and sciences among its inhabitants, and on the language
which they speak, the accents of which furnish the skel-
eton and nerves of all vocal melody; great perfection

cannot be expected in the music of Europe during the
Middle Ages, when the Goths, Vandals, Huns, Germans,
Franks, and Gauls, whose ideas were savage, and language
harsh and insolent, had seized on its most fertile prov-
inces."[57] Since for Burney, there are no written remains
of secular polyphonic music before the 14th century,[58]
his discussion of secular music before the invention of
printing is chiefly devoted to monophonic music (polyphonic music is dispatched in three pages). Like
La Borde, Burney begins with a history of language that
is, to say the least, erratic. Unlike La Borde, Burney
gives pride of place to the troubadours, to whom he
devotes half of his secular music chapter.

If Burney is more methodical than La Borde, he still
confuses fact and fiction, medieval and pseudo-medieval,
and has at his disposal no techniques to transcribe the
music. In the short section on the trouvères, for example, he places a curious pseudo-medieval composition
called the "Song of Roland," attributed to the Marquis de
Paulmy, beside songs of the Châtelain de Coucy or Thibaut
de Champagne.[59] During his perusal of troubadour songs,
he is overjoyed to come upon the story of "our Richard
the First" and seizes the opportunity to feed into his
history the tangled legend of *Richard Coeur de Lion*
first appearing in a romance in 1705 entitled *La Tour
Ténébreuse.*[60] The story of Richard brings Burney to
Gaucelm Faidit's *planh*, whose melody he presents as the
most ancient he has been able to find. The transcription of the melody illustrates Burney's method. He first
gives the melody and original text in what he calls "a
facsimile." Then he cooks up a rhythmic transcription
"with a base, in modern notes, to which the translation
is adjusted."[61] This makes a curious piece, with no better conception of the value of the original than we found
with La Borde. Burney does give Old Occitan original
texts with his translations, but he has no love for troubadours. He characterizes them as licentious, "rapacious
and corrupt artists without talents."[62] Although Burney
is even less interested in 14th-century polyphony than in
monophonic song, he does attempt a transcription, com-
plaining the while, to excuse himself, that he had been
promised transcriptions of some Machaut songs by a

correspondent in Paris, but the transcriptions hadn't
arrived, and he could hardly hope to succeed "in solving
enigmas which have already defeated superior sagacity"
(the "sagacity" of Caylus or even of La Borde, about
whose work he has some sharply critical remarks to
offer).[63]

While 18th-century medievalists collected an enormous amount of information about the past, their guiding
approaches were through language and history: even discussion of secular music was largely discussion of vernacular texts. In the century's crucial debates over the
idea of progress, the Quarrel of the Ancients and the
Moderns, and the Guerre des Bouffons, medieval song was
largely rejected or misunderstood. Between the Greeks and
the Moderns, it still occupied, as it had in the Renaissance, a barbarous wasteland. Progress resided in the invention of harmony, and only from the 16th century could
this invention be recognized for what it was. The path
from Greek monody to modern opera was easily found; but
it did not pass through medieval song. What enthusiasm
there was for medieval texts came from those Moderns who
sought the roots of their modernity in the childhood of
their nation. Thus despite the elements of knowledge
assembled, many confusions remained and the dominant
value judgments about poetry and melody stayed pejorative. Medieval monophony is simply monotonous; medieval
polyphony simply puzzling. So the *Encyclopédie ou dictionnaire raisonné des sciences des arts et des métiers*
of D'Alembert and Diderot, that great center of 18th-
century intellectual activity and re-shaper of episte-
mological paradigms, having informed us in the article
"Motet" that the term refers to "musique faite sur des
paroles latines à l'usage de l'église," then warns: "Je
dois avertir que les musiciens des XIIIe et XIVe siècles
donnaient le nom de *motetus* à la partie que nous nommons
aujourd'hui *haute-contre*. Ce nom et plusieurs autres
étranges causent souvent bien de l'embarras à ceux qui
s'appliquent à déchiffrer les anciens manuscrits de musique qui ne s'écrivent pas en partition comme à présent."
The *Encyclopédie* article "Chanson" opts for the preeminence of France in the development of the genre since the
Greeks because of the "galanterie aisée" that reigns in

French society. And in his *Dictionnaire de Musique,* Jean-Jacques Rousseau elaborates on this idea. Moving from the Anciens, to whom he has devoted most of his article on the "Chanson," to the Moderns, he marks the preeminence of France, witness the troubadours: "Cet heureux peuple est toujours gai, tournant tout en plaisanterie: les femmes y sont fort galantes, les hommes fort dissipés, et le pays produit d'excellent vin: le moyen de n'y pas chanter sans cesse?" And without making any clear demarcation between troubadours and trouvères, Rousseau continues: "Nous avons encore d'anciennes *chansons* de Thibault, comte de Champagne, l'homme le plus galant de son siècle, mises en musique par Guillaume de Machaut."[64]

Nonetheless, throughout the 18th century, scholars worked from manuscripts which they consulted and collected themselves; they were gentlemen scholars, and Sainte-Palaye is the most outstanding example. By the end of the century, the troubadour manuscripts were reasonably well catalogued, the trouvère manuscripts were fairly well known, but, except for Machaut, polyphonic sources were generally not catalogued at all. There were some conceptions of text editing in place; the editing of music, mainly because of the continuing mystery of notation, lagged far behind. As Burney noted, texts were more accessible. The thorny questions of how to bring manuscripts into printed books were scarcely raised on a theoretical level, and certainly not resolved on a practical level. Seeking approaches to these questions would be the work of the 19th century, continued in the early 20th.

The Nineteenth and Early Twentieth Centuries

Two dominant ideologies undergirded the 19th-century movement toward systematic procedures of text editing: romanticism and positivism. Both of these ideologies, to be sure, embraced many more issues than the question of establishing texts. But both shaped the conception of what a printed text should be and should do, as well as the notion of who should be producing edited texts and for what reasons. Romanticism reached for origins: along

with the idea of an oral poetic tradition reliable enough
to allow the recovery of "origins," romanticism nourished
a conception of genius and creativity that presumed for a
text, however diverse its manuscript tradition, a creating moment, an author's original that could authenticate
a printed version. Important to romanticism also was the
linking of national language and national soul. As Michel
Foucault has pointed out, the rooting of language in the
speaking subject, the notion that "language manifests and
translates the fundamental will of those who speak it,"
depends on the idea that language springs from the people
and carries a given people's unique destiny.[65] Positivism
provided a conceptual framework for recovering texts
based on the views that the weighing of evidence (in this
case manuscript evidence) can bring us to the truth (in
this case authentic text), and that complete objectivity,
achievable through sound training, is without problem or
bias.[66] Positivism proceeded according to scientific models and aspired to the reliability of scientific findings. It emphasized the value of scholarly expertise--
sound training--and looked askance on the crossing of
disciplines, perceived as amateurish.

These two dominant ideologies were not simultaneously
applied to poetry and music; troubadour and trouvère
poetic repertories became much more rapidly a main focus
of critical attention than medieval secular music. The
music, especially polyphonic music, was deemed more difficult of access and remained largely unappreciated by
scholars avid for texts. By century's end some firm principles of editing and publishing had been devised for
both halves of our subject, but the scholarly divisions
between them had become institutionalized. To trace this
story, given such divisions, it will be convenient to
treat first poetry and then music, and to maintain the
distinctions between troubadours and trouvères on the basis of language, and between monophonic and polyphonic
textures on the basis of accessibility. These distinctions will allow lines of development to be more clearly
drawn.

Troubadour poetry entered the 19th century partly as
legend, partly as historical fact. The concept of the

"troubadour" belonged as much to popular mythology as to scholarly debate, with the one never quite divorced from the other. Troubadour song played a role in the elaboration of the idea of romantic love; the "genre troubadour" affected art, music, and novels, as well as lyric poetry. These diverse developments cannot be followed here; suffice it to emphasize that the so-called "goût troubadour" helped create a public for troubadour song, even as it simultaneously distorted that song. The prominence of troubadour poetry also made it a perfect vehicle for the expression of nascent provincial nationalistic leanings. These strains converged to bring Occitan poetry and language to the forefront of the young discipline of Romance Philology.

François-Just-Marie Raynouard has sometimes been called the first modern philologist.[67] He was a lawyer by training and thus fitted more into the model of gentleman/scholar than into that of professional philologist. Nevertheless, his *Choix de poésies originales des troubadours* (6 vols. 1816-1821) and his monumental and still useful *Lexique roman* (6 vols, 1836-1844) mark the beginning of modern Occitan studies placed in the context of the romance languages. The former gives us complete texts in the original language (as opposed to the *Histoire* by Sainte-Palaye and Millot), while the latter provides a *Dictionnaire de la langue des troubadours*, indispensable to the understanding of the original texts.

The title of Raynouard's *Lexique* reveals his program. He was born in the Midi, and his approach to the history of romance languages reflects the emerging 19th-century Occitan nationalism. For Raynouard, a common *langue romane* had already displaced Latin by the time of Charlemagne, and this *langue romane* was identical to, or preserved by, Old Occitan. Other romance languages grew from this common source. Raynouard's use of the term *langue romane* thus had nationalistic and political overtones; by defending the linguistic priority of Occitan, he gave the troubadours pride of place, and thus reformulated the 18th-century debate on different grounds. Without stating overtly what he was doing, Raynouard placed greater value on language than on literature. He surely

recognized the originality of troubadour poetry.[68] But
this "originality" was a function of its position at the
beginning of European literature and no more. Raynouard
considered the troubadours inferior to the Ancients. Indeed, curiously enough, one of the reasons he gave for
their "originality" was their inability to understand and
hence to imitate the Ancients.[69] According to Raynouard,
a sufficient idea of the poetic talent of the troubadours
can be provided by the few translations of selected stanzas which he groups as an introduction to troubadour
texts in the original language.[70] The choice of texts in
his anthology was calculated to further his linguistic
and political goals: he included the oldest monuments of
the *langue romane,* beginning with the *Serments de
Strasbourg,* and troubadour texts selected with a view
toward justifying the glory of the poets, hence the su-
periority of their language.[71] Raynouard lists the manuscripts he used, but gives no manuscript sources for
individual texts and proposes no objective method for
establishing such texts. Thus, if Raynouard can be called
the first modern philologist, he certainly did not produce what could be termed a modern critical edition.

In response to the early volumes of Raynouard's
Choix, August Wilhelm von Schlegel wrote his perspica-
cious essay "Observations sur la langue et la littérature provençales" (1818). He criticized Raynouard's
politicized use of *langue romane* to refer only to Old
Occitan. But his debate with Raynouard and his own emphasis on linguistic questions sharpened both the focus on
language *per se,* and the notion of linking language and
national (or even personal) destiny. Schlegel continued
the 18th-century notion that troubadour texts offered
source material for the historian, particularly in the
sense that these texts "contiennent un trésor de souve-
nirs nationaux."[72] Yet he had a keener appreciation of
the poetry than Raynouard, and he recognized the integral
role of music: "Comme les chansons, les tensons et les
sirventés étoient également destinés à être chantés, il
seroit intéressant de connoître le rapport entre l'ordon-
nance des strophes et la composition musicale. L'un des
manuscrits de la bibliothèque royale (No 2701) contient
des airs de musique en assez grand nombre. Il est à

désirer que M. Raynouard veuille en donner quelques-uns, en les faisant transposer par une main savante dans la notation actuelle."[73]

The program that Schlegel advocated was never realized by Raynouard, nor even by any other scholar before the end of the 19th century, when Antonio Restori published his articles on troubadour music (1895). The focus of troubadour scholarship remained textual and linguistic, emphasizing the place of troubadour poetry in the history of romance languages and in the emergent Occitan nationalism.

It was Goethe who, perhaps inadvertently, inaugurated the discipline of Romance Philology by drawing the attention of a young Friedrich Diez to Raynouard's *Choix*. Diez, more than Raynouard, became the founder of Romance Philology and, more importantly, drew troubadour poetry into the orbit of the developing institutionalization of romance studies in Germany. Raynouard remained a private scholar to the end; Diez would profit from a teaching post at Bonn. The important place that troubadour studies have occupied in the work of German scholars after Diez, who established the basis of modern "scientific" study of medieval poetry, may be explained in part by the fact that the interest in a cultural Occitan past that motivated Raynouard's work was similar to the interest in a cultural German past, "out of which German national historiography took shape," that motivated German scholars.[74] So it was that much of the early work on troubadours was done in Germany. Karl Bartsch's edition of Peire Vidal's poems, published in 1857, was the first scientific edition of a troubadour corpus. And it was Bartsch who in 1872 drew up the list of troubadours that served to identify them until 1933, when the list was reviewed and revised by Pillet and Carstens. The work of Bartsch and Gröber on manuscripts, and the studies on language produced by the great German philologists, provided indispensable research tools. All, however, were clearly centered on texts.

By century's end in Italy, there was also a strong tradition of troubadour scholarship, illustrated by such names as Cesare de Lollis, U.A. Canello, Ernesto Monaci, Vincenzo Crescini or Pio Rajna. Principles of editing carried over from classical philology were readily adopted in Italy where they drew on a rich classical and humanistic heritage.

The development of "scientific" scholarship in France, as in Germany, was linked to nationalistic interests, but of a different sort. Raynouard had no immediate followers of his stature in Occitan studies. His successor in the Académie des Inscriptions was Paulin Paris, noted medievalist, professor at the Collège de France, and father of the even more noted medievalist Gaston Paris, who would succeed his father at the Collège de France. Gaston Paris studied in Germany with Diez, returning to Paris before the Franco-Prussian war. This war stimulated French nationalism; and partly in a desire to correct a perceived inferiority of French scholarship, Gaston Paris and his colleagues espoused German scientific and positivistic models based on classical philology. Gaston Paris thus came to stand for the implantation of scientific teaching and scholarship in France, inaugurating a period of intense compilation, cataloguing and editing that would dominate, though not without debate, the late 19th and early 20th centuries.

Gaston Paris himself was not drawn to the troubadours. It was his contemporary, Paul Meyer, professor at the Collège de France and at the Ecole des Chartes, of which he became director in 1882, who disseminated scientific approaches to both the language and the literature of the Midi. Of even greater importance for troubadour studies was the appointment of Alfred Jeanroy to the Sorbonne in the early 20th century. Jeanroy is best known today for his *Poésie lyrique des troubadours* (1934). And yet, although Jeanroy gave priority to the southern lyric, his doctoral thesis, published in 1889, *Les Origines de la poésie lyrique en France au Moyen Age,* sought to infer the nature of early northern lyric from sources such as refrains or later French popular poetry that were largely uninfluenced by southern art forms. This thesis reflected some of the concerns of Jeanroy's master, Gaston Paris, and rephrased once again the debate on linguistic priority, south or north. Not only had Paris espoused scientific scholarship as a nationalistic endeavor; he had also turned to the epic with its rich patriotic overtones as a vehicle for French national identity. Through the epic, the French language took its place in the sun as a vehicle for innovation; and since by this time, Old Occitan had been dislodged from the position of *langue romane* given it by Raynouard, a new paradigm could emerge: if priority can be granted to Old Occitan for the lyric, priority must be given to Old French for the epic (and later for romance), and a "true" Old French lyric could be sought as well. From the time of Gaston Paris, and despite the work of eminent scholars such as Meyer or Jeanroy, the increasing institutionalization of Old French studies would ultimately and very gradually marginalize the study of Old Occitan in France.

As we have seen, initial confusions between trouvères and troubadours usually redounded to the glory of the troubadours. There was no "genre trouvère"; northern poets never attained mythic status. Yet if it can be argued that trouvère studies developed in the shadow of troubadour prestige, it must be recognized that from the start, approaches to editions of trouvère songs differed from those adopted for troubadours.

First, and doubtless because more music survived, early trouvère editions included music; they were less exclusively textual than troubadour editions. Already Levesque de la Ravallière's edition of Thibaut de Champagne in the 18th century, mentioned above, provided music for nine songs. An edition of the works of the Châtelain de Coucy appeared in 1830: *Chansons du Châtelain de Coucy, suivies de l'ancienne musique, mise en notation moderne avec accompagnement de piano* prepared by François Perne. And later in the century, we may note Coussemaker's landmark edition of the songs of Adam de la Halle (1872).

Second, if there was no early 19th-century champion of trouvères such as Raynouard for troubadours, there was a steadier stream of publications and editions, primarily by French and German scholars, particularly emphasizing genres and regions, but later individual poets as well. To a degree, French scholarship on the trouvères proceeded from nationalistic concerns. But, as we have seen, epic was the main vehicle of French nationalism; and the language of the lyric *per se* was never as high on the French political agenda as the language of the Occitan lyric on the agenda of the Midi. By mid-century, Paulin Paris had surveyed trouvère manuscripts (*Les Manuscrits de la Bibliothèque du Roi*, VI, 1845) and begun substantial articles on trouvères in the *Histoire littéraire de la France, ouvrage commencé par des religieux Bénedictins de la Congrégation de Saint-Maur et continué par les Membres de l'Institut (Académie royale des Inscriptions et Belles-Lettres)*.[75] The *Histoire* should have reflected scholarly work on the troubadours as well, but no competent scholar could be found to participate in the enterprise.[76] Old French was, of course, a part of Friedrich Diez's *Grammatik der romanischen Sprachen* (1836-38); by the end of the century, specialized studies of Old French began to appear as well as the still irreplaceable collection of texts that constitute the Bartsch *Chrestomathie* (1866). And the manuscripts were subjected to examination and ordering by Raynaud and Schwan.[77]

But if work thus went on apace, the results were somewhat scattered. The Old French repertory was less compact than the troubadour repertory, more difficult to limit in space and time and hence to cultivate. The limitations placed on the troubadour repertory were to a degree artificial and cut off serious study of poetry after the Albigensian Crusade. But sharp definition of the field fostered clear focus on poetic personae. Although trouvère poet/composer personae on the troubadour model first caught scholarly attention, the trouvère repertory is characterized by a greater diversity of genres and many more anonymous pieces. It is further the vehicle of two crucial and related transitions during the 13th and 14th centuries: from monophonic to polyphonic song, and from song to poem, the first increasing the complexity of the musical element, the second abandoning actual music altogether. In these characteristics reside many of the difficulties from which the trouvère repertory has suffered, and they help explain why that repertory is not fully known and appreciated even today.

While the troubadour poet/composer paradigm, and the trouvère songs it carried in its wake, as well as some anonymous trouvère compositions, could fall into romantic notions of poetic creation and thus maintain public and scholarly interest, the poetry itself, and especially the more formalistic genres of the 14th century, continued to be seen within the general perception that the medieval period was ignorant and its poetry tiresome and repetitious. This perception was particularly pernicious for texts joined to early polyphonic textures because the polyphony itself suffered from an even greater lack of understanding. Thirteenth-century motet texts were all but eliminated from scholarly gaze and a persistently pejorative tone was preserved in discussions of Machaut and some of his contemporaries.

The first motet texts were published by the musicologist Gustav Jacobsthal (1879-80) and by Raynaud (1881-3). Even before these editions, Paulin Paris, in an article on Adam de la Halle for the *Histoire littéraire de la France* recognized some of the motet's intriguing features but without understanding the genre.[78] The *Histoire littéraire de la France* never reached the 14th century so we cannot know what general views Paulin Paris might have expressed about Machaut. Fourteenth-century lyric texts including works of Machaut were available in Prosper Tarbé's *Collection des poètes champenois antérieurs au XVIe siècle* (1849). Paulin Paris himself edited Machaut's *Voir Dit* (1875).[79] In the "Notice" to this edition, we may catch a glimpse of his attitude. Although he characterizes Machaut as a clever poet and a musical composer without peer (x), he finds that the admiration Machaut inspired in his own day is not likely to be duplicated in modern times (x, xxxi). Tastes have changed; and one detects in the "Notice" a faint tinge of surprise that such great respect could have been granted Machaut by his contemporaries. As for late 14th-century repertories contained in sources such as the Chantilly Manuscript, they were unknown until the 20th century.

Two literary histories of the late 19th century can

serve as a summary of the views I have indicated. Gaston
Paris's influential *Littérature française au moyen âge
(XIe-XIVe siècle)* covers the period to 1327.[80] The work
was criticized because it covered neither the 14th and
15th centuries nor Old Occitan, but precisely these
choices determined subsequent perceptions. Gaston Paris
had no great love for lyric. According to him, the trouvère courtly lyric (and one will remember Paris's role in
the establishment of the term "courtly" in critical discourse) simply died during the 13th century. Machaut then
created a new style which would be imitated by his successors.[81] Gaston Paris sandwiched the motet between
chansons de toile and rondeaux, devoted a mere five lines
to it, and did not make it entirely clear that there are
French as well as Latin motets.[82]

Petit de Julleville's *Histoire de la langue et de la
littérature française des Origines à 1900* (1896) devotes
2 volumes to the Middle Ages, from the origins to 1500.
The first of these volumes has a substantial article by
Alfred Jeanroy on "Les Chansons" with a note about music
at the end. The second volume devotes some twenty pages
to 14th-century poetry in an article by Petit de
Julleville. Jeanroy judges the "chanson courtoise" with
what would become his customary severity. Motets are
characterized in a few lines as of little interest: "Au
point de vue littéraire, ils n'offrent guère . . . d'autre intérêt que celui de présenter une grande variété de
versification et de rouler parfois sur des thèmes popu-
laires ou demi-populaires."[83] The note on music relies
heavily on Coussemaker for the motet, recognizes the
importance of the Montpellier manuscript, but finds that
the music can only "heurter toutes nos habitudes harmo-
niques et nous ne trouvons pas excessives les invectives
éloquentes que lui ont adressées des musiciens de premier
ordre comme Fétis."[84] Petit de Julleville's article on
14th-century poetry begins with the received (from Paris)
wisdom that all 13th-century styles and forms were dead
or decadent by the 14th century. In their place came the
fixed forms, whose poets were more and more inspired
by "une habilité purement mécanique."[85] Machaut is
viewed as prosaic and prolix, sometimes sincere in the
expression of feeling, but in the end so tedious that
the interest his work aroused in its own time appears

surprising. "Ces sentiments sont exprimés avec grâce quoiqu'un peu trop longuement, car Guillaume de Machaut sut quelquefois écrire, mais il ne sut jamais se borner."[86] The article bows in passing to Philippe de Vitry with no mention of the *Roman de Fauvel*, although the work was known. But music never retains Petit de Julleville's attention.

These histories did not take into account any of the new editions which began to proliferate at the end of the century in response to new scientific methods. In his article for the Petit de Julleville history, Jeanroy offers the flat opinion that critical editions will not change our appreciation of trouvère lyric: in his view "après comme avant les éditions critiques que nous souhaitons plus que personne de voir paraître," we will still find the trouvères monotonous.[87] In a way, he was correct. Positivistic editing techniques were not calculated to bring more sophisticated interpretations of the texts to which they were applied.

As I mentioned above, Gaston Paris stands for the introduction of scientific methods of text editing into French scholarship, with, especially for Old Occitan, his colleague Paul Meyer. The method they championed is usually known as the Lachmann method. It has as its goal the reconstruction of a text as the author's original; the goal is to be reached through rigorous and objective criticism and classification of manuscripts.[88] The method held sway not only in France but also in Germany, its country of origin so to speak, and in Italy. It undergirded many editions appearing in the late 19th and early 20th centuries. But in the early 20th century, this method was challenged by the French scholar Joseph Bédier. As is well known, Bédier sharply rejected the Lachmann method in his 1913 edition of Jean Renart's *Lai de l'ombre,* in favor of the "best manuscript" method, opening a debate that is still far from resolved.[89] The debate was chiefly focussed on epic and romance, not on lyric, which poses special problems of its own. The two methods reflect different concepts of what constitutes a text and of how these concepts of the text are related to manuscripts. The clash of concepts brought into clear focus

the impossibility of reducing manuscript traditions to a
single printed text.

   While, in general, the study of music followed a tra-
jectory similar to that of poetry, medieval music suffered from the specific handicap of appearing more inac-
cessible than the text, and misunderstandings surrounding
notation, not to mention performance practices, inevitably led to pejorative judgments. Given the highly text-
oriented thrust of positivistic methods with their emphasis on the written, it is not surprising that notation
became a central focus of 19th-century investigations. As
the *New Grove* article "Historiography" points out, "The
music of the Middle Ages was considered a lost, barbaric
art, and to an increasing extent, it was studied only for
its relevance to the history of European musical notation
. . . and for medieval writings on theory" (596). To a
degree, this is analogous to the study of literary texts
for what they can reveal about the development of language, except that when one stops at the level of notation, one never reaches the musical language as such.

   To convince oneself of the disfavor in which medieval music was held during the 19th century, one has only
to consult the major music historians. Christian
Kalkbrenner, writing at the close of the 18th century
but translated into French in the early 19th, traces the
discordant quality of 14th- and 15th-century music to the
fact that the *basse générale* and the *art de l'accompagnement* were as yet unknown.[90] Although a musician like
Raphael Georg Kiesewetter participated in an effort,
about which more below, to perform "early" music, his
Geschichte der europäisch-abendländischen . . . Musik
(1834) is scarcely flattering to medieval lyric. The
history is organized by "great names," such as the "Epoch
of Guido." Through the Middle Ages, these names are theorists; beginning with Dufay, they are composers. The 12th
century is an epoch "not distinguished by the name of any
particular individual."[91] Kiesewetter considers the segment he knew of Machaut's *Mass* the work of a dilettante,
adept only at versification. Surprised to learn that the
Mass was performed at the coronation of a king, he at-
tributes this circumstance to the low level to which

music had sunk in the years immediately following
Johannes de Muris.[92] At the end of the century, August
Wilhelm Ambros's ambitious *Geschichte der Musik* (4 vols,
1862-78) which aims to relate music to cultural history,
mentions a number of by now familiar troubadour and trouvère names, opts for placing Machaut before Adam de la
Halle in chronological sequence, and deplores the inability to understand the notation.

One of the main voices of 19th-century music historiography was F.-J. Fétis (1784-1871). In his two major
works, *Biographie universelle* (8 vols., 1835-44) and
Histoire générale de la musique (5 vols., 1869-76), Fétis
set forth a philosophy of music history and approached
the subject from two different but related directions:
biographies of major figures and chronological presentation of styles and techniques. Fétis was opposed to the
global application of the idea of progress: "La musique
se transforme . . . elle ne progresse que dans ses
éléments matériels."[93] This view, which denies progress
to art but permits it with respect to the techniques or
"science" of that art, explains Fétis's attitude toward
medieval secular lyric. The most important transformation
during the medieval period was the discovery of polyphony, "le principe de l'harmonie des sons simultanés."
This discovery would lead to the birth of true art. At
first, however, those who used it "n'en firent qu'une
chose barbare dont notre oreille serait blessée, mais qui
eut alors ses partisans à cause de sa nouveauté." Through
slow progress, the principle of polyphony "finit par se
dégager de sa grossière enveloppe" and created finally
"l'art des successions dans l'harmonie."[94] From that
time, from about the 15th century, music was free to develop and serve the needs of men of genius. The number of
occurrences of words such as "barbare" or "grossier" in
this passage of the "Préface" clearly betrays Fétis's
fundamental attitude. Monophonic song is perceived as
peripheral; polyphonic song prior to the 15th century was
still in its "grossière enveloppe." It is not surprising
that Fétis's treatment of individual troubadours and
trouvères in the *Biographie* is anecdotal and of little
value. Adam de la Halle is "un premier pas vers le
mieux."[95] Fétis claims to have made known the *Roman de*

Fauvel containing works of Lescurel.[96] As for Machaut,
the mass and motets "offrent de nombreux passages remplis
de mauvaises successions d'harmonie" but Machaut had the
virtue of having "précédé de peu Dufay, Dunstable et
Binchois, dont les ouvrages sont purs de ces fautes
grossières."[97]

The 5th volume of the *Histoire générale de la musique*
is devoted to the Middle Ages, rather more to the 12th
and 13th than to the 14th and 15th centuries. The same
themes are apparent. Troubadour poetry is boring, the
music is equally dull; troubadours and trouvères lacked
the notational symbols needed to write their music down;
nevertheless troubadours helped to extinguish barbarity
and initiate a movement toward a kind of art song, so
their historical importance must be recognized even if
great value cannot be assigned to their work.[98] The development of secular polyphony and the transformations
that will allow true art to follow false art at the beginning of the 15th century are laid out succinctly in
the chapter of the *Histoire* treating 14th-century
music.[99]

Nineteenth-century approaches to music included not
only writing about music but performing it, a kind of
revival of "early music" that had ramifications for
research. Given the attitudes described above, it is not
surprising that these "early music" performances rarely
included the Middle Ages but rather furthered Renaissance
studies. A prize offered by the Royal Academy of Sciences
and Arts of the Netherlands in 1824 for the best essay on
the merits of the Netherlands composers in the 14th,
15th, and 16th centuries set off a rivalry between the
winner (Kiesewetter) and the honorable mention (Fétis)
that would stimulate research on 15th- and 16th-century
music in 19th-century nationalistic traditions. Both
scholars supported early music concerts. But the rules
of the *Concerts of Ancient Music* that had flourished in
London from the end of the 18th century give an idea of
what "ancient" could mean: no work was admitted to the
concerts unless it had been composed more than 20 years
previous.[100] Performances of medieval music flourished
in another domain: pseudo-medieval revivals. The "genre

troubadour" continued to captivate imaginations; melodies
were arranged with accompaniments to please the contemporary public; at the turn of the century, the "Belle
Epoque," the French *diseuse* Yvette Guilbert included
arranged medieval songs in her repertory.[101] Guilbert
produced one of the earliest "editions" of Marcabru's
pastorela "L'autrier jost'una sebissa"; and if one is to
judge from her few surviving recordings, whatever the
"authenticity" of her transcriptions, she must have been
a formidable interpreter of that song.

The 19th century also saw a push toward the establishment of conservatories, but this did not especially
benefit medieval secular music. Jacques Chailley would
point out that if one excepts Gregorian Chant, young
musicians studying at the Paris Conservatory a century
later, in the 1930s, were quite unaware that there was
any medieval music worthy of their attention.[102]

In this unfavorable climate, what medieval musical
works were indeed published? Setting aside the domain of
Chant, in which crucial work was being done (particularly
at Solesmes), and the important publication of medieval
theoretical treatises by such specialists as Gerbert
(1784) and Coussemaker (1864-76),[103] one must admit that
compared to the founding of Occitan textual studies and
the steady growth of trouvère text publications, the musical harvest is discouragingly meager.

In the first part of the century, François Perne
edited the melodies of the Châtelain de Coucy, as I noted
above, but with piano accompaniment, thus following his
18th-century predecessors and with concessions to contemporary tastes. The first serious work of modern French
musicology in our domain--but one should remember that
the discipline took shape only in the late 19th century
and the term "musicology" gained currency only in the
20th--can be attributed to Charles-Edmond-Henri de
Coussemaker (1805-1876), a lawyer by training who devoted
most of his energies to musical scholarship. His edition
of the works of Adam de la Halle (1872) opened new paths
of musical research, if textually it left much to be desired.[104] In *L'Art harmonique aux XIIe et XIIIe siècles*

(1865), Coussemaker described and situated the Montpellier manuscript H 196 with respect to the development of the motet, identified trouvères whose compositions he thought the manuscript contained, and appended facsimiles and transcriptions.[105] But Coussemaker's model would not be developed in French musicology until around 1900.

Before that, the first "essai d'ensemble"[106] on troubadour music appeared as a long article by Antonio Restori in the *Rivista musicale italiana*.[107] Though usually ignored by the literature, Restori's article breaks new ground. He comes to the study of music through the study of literature and raises a number of important questions. His criticism of inaccuracies in the work of Fétis and Ambros is sharp and justified. He gives a clear survey of musical sources and makes the perceptive observation: "Dal Laborde, dal Forkel, dal Burney, vecchi storici della musica ed editori di melodie de trovieri francesi, fino ai recentissimi Lavoix, Tiersot, T. Galino, nessun musicista dubitò dell'autenticità delle melodie dei canzonieri."[108] Restori is the first to focus on the opacity of the sources. He undertakes a discussion of different melody versions, and he attacks Fétis's pronouncement that troubadour notation was just inadequate. For Restori, the notation fitted the object it was intended to represent, an object different in nature from polyphonic music.[109] It follows that Restori in no way foreshadowed the theory of modal rhythmic transcription that would soon sweep the field; he was closer to the views of a Carl Appel, or even to perceptions that have more recently come into prominence.[110] But he touched on most of the "classic" problems that the 20th century would debate.

As for text editing, so for music, the late 19th and early 20th centuries saw the adoption of paleographic and philological principles largely drawn from positivistic literary study. For medieval secular song, several important strands came together. Manuscript materials were better understood, and medieval notation benefitted from the important studies of a Hugo Rieman (*Studien zur Geschichte der Notenschrift*, 1878) or Johannes Wolf (*Geschichte der Mensural-Notation von 1250-1460*, 3 vols, 1905).

Early developments in editing were associated with a pivotal figure and a pivotal place: Gustav Jacobsthal, Professor at Strasbourg. Jacobsthal was trained as an historian and a musicologist.[111] He came to the University of Strasbourg, newly founded following Strasbourg's annexation by Germany after the Franco-Prussian war. He became interested in applying methods of history and philology to medieval sources. His own work had no immediate repercussions; but among his students was a man who would rank among the most outstanding specialists of medieval music: Friedrich Ludwig. Ludwig was also trained as an historian and a musicologist. He would follow his mentor in the post at Strasbourg before going to Göttingen when Strasbourg again became French. And among Ludwig's pupils at Strasbourg were Jean Beck and Friedrich Gennrich. Although Pierre Aubry did his work at the Ecole des Chartes in Paris, his ideas were probably influenced by Ludwig as well. Thus the "Strasbourg school" was born, and from it came the scholars who would change the face of medieval lyric.

Friedrich Ludwig's most remarkable achievement was a continuation of Jacobsthal's research on 13th-century polyphony, culminating in the still indispensable *Repertorium organorum recentioris et motetorum vetustissimi stili*, part 1 containing a systematic analysis of manuscripts and part 2 a listing of music and text incipits, left unfinished at Ludwig's death and subsequently edited and published by Gennrich. Ludwig also produced the first complete edition of Machaut's works (1926-29), an edition many specialists still consider authoritative.[112]

One of the more flamboyant inventions of the young century was the modal theory of transcription of troubadour and trouvère monophonic music. Variously ascribed to Aubry, Beck, and Ludwig, the theory applied the rhythmic modes used for early polyphonic music to monophonic melodies. Gustave Reese would later characterize it as "the only scheme available to us for transcribing into modern notation, *in accordance with a reasonably methodical system*, the melodies not measured in the MSS."[113] Since the theory seemed to offer a valid solution to a frustrating

problem, it was adopted with enthusiasm by its adherents.
Yet it was never entirely satisfactory to all specialists. When Carl Appel was finally able to publish his
edition of the melodies of Bernart de Ventadorn (1934),
begun during World War I, he eschewed modal rhythm,
choosing instead for his edition a non-mensural notation
similar to that adopted by more recent scholars such as
Van der Werf, and which Appel was the first to use for
the troubadour repertory. Since Appel indicated text
rhythms for the first two lines of each poem along with
the melodies, his edition remains the most useful starting point for study of the rhythm of troubadour songs.[114]

Both Jean Beck and Pierre Aubry published studies on
troubadour and trouvère music that were long authoritative, and their manuscript facsimiles, though never completed, are still indispensable.[115] Both collaborated
with Alfred Jeanroy or Joseph Bédier on editions of monophonic songs. Aubry published a facsimile of the *Fauvel*
manuscript and, in the same year, his *Cent motets du
XIIIe siècle*.[116] But the Beck/Bédier edition of the songs
of Colin Muset (1912) illustrates both the usefulness of
interdisciplinary collaboration and its fragility: when
the second edition appeared in 1938 (the edition now usually available) the music had vanished. One thinks of the
fate of Ronsard's *Amours*, from which the music also disappeared in a second edition.

The name most readily associated with philologically
based, positivistic approaches to medieval lyric is
Friedrich Gennrich. He was the most uncompromising pro-
moter of the modal theory for rhythmic transcriptions of
monophonic music. His aim was to transfer scientific
principles of text editing to music. His best known
effort is the edition of troubadour melodies: *Der musikalische Nachlass der Troubadours* (1958-65). He also attempted to apply scientific principles to analysis and
classification in order to delineate formal structures
of melodies and texts. The results obtained and published
in *Grundriss einer Formenlehre des mittelalterlichen
Liedes* (Halle: Niemeyer, 1932) were long considered
authoritative, presented as such in Gustave Reese's
influential *Music in the Middle Ages* (New York: Norton,

1940). By the early 20th century, therefore, if one may take Gennrich as an exemplary figure, positivistic principles of text editing had spread to music, and both disciplines were moving toward the goal of objective and reliable findings about the Middle Ages based on disciplinary expertise.

The story of the perceptions of medieval music and poetry from the Renaissance to the early 20th century here briefly sketched out reveals the pervasive influence of two central notions: (1) the concept of the Middle Ages as barbarous; and (2) the concept of the manuscript as a source of information, as a transparent window on a past divided off from the present.

The first of these notions lingered despite the re-evaluation of the Middle Ages grounded in the romantic desire to recover cultural "origins," with the impetus this desire gave to the study of languages as part of a nationalistic political agenda. The re-evaluation ultimately turned back against itself, however, by creating a Middle Ages viewed as "childlike" or "naive" and thus inferior.[117] Moreover, the romantic idealizing and mythologizing tendencies that assigned positive value to the Middle Ages seized only upon those segments of the medieval period (troubadour song, for example, or in another domain, Joan of Arc) that could be used to support their goals. Other segments, such as poetry in fixed forms, the motet, or polyphony in general, were still not deemed worthy of attention.

The concept of the manuscript as a source of information is linked to historicizing approaches and in particular to nationalistic fascination with cultural heritage. It led to the tremendously important work of cataloguing and learning to decipher manuscripts that was a major achievement of positivistic scholarship. Under this concept, the manuscript as a whole was less important than the pieces one could extract from it--text, music, illustrations--all these could be safely studied separately without reference to the others. In a slightly different

vein, the idea of manuscript as source undergirded the
romantic theory of "Urtext," or "author's original," to
which the manuscript, or more properly a manuscript tradition, could lead the scholar. To retrieve an original
that existed prior to manuscript compilation, one looked
through the manuscripts and not *at* them, and the notion
of author's original legitimized the single, standardized
version of a text thus obtained. The idea of author's
original was admirably suited to the printing press. This
19th-century meshing of ideology and technology completed
the transformation of text into object, completed, that
is, the reification of the song.

The ramifications of this transformation were numerous; I wish here to emphasize two. First, as the printed
edition came to serve as a reference for both teaching
and scholarship, it became routine to study the poetry of
Baudelaire and of Bernart de Ventadorn from the same type
of book. This brought the latter into the conceptual universe of the former. To be sure, knowledgeable philologists who practiced the art of editing medieval texts
knew well what vast differences separated the two "authors" in the composition and preservation of their
"works." But these differences were rarely theorized or
made an explicit part of critical discourse. They became
"invisible." The printed edition, when theoretically
unexamined and hence presumably unproblematic, could be
substituted both for manuscripts and even more importantly for any effort to recover medieval ideas about
the nature of song reflected in manuscripts. The substitution influenced teaching and student perceptions, as
well as those kinds of scholarship concerned with interpreting rather than editing texts.

The effect of this prioritizing of the printed book
can be best judged in the light of another influence
which I shall only mention here as my second point. The
value accorded the printed book, and its train of associations with fixity and authenticity, was reinforced by
estheticizing tendencies of the late 19th century such as
the "art for art's sake" movement. These tendencies had
the result of divorcing the work of art from its cultural
context in order to make of it an esthetic object held up

in splendid isolation as a focus for scholarly and peda-
gogical attention. Since medieval works were rarely
looked upon as works of art until well into the 20th
century, these tendencies did not initially affect them.
But as we shall see they did lead to critical attitudes
that figure importantly in 20th-century dialogues.

The 20th century would take aim at both romanticism
and positivism in order to define new approaches. However, it is useful to remember that the apparent certainty of positivistic rigor met resistance even as it was
being set in place. Positivistic approaches contained at
their core a set of stubborn problems that made them constantly vulnerable to attack. To the degree that Lachmannian procedures can be seen as the essence of positivism,
the critique by Joseph Bédier opened a breach in established positions. On the musicological side, Pierre Aubry
raised crucial issues in his portion of *Les Chansons de
croisade* prepared with Bédier in 1909 (B187). His arguments turned on the notion of "common error" used in the
Lachmann method to classify manuscripts. In the first
instance, he pointed out that the notion of error varies
with different musical repertories or languages: criteria
based on notation of durations can be invoked for polyphonic music, but are largely inoperative for monophonic
pieces. Further, the notion of error itself is virtually
without meaning for distinguishing between different
melody versions of the same piece: "nous avons affaire
moins à des fautes qu'à des variantes légitimes" (xxiv).
Aubry's conclusion was that philological methods could
not be applied to monophonic songs (xxxiii). Friedrich
Gennrich did not heed Aubry's conclusions but proceeded
apace following his own agenda. But even as Gennrich was
publishing his final word on the troubadours, new approaches were beginning to make his word obsolete.

These approaches did not come from text editing but
from the increasingly important disciplines of literary
criticism and theory which I shall review in Part II of
this Introduction. But in order briefly to sum up mid
20th-century reflections on medieval song, let me point
out here that while the first part of the century was
dominated by New Criticism (at least in Anglo-Saxon

countries), by the middle of the century French structuralism had become a potent force. Both of these would come
under criticism, and the attack on structuralism would be
sharp. But it is important to recognize that structuralist and formalist approaches first placed positive value
judgments on medieval lyric. By focussing on lyric works
themselves, and not on what can be learned through them
about cultural phenomena, linguistic developments, or
notational systems, structuralist and formalist critics
sought a better understanding of these works on their own
terms. One could even cite, for the monophonic repertory,
Friedrich Gennrich's *Formenlehre* which in its way reha-
bilitated medieval song despite the rigidity of its categories, which have ultimately had to be abandoned. But
the most potent formalist influence came from the literary scholar Robert Guiette. With his seminal article
"D'une poésie formelle en France au moyen âge" (1949),
Guiette reacted against romantic devaluation of medieval
lyric (boring, conventional) and prepared a veritable
renaissance of structuralist oriented research on medieval poetry, which includes the work of Dragonetti on
trouvères, of Pierre Bec on troubadours and trouvères,
or the seminal book by Paul Zumthor, *Essai de poétique
médiévale*.[118] This "rehabilitation" of lyric did not extend to polyphonic music. In the early part of the century, polyphonic repertories could not yet be brought
into the purview of criticism. Far too much work was yet
needed to decipher the musical notation. And if the motet
texts were integrated into the systematic analyses of
Zumthor or Bec, this integration elicited no rush of
scholarly research on the genre. But on the textual side,
for the late medieval period, one must cite the work of
Daniel Poirion. His study *Le Poète et le Prince* (1965)
constituted a powerful re-evaluation of existing judgments of 14th- and 15th-century works. While Poirion af-
firmed the importance of structure following the work of
Guiette ("La structure formelle ... nous donne le seul
critère positif des genres lyriques"), he yet refused to
take refuge in structure alone and called upon other humanistic disciplines in order to place the lyricism of
the late Middle Ages in its social context: the court
("le lyrisme que nous étudions se définit en fonction de
la société de cour").[119] Thus Poirion pointed already to

some new approaches that would significantly influence attitudes toward medieval lyric in general.

PART II
RESEARCH IN THE 1980s AND 1990s

The most important feature of late 20th-century approaches to medieval song is the rise of interpretation, or more precisely the rise of medieval song as an object of interpretation. The song could be theorized, problematized, criticized just like any modern work and thus became accessible to the interpretive strategies proposed by new developments in literary theory and criticism. But since the song is a musical as well as a literary object, its interpretation depends on musical as well as literary methodologies. The disciplines of literature and music do not always adopt the same interpretive strategies, nor did the development of new methodologies in both fields proceed at the same pace. Consequently, before taking up specific aspects of medieval song upon which current research has focussed, it will be useful to map out very schematically comparative itineraries of literary and musical thinking.

In his influential introduction to literary theory (1983), Terry Eagleton proposed roughly periodizing the history of modern literary theory in three stages: "a preoccupation with the author (romanticism and the nineteenth century); an exclusive concern with the text (New Criticism); and a marked shift of attention to the reader over recent years."[120] Let me take this literary periodization as a starting point and suggest some comparisons with music. But first, a word about vocabulary. I will not use the term "music theory" in my discussion, since this term normally designates an area of music study and is not comparable to the term "literary theory." I will, however, adopt the term "music criticism" which, along with its journalistic usages, can take on a meaning comparable to that of "literary criticism."[121] Now to Eagleton's periodizations. The first can be dealt with

straightforwardly. Romantic paradigms undergird both musical and literary criticism in the 19th century. They
still pervade much thinking about medieval song. If the
quest for origins and cultural information has diminished, and the preoccupation with the authors, where
there are authors, has changed focus, the organicist
models of birth, growth, decline, and the historicist
ideas of progress and linear development growing out of
romanticism are still powerful influences in both fields.

Eagleton's second stage is trickier. For my purposes
here, it will be useful to place structuralism with New
Criticism, given the importance of structuralism in
France and the impact of literary structuralism on medieval song. Both structuralism and New Criticism, but for
different reasons, tended to separate the work from writer and reader in order to analyze its inner workings and
perceive its value: they were chiefly concerned with the
text. Both sought the objectivity of science, although
New Criticism staunchly defended the esthetic value of
literature. Both viewed literature as devoid of social
function. But because they saw the work of art as unique-
ly determined by systems of relations of which the work
is a part and a reflection, and because they focussed
primarily on structures and processes that produce meaning, structuralists proposed a more radical elimination
of the author and adopted a more resolutely a-historical
stance than the proponents of New Criticism.[122]

Analogies can be drawn between New Criticism and
structuralism in literature and formalism in music. All
these approaches focus on the "work." The analogies and
the differences may be most readily brought out by briefly reviewing the ways the labels and the techniques they
represent are used in the two fields. Although some musicological writing shares the tenets of New Criticism,[123]
New Criticism as a term is not used in music. Structuralism is, but rarely. Structuralist methodologies *per se*
are not given prominence in music criticism, although as
Ian Bent remarked in the single short paragraph devoted
to "Structuralism and music" in the *New Grove*: "music
lends itself to structuralist analysis because it is so
manifestly concerned with interrelationships between mu-

sical ideas rather than with 'meanings'."[124] To be sure,
one of the dominant figures in 20th-century musical analysis, Heinrich Schenker (1868-1935), can be aligned with
structuralists. Like Lévi-Strauss or Jacobson, Schenker
sought to discern hierarchies of relationships and lo-
cated basic musical structures not on the surface but
beneath it. The concepts Schenker developed, "background,
middle, foreground," are not unlike the linguistic concepts of deep vs. surface structure.[125] And as structuralist poetics in its most purist phase sought, in the
name of "science," definitive analyses of literary works,
so Schenker sought definitive analyses of musical works.
Arnold Whittall has again recently underscored this aspect of Schenker's work: "Surely analyses do not come any
more finite and definitive than, for example, Schenker's
wordless graph of Bach's C major Prelude from Book I of
the Forty-Eight."[126] Yet Schenker was not, strictly
speaking, a structuralist, nor can other major musical
thinkers be specifically so defined.

In part, the discrepancy in terminology has to do
with the tendency to identify structuralism with semiotics (or semiology) in musical thinking.[127] The two are
close, the chief difference being that the systems determining literary structures in semiotics are identified as
linguistic systems. Since there is a long history of relationships between music and language, the turn toward
semiotics in music criticism is hardly surprising. Two
of musical semiotic's early practitioners, Jean-Jacques
Nattiez and Nicolas Ruwet are still powerful influences
in the field.[128] Although at first, musical semiotics
met with a hostile reception, it subsequently underwent
remarkable expansion, completely overshadowing structuralism *per se*.

But the differences in approach and terminology between musicological and literary developments have also
and perhaps more to do with the fact that two other concepts are firmly entrenched in musicological thinking:
style and form. Style became a central focus of music
historians with the work of Guido Adler who published *Der
Stil in der Musik* in 1911.[129] Style for Adler encompassed
form; it included all the features of a work from rhythm

to performance practice. The methodological procedure he termed style-criticism was based on the determination of a system of laws that could account for the organic development of style, so that style emerged as the key concept in both synchronic and diachronic studies of music.[130] Form, on the other hand, entered musicology from theory, where study of form had long served as training in composition. In the late 19th and early 20th centuries, with the work of Ebenezer Prout and Hugo Leichtentritt, *Formenlehre* ceased to be viewed only as a prescriptive training for composers and was taken over as a musicological analytic tool, in which function it became firmly ensconced.[131] Style and form are important concepts in literary criticism, too; but they do not there play the dominant role that falls to them in musical discussions. The general concept of formalism is of broader application in music than in literature. Literary formalism sought to rescue literature from history;[132] it can be aligned with New Criticism. But literary structuralists tended to replace the term "form" by "structure,"[133] thus restricting the scope of "formalism." Music never served as a source of historical information and did not need rescuing. What the young discipline of musicology needed were methodologies to define its purpose. Style and form served musicology's initial needs admirably; thus they have persisted and continue to exert strong influence.[134] With some adjustment, therefore, to recognize the specificity of musical concepts and discourses, one may affirm the validity of a rough analogy between a certain formalism in music and New Criticism and structuralism in literature.

With Eagleton's third stage, however, marked by a shift of attention to the reader, we come to major discrepancies in literary and musical discourses, terminological but especially chronological.

In the late sixties and seventies, as is well known, radical changes began to sweep over the literary disciplines, changes so diverse as to constitute a dizzying deployment of "literary criticisms": reader-response criticism and *Rezeptionsästhetik;* hermeneutics; semiotics; deconstruction; psychoanalytical criticism; feminist criticism; new historicism; and so on. This state of affairs led Dominick LaCapra (1985) to question the possibility of even conceptualizing a "history" of modern literary criticism. He placed his own effort to do so under the sign of Montaigne: "Il y a plus affaire à interpréter les interprétations qu'à interpréter les choses (there is more to-do about interpreting interpretations than about interpreting things)."[135] In an oversimplified way, one can characterize the reactions of the sixties and seventies as a destablizing of the projects of New Criticism and earlier structuralism, and ultimately as a rejection of all positivistic enterprises claiming that systematic knowledge is possible. The attack eventually undermined reading as an "*innocent* activity" by insisting that reflection on readers and reading is crucial to understanding.[136] Many of the changes in literary critical and theoretical modes can be grouped under the labels of post-structuralism or postmodernism. Viewed as reactions to previous theories (which they however also prolong), these new modes attempt to dismantle totalizing conceptions. Postmodernism in its many varieties, might be seen as an abandonment of the effort to draw meaning from incoherent and fragmentary phenomena, a critique of the assumptions about the power of reason that date, at least, from the Enlightenment. Post-structuralism, in its several manifestations, can be seen as a reaction against systems, or structures, claiming universal validity. Such distinctions function tolerably well for literature. They are less satisfactory for music.

Music criticism saw changes beginning in the sixties and seventies, too, but they overtook the field at a far slower pace compared to developments in literary theory. The firm entrenchment of the concepts of form and style and of positivistic methodologies surely contributed to the slowness of change in music. But one must consider also the status of the musical "reader" and of the "text" to be read: the shift of attention to the reader characterizing literary studies cannot be exactly transferred to music. A musical "reader" may read the score; but arguably a score is not the work in the same way that a literary text is the work. A musical work needs to be heard. So the concept of "listener" is as important as that of "reader." (This view seems particularly pertinent to medieval song.)

The ramifications of this observation cannot be discussed here. I simply wish to offer two brief remarks before proceeding to the matter of changes in music criticism. The first remark concerns musical modernism. From the outset but particularly after the Second World War, musical modernism provoked anti-modernist reactions due not only to the strangeness of the musical techniques but also to the strangeness of the listening experience. Instead of inviting new modes of music criticism, the "crisis of modernism," to use Joseph Kerman's term, reinforced entrenched conservative stances among musicologists.[137] The term "postmodernism" has a very different resonance in musical thinking as compared to literary theory.

My second observation concerns an aspect of modernism that would have far-reaching consequences for the musical half of our subject: the development of the mechanical reproduction of sound. Andrew Bowie has even gone so far as to suggest that "one might, indeed, almost be able to define the modern period in terms of the increasing public availability of all forms of music."[138] This development did not immediately affect the musicological enterprise; but it transformed the performance practices and the possibilities of reception of early music and redefined the function of "listener." The debate over "historically informed" performance rejoins some of the larger issues of music history I will presently touch on. And to at least one critic, all modern renditions of medieval music, given their great variety, could be termed "postmodern" to accentuate the notion that any modern performance of a medieval song is but one realization among many undertaken to give the song renewed existence.[139]

Many of the important changes that would affect the disciplines of musicology beginning in the sixties took place in the field of music history. For example, Leo Treitler began to formulate questions about how one "does" music history, taking a stand against positivistic and evolutionary history in a way that could be related to post-structuralist critiques of historicism.[140] In 1977, Carl Dahlhaus published his *Grundlagen der Musikgeschichte,* translated into English in 1983 as *Foundations of Music History.* Writing in Berlin after the upheaval of the sixties, Dahlhaus took account of the influential literary developments in Germany which have come to be labeled "Reception Theory," and of the work of their important predecessor, the philosopher Hans Georg Gadamer.[141] Dahlhaus's wide-ranging discussion of what it means to be a music historian drew on much more than Reception Theory (indeed it drew on most of the major philosophers of history), and it concludes with an assessment of the problems raised by reception history. But one of the threads of its arguments constitutes a critique of the historicist/positivist paradigms that can also be aligned with approaches that would come to be labeled post-structuralist. And some of this thinking about music history parallels the literary movement labeled "new historicism." "The very sound of the label," Brook Thomas has argued, "serves rhetorically to displace the most influential brand of criticism that preceded it: the New Criticism."[142] Without being merely a facet of post-structuralism or postmodernism because it has its own identity (revealed, if in no other way, by the use of "new" vs. "post"), new historicism nevertheless shared their distrust of what Jean-François Lyotard has called the "grand narratives."[143] New historicism, like post-structuralism, sought to dismantle the notion of history-as-master narrative, with its emphasis on progress or finality, and to replace it by a concept of history as interplay of interpretations in which the interpreter is as much a part of the "history" as what might have formerly been considered "historical fact."

Revisionist thinking about music history, roughly parallel to some developments in literary thinking, thus appeared in the sixties and seventies. But it must be recognized that music historians' reflections on how one "does" history and how one can situate "texts" came into greater conflict with the idea of the autonomous work of art than was the case with literary reflections, since estheticizing concepts remained more firmly entrenched in music. The question was clearly raised by Dahlhaus: is the significance of music historical or esthetic?[144] Comparing a political event to a musical work, Dahlhaus argued that a musical work has a continual present-ness that a political event inevitably loses: the esthetic presence of a work of music can be "recaptured in later performances," whereas the political and social fabric dies beyond recall.[145] The issue Dahlhaus raises is fundamental; but it intersects with and is complicated by the issue of what kind of "authentic" present-ness can be attained in performance of music whose performance tradition has been lost. And the issue raised by Dahlhaus is doubled by another paradox: how does one specifically separate out the musical from the non-musical? This problematic has been developed by Lydia Goehr in a wide-ranging review of the work of Dahlhaus, Treitler, and Leonard B. Meyer.[146] Thus tension between the esthetic and the historical pervades musical discourse on history, giving it a coloration quite distinct from literary discourse.

Arguably, then, although musical criticism did not change as rapidly as literary criticism, and although terms such as post-structuralism or postmodernism are less satisfactory for music than for literature, the winds of change still transformed musical thinking. Can we arrive at a periodization for music? Writing in 1983, Joseph Kerman was able to structure a thoroughgoing critique of musicology around the notion of the persistence of positivism in the field. Pointing out (as have others) that musical thinkers lag behind general intellectual life, Kerman then stated: "Semiotics, hermeneutics, and phenomenology are being drawn upon only by some of the boldest of musical studies today. Post-structuralism, deconstruction, and serious feminism have yet to make their debuts in musicology or music theory."[147] But writing in 1991 about "American Musicology in the 1990s," Kerman explicitly recognized that the 1983 statement would have to be revised, for many musicologists had by then begun to absorb more recent intellectual approaches into their work.[148] As one piece of evidence for the revision he proposed, Kerman cited the

collection *Music and Society: The Politics of Composition, Performance and Reception* (Cambridge: Cambridge
University Press, 1987) in which the editors, Richard
Leppert and Susan McClary, extending boldly the concept
of historical and social contextualizing and drawing upon
recent cognitive methodologies, squarely took on the assumption, still pervasive in their view, that "art con-
stitues an autonomous sphere, separate and insulated from
the outside world" (xi). The essays in the collection are
interdisciplinary in focus and range over popular music,
MTV, electronic (vs. mechanical) reproduction, as well as
Bach.

But perhaps the most cogent illustration of the
degree to which recent intellectual movements and
particularly recent developments in literary criticism
have come to fructify and be fructified by musicological
discourse is the recent collection of articles from a
symposium held at Dartmouth College in 1988: *Music and
Text: Critical Inquiries* (Cambridge: Cambridge University
Press, 1992). As articulated by its editor, Steven Paul
Scher, the purpose of the volume was to demonstrate "how
musical and literary studies can combine forces effec-
tively on the common ground of contemporary critical
theory and interpretive practice" (xiv). Scher argues
that musico-literary analysis seems to "fare well in the
critical climate of post-modernism" (xiv), where the
practitioners of the diverse and disparate approaches labeled post-structuralism, hermeneutics, reception esthet-
ics, new historicism etc. seem willing to move beyond
disciplinary boundaries (xiii). The essays raise a variety of issues such as contexts of listening, literary
theory as a model for musical understanding, representation and semiotics, gender and convention.

One may deduce from the above remarks that the sea
change that transformed literary criticism in the late
sixties and seventies came to musicology in the late
eighties and nineties. Even yet, it has not thoroughly
shaken up the field. As we have seen, the change in music
is comparable to what took place in literary thinking
but by no means identical. If recent literary theories
all focus in one way or another on reading, musical

discourse, though problematizing the "reader" (that is, the critic) as interpreter in a manner analogous to literary theory, yet develops its focus more out of a tension between the historical and the esthetic, between situating texts in contexts vs. analysis of works themselves, than by developing models of listening. For our purposes, it is important to realize that the slower pace of musicological change coupled with the continuing seductiveness of literary structuralist analyses have meant that research on medieval song, text and music together, remains relatively conservative, drawing still on strategies characteristic of Eagleton's second stage, rather than advancing boldly into the third.

In her review article on "Writing Music History," Lydia Goehr remarked "Paradigms can continue to exert influence even after they have fallen from power. They do this by serving in our historical memory as the traditional standards against which we measure our new paradigms and constantly assert their difference. Formalism in music criticism and positivism in the philosophy and history of music currently fill this role. . . . They serve in our present as our legacy from the past."[149] The paradigm of positivistic thinking still influences the understanding of medieval song, even as newer practices of criticism and interpretation radically alter the understanding the older paradigm provided. The examination of specific parameters of medieval song, to which I shall now turn, will consequently involve assessing research in the eighties and nineties against the background of a latent romanticism and a persistent positivism, both challenged by a developing plurality of critical discourses. I will first review the topics I have found most frequently treated during this period, and then conclude by a brief discussion of the application and pertinence to medieval song of some of the critical discourses themselves.

EDITING

Editing has recently been a particular focus for the critique of positivism. To some, it represents the ultimate positivistic activity. So for Joseph Kerman, who has argued that the presentation of works of early music, not their interpretation, has been counted as the most notable achievement of a musicology that "dealt mainly in the verifiable, the objective, the uncontroversial, and the positive."[150] So for a Bernard Cerquiglini or for contributors to a volume of *Speculum* (January, 1990), who characterized philology centered on text editing as old or procrustean.[151] Reactions to such critiques have not been wanting. To Joseph Kerman's stance, Margaret Bent replied that the purely positivistic (in the pejorative sense) musicologist is largely "a straw man."[152] The image of philology as procrustean provoked a reactive reaffirmation of the value of text editing. As Mary Speer has argued "An edition is always an interpretation of a text, a provisional working hypothesis about its nature and its poetics."[153] The crux of the matter seems to be editorial awareness, and in particular theoretical elaboration of that awareness. While most editors know how complicated are the choices they must make, those who use edited texts, as I have already had occasion to note, and whose conceptualizations are marked by a print culture, may be led, by the very printed form of the edition, into believing that the edition is "definitive," the text "authentic." If an emphasis on theory has undermined "reading as an *innocent* activity,"[154] it has also undermined the preparation and use of critical editions as *innocent* activities, although it has no more abolished the necessity for editing than it has abolished the need for reading. I will here address some issues in editing that pertain to medieval song, on conceptual and practical levels, both to review what has been done and to assay relationships between editing procedures and scholarly research.

In the debate over the editing process, issues surrounding the editing of medieval song have received surprisingly little scholarly attention. For medieval song, considered as words and music together, the problem of defining the "text" to be edited from manuscripts is crucial. This theoretical problem is related to but distinct from the issue of the legitimacy of interpreting texts without music or music without texts. The questions to

which answers are needed turn on the conceptualizations
of "song" in medieval manuscripts and how and to what
degree those conceptualizations are to be translated
into the modern idiom of print (or, if one wants to look
toward the future, into modern electronic media). These
conceptualizations are expressed not only by the presence
or absence of music but also by the kinds of relations
established between text and music, by the different
choices and manipulations of different writing systems,
and by the variations inherent in manuscript culture.
They engage the use of illumination, where illumination
is present. Defining the object of a modern edition of
medieval song reaches beyond decisions about specific
techniques of text or melody editing, however important
those decisions may be. The editing process needs to har-
monize the competing demands of modern disciplinary specialists and lead to editions in which words and music
are integrated in ways best suited to the manuscript traditions of the different song repertories, each of which
exhibits specific features that determine editing needs.

For the monophonic repertory, beside the much debated
issue of rhythm, the central question is how to define
and present the "song" that emerges from a problematic
written tradition. A usual editing scenario is to give
priority either to words, in which case melodies are simply eliminated or joined in an accessory manner (transcriptions of one stanza in an appendix, a few manuscript
facsimiles), or to music, in which case the first stanza
alone is taken as the main subject of inquiry, with succeeding stanzas of text frequently ignored. On the one
hand, then, we have a concept proposing the text as the
song, on the other a concept proposing text and music
together, but only part of the text. The differing emphases of philologists and musicologists arise to be sure,
from the manuscript sources, where, if it is given at
all, music is given only for the first stanza. The musicologist's gaze is directed toward the initial stanza and
those texts with music; the philologist takes into consideration the entire written record of the text, with or
without music.

In the motet repertory, because the music and the

text(s) are co-termini, the problem of "leftover" text
segments does not arise. Instead there are problems of a
more complex musical notation system and the intriguing
phenomenon of polytextuality which adds another layer of
complexity. Moreover, the varying manuscript traditions
and the multi-form and experimental nature of the motet
itself make it difficult to think in terms of critical
editions of specific pieces.[155] The basic concepts of
editing motets have been musical, not only because the
music is intricate and the texts idiosyncratic, but also
because the relative disfavor enjoyed by the motet texts
has led to their neglect by philologists.

Still another set of questions arises with the 14th-
century *chansons*, some of which are again strophic. In
the normal process of consigning these *chansons* to manuscripts, texts were written first, followed by the music.
As Lawrence Earp has pointed out, when this technique was
applied carefully, it could produce unambiguous correlations of text and melody. Yet ambiguities could arise,
often from errors in the copying process, especially with
repeated copying. Moreover, only one segment of text--a
stanza, for example, in the ballade--is normally fitted
with music in the manuscripts; the remaining portions of
text are written out separately. Thus not only is the coordination of text and music, even in those segments of
the song where text and music are joined in the manuscript, sometimes unclear (unlike, say, the monophonic
repertory), but there are also text remnants not directly
given with music to be sorted out. Text underlay, the coordination of pitches and syllables, thus becomes a fundamental problem. There is also the question of whether
to apply text to untexted parts of the song (frequently
the *cantus* voice is the only one with text); but since
this question arises more in performance than in editing,
I will not directly address it here.[156] As with the
motet, so with the polyphonic *chanson*, the complexity of
the music is such that the song is chiefly the musicologist's preserve, and with the exception of Machaut, texts
are generally relegated to a secondary position.

In so far as techniques of editing medieval lyric
are concerned, a fundamental problem affecting monophonic

even more than polyphonic song, is the question of the applicability of the strictly conflationary Lachmannian method and its positivistic descendants to lyric repertories at all. With respect to texts, the issue was raised most succinctly by István Frank in a 1955 article on "L'art d'éditer les textes lyriques." In his view, the central tenet that one can recover an "author's original" is largely invalid for a repertory where oral transmission figures so importantly. As we saw above, Pierre Aubry similarly rejected Lachmannian methods for the melodies. The consistent lack of fit between Lachmannian methods and lyric sources would seem to push lyric editing into the Bédier camp.[157] But when one places music and text together in the troubadour/trouvère repertory, the choice of a single "best" source for both, following Bédier's techniques, can become problematic since the "best" choice for the musicologist might not always be the same as the "best" choice for the philologist.

These, briefly sketched out, are some of the editorial problems and choices encountered in the different repertories. I turn now to a few specific observations on joining text and melody in modern editions, including the use of supplementary materials such as translation or commentary to further modern comprehension. For general approaches to editing, and for good bibliographies, one can consult Foulet and Speer, *On Editing Old French Texts* (B440) and John Caldwell, *Editing Early Music* (B439). Foulet and Speer do not include lyric texts, following the general tendency of philologists to emphasize narrative works. Caldwell, however, provides a convenient starting point for my observations because he devotes the final pages of his chapter on "Medieval and Renaissance Music" to what he considers the "knottiest problem of all for the conscientious editor of medieval music: the presentation of the verbal text." From a musicological standpoint, he thus brings up our central problem: how to coordinate words and music. This problem, in his view, is raised in an acute form by Provençal or Occitan songs because the sources are complex and there are often cogent reasons why text and music editors would find it hard to agree on any single source or any method of conflation.[158] Let us therefore examine the issues posed by the

Occitan repertory, within the general context of troubadour and trouvère songs.

The monophonic repertories are difficult to fit into
a modern edition because they are resistant to fixity and
standardization. For many specialists, the ideal would
be to publish all the known versions of a given song or
group of songs, poetry and music. But this ideal has both
conceptual and physical drawbacks. With a small corpus,
such as the songs of Jaufre Rudel edited by Rupert
Pickens (B249), the approach can yield excellent results.
Inspired by the concept of *mouvance* elaborated by Paul
Zumthor (B430), reacting against the interventionism of
Alfred Jeanroy's 1915 edition (B248) which had become
standard, and affirming that it is "impossible to redis-
cover Jaufré's intentions (i.e. the extent of his personal involvement in the creation and regeneration of his
works)," Pickens considers each manifestation of a song
to be "in its own right, as valid a whole, complete poem
as any other version." This approach is guided by concepts of oral transmission and "authenticity" that posit
"mouvance" as "an aspect of the intention" of the
song.[159] Because the manuscript tradition of Rudel's
songs is rich, while the songs are few in number, Pickens
is able to provide a detailed study of transmission and
manuscript relations as well as several manuscript versions of each song, with translations. Pickens does not
include music. For the music, one must turn to Hendrik
van der Werf's *The Extant Troubadour Melodies* (B218)
which furnishes all the melodies in non-mensural notation
with the first stanza of text. With the songs of Jaufre
Rudel, then, edited by Pickens and van der Werf in two
separate publications, we find multiple text and melody
versions laid before us, and we can piece together what
is in the manuscripts as we have them. But the solution
adopted by Pickens can work on a practical level only
with a small repertory. And some of the conceptual defects of his edition are neatly summed up by Pickens himself (42): on the organizational level, "all of the poems
are collected in a single book, whereas all medieval collections extant contain only one version of a given
song"; on the level of editorial intervention, "it is
convenient to classify versions, to give explicitly and

implicitly prominence to some rather than others, and to collate, using traditional methods of establishing texts, several very closely related versions"; and on the level of what I have called manuscript image, words alone are found in his book without musical notation or illuminations.

Another approach to presenting songs has been adopted by the Garland Library of Medieval Literature series. Collaboration between text and music editors is sought, but the basic orientation is literary. Editorial policy follows the practice of selecting a best manuscript, not necessarily the same one for each text in all editions. A single version or a synoptic presentation of each extant melody is then appended, with commentary, variously integrated, by the music editor. This leads to mixed results, while having the virtue of drawing attention to the existence of music.[160] In the edition containing Jaufre Rudel's songs (Wolf and Rosenstein [B250]), the base manuscript selected for the poetry often produces a text at variance with the words underlaid to the melodies as they are appended (although the textual notes do give other text versions which fit some of the melodies). A curious disjunction is thus created between text and melody which is not directly addressed in the edition. This disjunction does not facilitate the study of text-music relationships. More careful coordination guides the edition of the songs of Gace Brulé by Samuel N. Rosenberg and Samuel Danon with melodies edited by Hendrik van der Werf (B285). Here, the melodies appended to the edition are generally, though not always, from the same source as the text, and there has been collaboration on the choice of source. Different melody versions are not given; neither are there different text versions (although textual variants are provided). But the size of Gace Brulé's corpus--82 poems and 67 melodies--renders an edition with all text and melody versions quite impossible for a modern printed book, and the compromises reached here, save the relegation of melodies to an appendix, provide in a clear and convenient format basic materials needed for initial study of text-music relationships.

Two recent editions of troubadour and trouvère song

place the melodies with the texts (not appended at the
end), presenting the complete song in one place. My study
of Raimon de Miraval's *cansos* (B627) is accompanied by an
edition of the *cansos*, texts and melodies together, but,
given the purposes of the study, not necessarily from the
same manuscript source. Basic supplementary material,
including English translation of the texts, supports the
text and music analysis undertaken in the book. Susan
Johnson's edition of the songs of Richard de Semili
(B304) also places texts and melodies together, taken in
all but one case from the same manuscript source, with
full critical apparatus and explanatory notes, a glossary
but no English translations.

The editions described above are devoted to a single
poet/composer. The collection of trouvère songs, *Chantar
m'estuet*, by Samuel N. Rosenberg and Hans Tischler (B210)
is intended to give a broad view of different types of
Old French monophonic song as well as to include music
along with texts where the music has been preserved. The
approach is clearly conducive to the study and performance of song as an entity; but problems arise on another
level. The melodies are given a metric-rhythmic transcription into modern notation that, whatever its vir-
tues, makes it impossible to know what was in the manuscript, to which one must therefore return to re-discover
the music. Texts are not translated, and the glossary
presumes both knowledge of modern French and some familiarity with Old French. Thus, while materials are there
to encourage examination of texts with melodies, they are
not always of easy access. The recent edition of *The
Monophonic Songs in the Roman de Fauvel* by Samuel N.
Rosenberg and Hans Tischler (B337) brings together music
and texts with text translations to facilitate immediate
comprehension. Supporting discussion of the narrative and
of the placement of songs within it, as well as the appended formal schemas, enhance the usefulness of the edition. But the edition also raises the problem of the relationship of the musical transcription, which is heavily
normalizing, to the diversity of the problematic notational symbols found in the original manuscript.

The main problems that emerge from this brief look

at a few editions arise from the kinds of choices one
must make, both theoretical and practical, to put music
and text together in a manner appropriate for a modern
edition. John Caldwell correctly argues that in making an
edition of Old Occitan songs, one's aim must be considered, and the two aims he proposes are important though
not exhaustive: "is it [the aim] to revive the songs as
current at the time and place of the source, or is it to
recover them as sung, say, 150 years earlier?" He further
argues against taking over an edited literary text for a
musical edition on the grounds that such texts can vary
substantially from texts in musical sources. Although the
variations are not always as substantial as Caldwell
would have us believe, the point raised is, of course, a
central one. Caldwell then pushes his argument to the
conclusion that one cannot present song as a musical-
textual entity unless one uses a musical source for both
text and music: the musical source "which may not have
primary value for the text editor, is . . . primary for
the musical-textual entity which is the song itself."[161]
Presumably by adhering strictly to the musical source,
the aim of "reviving the songs as current at the time
and place of the source," which seems to Caldwell to be
the preferable aim, will be achieved. In a similar vein,
Wulf Arlt, speaking about editions, argues that in the
case of European courtly song, if we are to understand
music-text relationships, it is required that both text
and melody come from the same source.[162]

Both Arlt and Caldwell seem to consider only text
editions based on collated sources and not the frequently
adopted single source approach. But beyond the question
of text editing methods, one must ask if an exclusive adherence to the same source for music and text is the only
way to produce an edition in which the song as a musical-
textual entity can be studied. The answer--and the feasi-
bility of adherence to a single manuscript--will be different according to different repertories. The trouvère
repertory offers a wider choice of versions, since so
many melodies have been preserved. It is usually likely
that one manuscript can be selected for text and music.
The problems in this repertory arise from the sometimes
quite sharp dissimilarities in melody versions and the

possible autonomy of text and melody transmission. For the troubadours, given the fact that fewer melodies have been preserved and in more precarious conditions, selecting a single manuscript for text and music is much more complicated; and strict adherence to a principle that would assign primary value to a musical source runs the risk of placing out of reach the very goal it apparently seeks: understanding the song as a musical-textual entity.

The major question pointed up by the troubadour repertory is how to define the musical-textual entity and what relationship this entity bears to what has been written in manuscripts. Given the characteristics of the troubadour manuscript tradition, we can fully satisfy neither of the aims proposed by Caldwell: we cannot be sure that in following slavishly one manuscript we are reviving the song as current at the time and place of the source; neither can we recover what may have been sung some 150-200 years earlier. As Wulf Arlt points out, the music and text scribes were often different people, and the music may have been written later than the words and acquired from a different source.[163] The whole process of writing down the troubadour songs was an effort, so far as we can judge, to recuperate a past art in a cultural climate innocent of modern notions of authenticity or of concepts that specific melodies must accompany specific texts. To be sure, one has to imagine that the medieval scribe sought to associate melodies and texts in consistent ways according to his understanding of what he was about. Thus careful consideration of text-music relationships in musical sources is surely essential. But it is unwise to assume that this is the only path to understanding these relationships. Placing emphasis on musical sources, as we have seen, often goes hand in hand with the prioritizing of one stanza, the first, over all other stanzas. But is it only in the first stanza that the musical-textual entity is to be found? Arlt seems to suggest not when he advocates the return to sources to prepare a performance if an edition (such as van der Werf's *Extant Troubadour Melodies*) contains only one stanza.[164] However, if one returns to the *musical* source for, say, the Comtessa de Dia's "A chantar m'er," all one will find is the first stanza because the manuscript (W) has no others. In that case, recovering the musical-textual entity in the full panoply of its unfolding re-quires a leap of faith into sources that preserve only texts, the faith that even if no melody has been written down there, the song might at some point have been sung all the way through to something like the melody pre-served in the musical source. Prioritizing the first stanza--with the implicit assumption that since it is the only stanza to which music was actually affixed in a medieval source, it is the only stanza that can yield valuable results in analysis--neglects a key feature of strophic composition: how the musical-textual relation-ships play themselves out through an entire song.

The notion of repeating the same melody for different strophes is distinguishable in degree but not in kind from the practice of using the same melody for slightly different texts or even for completely different songs, as occurs with *contrafacta*. Such practice is widely docu-mented in medieval sources; and the existence of this practice, coupled with the possible scribal practice men-tioned above of taking a melody from one source to use it in another, should caution us to beware of attaching to troubadour manuscript traditions a fixity more appro-priate to printing, so that we categorically exclude the joining in modern edition of a melody and a text from different medieval sources. The technique of taking text and music from the same source emphasizes a medieval wit-ness; but the technique of using different sources is not inconsonant with what we know of medieval practice. If a poem is only fully represented in a manuscript without music, the goal of seizing the complete musical-textual entity we desire to study can be met only if text and melody are taken from different sources.

Arguably, then, the notion that music and text must always come from the same manuscript source if we are to recuperate a musical-textual entity cannot constitute an unexceptionable editorial principle for vernacular mono-phonic song. Surely with the troubadour repertory, some-times with the trouvères, complex questions of transmis-sion and of how melodies and texts came to be deposited in manuscripts preclude clear-cut editorial rules. An approach taking flexible account of the problems while seeking to provide an adequate conception of the song would seem the best editorial goal. But we should entertain no delusions about what we are up to. If an editor takes melodies from one source and texts from another, the editor is not necessarily seeking the authenticity of an actual performance, either at the time of the source or earlier. But then the manuscripts from which we must work do not necessarily do that either.

In sum, the Old Occitan lyric raises in an acute form not just the question of how a musicologist should present a verbal text, but how editions can best present songs as musical-textual entities, drawing from manuscript witnesses a vision (if not a single authentic version) of the songs, while avoiding the unexamined substitution of that vision for the diverse realities of the sources.

If problems of joining text and music in editing are acute with Old Occitan songs, such problems are by no means absent from later repertories. In the edition of polyphonic repertories, it is generally the music editor who is responsible for the outcome, and understandably so, as I pointed out above, given the intricacy of the musical component. Although texts frequently benefit from their own editor, they are not always as carefully scrutinized as the music. Partly this is due to lack of interest on the part of philologists, whose attention has been absorbed by major figures such as Adam de la Halle and Machaut. The issue of philological interest in polyphonic song texts is a question to which I will return in a later section. But even if more research were done by philologists, how should editions best integrate music and text?

Current practice includes several procedures. Sometimes texts are given in a separate section, with translations and commentary, as in Hans Tischler's edition of the *Montpellier Codex* (B316), or in the *Five Ballades for the House of Foix* edited by Peter Lefferts and Sylvia Huot (B334), or without translation and commentary, as in

Willi Apel's *French Secular Compositions of the Four-teenth Century* (B330). The procedure incorporating trans-lations and commentary seems to offer good prospects for studying texts along with music. The Lefferts/Huot edi-tion provides brief literary analysis as well as transla-tion of the texts. But for the Tischler edition, the text commentary was apparently added late (xv), creating a disjunction between music and text editions, and the text editor's treatment of the French texts is not abreast of recent scholarship.

Another procedure is followed in the important series *Polyphonic Music of the Fourteenth Century*. Text is given only as underlay, that is, all text is underlaid in the edition whether it was underlaid in the manuscript or not, and although there may be brief critical comments, no separate text section is provided. This practice is useful for singing. But since it does not reflect what is in those original sources where all text is not under-laid, it is not conducive to the serious study of text-music relationships. The text in such editions merely ap-pears as a collection of syllables attached to notes. And as John Caldwell has pointed out (B439, 43), the attempt to underlay several stanzas can lead to illegibility as well as misunderstanding, if the editor has not fully considered the various, often perplexing, technicalities of syllabication in Old French. Clearly, where text un-derlay is one of the main areas of investigation, it is useful to have sorted out what the manuscript offers from what the editor adds. Few editions attempt such sorting-out in a consistent manner, although Willi Apel's *French Secular Music of the Late Fourteenth Century* constitutes a partial exception.

A third editorial practice can be observed in Nigel Wilkins' *Armes, Amours, Dames, Chevalerie* (B212), in-tended to be a performing edition. It groups all informa-tion pertinent to a song with that song: music, full text, translation, commentary. His conception allows for easy consultation of all components of the song, al-though the transcriptions of medieval notation and the "re-organizing and rationalizing" (ix) of text underlay in many cases make difficult an understanding of what the manuscript sources provided.

In the polyphonic repertories, the particular issue of using the same source for text and music is not foregrounded as it is in the monophonic repertories. To be sure, the issue of separability of text and music pertains in a general way to the 14th-century *formes fixes*. In the Machaut manuscripts, for example, many poems do not have music, and lyric pieces inserted without music, say, in the *Voir Dit* are given with music elsewhere in the same or another manuscript. Still, choice of a single source is not the main issue. The polyphonic repertory foregrounds the question of integration in editing: are the words merely syllables on which to hang musical notes or should consideration of their shape and texture in the manuscript traditon be a part of the editing process? Do the changing relations of text and music in polyphonic manuscripts correspond to changing concepts of song that could profitably be elaborated as part of an edition or at least reflected in the editing process? If we are to "revive songs as current at the time and place of the source,"[165] which is a strong consideration for the polyphonic sources since they are less antiquarian than many monophonic sources, then we need to consider fully concepts of text-music integration that may be contained in them.

The move from printed book to electronic book, now more and more discussed, will surely offer new options for editors. Charles Faulhaber has described some of the desiderata and new vistas of electronic critical editions. Using the models of hypertext, or of a complete hypermedia system, one could conceivably produce not only the critical text, backed up by all manuscript versions-- the text and its complete environment, so to speak--but also manuscript illumination and musical sounds.[166] Thus we could have the complete song in all of its ramifications, and no edition would be complete without sounds and images. This new way of editing would call for a reconceptualization of what the song is or should be; for just as manuscripts and printing press offered different images of song, so will hypertext and hypermedia. Recovering texts or illuminations is quite a different operation from recovering sounds: texts and illuminations survive from the Middle Ages; sounds are gone. Yet hypermedia systems might permit access to different *modern* sung versions, thus enabling us better to imagine the variability in performance that surely must have been common practice in the Middle Ages for certain repertories. The exciting possibilities of the hyperedition only make examination of theoretical positions the more urgent, so that in the move from text to hypertext we do not again, by recapitulating past misconceptions, lose the song.

Although the manifold problems of editing have merely been sketched out here, even this brief review of existing editions reveals that we rarely find in one edition all material necessary for study of text and music: the concept of presenting songs as musical-textual entities has rarely been set as a goal, theoretically elaborated, or practically realized. Setting this goal at a moment when new technological vistas are opening up could invite a clearer focus on the song as an esthetic whole and suggest new perspectives on text-music relationships.

RHYTHMS AND SOUNDS

Turning now to specific aspects of text-music relationships, I will first examine basic concepts of rhythms and sounds and then take up style, forms and structures, and genres. Scholarly energies have traditionally been applied to discussion of rhythmic elements of lyric repertories. But recent research has also concentrated on sonorities, particularly with regard to 14th-century music.

Considerations of rhythm, as is well known, have posed some of the knottiest problems for the monophonic repertories, with which I will begin. These repertories have suffered from the negative perception that the notation of the monophonic chansonniers was somehow deficient. From this perception of deficiency grew the various methods of overcoming it, the most spectacular of which was the theory of modal rhythmic transcription devised at the beginning of the century. The debates which ensued have themselves been debated and summarized many times.[167] It is unlikely that any final and unequivocal resolution of the numerous questions raised by the notation of monophonic repertories will be attained. But in the wake of the diminishing credibility of the modal theories of rhythmic transcription, new lines of inquiry have opened up, which have been shaped by a distrust of positivistic editions and a return to the manuscripts themselves to reassess the information they furnish. In this context, the rejection of positivistic editing methodologies takes the form of an anti-normalizing stance.

The findings of Hendrik van der Werf, his continuing criticism of modal theories, his staunch defense of the use of nonmensural notation in the transcription of troubadour and trouvère music, and his elaboration first of the idea of "declamatory rhythm" and more recently of the notion, that, in performance, all pitches should be of approximately equal duration, proceed from close scrutiny of manuscripts and particularly of musical "variants" that are left out of normalizing editions.[168] The approach adopted by John Stevens calls for examination of the monophonic notation on its own terms, moving from the manuscripts themselves to a consideration of the rhythmic properties of the song. Taking note of "the lack of attention to the actual notation of non-liturgical monophonic music," he devotes a chapter of his book on *Words and Music in the Middle Ages* to "Palaeography, Notation and Presentation." There, he raises most of the pertinent issues, at least in summary form. He points out the consistently "syllabic" presentation of text and music; the flexibility of the notational signs; the putative relationship of variants to an oral art.[169]

Beyond the manuscript tradition itself, evidence from the Middle Ages concerning rhythm could come from theoretical writings on music. But, as a general rule, medieval theorists do not shed unequivocal light on the rhythmic properties of monophonic secular song. Medieval musical treatises are not usually concerned with problems of secular monophony, with the exception of Johannes de Grocheio whose oft-quoted suggestion that the notes of certain songs were not precisely measured would tend to support, albeit indirectly, a concept of "free" rhythm.

Yet, basing his arguments on medieval rhythmic theory and on Grocheio's discussions, John Stevens establishes opposition between two main traditions of rhythm in song: *musica metrica* which "describes sounds which are measured in longs and shorts and grouped in 'feet,'" and *musica ritmica* which "specifically excludes durational values and deals with the organization of strictly counted syllables, unmeasured, into harmonious and balanced wholes" (B415, 415). *Musica ritmica* becomes the basis of his concept of isosyllabism (equality of syllables). Some of these same theorists had been adduced by Georges Lote to support his view of the syllabic nature of medieval French verse, although Stevens does not mention Lote.[170]

John Stevens argues that the evidence he has adduced from paleographical analysis and the theoretical sources (including vernacular treatises, especially Dante) indicates that music and text in the repertories he is considering are clearly and consistently "syllabic" in presentation. With this argument one can have no quarrel; there is strong evidence, ably marshalled. Stevens, however, uses his evidence to develop a theory of *iso*syllabism. Although he recognizes that "syllabic" presentation is not the same thing as "isosyllabic," "even if the presentation is as apt a representation of isosyllabic melody as could be desired" (B415, 457), he yet easily makes the leap from the one to the other. He sees both as based on number, on counting; and for Stevens, number is the crucial parameter: "The notes and the words are not so much related to one another as related both to a single numerical idea" (B415, 499). The abstract position adopted by Stevens clears the air of many foggy notions, but in itself is not of easy application. On the practical side, performance with absolutely equal syllables can become stilted, running contrary to the nature of language rhythms, which do not usually arise from units susceptible of exact measuring. Stevens does qualify the concept of isosyllabic movement by asserting that it is not "inflexible, rigid or metronomic" (B415, 504). But we are left with the question of how flexibility can be achieved.

As recent approaches to musical rhythm in the

monophonic repertories have more and more discredited
the "modal" theories that previously held sway, the
tendency has become to look toward the text for rhythmic
definition. This tendency poses problems of its own; but
many of these problems could be usefully addressed, leading to more sophisticated analyses of text-music coordinations in all repertories here under consideration,
through a clearer appreciation of vernacular versification. John Stevens, for example, virtually eliminates
vernacular versification from his considerations. Understandably, he shies away from the uses to which versification has been put by devotees of "modal rhythm" who
would derive regular patterns from scansion of certain
verse-lines (B415, 494-6). He opposes to such regular
patterns Carl Appel's analyses of the poems of Bernart de
Ventadorn, but without drawing from Appel's analyses information about versification that could flesh out the
idea of flexibility in a basically syllabic rhythmic
style.[171]

It might be thought that medieval treatises on vernacular poetry would help clarify the issues. The tradition of medieval and grammatical treatises on the vernacular begins in Catalonia around 1210 with the *Razos de
trobar* by Raimon Vidal de Besalú. The most famous of the
Occitan treatises is the *Leys d'amors,* composed in Toulouse, 1330-56. Between those treatises is situated
Dante's *De vulgari eloquentia,* c.1304-06. Neither the
Leys d'amors nor Dante's work has as its true object the
earlier song tradition, although much modern critical vocabulary is drawn from them. The treatises support counting of syllables as a first requisite of song composition. The *Leys d'amors* also consider accent: word accent;
the role of accent in determining verse structure and
designating verse types; and accents of music and verse
in an initially puzzling statement that becomes more
comprehensible when one realizes to what degree the *Leys*
treat vernacular accent through concepts drawn from Latin, all the while realizing that vernacular accent differs from Latin.[172] The *Leys* provide a lengthy definition
of accent.[173] The definition begins by calling accent
"melody": "Accens es regulars melodia o tempramens de
votz lequals estay principalmens in una sillaba." This

"melody" created by the rising or falling of the voice
in reading is immediately distinguished from "can de
musica." The "can de musica" refers to the melodic line
alone, which does not always observe word accents, and
the example given is, characteristically, a Latin one, a
Responsory, in which groups of notes occur with unaccented syllables and single notes with accented syllables,
thus lengthening what should be short and shortening what
should be long. The term "can" is used with language spoken or read only by analogy ("per alcuna semblansa"),
because as in singing, so in speaking, one can discern
pitch, stress and duration: "en ayssi co hom eleva la
votz fortmen quan canta, ayssi meteysh en la sillaba on
cay le principals accens, eleva hom la votz mays e plus
fortamen, fazen major demora de temps." The author of the
Leys has a problem not only with differentiating the vernacular from Latin but also with extracting poetry from
music, similar to the problem faced by his slightly later
northern confrère, Eustaches Deschamps (*Art de dictier*,
1392). Much of the discussion about accent in the *Leys*
is informative; but none of it is entirely clear, and it
would repay further study.

By way of suggesting how closer attention to versification might enrich understanding of what flexibility
could mean in a syllabic rhythmic style, let me briefly
review some basic features--syllable count, the nature
and role of stresses in a syllabic line--pertinent to
rhythmic issues but not always given full weight in
scholarly discussion. Counting syllables is, of course,
essential to Old Occitan and Old French versification.
But it is not an entirely simple operation. Medieval
scribes did not always adopt the same writing conventions
--particularly with regard to the final "a" in Occitan,
the mute "e" in French, or the handling of diphthongs;
and musical scribes, particularly if their native language was not that of the song in question, diversely
interpreted diversely written texts. Normalized syllable
counting, which has usually pertained in editions and is
to a large extent justified by the nature and development
of the poetry as well as by the prescriptions of the *Leys
d'amors*, is reflected in the two modern versification
guides through troubadour and trouvère song: István

Frank, *Répertoire métrique de la poésie des troubadours*
(B12) and Mölk/Wolfzettel, *Répertoire métrique de la
poésie lyrique française des origines à 1350* (B20). However, the inadvisability of normalizing all texts of
whatever genre has been cogently argued in the recent research of John Marshall (B560-3) and incorporated into
the theoretical work of Dominique Billy (B471). Frequently, versification irregularities have been excluded because it was thought that they could not be sung. That
this view proceeded from an inadequate comprehension of
musical properties, or, indeed, precluded adequate comprehension of the music is evident from Marshall's
work.[174] It seems clear that the reaction to normalizing
should not obscure the need to sort out irregularities
that could be considered (scribal) error or mere spelling differences; but it is equally clear that in the
sorting-out process, all irregularities of syllable
count should not be swept under the rug. Theoretical
recognition of irregularity problematizes the concept of
isosyllabism as an unexceptionable analytical tool in
rhythmic analysis.

The relationship of syllable count to line of verse
raises some issues related to irregularity that need
resolution in the practical working-out of text-music
rhythms. The syllable is the defining unit of the line
of verse; but designations of verse types do not always
correspond to actual number of syllables. This point,
joined to the role of accent in defining verse types,
has not always been clearly perceived. I will thus describe here the main issues that could profitably be
incorporated into the text-music research agenda.

At least as early as the *Leys d'amors,* and likely
earlier, we have evidence that conventions governing
verse types in Old Occitan were, like those pertaining to
French, based on the oxytonic (accent on the final syllable) character of the language--in contrast, say to Italian or Spanish where word accents are commonly paroxytonic (accent on next-to-last syllable). The importance
of stress in classifying verse type is set forth in the
Leys d'amors (I, 100): the number of syllables defining a
verse always refers to verses ending in the "accen agut"

or oxytonic word; if there is an "accen greu" (*natúra,
cortezía*), that is, a paroxytonic word, the line will
have an extra, uncounted syllable.[175] The line of verse
is thus defined by its final accent: a 10-syllable line,
for example, will have its final *accent* on the 10th syllable, whether masculine or feminine. But in the feminine
line, there will be a concluding *uncounted* and *unaccented*
syllable, indicated here by "x":

10-syllable Occitan:

Masc: Tan m'abellis l'amoros pessamens
        1   2 3 4   5 6 7 8 9 10
Fem: Que s'es vengutz e mon fin cor assire
        1   2   3 4   5 6   7   8 9 10 x
                (Folquet de Marseilla, B239, 15)

8-syllable French:

Fem: Fine   amours et bone esperánce
        1   2   3   4   5 6   7 8 x
Masc: Me   ramainne joie et chantér
        1   2   3 4   5 6   7 8
                (Gace Brulé, B285, 154)

A remark is called for at this juncture on terminology. In syllabic versification systems, the word "meter"
refers only to number of syllables; this usage is to be
carefully distinguished from the various meanings of
"meter" in musical terminology or for other versification
types. It should also be noted that the term "feet" drawn
from classical terminology, is sometimes used to refer to
syllables. In general, it is better to retain the word
"syllable."

Because the definition of the line of verse is a matter of accent as well as counting, the interplay of masculine and feminine line endings can become a source of
subtle rhythmic effects in relation to musical settings.
A series of 8-syllable masculine rhymes with accent always on the last syllable is to be rhythmically differen-
tiated from the frequently encountered combinations of 8
(masculine) + 7' (feminine) syllables where the number of

syllables is the same, but the text accent is now on the last, now on the next to last syllable. One thinks not only of troubadour song, but also of Machaut's ballade from the *Remede de Fortune,* "Dame de qui," in which the *clos* cadence of the first part is musically identical to the final cadence--but the rhyme and thus the text accent has changed: "ir" for the first part, thus masculine with accent on the last syllable; "oi-e," for the final cadence thus feminine, with accent shifted to the next to last syllable. The sweetness and joy of the expectation of love together with its instability cannot be better expressed than through this juxtaposition.

The difference between actual number of syllables and conventional designations of verse types brings a certain amount of confusion to John Stevens's isosyllabic system: he finds it necessary to come out with two different total syllable counts for songs where there are feminine lines, the undergirding concept of accent being inadmissible in his system.[176] How his analyses might be modified if the reasons determining the conventional designations of verse types were taken into consideration is a matter for further discussion.

Beyond counting of syllables and attention to final stress, the caesura must be considered in describing different lines of verse. Only lines of 10 or more syllables have a regular caesura; the 10-syllable line is the only important one for lyric poetry. The nature of the caesura --actual fact or theoretical concept, accent or pause-- has occasioned some debate; the normal place for a caesura in the 10-syllable line is at the 4th syllable, although 5 + 5 or 6 + 4 can be noted. But there is a further consideration. Other types of caesura were used until the 16th century when it became customary to restrict feminine endings at the caesura to those that could be elided, as in:

Et rien de Ro/me en Rome m'aperçois
1   2   3 4   5   6 7   8 9 10
        (Du Bellay, *Les Antiquités de Rome*, III, 2)

Old Occitan and Old French could treat the caesura like

a verse ending and admit there an extra uncounted syllable. This is the *epic caesura*:

> Nos iove ómne / quandius qu'e nos estam
> 1   2 3 4   x   5   6   7   8 9 10
> (*Boeci*, cited in B480, 2).

Also in use was the *lyric caesura* which involves the
placement of a syllable without accent at the cesura and
counting it in the verse:

> Oimais ármas / ni fort tornei espas
> 1   2   3   4   5   6   7 8 9 10
> (Gaucelm Faidit, B240, 416).

For the lyric caesura, there is a shift of accent from
the 4th to the 3rd syllable. These different caesurae
lend rhythmic variety to the verses. The lyric caesura
does not change the relation of syllables counted inside
the line to the meter determined by the count; however
the epic caesura does alter this relationship. The 10-
syllable line can have 11 actual syllables if it is feminine or has an epic caesura; 12 actual syllables if it
has both feminine ending and an epic caesura. But these
extra syllables do not change its status as a 10-syllable
line. In strophic song, the presence of an epic caesura
means melodic readjustment where the caesura occurs. Not
many songs exhibit the device; one of the more celebrated
is "Bele Doete" (B654, 89). The first stanza, underlaid
to the melody, has 10-syllable lines with masculine endings and 3 epic caesurae:

> I   Bele Doete as fenestres se siet
>   1 2 3 4 x 5   6 7   8   9 10
>   x = epic caesura with hiatus indicated
>   by number of notes in the manuscript
>   Lit en un livre, mais au cuer ne l'en tient
>   1   2 3   4   x   5   6   7   8   9   10
>   x = epic caesura
>   De son ami Doon li resovient
>   1   2   3 4 5 6 7 8 9 10
>   normal caesura

Q'en autres terres est alez tornoier
1   2   3   4 x   5 6 7   8 9 10
                 x = epic caesura
E, or en ai dol.

The second stanza has 10-syllable lines with feminine
endings and one epic caesura:

II Uns escuiers as degrez de la sale
    1 2 3 4   5   6 7   8 9 10 x
                  x = feminine ending
    Est descenduz, s'est destrossé sa male
    1   2 3 4   5   6   7 8 9 10 x
                  x = feminine ending
    Bele Doete les degrez en avale
    1 2 3 4 x 5 6   7 8 9 10x
                  x = epic caesura and feminine ending
    Ne cuide pas oïr novele male
    1 2   3   4   56   7 8 9 10 x
                  x = feminine ending
    E, or en ai dol.

The actual number of syllables thus varies from 10 to 12,
and a certain number of melodic adjustments are needed
for the succeeding strophes. It is noteworthy that the
epic caesura serves most importantly to highlight the
name "Bele Doete" with very subtle rhythmic effects.

The elements of verse thus far addressed, though they
have provided some controversy, are nevertheless reasonably supported by medieval evidence. The same is not true
of the kinds of accentuation one may posit in addition to
the fixed accents of caesura and rhyme. These accents are
sometimes called "mobile accents" and they are a function
of syntax and performer's delivery as much as of any versification rules. Some indication of how the system might
have worked is furnished by the *Leys d'amors* where we are
told that in verses without necessary caesura, pauses
(later defined as accents) are optional ("E devetz saber
quen alqus bordos pot hom far pauza quis vol, en alcus no
et en alqus es de necessitat quom fassa pauza" (B181, 1,
130). Moreover, there is a distinction between pauses "to
catch one's breath" which can occur anywhere and pauses

related to meaning and syntax (1, 130). Thus there is a
linking of accent and pause not only to verse type but
also to meaning and the simple necessity of breathing;
this points to relationships between accentuation of
words, word groups, or syntactical features and the exi-
gencies of meter that could give some insight into the
characteristics of vernacular verse, at least as the
14th-century author of the *Leys* saw them.

In the absence of native-speaker models, scholars
have turned for information to manuscript evidence and
what we know of the phonological development of the languages. In the manuscripts, we can perceive some word
linkages that perhaps reflect speech habits at least to
some degree.[177] From the phonetic development of the languages, it seems evident that word stress in Old Occitan
and Old French was stronger than in their modern counter-
parts, yet it was not strong enough to become the basis
of a versification system. Mildred Pope proposed that
during the period beginning roughly at the end of the
11th century and including Old and Middle French, "the
whole rhythm of the language was gradually changed; the
intensity of the tonic stress was gradually diminished,
and there manifested itself with increasing strength a
tendency to link closely together words closely associated in thought" (B59, 103, §223). Thus we could posit as
early as the 12th century language rhythms that resist
any imposition of regularly recurring metric accent but
support the concept of flexible accents--beyond caesura
and rhyme--determined by word groups and syntax on the
one hand, by diction on the other. The Old Occitan and
Old French poets play with varying accents across a fixed
number of syllables, in contrast to English poets who
work with stress patterns which, while they can be rear-
ranged for rhythmic effect, provide an expectation of
pattern predictability. And in Old Occitan and Old
French, unlike English, rhythm and syntax go hand in
hand, since rhythmic units corresponding to sense units
largely determine the mobile accents. Moreover, since
rhythmic units and sense groups largely coincide, and
since the one stable poetic accent is always at the
rhyme, there is a strong tendency for lines of verse and
grammatical units to coincide as well, concluding at the

rhyme. This makes the use of run-on lines (*enjambement*) a more forceful stylistic feature in Old Occitan and Old French than in modern English.

Certain rhythmic features of the line of verse are thus stable: it is defined by number of syllables; verse-type classification is linked to end-line accentuation, oxytonic or paroxytonic; obligatory accents occur at the rhyme and, where necessary, at the caesura. The idea of mobile accents linked to syntax can reasonably be posited, although it rests on evidence that, while persuasive, yet remains elusive. These concepts linking regularity and flexibility can permit a better understanding of how syllabic song structures can achieve rhythmic variety, allowing music and poetry to flow together naturally as a single expressive unit.

The elusiveness of the "mobile" accents has led Roger Pensom to attempt, for the 10-syllable line, an elaboration of rules that would eliminate random accentuation and permit a concept of varied but ordered distribution of accented and unaccented tones and syllables (B589). His approach differs from van der Werf's free declamation and Stevens's isosyllabism. Pensom's theories, applied so far only to decasyllabic verse and especially to the poetry and music of Thibaut de Champagne, are provocative but as yet inconclusive. They demonstrate, however, the kinds of new insights to be gained from incorporating issues of linguistic accentuation into the text-music research agenda.

Now to turn to sounds. Sound and rhythm are linked because the final accent that punctuates the line of verse is also a function of rhyme. One must distinguish between rhyme schemes, which are abstract formulae, and the rhyme sounds that constitute sonorous reality. The importance of rhyme is revealed by the subtleties of both theory and practice lavished upon it: the *Leys d'amors*, for example, luxuriate in rhyme terminology, and the pyrotechnics of the troubadours are well known. The styles of *trobar car* or *trobar ric* ("rich" or "rare" styles) call for the use of unusual sounds, artistic rhymes, and recherché vocabulary. Interstanzaic sound

sequences established by end-line repetition patterns
shape different stanza types; intrastanzaic repetition
can link stanzas together (Billy, B471). Similar sounds
in positions other than at the rhyme can reverberate
within the line or stanza, a kind of sound echoing capable of the most sophisticated effects (Smith, B622).
What is at stake here is the delight taken in sound itself. Rhyme is the central poetic focus of the exuberant-
ly joyful sound play that characterizes medieval song.
The "melody of rhymes" in trouvère song has received
lengthy analysis by Dragonetti (B492, 404-57). But the
song itself integrates both music and text sounds not
only at the rhyme but also throughout the song, and part
of the pleasure of listening to it must have arisen from
that integration.

If text sounds have been a focus of research, the
sonorous dimension of vernacular melodies has taken a
back seat to the question of rhythm. To a degree, this
is because only one tonal characteristic lends itself to
analysis: pitch. Dynamics and tone quality are far more
elusive and perhaps in the last analysis escape us entirely. No more than we can know the exact quality of
vowel sounds can we know the exact quality of musical
sounds. Study of tonal characteristics has tended to veer
toward organizations of pitches, study of intervals, tonal arrangements, or hierarchies of pitches. And this type
of study usually proceeds against the background of Chant
and Chant methodology. Similarly, the study of melodic
properties moves toward the analysis of sounds in structures, a point to which I will return later.

For the monophonic repertory, there has been continuing debate about the vernacular use of scales and/or
modes. Ian Parker (B583) pointed out the drawbacks of the
medieval modal system as applied to the secular repertory, but saw no way around using this system as a point of
reference. Parker also assessed the third-chain principle
developed by Curt Sachs, without finding it entirely satisfactory either. This principle had been adopted by van
der Werf in his *Chansons* to elucidate vernacular compositional processes (B645, 47). Van der Werf also posited
the existence of two basic medieval scales for the

secular repertory: "medieval major" and "medieval minor" (53-9), avoiding the term "mode" altogether. In his recent article "The Troubadours Singing their Poems," Leo Trietler has broken down the concept "mode" into two aspects: "melody type" and "octave species," arguing that these two aspects overlap to form a basis for establishing a musical syntax (B640). Treitler also sees in Curt Sachs's third-chain principle an instrument adopted by the troubadours in the elaboration of their melodies.

Semioticians and thematic or motivic analysts have been concerned with melodic properties chiefly as they reveal themselves in patterns. The work of Donna Mayer-Martin on Gace Brulé (B564) or of Elizabeth Aubrey (B452) is focussed on motivic process. Aubrey also investigates how the study of melodic variants can yield information about the manipulation of sounds as well as about rhythm. In his article on "Distributional Structure in Troubadour Music" (B516), based on linguistic methods, but related by its emphasis on frequencies of occurrence to feature analysis, David Halperin gives statistics on melodic intervals and isolates melodic formulae, without, however, grounding his findings in larger theoretical issues.

These approaches to sonorities and to organization of sonorities allow the identification of essential musical sounds to which textual sounds can then be related in the fabric of the song. But there are other approaches that could be exploited in research on medieval song which emphasize the notion of the importance of listening. Don Ihde in his *Listening and Voice: A Phenomenology of Sound* points out pertinently that western thinking is dominated by visualism, which has led to a neglect of the invisible to which listening attends: we need an "ontology of the auditory." Ihde's purpose is to move towards "a radically different understanding of experience, one which has its roots in a *phenomenology* of auditory experience."[178] The intellectual movement of phenomenology, which in part undergirds reception and reader-response theories (notably in the work of Wolfgang Iser), has only slowly affected musical thinking.[179] One of the more important recent studies is Thomas Clifton's *Music as Heard*. Clifton calls upon phenomenology to develop a theory of music as a phenomenon and to find ways of analyzing this phenomenon. Although Clifton's focus is on modern music, he uses several examples from Chant to propose ways of talking about the concept of musical line, including text.[180] Since the experience of listening was surely central to medieval song, as Paul Zumthor's recent books on the voice in medieval "literature" have reminded us (B431), the approaches represented by Ihde and Clifton, though not specifically directed toward medieval song, point to new ways of describing it as an irreducible amalgam of textual and musical sounds taken in by the ear.

Using more traditional methods, a number of analyses have been carried out on the linked functionings of musical and vocal sonorous qualities. In my study of Raimon de Miraval's *Cansos*, I examined the interplay of melody and rhymes, both rhyme sounds and rhyme schemes (B627, 108-14). Stephen Nichols proposed a detailed study of sound effects in Marcabru's "Dire vos vuoill ses doptansa" (B576). Bernart de Ventadorn's songs have been the subject of studies by Joan Ferrante, who places primary emphasis on the text of "Ab ioi mou lo vers e.1 comens" but considers also the music (B500, 113-41), by Nicoletta Gossen, who emphasizes primarily the music (B510), and by Vincent Pollina, who has examined words and music in "Era.m cosselhatz, senhor" (B598). From another viewpoint, that of performance practice, Christopher Page has called attention to the importance of vowel color in medieval polyphony (B763, 84); mutatis mutandis, many of his observations could also be valid for monody. Thus not only rhyme but the complete spectrum of vernacular sounds interact with music on different levels; and this interaction is in need of further refinement through research.

To this point, I have chiefly discussed monophonic song, though much of what I have said, especially on vernacular versification, is pertinent to polyphonic song as well. But I would now like to focus specifically on polyphonic repertories. New textures bring new rhythmic complexities, new sounds and combinations of sounds. The notation of rhythm, explored with ever increasing

sophistication both in clearly mensurally notated monophonic song and in polyphonic song, gave music and text
the potential to follow independent, though perforce
still coordinated, rhythmic lines. When music has an accentual system of its own, independent of text and expressed through a coherent notational system, word-music
relationships are profoundly modified. The kinds of juxtapositions and coordinations of musical-textual lines
that then become possible constitute a new art of song.
The radical difference of this art is obscured by the
modal theory of rhythmic transcription of courtly songs
which presumes for these songs musical rhythmic properties that manuscript notation simply fails to record. In
support of rhythmic transcriptions of courtly song, Nigel
Wikins, for example, has argued that because in the 13th
(and even into the 14th) century monophonic and polyphonic styles overlap and because there are numerous ex-
changes between the two repertories, it "seems odd to
suggest that Lescurel or Machaut, in their secular monodies, should have an utterly different idea from their
predecessors of only a few years before" (B371, 183). If
Lescurel's monophonic songs possess rhythmic properties
reflected by the musical notation, so goes the argument,
then trouvère song must have had similar properties, although the notation does not reveal them, because the two
kinds of song are roughly contemporaneous. This kind of
reasoning blurs the esthetic implications of important
differences in notational systems. It is precisely an
"utterly different idea" as Wilkins puts it--the linking
of verse to a *measured* melody--that defines a new art.
Adam de la Halle used different notation systems for
monophonic and polyphonic music; Lescurel, a few years
later, uses the new rhythmic notations for his monophonic songs. Adam de la Halle's monophonic songs were mainly
chansons which look back to a tradition of love songs.
Lescurel's compositions are no longer "courtly" songs in
the old sense: they are rondeaux, ballades and virelais;
the styles have changed. The 13th century indeed saw
overlap and exchange, but also the development of a new
musical notation to represent musical rhythms, with which
text rhythms would react in distinctive and radically
different ways.

Although a few studies have been undertaken, relatively little work has been done on textual rhythms and
sounds in the 13th-century vernacular motet. Consideration of rhythmic aspects of versification in motet editions has chiefly served to determine how to print texts
under melodies, not as part of an appreciation of rhythmic subtleties. Musicologists Yvonne Rokseth and Ernest
Sanders posited connections between development of musical rhythmic styles and specific properties of the French
language.[181] Louisa Spottswood has inquired into possible
relationships between pronunciation of Latin and Old
French (B694). Some fifty years ago Hans Nathan proposed
that motet texts, Latin and French, might have been chosen precisely for their coordinations of vowel sounds,
rather than for meaning.[182] In her 1983 dissertation and
in subsequent articles, Beverly Evans goes deeper into
this question, emphasizing textual values and carefully
examining the esthetic effects of textual sound patterns.[183] In an influential article published in 1986,
Dolores Pesce reexamined "The Significance of Text in
Thirteenth-century Latin Motets" to argue that the sound
and sense of the texts, along with the music, were woven
by motet creators into a sophisticated musico-poetic fabric (B685). In a different vein, from the standpoint of
performance practice, as I mentioned above, Christopher
Page has examined the importance of vowel color: vowel
qualities play an essential role for tuning, for the
articulation of contrastive and concordant sounds and
meanings in the different voices, and for the coloring
of cadences (B763, 84). Yet despite these suggestive
studies, it cannot be said that the 13th-century vernacular motet has yet been fully constituted as a subject
for serious study of textual values, especially rhythmic
values. There is still a tendency to consider motet
texts inferior because these texts do not exhibit the
conventional characteristics of versification found in
courtly song. But with the new light cast on motet texts
by recent anti-normalizing approaches to Old French versification, no longer can one even tacitly agree with
Lote that the motet, by virtue of its irregularity
"n'apporte rien de bien notable à l'histoire de la
métrique" (B433, 2, 216). On the contrary, the study of
motet versification can now enter the mainstream of

research on versification, allowing reformulation of
questions involving the relationship of vernacular motet,
versification and prosody, to courtly song. Although vernacular motet texts use themes from the courtly repertory, the fact that their versification is different
(short, irregular lines, for example) colors the themes
and distances the motet from courtly songs in ways that
need to be explored. On grounds of versification alone,
not to mention tone and diction, the idea that motet
texts are virtually indistinguishable from trouvère
songs, taken collectively, is questionable. These and
related issues are in need of the refinement that their
incorporation into future research agenda could provide.

On the musical side, for the 13th-century repertory,
the conceptualization of new rhythmic properties as it
is expressed through musical notation is well understood
in its main lines. However, recent research has turned
toward finer details of both practice and theory in the
effort to understand more fully not only the notation but
also the rhythmic practices of which it is a representation.[184] The analysis of sonorous qualities, however, has
suffered from stereotyped views both of motet composition
and of the kinds of sonorous effects achievable in music
that is not tonal, a question addressed by Dolores Pesce
in a recent article on the sonorous coherence of the
13th-century double motet (B686).

While accurate appreciation of specific features in
text or music taken separately is important, coordination
of poetic and musical rhythms and sounds raises other
issues as well. Some of these issues turn on the question
of non-synchronized phrasing. For courtly song, and for
the fixed forms, though with different results, one posits equivalence of poetic verse and musical phrase, which
results in a clear articulation of phrase structure. For
early motet styles, this principle is largely valid; but
later styles employ overlapping, non-synchronized phrases
to create a multi-layered texture. The diverse effects of
this sophisticated multiple layering of textual and musical rhythms and sounds--and of different languages in
polytextual motets--have yet to be fully examined and
tested in scholarly research, both on the purely

technical level and on the level of esthetic appreciation.

The 14th century has not suffered from the same neglect. Musically, this period presents itself under the
sign of rhythmic renewal and experimentation. The first
part of the century is generally called the Ars nova; the
name given to the more intricate late 14th-century rhythmic styles is Ars subtilior. On the literary side "subtlety" is also a governing concept (Cerquiglini, B720),
realized in the development of the "formes fixes." Possibly because it offers fertile ground for the deployment
of interpretive strategies associated with postmodernism,
as Robert S. Sturges has suggested,[185] the 14th century
is experiencing a veritable renaissance, from the sump-
tuous new facsimile edition of the *Roman de Fauvel* by
Edward Roesner, François Avril, and Nancy Regalado
(B118), to a proliferation of studies on Machaut, his
contemporaries and followers.

The early 14th-century *Fauvel,* with its mixture of
styles, forms and techniques is a pivotal work. It is a
satirical and allegorical piece. The version in BN fr 146
is related by the technique of musical insertions to the
lyric-insertion romance inaugurated by Jean Renart's *Roman de la Rose* (or *Guillaume de Dole*) in the early 13th
century and cultivated by Machaut in the *Remede de Fortune* and the *Voir Dit.*[186] But the *Fauvel* has the most
copious and heterogeneous collection of interpolations--
monophonic and polyphonic--of any of the works using the
insertion technique. In his introduction to the facsimile
edition, Edward Roesner suggests that despite the importance of the manuscript as a pivotal source, "the musical
notation of MS fr 146 has not been studied in the detail
that its historical significance warrants" (B118, 30).
The manuscript contains a remarkable collection of vernacular monophonic pieces transmitted in mensural notation; this notation awaits the scrutiny that could situate it in relation to notational systems used by Adam de
la Halle, or to the notation of troubadour and trouvère
song collections, leading to a better perception of relationships between mensural techniques and the contemporaneous rhythmically neutral notation used in the courtly

chansonniers (31). The manuscript also bears witness to
the rapidly expanding rhythmic vocabulary in the early
14th century and to the new tendencies toward rhythmic
detail and intricate craftsmanship that are manifestations of fundamental changes in the nature of the rhythmic systems (30). The variety of texts appearing as
interpolations in the *Fauvel* raise their own sets of
questions concerning versification types associated with
a variety of musical settings. A brief guide to these
heterogeneous literary materials, prepared by Nancy
Regalado, also forms part of the introduction to the new
facsimile edition of the *Fauvel*.

The term "isorhythmic" is often used to refer to a
principle of composition characterizing 14th-century
motets. This principle was based on the manipulation of
pitch and rhythm as separate elements. Certain generally
repetitive patterns were used as structuring devices: a
rhythmic pattern called *talea* and a pitch pattern called
color. These patterns could be of varying lengths and
complexities and juxtaposed in diverse ways; they reflect
emphasis on number and proportion to create large compositions. When one also includes text rhythms, the juxtapositions can become very sophisticated indeed. Generally
speaking, discussions of the isorhythmic motet emphasize
the musical properties, without fully integrating sonorous or rhythmic text elements. But the recent study of
Daniel Leech-Wilkinson, *Compositional Techniques in the
Four-Part Isorhythmic Motets of Philippe de Vitry and His
Contemporaries* (B753) provides rich new insights into the
kinds of complex text-music correlations we may discern
in the early 14th-century motet (1315-1365). Although sonorous text elements are not played out to their fullest
power in the book, Leech-Wilkinson inspects and explains
structural text/music relations including how some text
meanings are taken up by the music.

Mapping out the dual evolutions of textual and musical rhythms and sounds has been of concern to Machaut
scholars. The work of Steven Guthrie, "Meter and Performance in Machaut and Chaucer" (B744) is focussed on textual rhythms in relation to musical performance. In an
article on "Machaut and Chaucer: *Ars Nova* and the Art of

Narrative" (B717), Thomas Campbell exploits textual and
musical rhythmic and sonorous subtleties to bolster up
his argument about narrative. Robert L. Gieber analyzes
poetic rhythms in Machaut's ballades, rondeaux, and virelais, arguing that these are reflected in musical lines.
And in the special Machaut issue of *Sonus* (12:1991),
articles by Alejandro Pulido (B766) and Daniel Leech-
Wilkinson (B754) address questions of rhythm in text-
music relationships.

To be sure, the figure of Machaut dominates the Ars
nova period. Other contemporaneous and later repertories,
including the Ars subtilior, have been less studied from
the standpoint of music and text. Musical rhythm and
notation have been particular concerns of Ars subtilior
specialists. The texts of lesser known repertories have
rarely been taken seriously as esthetic objects by literary scholars. However, the collection of essays *Musik und
Text in der Mehrstimmigkeit des 14. and 15. Jahrhunderts*
edited by Ursula Günther and Ludwig Finscher (B82) explores text/music relationships from several points of
view, touching on late 14th-century French polyphony but
not limited to it. The edition of *Five Ballades for the
House of Foix* by Peter Lefferts, with text edition and
commentary by Sylvia Huot (B334), as well as Lefferts's
article on "*Subtilitas* in the Tonal Language of *Fumeux
fume*" (B756) display the richness of late 14th-century
pieces. These constitute forays into a field that could
well repay further cultivation; and were these developments placed against the late 14th-century disengagement
of important lyric poets from music, we could form a
clearer picture of the so-called separation between
poetry and music and the growing musical specialization
that brought about a differentiation between those who
wrote only poetry, such as Deschamps or Froissart, considering themselves incapable of following the new music,
and those, primarily musicians, such as Solage or Trébor,
who may well have written both. Modern literary scholars
have concentrated on the known poets and have disregarded
the texts that may have been composed by musicians. A
fresh look at this question could bring a re-evaluation
of the "separation" of poetry and music in the late 14th
century.

Although scholars have placed heavy emphasis on
rhythmic features for both 13th- and 14th-century music,
the development of tonal language is equally important.
The tonal organization of the motet, starting from the
tonal organization of the tenor and including upper
voices that may be modally independent, often projects
an ambiguity into which separate movements of textual
sonorities may play. But Richard Crocker has pointed out
that one may well conceive of tonal organization in the
broad sense of "planned relationships among tones or
pitches," and in this sense "a clear concern for tonal
organization is apparent in all but some inept or corrupt motets" (B664, 667). One of the problems, Crocker
argues, is that "medieval research still needs to discover the appropriate terms in which to conceive and describe" the balance between independently active voices
and overall organization that characterizes the motet
(667). Referring to a similar problem in later developments, Sarah Fuller has called for the elaboration of
concepts and terminology appropriate to discourse about
sonority in 14th-century music whose riches, despite considerable work on harmony in Machaut's music, are as yet
not fully understood. Fuller sees sonority as a significant structural resource; she takes up questions of the
nomenclature of sonorities; of syntax viewed as prolongation, progression and cadence; of terminations or points
of repose. She concludes that: "Much remains to be
learned about syntax between sonorities in the works of
Machaut and his contemporaries, and about tonal relationships engendered from interactions among sonorities."[187]
Fuller's work engages crucial questions of composition in
Machaut's songs, viewing a Machaut piece as a coherent
sonorous whole to whose main outlines all elements contribute. Like the work of Dolores Pesce on 13th-century
motets, the work of Sarah Fuller points to new ways of
examining sonority and in particular to the concept of
coherence applied to medieval compositions, a coherence
obscured by the imposition of modern definitions.

This discussion of rhythms and sounds has focussed
on some of the elements that can be combined in different
ways to create sound structures through movement in time.
Rhythms have attracted greater scrutiny than sounds. But

more careful analyses of textual rhythms, in the light
of clearer appreciation of language characteristics and
anti-normalizing conceptions of versification, await
further scholarly attention, especially in the motet repertory. Respect for diverse types of notation and the diverse rhythmic perceptions that may undergird them reflects what could be termed an anti-normalizing view of
notation; and by undermining previous opinions, it opens
the way to a renewed study of musical rhythm. Particularly needed, then, are syntheses of music/text relationships based on new perceptions of their dual rhythmic
properties, for all repertories, singly and comparative-
ly. As for sounds, much remains to be done on monophonic
melodic analysis and on the concept of polyphonic sonorous coherence. Complete integration of sounds and
rhythms, examination of how "disciplinary" features merge
into "interdisciplinary" coordinations, is still a tanta-
lizing goal for further research.

STYLE

   Style focusses on the work of art and its esthetic
properties yet comes into being in circumstances that
must be deemed historical. It emanates from the individual yet reflects a discourse community. As an expression
of individual personality, style is mainly a romantic notion; for some modern, particularly postmodern theorists,
"style" disappears into "discourse." Thus the issues
surrounding style reflect the shifting critical stances
of the practitioners of stylistic analysis. My purpose
here is to single out a few of the issues that have been
raised in recent research on medieval song, particularly
regarding tensions between the esthetic and the historical and between the individual and the group.

   As we have seen above, in the introductory discussion of 20th-century critical approaches, style became a
central focus of musicology at the beginning of the century with the work of Guido Adler. Adler sought to establish the study of music on a "scientific" basis of laws
and rules drawn from "observation" of musical "facts." As
Carl Dahlhaus has pointed out, stylistic history growing

from Adler's initial impulse did contrast with positivism by going beyond the mere *accumulation* of facts; but
to the degree that the historiographical principles were
"rooted in art itself,"[188] such stylistic history valued
the esthetic and drew on a concept of style as normative
and formalistic, as a set of features characterizing a
group of works from the standpoint of typology or of
historical period. Thus was raised the issue of the relations between style normatively conceived and historical
understanding, since to root the study of music in music
itself was to pose it as an esthetic object and cut it
off from its "historical" contexts.

This problem has been largely responsible for the
current disrepute of the style analysis model set forth
by Adler. Not that style has been entirely abandoned:
instead, the task has become to redefine it. One could
view from this perspective Leonard B. Meyer's most recent
book on *Style and Music*.[189] The purpose of the book is to
set discussions of style into wider contexts of history
and ideology. Recognizing the difficulty of relating specific musical features such as pitch or rhythmic patterns
to cultural contexts, Meyer still argues for the importance of the task. Without integration of external parameters, any history of style is merely "a series of
synchronic style-frames ordered chronologically on some
hierarchic level."[190] Change for Meyer is a function of
musical choices; choice is dependent on sets of constraints that establish compositional options. History of
style will then be the setting forth and explanation of
individual choices made within the context of all possible contemporaneous choices.

A similar tension between the esthetic and the historical undergirds the concept of styles and values developed by Daniel Poirion in Volume 8 of *GRLMA*. Positing
a contradiction between (1) the esthetic and normative
definitions of genre that had served to organize *GRLMA*
volumes on earlier centuries and (2) the historical perspective of late medieval French literature, Poirion
argued that to respond to new modes of textual production
in late medieval literature, new approaches were needed:
the normative must yield to historical understanding. In

an article for that volume ("L'Epanouissement d'un Style:
Le Gothique Littéraire" [8: 29-44]), Poirion further
elaborated these perceptions. Careful to preserve
esthetic values from mere reduction to the surrounding
contexts, Poirion nevertheless asserted that it is in the
"matière historique ... que s'inscrivent, parallèlement
aux formes de l'art et de la littérature, les styles de
vie qui leur prêtent un sens" (8, 29). "Styles littéraires" can thus be linked to "styles de vie," defined as
systems of values--forms and manners--that achieve coherence, as far as we can perceive such coherence, within
particular limits of time and space. From the juxtaposition of "styles littéraires" or "styles d'écriture" and
"styles de vie" can emerge a deepened comprehension of
literary history.[191]

From quite different points of view, both Leonard
Meyer and Daniel Poirion raise and attempt to resolve
problems of the esthetic vs. the historical as they apply
to style. For our subject, equally intriguing issues turn
about relationships between the individual and the group.
If in musical discussions, style has fallen into disrepute because of its normative emphases, in literary criticism the idea of individual style, which posits an
"author" and an author's "intention" or "characteristic
expressions," has retreated, with the notion of "author"
itself, before such concepts as "discourse" which emphasize functions of language rather than intentions of authors. Medieval conceptions of style, chiefly elaborated
under the rhetorical category of "elocutio," were predominantly normative or prescriptive: certain ways of speaking, writing, composing conformed to certain genres or
made possible desired effects in communication. To a degree, medieval rhetorical theory and modern structural
linguistics coincide in their emphases, though not in
their methods. Rejecting the identification of vernacular
style with rhetorical figures, Paul Zumthor proposed instead, as is well known, the notion of register, defined
as "a network of preestablished relationships between
elements belonging to different levels of formalization,
as well as between the levels themselves."[192] Pierre Bec
(B458) applied the concept of registers to the French
lyric of the 12th and 13th centuries, distinguishing in

this repertory two main registers: "aristocratisant" (into which would fall the *grand chant courtois*), and "popularisant" (into which would fall most songs outside the *grand chant courtois*). Zumthor has even argued that it cannot be assumed that *individual* stylistic differences would have been perceived by contemporary audiences.[193] But already in 1959, S.C. Aston warned against seeing in troubadour poetry, for example, a uniformity that study of the actual works of the troubadours quickly dispels: the individual must yet be contended with.[194] For a portion of the medieval repertories here under study, the concept of individual (composer's) choices (which may be choices of performers or scribes) remains problematic, and the possibility of discerning actual choices more debatable still. We can more readily define and contextualize collective styles. But exploring relations between the individual and the group, conceptually and historically, could yet underscore the significance for style of the selection of alternatives within stylistic norms, even there where the selection is transferred to the level of "discourse."

A certain number of recent critical studies have been devoted to style *per se* in individual poets and composers, primarily in the estheticizing mode. An article by Chantal Phan, "Le Style poético-musical de Guiraut Riquier" (B590), distinguishes characteristics of a composer for whom we have what is apparently his own dating of his works. Or again, taking a well-known trouvère, Thibaut de Champagne, Hans-Herbert Räkel has sought to describe melodic invention in the songs of Thibaut as compared to one of his predecessors, Blondel de Nesle (B607), while Charles Brucker has examined his stylistic innovation through the use of adjectives (B474). Donna Mayer-Martin has investigated stylistic features of Gace Brulé's melodies with a view toward isolating elements that could be considered original (B564), while Marie-Henriette Fernandez demonstrates the variety of melodic invention in the works of Guillaume le Vinier (B495). The 14th century provides a surer basis for the comparative study of individual styles and style change, a task undertaken by Wulf Arlt in his article "Aspekte der Chronologie," where Lescurel and Machaut figure prominently (B704).

That the troubadours as poets were stylistically
self-conscious is clearly illustrated by their debates
over such style-defining terms as *trobar clus* ("closed
style") or *trobar ric* ("rich style").[195] These were exclusively literary debates; they could not arise on the
level of music alone. The question of possible influences
of such stylistic debates among the troubadours on issues
involving music/text relationships has not been raised.
For the 14th century, however, with a term such as "soutil" ("subtle"), a suggestive linking of poetic and musical concepts has been established, if in no other way
than by the placing of the late 14th century under the
sign of Ars subtilior (Cerquiglini, B720; Lefferts,
B756).

Given the problematic status of the individual poet/
composer in our repertories, it is not surprising that
scholars have treated collective styles more extensively
than individual styles. The wide (thought not always
felicitous when the effect is to screen out individual
values) use of Zumthor's "register" to discuss trouvère
styles is illustrative. In a slightly different vein, for
the period 1100-1300, Christopher Page (B407) proposes a
very general synchronic typology, taking the idea of
"style" in a large sense, related to medieval rhetoric.
He separates "high style" *canso* from "lower style" dance
related songs, basing the distinctions on poetry as well
as music. For the motet, where anonymity prevails, style
must clearly be viewed differently than, say, for the
early troubadours; thus for the motet, stylistic analysis
is most fruitfully carried out on works and genres.[196]
For a later period, another type of collective style has
been described: the "international style," debated, for
example, at a recent conference and elsewhere (B65). As
these samplings suggest, the styles characteristic of our
different repertories have been described and assessed
in broad outline, frequently from the separate viewpoints
of music and poetry, more rarely taking both into consideration.

What then remains to be done? Certainly further
investigation of the concept of style as it can be
applied to music and poetry simultaneously could yield

new insights. A future research agenda could profitably include further analyses of individual styles where that is possible; closer delineation of the differing parameters, textual and musical (rhythms and sounds), that characterize collective styles; and, more particularly, given the thrust of current methodologies, the integration (to use the terminology of Daniel Poirion) of style and values, or (on the views of Leonard Meyer) of internal and external contexts.

FORMS AND STRUCTURES

Under this topic, we find a rich harvest of recent studies, not surprisingly given the prominence of form in medieval theory and practice and the continuing influence on medieval song of modern formalist and structuralist approaches. For the convenience of my exposition, I will use the terms "form" and "structure" interchangeably. While many of these recent studies approach analysis of forms and structures in the traditional ways that can still yield valuable findings, others, paralleling the intellectual movements of post-structuralism or postmodernism, seek to devise new ways of interpreting text-music relationships. The major trend in all these studies, whatever the methodology, is toward greater refinement in our appreciation of how songs work.

It has been customary when treating formal aspects of music and poetry together in monophonic song or polyphonic *formes fixes* to employ different schemata that juxtapose in diverse ways specific pieces of information about music and texts. Thus, conventionally, a musical segment can be represented by a capital letter, textual rhymes by a small letter, and number of syllables by a figure with a superior stroke to show feminine ending. Using these conventions, one can draw up summary diagrams such as: (a) for a monophonic song, when the capital letter indicates a single musical phrase

```
AB   AB   CDEF
ab   ab   ccdd
88'  88'  6688
```

or (b) for a 14th-century ballade, where capital letters
indicate musical segments, the small subscript letters
"o" and "c" *ouvert* and *clos* endings, and the last itali-
cized small letter shows the refrain:

A_o A_c B
a   b   a   b   c   c   d   *d*
10 10   10 10   7 10 10' 10'.

The diagrams vary to insist on different pieces of information. Although invented by modern critics, this
diagrammatic practice can be said to have roots in the
medieval sources that have furnished concepts and a critical metalanguage for modern analysis.

For monophonic song, the most important theoretical
sources of information from the medieval period are
Dante's *De vulgari eloquentia* (B175) and the *Leys d'amors*
(B181-2). Dante's treatise has exerted a particularly
strong influence on text/music relationships, extending
even through the *formes fixes*. On a concrete level,
Dante's discussion of song centers on the stanza, the
"receptacle" within which the whole art of song is contained. His concern is with the arrangement and distribution of parts (B175, II, x-xiii). In his view, some stanzas have a divison, *diesis,* and some do not. The presence
or absence of *diesis* depends on the melody, the *oda.* If
there is no melodic repetition, and thus one *oda continua*
from beginning to end, then there is no *diesis.* But if
melodic repetition occurs at the beginning or the end of
the stanza or both, there is *diesis.* An initial stanza
portion without repetition is called *frons* ("front"); if
the initial portion has repetition, it is called *pedes*
("feet"); a final stanza portion without repetition is
called *cauda* ("tail" or "coda"); a final portion with
repetition is called *versus* ("verses"). Although Dante
himself does not use such diagrams, his concept of
"pedes" with "cauda," for example, is conveniently
represented by AB AB CDEF or "pedes" with "versus" by AB
AB CD CD. On another level, Dante captures the medieval
fascination with form viewed as the harmonious relations
of parts or *harmonia.* This aspect of Dante's thought
provides the starting point for the powerful recent

argument for a theory of number and harmony as fundamental esthetic principles elaborated by John Stevens (B415, 19).

Not only medieval theory, as exemplified by Dante, but also medieval practices reveal an exuberant preoccupation with form. One thinks of the technical innovations of the troubadours and trouvères or of the elaborate codifications of the *formes fixes*. But these very practices are invoked by those who react against both medieval theoretical writings and modern formalist/structuralist approaches: through such theoretical or formalist lenses, it is argued, we are unable to seize the enormous varieties of medieval formal imagination as *practiced* by poet/composers. Two topics will illustrate the issues implicit in these critical reactions: (1) the questionable relevance of Dante's descriptions to vernacular practice; (2) the inadequacy of formalistic schemata as tools of analysis.

There have been consistent objections to over-reliance on Dante's work as a source of information about earlier medieval song practice.[197] Reservations center on two aspects of Dante's treatment of the stanza: the notion that stanza construction is determined by melody; and the usefulness of Dante's terminology.

The problem with respect to the role of melody is that Dante speaks of music only ambiguously at best. His most recent translator, Marianne Shapiro, points out that he makes no clear-cut distinction between metrical structure and melody (B414, 40-1). Music alone in Dante's treatise appears more as an abstract idea than as a sonorous reality; harmoniousness is perhaps more of words than of music. And if melodic repetition is given as a determining feature of stanza construction in chapters 9 and 10 of the treatise, the continuation of the discussion in chapters 11 and 12 makes it clear that the terminology devised grows also out of metrical considerations such as syllable count and arrangement of different lines (the treatise breaks off at chapter 13 before rhyme can be considered). Thus to understand melody--actual music-- as the single determinant of stanza structure is to seize only part of Dante's meaning.

The problem with Dante's terminology--*oda continua,
frons, cauda, pedes, versus*--is that it only partially
corresponds to the reality of courtly song, that is to
the actual stanza shapes, musical and textual, that we
encounter. Consequently the adoption of Dante's terms
leads not only to misunderstanding but also to false
normalization. Take, for example, the most frequently
exploited combination of terms: *pedes* and *cauda*. These
terms are usually taken to correspond to a structure
with direct rhyme repetition (ab ab) that could be
diagrammed:

```
A B    A B    C D E F
a b    a b    c c d e
8 8'   8 8'   6 6 8 8
```

But then the question can arise: is another closely related structure, with inverse initial order of rhymes,
equally valid?

```
A B    A B    C D E F
a b    b a    c c d e
8 8'   8 8'   6 6 8 8
```

The inverse order of rhymes (ab ba) corresponds less to
Dante's definitions--although since he does not discuss
rhyme schemes we cannot know--yet more to courtly reality. The custom among critics, when using Dante's terminology, has been to associate direct rhyme repetition to
direct melodic repetition; the inverse is quietly taken
as less valid.[198] Songs combining ABAB with abba are
pushed away, as it were, without full theoretical justi-
fication, from the mainstream of scholarly reflection.
The association of direct melodic repetitions with inverse rhyme order is a different process from the association of direct repetitions of melodic and rhyme sounds
(Switten, B627, 102). It is true that one can perceive
in medieval song itself a tendency to associate direct
rhyme repetition with direct melodic repetition, but this
tendency manifested itself over time, and the fact that
it has a history (which has not yet been written) is
masked by the assumptions derived from specific applications of Dante's terminology. Or again one could call

attention to the inadequacy of the simple designation *oda continua* for melodies without repetition of entire phrases, whose designs yet grow from features such as repetition of small motifs or of sequences of cadences (Arlt, B381, 187; Switten, B627, 39). Using a simplistic concept of *oda continua*, it can be stated that the *oda continua* melody is proportionally more frequent among troubadours as compared to trouvères. But some 40 percent of such "true" *oda continua* troubadour melodies are found in songs attributed to three poets: Peire Vidal, Folquet de Marseilla, and Gaucelm Faidit (Switten, B627, 104 n.14). And even with these poets, different kinds of highly experimental melodic formal processes, some of which include motivic or cadential repetition, are obscured by the imposition of the *oda continua* label on the melodies.

Perhaps because of the use to which Dante's terminology has been put, perhaps because later developments in the trouvère repertory, particularly the *formes fixes*, led to the expectation of certain norms, modern notions of how metrical and musical structures "go together" have sometimes been characterized by a certain rigidity, reinforced by the use of schemata. For later trouvère repertories it may be plausible to propose that text/melody agreement can be indicated by coincidence of letters designating rhymes with letters designating melodic lines (e.g. abab with ABAB), and that if such coincidence is not possible diagrammatically, then text and music do not "go together." For earlier repertories, however, this approach is simply misleading. The fact that earlier repertories are more flexible and less amenable to schematization does not mean that in them text and melody follow separate ways. It means rather that inventiveness and formal experimentation express themselves differently. If, for example, in a series of 8-line stanzas one encounters abab cdcd for the rhyme scheme, ABCDEFGH for the melody, and syntactical text divisions sometimes 4 + 4, sometimes 3 + 5 or 5 + 3, it is not helpful to assert that music and text do not "agree." The more interesting point is how we can understand and interpret their coordinated unfolding.

It is precisely the unfolding of song in time that has been obscured by diagrams which reduce process to a static mold. Hence the dissatisfaction with schemata as tools of analysis, my second topic. Diagrams leave out important information and often impose on musical phrases a deceptive normalization: when "A" is "A" and not "B" is often a matter of interpretation. Sensory reality cannot be reduced to abstract category without loss. Moreover, as Eero Tarasti has pointed out, the use of letters to symbolize musical units following each other in a linear chain cannot capture the full significance of temporally unfolding sound forms. "One of the basic properties of the temporal course of music is its irreversibility. Because of this fact, there is not symmetrical repetition in music at all, and even in the ordinary *lied* form ABA the second A differs from the first" (B420, 109). There is no *identical* "second time" for the music listener: a repetition, just by virtue of the fact that it is a repetition, differs from an initial statement. Approaching the same problem from another point of view, Leo Treitler has argued that abstract formalist approaches pay "little attention to time-process and time-sense."[199] Such arguments need not lead us to the conclusion that schemata or formalist analyses are useless; they caution, rather, that discussion of text/music relationships should not rely on schemata alone, but should seek to discern, beyond the schemata, the playing out *in time* of textual and musical elements.

What, then, shall be put in the place of diagrammatic analysis? The most promising approaches concern the assessment of rhetorical purpose, diversely expounded and practiced. Leo Treitler has criticized the formalistic claims that medieval music does not respond to language on semantic or syntactic levels (B425, B640, B641) in order to develop a concept of music as sung language which opens up to analysis a range of musical responses to poetic texts. In a discussion of Jaufre Rudel's "Lanquan li jorn," for example, Treitler shows that dynamic melodic tensions subtend the entire song (B640, B641). This kind of analysis focussing on the composer as a "reader" and "interpreter" of poems can include formal, syntactic, and semantic elements as they interact in time: no one element excludes the others.[200]

From somewhat different points of view, working on the level of the stanza and emphasizing the initial strophe where text is underlaid to the melody in manuscripts as well as different manuscript versions, Vincent Pollina, in recent studies on Gaucelm Faidit (B600, B602), and Nicoletta Gossen, examining the songs of Bernart de Ventadorn (B510), have brought out the way in which syntax, meaning, language sounds, word play, and melodic inflection can work together. In discussions of Marcabru both Wulf Arlt (B381) and Vincent Pollina (B603) have related melodic style to genre. Arlt separates the *pastorela, sirventes* and crusade song, on the one hand, from the *canso.* He further pursues relations between melodic inflection and text in Jaufre Rudel's "No sap cantar" and Giraut de Bornelh's "Reis glorios."

The type of analysis that reposes on rhetorical purpose and emphasizes process encounters two difficulties that invite further research. The first is the widespread use of *contrafacta* or borrowing and exchange of tunes and texts. If text and melody are related only on the level of form, then texts and melodies are easily interchangeable when formal structures correspond. If, however, specific melodies are seen as responses to specific texts, then interchangeability poses a theoretical problem needing resolution. The second difficulty, not unrelated to the first and pertinent only to strophic song, is to examine how music and text may be coordinated in the stanzas following the first, since the melody in the manuscript is given only for the first stanza. Certainly there is more involved than simply coordinating notes and syllables, as formalists might view it. Yet if the melody is conceived as a response to the first stanza, how does it "respond" to the others?[201] Much depended, doubtless, on the performer's inflections. As the melody is repeated, it is cast in a new light by association with different texts in succeeding stanzas: here the concept of irreversibility, bringing with it the impossibility of exact repetition, can figure importantly.

To briefly illustrate an approach to the second

difficulty, one might propose the linking of form and
process in an interpretation of Marcabru's *pastorela*.
The formal structure could be roughly diagrammed

A	B	A	B	C	C	D
a	a	a	b	a	a	b
7'	7'	7'	7'	7'	7'	7'
issa	issa	issa	ana	issa	issa	ana

although Arlt's analysis clearly demonstrates that the C
phrase picks up motifs from A and B phrases; only the D
line is different (B381). In Richard Hoppin's view, "the
music completely ignores the refrainlike function of the
"b" rhyme particularly in the fourth line of each stanza"
(B359, 278). In this fourth line, indeed, there is not
only the "refrainlike" rhyme sound "ana" but a refrain
word, "vilana." Throughout the song, the rhyme sound "a"
changes every two stanzas (technically *coblas doblas*)
while the unchanging "b" rhyme anchors the song. The
first appearance of this "b" rhyme is, in a way, a surprise: one might think that aaaa or abab would "go better" with the melody, and this feature is the source of
Hoppin's observation. But the very appearance of a new
rhyme sound with melodic repetition can be interpreted
in a different way: it breaks an expectation of symmetry
created by the melody as we have so far heard it. This
propels the song forward by bringing it into a new paradigm, and, at the same time emphasizes the word "vilana."
The echoing "ana" at the end of the stanza, with new musical material, effects closure. But we do not know upon
hearing the first stanza alone that "vilana" is a refrain
word. That only becomes clear as the stanzas succeed each
other. Nor can we know that in the 12th and final stanza
the shepherdess will be portrayed as claiming her final
victory by taking over this refrain word in her own voice
(the knight had sung it until then). The music does not
"ignore" the refrain; rather, the positioning of the refrain word at a specific point of melodic repetition and
in a series of rhyme sounds where it initially surprises
but ultimately defines the form becomes one of the key
features of the song's unfolding and generator of its
essential meaning.

Such dynamic processes can be explored in polyphonic music as well, although different kinds of coordinations will present themselves, since the music offers much more complex structures of its own. Moreover, the textual designs of the fixed forms, unlike those of troubadour *cansos*, are known in advance, or at least are more readily deducible from the initial portion of the song. Arguably here, too, the first stanza of the ballade or the refrain of the rondeau will receive the most careful musical response (Fuller, B732; Arlt, B704, 235-6; Randel, B767). But here, also, the music first heard to one set of words is subsequently heard to another, and this continuous interplay of textual/musical sounds and syntax ultimately shapes the whole song as we hear it through time.

A brief sampling from Machaut's ballade "Dame de qui" from the *Remede de Fortune* will illustrate this point. Without pretending to do justice to the song's intricate web of poetic imagery, melodic and rhythmic properties, or tonal relations, I will comment on two settings in the first stanza surrounding the key concept "Dame." This ballade has the normal three stanzas with refrain; it may be diagrammed:

$$
\begin{array}{llllllll}
A_o & & A_c & & B & & & \\
a & b & a & b & c & c & d & d \\
10 & 10 & 10 & 10 & 7 & 10 & 10' & 10'
\end{array}
$$

The verse that opens stanza 1 veers expressively away from a typical 10-syllable pattern. A strong accent falls on the first syllable of "Dame," while the 4th-syllable caesura, "qui," is weakened: "Dame, de qui toute ma joie vient." Other lines in this and the following stanzas which this music will accompany have regular caesurae. Looking only at the cantus part, we find that Machaut sets the first accented "Da-" with a graciously cascading melisma, then a long value for the next syllable "-me." The word "qui," the normal caesura point, has a brief melisma on the highest note of the phrase. Then, with initial syncopation, the remaining words of the verse follow in rapid-fire syllabic style. Machaut's strategies accomplish two things: (1) they clearly set

the ballade under the sign of the Lady, and with each
return of the melisma to new words, the words will relate
back to the Lady as they are infused with her musical
presence; and (2) the setting of the word "qui," while
clearly subordinate to "Da-," is sufficiently spacious to
allow the regular caesurae to emerge. As the song plays
itself out, initial hemistiches of the 1st and 3rd lines
of each stanza bathe in the memory of the Lady; this
brings effects such as the musical linking of "Et dedens
moy" (Stanza 2) and "Lonteins de vous" (Stanza 3--the
last appearance of the melisma) to the Lady in order to
develop the central theme of presence in absence. The
Lady is mentioned also in the second half of the first
stanza: "car le gracieus espoir / Douce dame, que j'ai de
vous vëoir." The short 7-syllable line and the normal
10-syllable line are treated musically as a segment push-
ing through to a cadence on "vëoir," but with a brief
rest in the cantus after "dame" which marks the lyric
caesura of the longer line--almost as though the lines
were playfully turned about: a 10-syllable feminine line
followed by a 6-syllable masculine one: "Car le gracieus
espoir, douce dame,/Que j'ay de vous veoir." In any
event, "Douce dame," set here syllabically to a portion
of a recurrent rhythmic motif, is highlighted. The play-
ful ambiguity of this setting will serve to marvelous ad-
vantage in the final stanza where a series of enjamb-
ments, one of which runs over the *clos* musical cadence,
spanning the two sections of the stanza, emphasize the
lover's desire and his anticipated joy, the emotional
climax of the song, before swinging into the final statement of the refrain, rendered now even more powerful in
its new and final context.

The argument has recently been advanced by Marie
Louise Göllner that Machaut cultivates an especially
close relationship between poetry and music in his refrain forms using procedures that, paradoxically, treat
poetic line and musical phrase as individual elements,
but, in so doing, achieve a series of balancings and
counterbalancings that enable music to enhance poetry and
vice versa. The conception of musico-poetic structures as
reposing on simple coordination yields to a refined notion of sophisticated interweaving. Göllner gives a close

reading of three virelais (Nos 3, 8 & 19) and three ballades (Nos 7, 25, & 28) to reach the conclusion that "the
musical fabric does not serve simply to reinforce features of the poetry, but rather sets up a structure of
its own to counterbalance that of the text" (B738, 75).
Göllner considers the relationships between text and music she describes to be an achievement unique to Machaut:
in her view, there were no predecessors and there would
be no successors.

If, then, labels and diagrams are handy devices for
the discussion of form, recent approaches open up sophisticated ways of moving beyond such devices. In the above
discussion, I have focussed on repertories of stanzaic
song. The precise points elaborated do not entirely fit
non-stanzaic types such as the motet. But approaches emphasizing form as process rather than as static mold and
privileging the playing out in time of textual and musical elements, simultaneously interwoven, are applicable
to all of our repertories. Further investigations in the
directions just outlined--and others that will surely be
invented--can make us see medieval text/music forms as
more intricate and diversely elaborated than normalized
analysis might lead us to suspect.

GENRE

In his article "Medieval Song" in the revised *New
Oxford History*, John Stevens refers to formal categories
(elaborated mainly by Gennrich) as "basic" to monophonic
song, but he elects not to follow them strictly, prefer-
ring to "develop the concept *genres*, which allows more
flexibility and corresponds more naturally to the complex
realities of the huge repertory of European song" (B625,
363). But genre analysis brings its own set of problems
which have increasingly come into view as the concept of
genre has been exploited by medievalists.

"Genre" has been primarily a literary term: the *New
Grove* does not give it a separate entry. But musicologists use it in their research, if it does not yet
appear in their dictionaries. For musicologists, it is

more difficult to separate "genre" out from style and
form than for literary critics. Semantic concerns which
often loom large in literary distinctions cannot similarly help define musical genres.

It has been argued that all genre theory is in some
sense Aristotelian.[202] Whether one agrees with it or not,
that view has important repercussions for the Middle
Ages: a crucial problem encountered when modern critical
theory examines the medieval period is precisely the fact
that medievals were generally not Aristotelian. The medieval period is more a time of generic transformation and
re-invention than a time of respecting ancient norms and
conventions, particularly in the vernacular. This creates
a situation of critical "alterity" well summed up by
Fowler: "With medieval writers we have to cope with quite
unfamiliar genre terms, or with classical terms used in
an unfamiliar way. These make up an entire system that is
strange."[203] The lyric repertories constitute an acute
case of this unfamiliarity. As Pierre Bec pointed out on
the occasion of a Round Table on genre for the XVIIIth
International Congress on Linguistics and Romance Philology (1986), categories that he designated *micro-
structures (lai, cobla, cantiga de ultramar, bestiaire*
and the like), generally in verse, were all applied only
to medieval works, whereas categories he called *macro-
structures (roman, théâtre, épopée, autobiographie)* were,
at this Congress, applied chiefly to post-medieval literature.[204] The category "lyric" does not exist in the early Middle Ages, and the terms used by medievals to speak
of what we call lyric have survived only with considerable modification, if they have survived at all. As Ritva
Jacobsson and Leo Treitler have observed in another context, instead of taxing the medievals with confusion or
failure, "we might consider that our expectations in nam-
ing and classifying are inappropriate to the early medieval way of organizing materials, and look for alternatives that may bring us closer" to their way.[205]

This raises the issue of what one might call historical specificity. An important feature of medieval thinking is the conflation of style and genre. More exactly,
distinctions of style level tended to take precedence

over distinctions of genres in medieval theoretical
discourses. Thus the tripartite division--low, middle,
high, coming from Cicero via Quintillian--became an
essential analytic category, taken up notably by Dante.
This emphasis on style analysis is doubled by a tendency
toward proliferating classifications, which are especially messy for the lyric, where terms overlap for reasons
not always clear to us. In the vernacular, especially, we
are not dealing with genres operating under fixed norms
but with genres that are constantly coming into being.
For these reasons, the contrast, or conflict, between
abstract theory and historical practice is a particularly
acute problem for medieval music and poetry.

Literary discussion of medieval genre theory has
often taken as a point of departure the seminal article
by Hans Robert Jauss first published in French as "Littérature médiévale et théorie des genres" (Poétique 1:
1970).[206] Jauss argues that we cannot do without genre
because genre constitutes a "specific situation of understanding" (79) without which literature would be un-
intelligible. On the other hand, purely normative or
classificatory concepts of genre do not allow consideration of historical process and transformation. To develop the idea of historical process, Jauss utilizes the
concept of "horizon of expectations" (from his theory of
Rezeptionsästhetik, in this context meaning the reader's
generic expectations). If in the place of a substantial-
ist notion of genre one poses the historical concept of
a continuity, "then the relationship between the individual text and the series of texts formative of a genre
presents itself as a process of the continual founding
and altering of horizons" (88). A new text evokes for
the reader or listener both the "rules of the game" and
new variations of those rules (unless it is a simple reproduction of the existent "game"). The metaphorics of
development, function, and decay can be replaced by "the
nonteleological concept of the playing out of a limited
number of possibilities" (94). As a way of categorizing
genres amidst the variability in historical appearances
and also in relation to the medieval habit of mixing
genres, Jauss adopted the notion of the generic "dominant" (81), according to which a medieval genre can be

characterized by a group of features, one of which will emerge as the dominant and therefore the shaper of the system (82).

Jauss's effort to reorient thinking about medieval genres did not entirely displace the linguistic and structural approaches represented by Paul Zumthor's influential *Essai de poétique médiévale* (1972).[207] Pointing out the ambiguity of the term "genre," which he, too, sees as a post-medieval concept elaborated from classical Aristotelian views, Zumthor also seeks classification principles based on medieval literature itself (160-4). But he is not concerned with historical continuity. For Zumthor, the concept "genre" can profitably be replaced by "formes du discours" (170-85). This permits the development of language-based criteria to classify works into different systems ("modèles du discours"). From these systems not only historical references but authors as well have all but been eliminated, although there is mention of the "comportement textuel" of poets and of their public (190). Zumthor's point of view is thus radically different from that of Jauss. Central to his thinking is the notion of "registre." The genre is a larger discourse structure realized through registers.[208] Exploitation of the concept of register allows Zumthor to integrate his fertile notion of "mouvance" into formalist analysis; it explains why "la *mouvance* même de l'oeuvre, de texte en texte, de variante en variante, ne modifie jamais ce qu'a d'essentiel le poème" (*Essai*, 240). Zumthor's essentially structuralist-semiotic approach has had wide appeal for medievalists, despite the drawbacks inherent in a method that tends to reinforce by resituating it the earlier appreciation of song as merely conventional.

For systematic discussion of genre in early Old French lyric, one turns to Pierre Bec's *La lyrique française au moyen âge XIIe-XIIIe siècles* (1977), where the approach is structuralist/semiotic in its use of register to elaborate a generic system (B458, 33-43). Although its subject is Old French lyric, it also points to ways in which research could proceed in order to achieve finer differentiations between troubadour and trouvère reperto-

ries. Bec classifies genres according to (1) the presence
or absence of music, (2) the relative importance of thematic material ("genres à pertinence thématique"), or (3)
formal musical and poetic structures ("genres à pertinence lyrico-formelle") (36-40). But having separated out
the different classes and sub-classes, Bec immediately
notes that there is often crossing of genres so defined.
Thus if the motet is a prime example of a genre "à pertinence lyrico-formelle," it can also be placed with songs
typical of genres "à pertinence thématique" because of
the themes it treats (38-9, 214). Bec's analyses are both
systematic and flexible, and they provide an essential
starting point for genre research on trouvères.

The most thorough-going approach to medieval lyric
through genre has been carried out in the work for which
Jauss's article served as part of the introductory considerations: the *GRLMA*. The second volume of this monumental work, entitled *Les Genres lyriques,* begun in the
60s and directed by the late Erich Köhler, took as its
subject lyric "genres et formes" up to the end of the
13th century. For our domain, only *La lyrique occitane*
has been completed, in several fascicules, for the most
part dating from the 1970s. Blending sociological and
structuralist approaches, recognizing the historicity of
genres but also their internal structures, *La lyrique
occitane* attempts to arrive at a systematic genre
classification: fifteen genres are identified and each
is given separate discussion.[209] In 1990, under the
direction of Dietmar Rieger, an associated documentary
volume was published. This volume is also rigorously
organized by genre. Indexes regroup the material by
author, referenced then both to the earlier discussions
and to the documentary volume. In this way, one can
perceive which troubadours utilized which genres (as
they are set out in the *GRLMA* fascicule) and where one
can find information about them.

As we have seen above in the discussion of style,
Daniel Poirion and the contributors to Volume 8 of the
GRLMA, devoted to the later Middle Ages and published in
1988, decided to modify the systematic genre organization
originally projected for all volumes. They argued that

for their period, "la grille des 'genres' traditionnels
s'est avérée mal adaptée à la classification des textes"
(*GRLMA* 8, 11). Thus, the eighth *Grundriss* volume treats
traditional genres such as the rondeau, the ballade or
the lai, but also includes the *dit*, and expands out to a
growing body of literature on medicine, astronomy, alche-
my. The differing approaches to genre in the *GRLMA* volumes reflect not only different editions but also different moments in the development of critical approaches.

The current research activity for our repertories
has emphasized fine-grained analyses of specific genres.
Sorting out medieval terms and the realities to which
they presumably refer is an ongoing concern. Since vernacular genres do not reflect ancient models, the only
way to define them generically is to proceed from analysis of the extant works. So it is that a number of recent
studies have redefined established genres or have proposed new ones when considering what criteria may be used
for such definition. An issue of particular interest for
song is the relative weight to be assigned to music or
text. Genres that have recently come under renewed scrutiny include the *balada* (Bec, B463); the *canso redonda*
(Billy, B467); the *alba* (Poe, B593-5); the lai and
descort (Billy, B466, B470; Cyrus, B488; Maillard, B555;
Marshall, B558; Tischler, B699); the *estampie* (Billy,
B469; Cummins, B487); the *pastourelle* (Doss-Quinby, B491;
Gérard-Zai, B506; Gravdal, B511; Paden, B580-1); the *jeu-
parti* (Gally, B502); the rondeau (Cerquiglini, B721);
the polytextual *chanson* as genre (Newes, B761).

In contrast to these genre-specific investigations,
a recent article by Peter Wunderli takes up directly the
question of criteria (B652). Commenting on the studies of
Pierre Bec and on the *GRLMA* fascicules dedicated to Occitan poetry, Wunderli argues that formal criteria are ambiguous and purely secondary for the classic Occitan lyric. He proposes a genre classification of Occitan poetry
based chiefly on "traits de contenu" and, secondarily, on
"traits de registre" (602). He excludes form, thus music
along with versification (602). "Comment distinguer sur
une base purement formelle la *canso* et le *sirventés,* la
tenso et le *partimen*, etc.?" (602). In adopting this

position, Wunderli remains close to Köhler and Bec but
rejects Zumthor (602). His method is drawn from structural semantics, and his focus is narrow, limited to the
period around 1200 he terms "classic" (601) and excluding
genres that are, according to his definitions, neither
"courtly" nor "classic" such as the *balada* or the *romance*
(603). Under these constraints, Wunderli proposes a blan-
ket system of genres in which the *canso-sirventes*, derived from the *vers*, serves as the "genre absolument non-
marqué du système" because it admits thematic variety and
reflects the "aspirations des *jovens*" (606). *Canso* and
sirventes then can be related to the *canso-sirventes* as
oppositional developments; each of these will have further subdivisions thus constituting a complete hierarchy
of "classical" genres. Since Wunderli rejects music, his
categorizations are of limited usefulness in the analysis
of poetry and music. But his rejection raises issues
that, though previously discussed, still await resolution. Wunderli's comments on form coincide with certain
basic difficulties encountered in all word/music studies
of troubadour song: (1) the difficulty (some would say
impossibility) of distinguishing formal melodic criteria
that could be used to make generic classifications among,
say, *canso* or *sirventes*; and (2) the terminological confusion that arises from the adoption of terms relating to
literary genres (such as *kanzone*) to designate musical
form.

It seems clear then that in genre analysis the inclusion of music for monophonic repertories demands a perspective different from structural semantics. Wulf Arlt
(B381) and Vincent Pollina (B603), for example, have
proposed distinctions between *canso* and *sirventes* based
on melodic properties. If we adopt a wider grid along
the lines proposed by the medieval theorist Johannes de
Grocheio, we can draw generic distinctions which oppose
courtly song on the one hand to more popularizing songs
for entertainment and dancing on the other. John Stevens
argues that such a distinction amongst the various
musical-poetical genres is important for an understanding
of rhythm (B415, 460). The fundamental distinction he
proposes would set a metrical tradition of anonymous
dance and dance-song (refrain, carole, rondeau,

estampie, etc.) against a numerical tradition of monophonic *conductus*, *chanson*, sequence and lai (461). The
former exhibit metric rhythm, the latter isosyllabic
rhythm. "Between the extremes of chanson and dance song,
are other genres even harder to pin down, such as the
pastourelle; but genre must always be seen as an important determinant" (B625, 362). Thus we cannot expect a
single rhythmic solution for all monophonic songs, nor
can we expect that the same melody will have "the same
rhythmic meaning in every context" (B415, 460). Although
working out the precise practical applications of these
theories would demand further elaboration, the perception that generic considerations can furnish information
about rhythm is a useful analytic tool for coming to
terms with the much vexed question of rhythm in monophonic song.[210]

In contrast to the monophonic repertories where it
can be set aside, the musical dimension is essential to
the motet. Since the *GRLMA* volume that would have treated
the motet was never completed, one cannot know whether
this genre would have been treated there as such. Indeed,
whether the motet is a genre or a form is debatable. From
the standpoint of music and text, taken together, the
13th-century motet is the least understood of all the
repertories here under consideration, particularly if
one seeks to separate the French motet from Latin, or
even decide where to draw the line when a motet is multi-
lingual. The motet's complex generic indicators have yet
to be sorted out. The considerable work done on the 13th-
century motet has chiefly focussed on music, yet as
Beverly Evans and others have pointed out, the motet
reflects textual as well as musical innovation.[211] If
much of the work done on motets has proceeded from a
perception of texts as worthless, now, as re-evaluation
of the texts reverses this perception, new scenarios can
emerge. And with a revised understanding of text, the
defining characteristics of the motet as a textual/
musical genre can be set forth with greater sophistication.

In his chapter "French Polyphony of the 13th
Century" in the revised *New Oxford History* (1990),

Richard Crocker focusses primarily on motets with French texts. What indeed is a French motet? While we can iso-late some tendencies differentiating French from Latin motets (discussed by Crocker), difficult problems still await elucidation, such as: What factors bring about these different tendencies? Who composed, performed, and listened to French texts and their music? How are motet texts related to the trouvère repertory (themati-cally and formally) and how does this relationship bring musical factors different from those of Notre Dame poly-phony? (B664, 638). What are the basic features of melod-ic and contrapuntal structure in 13th-century polyphonic repertories? (641). Answers to these questions might well map out investigative strategies that would enable a fuller appreciation of motet properties.

But can the French 13th-century motet be considered a single genre? This question raises the same kinds of terminological tangles that obtain in earlier reperto-ries, where a proliferation of terms, medieval and mod-ern, greet the researcher. In his fine study of 13th-century French motets, Mark Everist has argued that the usual classifications of motets according to number of voices or language of voices in the upper text, or both, while useful, are not sufficient. The classification by number of voices "leads to problems when attempts are made to establish more specific sub-genres for motets with French texts, using terms such as 'refrain motet,' 'motet enté,' 'refrain cento,' 'Kurzmotette,' 'rondeau motet,' or 'motet with terminal refrain,'" (B669, 1). The term "motet enté," for example, can refer to composi-tions with one to four voices. It is also difficult to be sure whether terms such as "motet enté" or "rondeau motet" refer to just one voice or a whole composition (1). Nor are medieval theoretical sources or even manu-script designations particularly helpful. Thus it becomes necessary to apply empirical criteria "such as the types of text employed, the number of voice parts, the use of refrains and the compositional origins of the pieces" in the effort to define sub-genres (3). Applying musical procedures, textual choices and manuscript provenance, Everist has been able to propose a more precise defini-tion for the rondeau motet and to argue that the eight

pieces he has so defined were probably composed around
Arras. Applying similar procedures to the "refrain
cento," Everist has argued that this "musical phenomenon
needs to be considered a technique and not a genre"
(B670, 188). In a book published by Cambridge University
Press, *French Motets in the Thirteenth Century: Music,
Poetry and Genre* (B672), Everist further elaborates the
application of genre theory to French motets, sorting
out genres from techniques, in order to assess tradition
and innovation within the motet repertory.

A point clearly needing further scrutiny is the mixing, conflation, and renewal of generic types brought
about by the absorption of trouvère textual material
(from themes to whole texts) into the motet, a point to
which one of the questions coming out of Crocker's chapter directs our attention. Crocker himself argues that a
direct and exclusive relationship between trouvère texts
and motet cannot be posited because the short, irregular,
rhyming lines characteristic of the Latin *versus* sometimes occur in motets and these cannot be explained by
trouvère art. The "maker of a French motet was between
the poles of a trouvère song and discant clausula, so it
is no wonder if at some time or other he tried all the
possibilities within that range. Of these possibilities,
however, that of irregular length verses is the one that
cannot be easily explained by trouvère art" (B664, 642).
However they came to be used, short, irregular lines determined the distinctive phrasings of the French motet
and opened new possibilities in the creation of rhythmic
patterns conjoining upper voice(s) and tenor. John
Stevens has argued that most of the French motet texts
are composed in a style that is distinct from that of the
trouvère courtly song (*grand chant*). In his view, of the
motet texts that are not freely composed, "far and away
the largest number come from the repertory not of trouvère song properly so called but of dance-song" (B415,
461). Important to Stevens's argument is the fundamental
concept of "rhythmic genre" (461): dance-songs have measured rhythm; courtly songs do not. Since dance-songs had
measured rhythm, they were easily adaptable to the motet
(462-465). But motet texts also need to be seen in the
light of irregular courtly songs now increasingly a focus

of attention, for the perception that some courtly songs may themselves have been irregular alters our assessment of relationships between courtly song and motet texts.

Although the motet is a genre whose definition has centered on music, the texts, so long neglected, are increasingly coming under scrutiny. The point of departure is the fundamental study of medieval lyric by Pierre Bec, who emphasized the contrastive internal structures of the motet. He defined the main contrasts as linguistic: (Latin/French); prosodic (divergent meters and rhymes); and semantic (juxtaposing different registers such as *fin'amor* and *bonne vie*). According to Bec, the essential characteristic of the motet is its polytextuality or intertextuality, and his call for further research along these lines is only now being answered. (B458, 214-7). Recent research by Sylvia Huot takes up the notions of intertextuality and "textual" polyphony. In her 1989 article "Polyphonic Poetry: The Old French Motet and its Literary Context" (B675), she examines several motet texts, arguing that they show close links to the larger contexts of 13th- and 14th-century poetry, and that these texts, as texts, are as avant-garde as the musical form is sometimes considered to be. Further research now being completed by Huot on 13th-century vernacular motets in the Montpellier Codex will provide striking illustrations of the interrelations between text(s) and tenor and will fully rehabilitate the texts as sophisticated literary compositions. Huot's approach has been challenged by Christopher Page in his *Discarding Images* (B409). In the two chapters Page devotes to the Ars antiqua motet, he raises the issue of why motets with Old French secular texts ever emerged (44). As a partial resolution of this issue, he proposes to see the motet as parody, as a part of the festivities enjoyed by clerics. Believing it is essential to define both the audience and the tone of motets, Page offers a sophisticated analysis of the vocabulary of Grocheio's treatise, newly edited by him (B165), particulary of the terms *vulgares laici* and *litterati* (B409, 43-111). Page emphasizes the way motets *sounded*, how they were *heard*. He firmly rejects the concept of intertextuality as an analytic technique applied to 13th-century motets.

Given the work forthcoming or in preparation by a number of scholars, one may conclude that the 13th-century motet is rapidly becoming a central research topic. Thus, if at present the motet is the least understood of our repertories, that situation is in the very process of transformation.

Speaking of the motet, I have circled around the question of refrains. These are among the more difficult forms or genres to circumscribe and identify. Recent work on refrains has both demonstrated their importance and underscored their ambiguity (Doss-Quinby, B490; Butterfield, B661; Everist, B670). "Refrain" is initially a textual term, applied analogously to recurring segments of musical forms. Therein lies one problem: is the refrain primarily textual in medieval song, or musical also? Some refrains are a regular part of song forms where they are regularly repeated. Others are interpolated or quoted in different works--romances, motets, monophonic songs. All scholars see the refrain as a stimulus to poetic invention and creativity.

The core feature of the refrain is repetition, not only within single pieces, but also from piece to piece as if to constitute a network of echoes. Therefore, of primary importance are those techniques of analysis that investigate the cumulative effect of repeated segments, not as mechanical restatements, but respecting the temporal difference that changes the significance of the refrain as it moves through new contexts. Equally important approaches can be developed from notions of intertextuality. Refrains that occur in courtly song or in dance or dance-related songs have benefited from considerable scholarly scrutiny; the insertion of refrains into romances, while well observed, is less well understood. The first romance with lyric insertions, the 13th-century *Romance of the Rose or of Guillaume de Dole* by Jean Renart, juxtaposes refrains, dance songs and courtly songs without refrains. Other romances have only refrain insertions. Sometimes there is musical notation in the manuscripts, frequently there is not. [212] The 14th-century *Roman de Fauvel* contains a veritable compendium of musical types, refrains among them, virtually all the known genres of its day. Refrains are also inserted into motets. The interaction between refrains and other songs in a single work as well as intertextual references among different works (the "citation" technique), have yet to be fully mined for what we can learn about the nature and function of refrains, musical and poetic. It seems clear that when the history of the 13th- and early 14th-century French vernacular song comes to be written, techniques of fragmentation and recombination inherent in the word "refrain" will figure importantly as part of its esthetic.

In the 14th century, the motet with French texts continued to be cultivated, but it was transformed: new musical techniques, notational and compositional, led to the isorhythmic motet, the main 14th-century vernacular motet genre. The generic marker of the 14th-century motet is thus melodic and rhythmic restatement; but Margaret Bent has recently warned against applying simplistic notions of sameness to the motet, where "repetition" could include astonishingly complex "variation," and has called for a redrawing of genre boundaries to "challenge some of the traditional confining and tidy definitions."[213] In the 14th-century motet, periodicity of musical structure brought about a somewhat more regular text structure than was the case for the 13th-century motet, although texts for different voices still tended to differ in length. More importantly for our purposes, there was a shift in language: whereas the main locus for experimentation in the 13th century was the motet with French texts, in the 14th century Latin became its chief linguistic vehicle. By mid-century, only Machaut still cultivated polytextual motets with French words, with considerable finesse, to be sure, as has been brilliantly demonstrated by two articles on motet No. 15 by Kevin Brownlee and Margaret Bent (B707, B715).

Beside the motet and eventually displacing it as a vehicle for vernacular expression and experimentation, there also appeared the *formes fixes*: ballade and rondeau especially, but also virelai, and lai. These *formes fixes* are simultaneously classifiable as form and genre because their generic markers were their forms. They are, so to speak, refrain-driven, except for the lai, so that

the genres are largely defined by the length and placement of refrains. The rondeau and ballade are usually
polyphonic, the lai and virelai more frequently monophonic, at least as cultivated by Machaut. Although as I have
pointed out, the *formes fixes* normally have one text, we
also find ballades in which different texts are used for
different voice parts, such as Machaut's "Quant Theseus/
Ne quier veoir" or the noted double ballade by Andrieu
(using a poem by Deschamps) on the death of Machaut,
"Armes, amours/O flour." The unity of such ballades, however, is underscored by a technique not available to
polytextual motets: both ballade texts have the same refrain. This technique is most strikingly exploited in
Andrieu's "Armes, amours/O flour" where the coming together of all voices in the words "La mort Machaut, le
noble rethouryque" produces a haunting effect.

What is the origin of the *forme-fixe chanson*? Due to
the lack of musical evidence, this question admits no
easy answers. It is the focus of recent research carried
out by Lawrence Earp, who views its appearance as a
"switch in the priority of genres" at the end of the
13th and the beginning of the 14th centuries, characterized by the virtual disappearance of courtly trouvère
songs and the rise of dance songs such as rondeaux and
ballades (B725, 101). Earp offers a plausible hypothesis
according to which the transformation would have taken
place in several stages. The late 13th-century dance song
was both monophonic and polyphonic, the former cultivated
at court, the latter chiefly by Adam de la Halle. Around
1300, one finds in the monophonic dance song of Lescurel
new musical complexities, rhythmic and melodic, that
constitute the first step toward a redefinition of the
genre: here we have a dance song unsuitable for dancing.
Freedom from the physical act of dancing favored the
elaboration of the more sophisticated poetic structures
from which the *formes fixes* would emerge at the beginning
of the 14th century. Simultaneously, at the beginning of
the 14th century, crystallization of complicated rhythmic
patterns into the isorhythmic motet placed sophisticated
new techniques at the disposal of composers. Application
of these new musical techniques to the new dance lyrics,
possibly facilitated by the fact that trouvère lyric had

already been incorporated into the 13th-century motet, resulted in the appearence of the *forme-fixe chanson*. The earliest musical evidence of the new genre is found in a song by Machaut datable to the 1340s (113-5).

The main current thrust of scholarly discussion regarding the poetic *formes fixes*--beginning already with Daniel Poirion's *Le Poète et le Prince* (1965)--has been to combat the concepts of fixity and decline. The fact that the form is "fixed" does not exclude dynamism and movement. For example, Jacqueline Cerquiglini ("Le Lyrisme en mouvement," B719) has sought to locate the mobility of 14th and 15th century poetry, as compared to the "fixity" of the *grand chant courtois*, in narrative movement through time created by linking separate pieces together, and in the use of multiple voicings which contrasts with the courtly song's single "I".

Genres, like forms, are a way of organizing our knowledge and experience of songs. They enable the poet-composer to express himself and the audience to understand what is expressed. But classifications and labels are more useful as critical tools than as prescriptive indicators of categories into which songs should fall. As much recent research has shown, the work of classification is both a medieval preoccupation and a modern critical necessity, and refinement and readjustment of the classifications we adopt is imperative. At the same time, classifications, medieval or modern, should not serve to screen out the sometimes bewildering variety of medieval creations.[214] Medieval song might almost serve as a model for the postmodernist challenge to boundaries and norms. Thus the task of research becomes to problematize, to historicize, and to analyze the concept of genre applied to medieval songs, even as specific genre classifications are used to understand the songs.

CRITICAL MODES AND THE INTERPRETATION OF MEDIEVAL SONG

So far, I have argued that scholarly debates about the specific features of medieval song directly or indirectly reflect developments in critical theory since

the 1970s. Now I would like to step back and consider
some of the critical modes themselves as they affect the
analysis and interpretation of our repertories.

It is clear, as I pointed out above, that literary
critics have embraced new methodologies with greater
alacrity than musicologists. Yet in the introduction to
a book published in 1980, *The Interpretation of Medieval
Lyric*, W.T.H. Jackson could still justify the enterprise
by stating: "There are many books about medieval lyric
but very few about its interpretation." Interpretation
means for Jackson "full interpretative studies of individual poems" as opposed to the tactic of using the poems
as evidence in elaborating theories about general concerns, such as origins or influences, or, particularly,
about the nature of "courtly love."[215] This is a very
specific definition of interpretation, focussed on the
works themselves and formulated before interpretation
theory had penetrated all scholarly communities. But it
raises points that would later take on considerable
significance.

Arguably one of the striking results of the application of new critical ideologies to medieval lyric has
been the "deconstruction" of what might be called the
"paradigm"--or even the "master narrative"--of "courtly
love," including its structuralist/semiotic embodiment
in studies such as the *Essai* of Paul Zumthor (B430).
Specialists have long known that medieval poetry was
more diversely inspired and composed than modern normalizing conventions would have us believe. And for the
troubadours at least, different varieties of love have
long been a subject of analysis. But recent theories
bring diversity itself directly into critical focus, in
particular through the adoption of theoretical positions
centered on the destabilizing of the sign and on notions
of linguistic play. To be sure, for the structuralists,
poetry was play, but play rather of forms and of formulae
than of signifiers. Centering the play on the linguistic
sign itself has opened the way to exploration of such
concepts as irony, multiple and intended ambiguities, or
subversion (Kay, B534; Gaunt, B504; Gruber, B513). This
re-focussing of analysis has been combined with a turning

away from concerns such as origins and influences toward the concept of intertextuality, about which I shall have more to say later.

With the undermining of structuralist analysis has also come a renewed interest in the "subject," evacuated by structuralism, no longer defined in the romantic manner as a suffering soul whose songs reflected "real" feelings (the autobiographical approach that guaranteed the "authenticity" of the song), nor in the formalist manner as a merely grammatical "I." The "subject" is now to be defined in the light of postmodernist criticism as a rhetorical and thus primarily linguistic construct which can adopt various "positions," only some of them autobiographical. This re-examination of subjectivity opens the way to renewed discussion of the "subject position" of women writers in a society dominated by male discourses (Lemaire, B399; Kay, B531, B533, B534).

These critical orientations have yet to be fully exploited in studies of music and text. More usually music/text studies view the texts in autobiographical or structuralist/semiotic modes. Yet if music is understood as a response to a reading of texts, then re-conceptualizing of the text should become a factor in renewed understanding of the musical response.

With regard to the music of our repertories, the most striking development has been the call for closer attention to the analysis of 14th-century songs. Discussing the ballade "Se Alixandre" by Trébor, Howard Brown remarked in a 1987 article: "It is only a slight exaggeration to say that we know everything about the piece except how it works" (B712, 77). In a 1982 Cambridge dissertation on the isorhythmic motets of Philippe de Vitry and his contemporaries (B753), and in an article on Machaut's "Rose, lis" (B752), Daniel Leech-Wilkinson has argued, in terms reminiscent of earlier literary New Criticism, that musicologists need to ask questions about "the music itself" instead of, or at least in addition to questions about "the discovery and evaluation of sources" (B753, 8). The close analysis in his dissertation provides the kinds of musical knowledge (chiefly stylistic)

that can refine and reshape standard notions of the development of 14th-century music and of the interactions
between different composers. His article on Machaut's
"Rose, lis" further presents the case for the application
of modern analytical techniques to medieval music on the
grounds that we should not allow ourselves to be limited
to the notion that a "historically correct" interpretation of medieval music is the only valid interpretation.
"Analyses of surviving works, while taking careful account of what we know of period techniques, have to proceed from, and seek to explain, what we currently see
and hear in the music. There is no other view available
to us."[216] Moreover, Leech-Wilkinson argues that we
should not be limited by the prevailing notion that
polyphony was always "constructed successively, one part
at a time, and that, as a result, vertical relationships
within the music are of very much less significance than
is the integrity of the horizontal lines" (B752, 9). His
reasoning subtends the argument that modern critical
terms are not necessarily anachronistic, if one discards
their context-dependent features and retains those which
are of more widespread validity (B752, 11-2). Thus the
techniques used in motivic analysis or, more particularly
for the case at hand, Schenkerian analysis, although
their application to medieval music has been criticized,
are not inappropriate if properly used. The example then
given of the Machaut rondeau indeed supports the argument
that modern approaches can help reveal complexities of
medieval style and compositional practice, and Leech-
Wilkinson's use of these approaches is everywhere judicious.

But if the general case for modern approaches to
medieval music is expertly made by Leech-Wilkinson,
difficulties yet cling to the application of Schenkerian
analysis to medieval song. The most telling reservation
arises from the fact that Schenker's system virtually
ignores the text and is hostile to pure melody, as, say,
in the Chant.[217] Indeed, Leech-Wilkinson was obliged to
disregard the text to carry out his analysis, with the
curious assertion that possibly in Machaut's own view
"musical form operated, to a large extent, independently
of textual association."[218] It is quite true that musical

constructs, on some level at least, can be analyzed without reference to texts; but it would seem that the richest analyses would take cognizance of Machaut's skill as a composer in "reading" literary texts and of the way his music can be shaped by those readings. Part of Leech-Wilkinson's argument that the text is expendable is based on the idea that while the "Rose, lis" text is resonant with evocations of the *Romance of the Rose* by Guillaume de Lorris and Jean de Meun, in our own reading of this romance, we can capture so few of these associations that seeking them is not a useful analytic procedure. This position has been brilliantly countered in the paired articles by Kevin Brownlee and Margaret Bent on Machaut's motet 15 (B707, B715). Brownlee provides a literary context while Bent gives a rich analysis of the way in which duplicitous and ambivalent musical structures in the motet reflect the duplicities of the text. If new analytical techniques, musical or poetic, are to bring fresh insights to medieval song as song, a steady interdisciplinary focus on text and music would seem most useful.[219]

For interdisciplinary work, language-based approaches such as semiotics offer good promise. But if semiotics has inspired a large outpouring of essays and books,[220] most of these do not concern medieval song *per se*. Those who apply language theories to music have tended to concern themselves with modern musical developments. In his wide-ranging critique of language-based approaches to music, Harold Powers has observed that "The new literature [on music as language] seems uninterested in older traditions of language models for musical analysis," although "the very notion that music is something that can be segmented and analyzed, and the traditional terminology for doing so, have deep and particular roots in historical language models for musical analysis that are peculiar to Western European culture" (B410, 9). And semiotic approaches have not always led to the richest interpretations. The sophisticated and rigorous analytical taxonomies sometimes generated by semiotics tend to void the song of its "expressive" content and throw it back, as it were, into the camp of the structuralists. The task facing semiotic analysis of medieval song is to

develop ways of understanding the union of words and
music as both structure and communicative process,
drawing on medieval use of language models for musical
analysis.

Despite the difficulties inherent in the method, one
could do worse for this enterprise than to re-examine
the seminal article of Nicolas Ruwet, "Méthodes d'analyse
en musicologie" (B412). The suggestion that we do so was
put forward by Mark Everist in his recent translation of
the article (B413). As Everist points out, Ruwet's
"Méthodes" constitute "one of the few sets of analytical
methodologies which initially address repertories other
than those of the 'common practice' era" (B413, 3). The
major difficulty with Ruwet's analyses of medieval song
is the concept of rhythm that undergirds them. Writing
in the 1960s, Ruwet took Gennrich's rhythmic transcriptions of monophonic song as a given, arguing that he was
interested in problems of method, not in problems of
transcription. Consequently Ruwet's analyses would need
to be re-focussed on the basis of more recent perceptions
of how melodies and texts work together rhythmically. As
Everist points out in the introduction to his translation, "It is unconstructive simply to dismiss an analytical methodology out of hand on these [rhythmic] grounds
alone. The assessment of the degree of variation between,
on the one hand, an analysis based on a 'free declamatory' edition of the song and, on the other hand, Ruwet's
original analysis would make a valuable contribution to
the development of the analysis of medieval song" (B413,
5). Ruwet himself deemed his methods inappropriate for
polyphonic structures. Lawrence Gushee's application of
semiotic concepts of paradigmatic diagramming to Machaut
and Adam de la Halle received a "skeptical response."[221]
Likewise, the analysis of Costeley/Ronsard "Mignonne al-
lons voir" by Jean-Michel Vaccaro (*Revue de Musicologie*
61, 1975) which drew upon Ruwet's methodologies, has met
with little critical comment.[222] Yet Everist's suggestion
that Ruwet's methods, despite their evident drawbacks,
could well "be given a much greater exposure in the
analysis of music composed before 1600" (B413, 7) points
the way to development of new analytical procedures for
medieval song.

Speech-act theory, another language-based approach sometimes described as semiotic,[223] holds out the promise of fruitful application to our repertories. This theory, due especially to J.L. Austin and John R. Searle,[224] makes a distinction between utterances that are con- stative (true/false) or performative (actions in them- selves); further, it describes utterances as different types of speech act, such as locutionary (grammatical), or illocutionary (actively accomplishing something by the very act of speaking). Arguing in a 1972 talk on "Methods, Style, Analysis," that "style is a concept about expression,"[225] Leo Treitler saw value for musical analysis in the notion of the "illocutionary" component of meaning (as developed by Searle) which sees meaning generated by the *way* things are said. Since illocutionary speech acts do something in the very saying (they are "performative"), adopting a speech-act perspective would mean emphasizing the fact that the musical work acts upon its hearers and is sustained by the social realities in which it is embedded. This aspect has been elaborated, with reference to the 19th century, by Lawrence Kramer (*Music as Cultural Practice*) who also draws on the con- cept of "illocutionary force" to show how musical pro- cesses can count as expressive acts. An expressive act can only be recognized as such "within the situation it traverses."[226] The situational signals found in literary texts have no exact parallels in music. Kramer argues that they do have inexact parallels which we need to learn to detect. Among the signposts leading to recogni- tion of expressive acts, Kramer recognizes "textual in- clusion," a type of signpost that includes texts set to music as well as such things as titles or expression markings (9). Kramer stresses the fact that text in vocal music does not "establish (authorize, fix) a meaning that the music somehow reiterates, but only invites the inter- preter to find a meaning in the interplay of expressive acts."[227] To be sure, analytic strategies drawn from speech-act theory pose particular problems when applied to our subject. Social realities, the situations a song traverses, are certainly different and more difficult to discern for medieval than for modern song. Yet speech-act theory usefully stresses the act of communication, the ability of music and language to convince, persuade, elicit reactions from hearers in specific situations, in short, to become "performative." Despite the methodological problem involved, therefore, its application to medieval song could generate valuable new insights.

The art of persuasion is, in a different though related vein, the art of rhetoric.[228] Despite the unquestionable importance of rhetoric, its value for the analysis of medieval vernacular song has been diversely appreciated, and application has been made to poetry far more than to music. Roger Dragonetti organized his influential study *La Technique poétique des trouvères dans la chanson courtoise* (B492) around rhetorical concepts, with particular reference to Dante. In contrast, Paul Zumthor devalued rhetoric in his *Essai*: "Rhetoric had a durable but uneven influence on vernacular poetry, and is therefore far from providing a general basis for interpretation; it has nothing to do with the underlying sources of poetics."[229] And in her book *Troubadours and Eloquence*, Linda Paterson argued that "the rhetoric of the troubadours was not necessarily the rhetoric of Dante, or of the medieval schools" (B586, 1). As we have seen in the discussion of Dante above, the gap between rhetorical theory and early vernacular practice is substantial. But for all that, has rhetoric no more to contribute to the modern understanding of medieval song?

The aspects of rhetoric most frequently emphasized are *inventio, dispositio*, and *elocutio* as the locus of tropes and figures. But the rhetorical system also includes two other parts: *memoria* and *pronuntiatio* or *actio* which have come under increased scrutiny in the context of communication and audience-oriented theories. The importance of *memoria* has recently again been underscored by Mary Carruthers.[230] Memory is more frequently discussed in its capacity to preserve and store than in its relation to *pronuntiatio* or *actio*, the art of delivery. But in rhetorical theory, effective vocal and gestural delivery depends on memory. Cicero's *De Oratore* makes clear that, however thoroughly gesture and intonation of voice be controlled, unless memory is "placed in charge of the ideas and phrases which have been thought out," all is wasted.[231] Rhetoric, through the category of *pronuntiatio*, was not alone among the liberal arts to emphasize gesture; music likewise is related to movement and delivery, as Jean-Claude Schmitt has recently reminded us in his monumental study on the meaning of gesture.[232] A fertile field is thus offered to the critic of medieval song. How has it been cultivated?

Interaction between memory and writing informs a recent study of the troubadour lyric by Amelia Van Vleck: *Memory and Re-Creation in Troubadour Lyric* (B647). Recognizing the crucial role of memory in the transmission of troubadour song, Van Vleck seeks to determine how "the style of troubadour poetry ... might have been influenced by available modes of transmission" (6). She focusses particularly on the tension between notions of or desire for textual integrity and the re-creative activity that characterizes transmission by (memorized) sung performance, and she seeks to show how the troubadours themselves thematized this tension. Did they attempt to impose textual integrity? Did they expect re-creation? Answers to these questions cannot be definitive; it is the tension itself that is important. The book comes down on the side of those who valorize performance and memory in the transmission and preservation of troubadour song.

Although facets of *memoria* and *pronuntiatio* figure importantly in her book, Van Vleck does not develop these rhetorical concepts as such. But they are taken as a point of departure in an article by Jody Enders, "Music, Delivery, and the Rhetoric of Memory in Guillaume de Machaut's *Remède de Fortune*" (B727). Enders draws on the relation between memory and delivery in rhetorical theory to examine the union of poetry and music in medieval song, arguing that "memory is, in fact, the conceptual birthplace of the commingling of rhetoric, poetry, and music that is paramount in lyric ontology" (453). This argument proposes a reintegration of *ars memorandi* into literary--and musical--criticism. To be sure, the importance of memory for medieval musical education, performance, or transmission has long been recognized. Specifically germane to our subject is the work of Ritva Jonsson and Leo Treitler, who use the arts of grammar

and rhetoric to develop a conception of performed music
as "sung language," "a single, unitary mode of expression" (B425, 1), where speaking and singing are collapsed
into a single notion: the cantus. These lines of inquiry
show how grammatical and rhetorical theory, particularly
the arts of memory and delivery, have emerged as fruitful
tools of analysis. The concept of memory as a locus for
composition, for the precise type of composition that
unites poetry and music, and the concept of rhetorical
delivery as a model for vernacular performance, both are
resources for our further understanding of musico-poetic
medieval genres.

To speak of rhetorical delivery is also to raise the
issue of orality. The notion of "oral culture," with the
problematic relations between orality and writing that
such a notion engenders, undergirds much of the research
just described. But the foremost proponent of a carefully
circumscribed "orality" is Paul Zumthor. In his recent
books, *Introduction à la poésie orale* and *La Lettre et la
voix* (B431), he forcefully argues for the "orality" of
medieval literature. If texts are sometimes written, and
"literate," they are yet always "vocal," that is "voiced"
through performance; they consistently have a primary vocal dimension.[233] And to the degree that voiced performance is the central medium, literature becomes theatre.
While Zumthor pursues his convictions with a single-
minded energy that invites critical nuancing of his
arguments, the arguments themselves provide stimulating
perspectives for research on medieval song.

One of the problems that arises with the entire
group of approaches that focus on communication and
communicative values, a problem that did not escape
Zumthor's attention, is the difficulty of recuperating
these values from medieval manuscripts. How can we recover the "vocal dimension" of medieval delivery? Timbre,
for example, cannot be represented by writing but only
produced. To what degree can we take "living speech"
situations as models for medieval song? If most theories
focussing on communication see literature as "situated,"
what effects can we draw from this "situatedness"? Unless
the fruits of research on song as communication are to

remain abstract and theoretical (Zumthor's solution), questions such as these need further investigation, even though final answers may always elude us.

For a somewhat different approach situating the work of art in social relationships, one can turn to important approaches deriving from the work of Mikhail Bakhtin. This is not the place to review Bakhtin's complex theories in detail. Suffice it to say that Bakhtin focusses on the specific utterances of individuals in particular contexts, viewing language as "dialogic," caught up in and understandable only through social interchange. In his work on Rabelais, he developed the concept of carnival, a world of humorous forms opposed to officialdom.[234] The idea of the joyous and endlessly ambivalent carnivalesque functions nicely as an analytic tool for a work such as the *Roman de Fauvel*. As I mentioned above, carnival and carnivalistic parody have recently been invoked by Christopher Page to characterize the 13th-century vernacular motet as a composition suitable for lay festivities (B409, 50-1). Perhaps more far-reaching than the idea of carnival is the concept of intertextuality. This concept was developed by Julia Kristeva from Bakhtin's theories, and it has become a dominant concept in much current thinking.[235]

Intertextuality permits the establishment of relations between texts while rejecting the romantic notions of origins, sources, and influences. But if intertextuality can be defined for literature with tolerable clarity as the various relationships one text may entertain with another text or texts, defining the term for music is much more complex and reposes on a wider meaning of the word "text." Any full definition must account for *contrafacta*, direct musical citations of all sorts, circulation and insertion of refrains into different types of works, and so forth. It has been argued that, given the multiple interrelationships of medieval melodies, there can be no musical intertextuality at all (Le Vot, B545). But that is an extreme view; and since in medieval song, music is to a degree textualized, the feature of text recall when one hears a melody can have an extraordinarily powerful effect (Switten, B629). The

application of the concept of intertextuality to medieval
song should account for the multiple possible intertextu-
alities of text *and* music.

A glimpse of the possibilities of this approach is
furnished by Jörn Gruber in his book *Die Dialektik des
Trobars* (B512). In this seminal study, Gruber argues that
troubadour song comprises a perpetual debate which reveals itself through an intertextual network of allu-
sions: semantic, metrical, and musical. Gruber's ideas
are shaped by another powerful approach to literary and
more recently musical analysis: reception theory, which
specifically refers to a cohesive undertaking associated
with a group of scholars at the University of Constance,
one of whose leaders was Hans Robert Jauss. In general,
reception theory can be situated in the shift from focus
on the author or work to focus on the reader; but Jauss's
focus is more particularly on the responses of a general
"receiving" public over time as both a condition and a
result of individual responses at precise times. Individual interpretation intersects with a general "horizon of
expectations" and from such intersections arise new
expectations.[236] Drawing upon a rich blend of reception
theory and intertextuality, Gruber is able to extend
intertextual networks from the troubadours to the trouvères, Dante, and Petrarch and to articulate a vision of
troubadour song that takes account of important aspects
of its "situatedness."

Like Gruber, Maria Luisa Meneghetti in her book *Il
pubblico dei trovatori* (B566) proceeds from basic tenets
of reception theory. She examines performance and reception of the early troubadour lyric, focussing particularly on the formation of dialogue genres. Her arguments
lead her toward elucidating the role of *vidas* and *razos*
and also toward iconography, which she uses as a key to
unlock contemporaneous "readings" of troubadour song. The
manuscripts are seen not only to preserve but also to
interpret troubadour song. They participate in creating
"horizons of expectations."

Meneghetti's use of manuscripts brings us to a newly
flourishing field of fresh emphasis on manuscripts, both

in the traditional sense of what they can tell us about
how medieval songs have been preserved and also with a
recent focus on the manuscript as a complete entity.
Study of manuscripts as sources of editions of text or
music proceeds apace, as the debates over editing strategies amply document.[237] The recent approaches look at
manuscripts not as sources of something else but as
"texts" in themselves. This way of viewing manuscripts
emphasizes the wholeness of the manuscript page and a
"dialogic" or "polyphonic" (in the Bakhtinian sense)
relationship between the visual/textual elements of that
page. In this view, to isolate one element (such as the
text) from the others is to distort the element isolated.
Works are more richly studied as manifested in manuscripts rather than as extracted from them. This approach
to manuscripts is essentially interdisciplinary, in sharp
contrast to the disciplinary dismemberment of the manuscript page. It draws also on reader-centered criticism,
considering scribes, copyists, compilers, and illuminators (like modern critics) as "readers" and "interpre-
ters" of texts. Focus on the manuscript page invites
renewed consideration of the function of "writing" and
"representation": words, notes, images. In the preface
to her study *From Song to Book*, for example, Sylvia Huot
argues that the medieval illuminated manuscript does not
merely describe events but rather stages them: it is
"performative" in the sense of the term developed by
speech-act theory (B392, 3). If, following reader-
centered critical approaches, one thinks of scribes,
compilers or illuminators as "readers," then an attempt
must be made to distinguish their work from the work of
an "author" putting together his own "book" (Bertolucci,
B465; Earp, B127). Such attempts rejoin traditional editing practices; and, indeed, the different ways of looking
at manuscripts are far from clearly separated out: they
could better be described as different lightings projected on the same scene. The full spectrum of manuscript
studies reflects both the variety and vitality in the
process of re-thinking manuscript culture that has developed under the influence of late 20th-century methodologies.

The new manuscript studies are but one outcome of

the consideration of contexts that has characterized a
number of post-structuralist movements and tends to identify itself particularly with the cluster of methodologies that advance under the umbrella of "new historicism." Literary studies devoted to the repertories here
under consideration have long taken contextualization
into account. But the impact of major thinkers who influenced "new historicism" has brought about a reconceptualization of connections between literature and culture, proposing that literature be no longer considered
a transcendent "foreground" to which "history" can furnish a "background." The concept of intertextuality
could be cited as a case in point. For musical studies,
"contextualization" is a more problematic process. I
have already addressed general relationships one might
propose between musicological reflections and new historicist thinking. Specific research on our repertories
proceeding from "new historicist" (in a very large sense)
critical orientations is a relatively new phenomenon.
Such critical orientations--attending to the historical
conditions of production--seem to be reflected in the
title of the Music and Society series edited by Stanley
Sadie (and in the *Music and Society* anthology edited by
Richard Leppert and Susan McClary mentioned above in the
introductory remarks on critical approaches). The series
edited by Stanley Sadie is designed to situate music in
the contexts of socio-political, economic, intellectual,
and religious life. In this series, stylistic discussion
per se is to be replaced by the consideration of different kinds of music as responses to different social
forces. One volume of the series is devoted to *Antiquity
and the Middle Ages* (B363). There are two chapters
covering our repertories: "Court and City in France,
1100-1300" by Christopher Page, and "Ars Antiqua - Ars
Nova - Ars Subtilior" by Daniel Leech-Wilkinson. Leech-
Wilkinson's chapter is more traditionally oriented
toward tracing styles and forms, which it nevertheless
relates to social contexts. The goal of Christopher
Page's chapter is to explain and differentiate the two
main loci of medieval monophonic song production. He
explores contexts as a way of understanding musical
"texts." But Page also underscores the work yet to be
accomplished in this direction by pointing out the lack

of a "social history of music in twelfth- and thirteenth-century France," mentioning, however, his *The Owl and the Nightingale* as "an attempt to provide one" (B363, 217).

Among the new approaches increasingly adopted for musical as well as literary criticism, one must place feminist and gender studies. To the degree that gender can be thought of as defined by social attitudes and practices, feminist criticism is powerfully related to methodologies of contextualization. Although there is no thoroughgoing feminist study of medieval song, there have been feminist readings of troubadour texts and editions of the trobairitz (Paden, B96; Rieger, B268, B610, B611; Kay, B534; Gaunt, B505; Lemaire, B399). Angelica Rieger makes the suggestive proposal that the female singing voice must have been an important facet of troubadour song (B610). As has already been mentioned, timbre as such cannot be recuperated. But on an abstract and theoretical level, it is tempting to speculate that qualities of voice might have delineated gender roles and established gender relations, carrying vernacular languages in ways opposed to Latin. The little we know suggests that timbre and voice quality were important for troubadour song. That there were female singers of courtly song and *jongleresses* is clear. But the gendering of voice is as yet an unexplored issue. In *La Lettre et la voix*, Paul Zumthor argues that it would be vain to seek a medieval theory of voice and of the social function of voice (B431, 142). Yet it is provocative to compare his discussion of medieval descriptions of voice (150-2) to the discussion of timbre and gender by John Shepherd in an article on "Music and Male Hegemony." Shepherd's analyses are largely based on modern popular song, and propose "softness" and "hardness" as gender specific vocal qualities. Shepherd also argues that timbre (sound as sound) is the aspect of music marginalized by classical theory. This marginalization for him is a result of the visual control of music by writing which "neutralizes" sound itself and ultimately leads to the articulation of male hegemonic processes through music.[238] But already in the Middle Ages, as we shall observe in a moment, writing led to the silencing of the female voice.

John Shepherd and Susan McClary, in different ways, have investigated how the mechanisms of classical tonality can be used to articulate cultural and musical hegemony.[239] Shepherd sees functional tonality as evolving from its *political* predecessor, pentatonicism, the hegemonic musical system of medieval Chant. Although Shepherd's treatment of Chant is summary at best, his effort to equate feudalism and pentatonicism focusses on the ideological implications of technical musical procedures.

One could point to other analyses of political and social control that have implicit or explicit bearing on gender. In his *The Owl and the Nightingale*, Christopher Page examined the ideological implications of the attitudes toward music held by 12th- and 13th-century clerical *litterati*, as compared to views of music contained in courtly romances, in order to argue that the *litterati*, who played a major role in "the invention of the state" (B408, 173), saw control over music, and in particular over the music of the laity, as important to the establishment of good governance. The "freedom of the court" in the romances is contrasted to the constraints arising from the religious convictions and political interests of the *litterati* (185). Although gender is not a focus of the book, the references to women in contexts criticized by the *litterati* suggest the possibility of a feminist critique. In the context of Page's reasonings, one may recall the differently oriented assertions made by John Shepherd that "the existence of music, like the existence of women, is *potentially* threatening to men." The phenomenon of sound emphasizes social relatedness (as opposed to vision, which distances) and implicitly demands a response. "When that happens, music reminds men of the fragile and atrophied nature of their control over the world." Music as heard, music as uncontrollable experience poses a threat to the "moral fibre" of the "rationalistic scribe-state."[240] Viewed in still a different way, the implications of social control over musical performance by women have been brought out in Maria Coldwell's essay on "'Jongleresses' and 'Trobairitz': Secular Musicians in Medieval France." In the 12th century, women may have composed and performed on a

relatively equal basis with men; but with the advent of
polyphony, women were excluded from the new groups of
(largely clerical) specialized composers and performers.
"During the same period when women's legal freedom and
economic power were declining, their musical status was
also being limited" (B484, 55-6). If there is as yet no
thoroughgoing feminist study of medieval song, the above
observations indicate some of the elements that might be
drawn upon for such a study.

Most of the approaches I have discussed have been
elaborated by literary critics or by musicologists. In
conclusion, I wish to turn briefly to performance. The
positioning of musical performance in historical contexts has, from its inception, informed the Early Music
performance movement. As Joseph Kerman, following Leo
Treitler, has remarked, "The Early Music debate can be
taken as a model for the negotiation of historical
interpretation in general."[241] In conjunction with the
development of recording technology, this movement has
focussed attention on earlier repertories, including, to
be sure, medieval song, in ways that writing about those
repertories cannot. In the case of song, the immediacy
of performance and the kinds of decisions, both linguistic and musical, that must be taken to enable performance, instantly provoke debate. The terms of the debate
vary according to the different repertories, but a central focus is always the attempted recuperation of
sounds, musical and textual, that scholarly discourse
either omits or does not confront as performable. It is
one thing to talk about sounds, quite another to produce
them. And although writing may seem to offer more reliable traces of literature than notation of music (thus
Kerman: "... a text is a much less complete record of a
work of art in music than it is in literature"[242]),
writing still reveals its inadequacies when tightly
questioned. It no more furnishes the *sounds* of early
literature than does the notation of early music. No
manuscript clearly transmits the exact sounds or speech
inflections that a performer must produce. And very
tricky situations can arise. Take, for example, a song
presumably dating from the late 12th century but preserved in a manuscript, let us say, from the late 13th

century, and set down, perhaps, by a scribe with his own
linguistic idiosyncrasies. Such a manuscript, presented
here as hypothetical but in fact a normative case for
much of the chansonnier tradition, would scarcely offer
a reliable record from which to perform the song. The
written records for music, depending on the repertory in
question, can be even more frustratingly sketchy. But
the domain of what Paul Zumthor has termed "vocalité"
(*La Lettre et la voix*, B431, 21) is problematic for both
words and music. Performance foregrounds the issue of a
song's situated existence in the past, of its very identity as sound, of its ontology, in short.

   Performance thus raises in a particularly acute way
the intertwined issues of historical understanding and
authenticity. For the medieval period, one may argue
that it is no more possible to achieve "authenticity" in
performance than to retrieve an "authentic" text in editing. But a written/notated "text" can be said to have
some "authentic" attachment to the past through its manuscript preservation; and the nature of the manuscript
witness determines the degree of "authenticity" obtainable. Sound, in contrast, is gone forever, as are performing situations and practices. A musical event cannot
be "authentically" reproduced. The act of performing, a
physical embodiment of the song, in which the distancing
of writing disappears, is inevitably subjective. That
does not mean that performances are *merely* subjective.
One can still view performance, to borrow Gadamer's term,
as "a fusion of one's own horizon with the historical
horizon."[243] Indeed, the performing dialogue with the
past is at its most convincing when the performance is,
to use current terminology, "historically informed." But
no degree of information will allow us to *reproduce* the
past. Modern sensibilities inevitably intrude, and it is
their reaction to the past more than the past itself that
we hear. The effort to translate historical understanding
into audible sounds contains within itself as a condition
of its occurrence the unavoidable distortion of the past,
without our ever being able to determine the precise nature of the distortion. Dahlhaus has neatly summed up the
situation: "There is no escape in sight from the dilemma
that to feel close to things past is to misconstrue them,

while to understand them is to sense their remote-
ness."[244]

Performance of medieval song involves not only
sensibilities of the performers but also those of the
listeners. A performance, to be successful as communication, must reach its audience. The only audience for
modern performance is a modern audience with its own
"horizon of expectations." Modern ears cannot grasp the
sounds of medieval languages nor divest themselves entirely of the sounds of modern (in the large sense)
music. Neither concert hall nor CD player provides an
"authentic" performing context. Yet modern performances
can shape modern audience expectations and accustom modern ears to new sounds. If the problems of performance
seem, on an absolute level, unsurmountable, the effort
to understand them sharpens our awareness of ourselves
and of our relations to the Middle Ages. What characterizes the Early Music movement at its best is the continuing dialogue that reveals new ways of reflecting on
and interpreting the past.

This possibility of historical understanding has led
to more probing discussions of performance practice, to
the degree that performance practice (and with it "applied musicology") is increasingly recognized as an important part of the study of early music (were performance also a necessary part of the study of philology!).
For instance, the Norton/New Grove book *Performance
Practice: Music before 1600* edited by Howard Mayer Brown
and Stanley Sadie (B445) defines performance practice as
a discipline in which both scholars and performers can be
engaged. "We shall never really understand a repertory
of music until we have learned how it sounds in performance, but good performances and 'understanding' alike
depend heavily on archival, literary, iconographical,
analytical, and purely philological studies" (B445, x).
The volume draws on the expertise of noted scholars. An
introduction by the late Howard Brown masterfully examines the major issues of performance. Chapters by Wulf
Arlt (secular monophony) and Christopher Page (polyphony
before 1400) discuss the repertories that are the subject
of this *Guide*. Though the book proceeds by gathering

together and refining some of the most lucid recent
thinking on the subject rather than by breaking new
ground, it nonetheless achieves the goal of situating
performance practice at the center of scholarly reflection.

    In their preface, Brown and Sadie affirm that:
" . . . the advent of recordings has changed radically
the way we can know about how music sounded in the past"
(x). But technology has also distanced us in new ways
from past performing situations and imposed constraints
of its own (as, for example, when the time limitations of
early recordings led to the performance of single stanzas
of troubadour songs). Further, sound technology brings to
music performance what printing brought to texts: absolute reproducibility. As Walter Benjamin has argued,
"Even the most perfect reproduction of a work of art is
lacking in one element: its presence in time and space,
its unique existence at the place where it happens to
be."[245] The quality of actual presence is always depreci-
ated in mechanical reproduction. A modern performance re-
situates medieval presence in time and space; mechanical
reproduction abolishes presence altogether. The issue of
authenticity returns at another level. By the same token,
as Benjamin has also pointed out, recording radically re-
structures the audience by "permitting [reproductions] to
meet . . . the listener in his own particular situation"
(221). Medieval song enters homes and classrooms; it
becomes in a new way commercially controlled (if a CD
doesn't sell within a month, it disappears from the
shelves). But in the end, the sheer possibility of wide
diffusion and the continuing experimentation guaranteed
by commercial demand and new technologies make reproducibility a powerful pathway to new knowledge.

NOTES TO THE INTRODUCTION

1. This manuscript contains chiefly Latin monophonic music: sequences, tropes, *versus*, dramas, lessons, responds, and antiphons, but some pieces are in the vernacular, including a few songs partly or entirely in Old Occitan. There are also some polyphonic pieces.

2. See for exceptions to this principle among trouvère manuscripts: Van der Werf, B645, 40; Stevens, B415, 451; Tischler, B700; Karp, B527; and the article "Troubadours, trouvères" in the *New Grove*.

3. I refer here to written coordination. I do not intend to suggest anything about duration of sounds in performance, which is a separate issue.

4. One may speculate that notators of monophonic music chose to preserve nuances that could not survive rhythmically specific notational techniques. Secular songs may have been notated by scribes accustomed to the notational techniques of liturgical books.

5. Fassler, B388.

6. See the remarks of David Hughes, "Music and Meter in Liturgical Poetry," *Medievalia et Humanistica*, 7 ns (1976): 36-37. Hughes points out that when notational means are required they can be rapidly invented.

7. This is a very schematic view. For a summing up of the far messier detail, see Edward H. Roesner's review of Hans Tischler's edition of *The Earliest Motets (to circa 1270)* in *Early Music History* 4 (1984): 362-75.

8. This process, probably initiated by the use of different texts in the upper parts, was described by Rebecca A. Baltzer in a paper read at the American Musicological Society Convention in Chicago, November 1991: "The 13th-Century Motet and the Role of Manuscript Makers in Defining a Genre." My thanks to Professor Baltzer for sending me a copy of the paper.

9. See Willi Apel, *The Notation of Polyphonic Music 900-1600*, 3rd ed. (Cambridge, MA: The Mediaeval Academy, 1945), 272.

10. A point made by Rebecca Baltzer in the paper cited in note 8.

11. Machaut composed several polytextual motets. For 14th-century polytextual *chansons* see Newes, B761.

12. Earp, B725, 112-3; See also B726.

13. In her paper for the AMS Convention (see note 8).
14. See Page, B409, 43-111, for a recent discussion of some of these questions with respect to the motet.
15. See Everist, B670.
16. Earp, B127.
17. For a discussion of *vidas*, *razos* and grammatical treatises, see Poe, B592. See also Huot, B392, 329, and ch. 2 for ordering in trouvère MSS.
18. See Meneghetti, B566, 334, 349, 350-1, 362ff.
19. See Bertolucci, B465; Bossy, B472.
20. *The Printing Revolution in Early Modern Europe* (Cambridge: Cambridge University Press, 1983). *The Printing Press as an Agent of Change: Communications and Cultural Transformations in Early Modern Europe*, 2 vols. (Cambridge: Cambridge University Press, 1979).
21. Eisenstein, *Printing Revolution*, 78ff.
22. Eisenstein, *Printing Revolution*, 81.
23. *From Script to Print: An Introduction to Medieval Vernacular Literature* (Cambridge: Cambridge University Press, 1945).
24. Translation in Strunk, B151, 199; see also Harrán, B148, 154n.67.
25. Ed. Henri Chamard (Paris: Didier, 1948), 108.
26. Raimon Vidal, B185; Deschamps, B176; *Leys d'amors*, B181-2; Dante, B175.
27. Alfred Jeanroy, "Les Etudes provençales du XVIe siècle au milieu du XIXe," *Annales du Midi* 43 (1931): 134. This article was taken up again as the Introduction to Jeanroy *La Poésie lyrique des troubadours*, 2 vols. (Toulouse: Privat, 1934).
28. Jeanroy, "Les Etudes," 135-7.
29. One should not forget the link between historical thinking and textual criticism for questions such as establishment of dating procedures and the separation of false from reliable documents.
30. See the article "Printing and Publishing of Music" in the *New Grove* for detailed discussion.
31. F.J. Fétis, *Biographie universelle des musiciens et bibliographie générale de la musique*, 2nd ed., 5 (Paris: Didot, 1875), 280. (Entry on Adrian LeRoy.)
32. Pierre de Ronsard, *Oeuvres Complètes*, ed. Paul Laumonier (Paris: Hachette, 1921), 4: 189.
33. Ed. Laumonier, 4: xix.

34. Lionel Gossman, *Medievalism and the Ideologies of the Enlightenment: The World and Work of La Curne de Sainte-Palaye* (Baltimore: The Johns Hopkins Press, 1968), 45 and 147.
35. See Gossman, *Medievalism*, especially 28-31 and 248.
36. See, for example, D'Alembert's *Discours préliminaire* to the *Encyclopédie ou Dictionnaire raisonné des sciences, des arts et des métiers*, or the historical works of Voltaire, such as the *Siècle de Louis XIV* (1751) and the *Essai sur les moeurs et l'esprit des nations* (1769), for pejorative views of the Middle Ages.
37. Jean-Baptiste de la Curne de Sainte-Palaye, "Mémoire concernant la lecture des anciens Romans de Chevalerie," in *Mémoires de Littérature, tirés des registres de l'Académie Royale des Inscriptions et Belles Lettres*, 17 (Paris: Imprimerie Royale, 1751), 787-99.
38. Gossman, *Medievalism*, 251, 263.
39. Gossman, *Medievalism*, 257-8; cf. Pierre Bec, "Mythe et réalité dans la vision des troubadours du XVIe au XVIIIe siècle," in *Mythes, images, représentations*, ed. Jean-Marie Grassin (Paris: Didier/Limoges: TRAMES, Université de Limoges, 1981), 247-253, especially 251.
40. Bec, "Mythe," 251.
41. Gossman, *Medievalism*, 263n.43; Albi Rosenthal, "Le Manuscrit de La Clayette retrouvé (Bibl. nat., nouv. acq. fr. 13521)," *Annales Musicologiques* 1 (1953): 105-7.
42. Throughout this period, Chant was the dominant monophonic model; compared to it, secular melodies were of secondary interest.
43. Abbé Jean Lebeuf, "De l'état des sciences en France, depuis la mort du roi Robert, arrivée en 1031, jusqu'à celle de Philippe-le-Bel, arrivée en 1314," in *Collection des meilleurs dissertations, notices et traités particuliers relatifs à l'histoire de France*, ed. C. Leber, 14 (Paris: Dentu, 1838 [originally published 1734]), 557-8.
44. Lebeuf, "De l'état," 558.
45. "Premier mémoire sur Guillaume de Machaut, poëte et musicien dans le XIVe siècle: contenant des recherches sur sa vie, avec une notice de ses principaux ouvrages," *Mémoires de littérature tirés des registres de l'Académie Royale des Inscriptions et Belles Lettres*, 20 (Paris: Imprimerie Royale, 1753), 404.

46. "Premier mémoire," 403.

47. "Notice sommaire de deux volumes de poësies fran-
çoises et latines, conservés dans la bibliothèque des
Carmes-Déchaux de Paris; avec une indication du genre de
musique qui s'y trouve," *Mémoires* ... *de l'Académie
Royale des Inscriptions et Belles Lettres*, 20 (Paris:
Imprimerie Royale, 1753), 377-8; 381-2.

48. *Les Poësies du roy de Navarre*, Vol. 1, 187.

49. *Essai sur la musique ancienne et moderne* (Paris:
Pierres, 1780; Reprint New York: AMS Press, 1978), BK IV,
Vol. 2: 265, 281, 287, 291.

50. *Essai*, BK IV, Vol. 2: 148.

51. *Essai*, BK I, Vol. 1: 149ff.

52. *Essai*, BK IV, Vol. 2: 146 note c. Cf. Jacques
Chailley, "La Musique médiévale vue par le XVIIIe et le
XIXe siècle," in *Mélanges d'histoire et d'esthétique
musicales offerts à Paul-Marie Masson* (Paris: Richard-
Masse, 1955), 1: 96. This article is taken up again in
Chailley's popularizing *40,000 Ans de Musique* (Paris:
Plon, 1961), translated by Rollo Myers as *40,000 Years
of Music* (London: Macdonald, 1964).

53. *Essai*, BK IV, Vol. 2: 444. Cf. Théodore Gérold,
"Le Réveil en France, au XVIIIe siècle, de l'intérêt
pour la musique profane du moyen âge" (*Mélanges de
musicologie offerts à M. Lionel de la Laurencie* (Paris:
Droz, 1933), 228.

54. *A General History of Music from the Earliest
Ages to the Present Period (1789)* (Reprint ed. Frank
Mercer, New York: Harcourt, Brace, 1935 [originally
published London 1776-1789]), Repr. Vol. 1 (Burney's
Book II), 526.

55. *A General History*, Repr. Vol. 1 (Burney's BK II),
704. It is noteworthy that Burney places the invention
of printing in a wide cultural setting.

56. *A General History*, Repr. Vol. 1 (Burney's BK II),
705.

57. *A General History*, Repr. Vol. 1 (Burney's BK II),
457.

58. *A General History*, Repr. Vol. 1 (Burney's BK II),
614.

59. *A General History*, Repr. Vol. 1 (Burney's BK II),
597. This notion was probably taken from La Borde, *Essai*,
2: 142-3. Cf. Chailley, "La Musique," 96.

60. *A General History*, Repr. Vol. 1 (Burney's BK II), 570. This story eventually culminated in Grétry's opera *Richard Coeur de Lion* (performed 1785). See Chailley, "La Musique," 99-100.

61. *A General History*, Repr. Vol. 1 (Burney's BK II), 574-6.

62. *A General History*, Repr. Vol. 1, 578.

63. *A General History*, Repr. Vol. 1, 615-6.

64. Cf. Marie-Elisabeth Duchez, "Jean-Jacques Rousseau historien de la musique," in *La Musique: du théorique au politique*, ed. Hugues Dufourt and Joël-Marie Fauquet (Paris: Klincksieck, 1991), 80.

65. *The Order of Things* (New York: Vintage Books, 1973); a translation of *Les Mots et les choses* (Paris: Gallimard, 1966), 290.

66. See Hans Aarsleff, "Scholarship and Ideology: Joseph Bédier's Critique of Romantic Medievalism," in *Historical Studies and Literary Criticism*, ed. Jerome J. McGann (Madison: University of Wisconsin Press, 1985), 94.

67. Pierre Bec, "Mythe," 252. Jeanroy elucidates Raynouard's role in "Les Etudes," 144-9.

68. François-Just-Marie Raynouard, *Choix de poésies originales des troubadours*, 6 vols. (Paris: Didot, 1816-1821; Reprint Slatkine, 1982), 2: i-ii. The word "original" has several meanings: standing at the origin, originality, and original language.

69. *Choix*, 2: ii.

70. *Choix*, 2: iii ff.

71. *Choix*, 5: i.

72. *Observations sur la langue et la littérature provençales*, Reprint of the 1818 publication with a foreword by Gunter Narr (Tubingen: Tübinger Beiträge zur Linguistik, 1971), 11.

73. *Observations*, 65.

74. Hans Ulrich Gumbrecht, "'Un Souffle d'Allemagne ayant passé': Friedrich Diez, Gaston Paris, and the Genesis of National Philologies," *Romance Philology* 40 (1986): 14.

75. Paris: Imprimerie Nationale, 1733-1938. 37 vols. Vols 20-23, published in the 1840s, contain material by Paulin Paris.

76. Jeanroy, "Les Etudes," 156-7.

77. Gaston Raynaud, *Bibliographie des chansonniers français des XIIIe et XIVe siècles*, 2 vols. (Paris: Vieweg, 1884) and Eduard Schwan, *Die altfranzösischen Liederhandschriften* (Berlin: Weidmann, 1886).

78. Jacobsthal, "Die Texte der Liederhandschrift von Montpellier H 196: diplomatischer Abdruck," *Zeitschrift für romanische Philologie* 3 (1879): 526-56; 4 (1880): 35-64, 278-317. Raynaud, B313. Paulin Paris, *Histoire littéraire*, vol. 20, 659.

79. Reprinted by Slatkine, 1969. For a discussion of editors of the *Voir Dit*, see Cerquiglini, B722.

80. Gaston Paris's *La Littérature française au moyen âge (XIe-XIVe siècle)* was first professed as a course in 1880-1, first published in Paris in 1889. I quote from the 3rd edition of 1905 (Paris: Hachette).

81. *Littérature française*, 207.

82. *Littérature française*, 194-5.

83. Louis Petit de Julleville, *Histoire de la langue et de la littérature française des origines à 1900* (Paris: Colin 1896), 1: 384.

84. *Histoire de la langue*, 1: 401. For Fétis, see below. Jeanroy finds troubadour music superior to polyphonic music because it is *popular*; he discusses formal structures and use of instruments.

85. *Histoire de la langue*, 2: 337.

86. *Histoire de la langue*, 2: 339.

87. *Histoire de la langue*, 1: 380.

88. See Alfred Foulet and Mary Speer, B440, 8-10, for a discussion of Lachmann.

89. Foulet and Speer, B440, 19-20.

90. Christian Kalkbrenner, *Histoire de la musique* (Strasbourg: Koenig, 1802), 2: 97. This is a French translation of *Kurzer Abriss der Geschichte der Tonkunst, zum Vergnügen der Liebhaber der Musik* (Berlin: Maurer, 1792). For secular monophony, Kalkbrenner follows the familiar judgment that it is a species of Chant, neither difficult nor demanding, adapted to courtly entertainment. Kalkbrenner constantly complains that since the notes are largely incomprehensible, and the performance tradition has been lost, it is impossible to understand medieval music.

91. Raphael Georg Kiesewetter, *History of the Modern Music of Western Europe*, trans. Robert Muller (New York:

DaCapo Press, 1973), Reprint of the first English edition, London, 1848. Table of contents, ix. Originally published as *Geschichte der europaïsch-abendländischen oder unserer heutigen Musik: Darstellung ihres Ursprunges, ihres Wachstumes und ihrer stufenweise Entwickelung; von dem ersten Jahrhundert des Christenthumes bis auf unsere Zeit* (Leipzig: Breitkopf & Härtel, 1834).

92. *History*, 101.

93. "Préface" to the *Biographie universelle des musiciens et bibliographie générale de la musique*, 2e ed. (Paris: Didot, 1873), 1: v.

94. "Préface" to the *Biographie*, 1: ii-iii.

95. *Biographie*, 1: 13.

96. *Biographie*, 5:282: N⁰ 6812 de l'ancien fonds, Bibliothèque impériale à Paris. This is the earlier numbering of BN fr.146.

97. *Biographie*, 4: 158.

98. *Histoire générale de la musique depuis les temps les plus anciens jusqu'à nos jours* (Paris: Didot, 1869-76), 5: 16, 13, 18.

99. *Histoire générale*, 5: 315.

100. See Vincent Duckles, "Patterns in the Historiography of 19th-Century Music," *Acta Musicologica* 42 (1970): 78.

101. See Jean Maillard, "The Many Faces of Medieval Musicology" trans. Brian Willis, *Studies in Music* [Australia] 4 (1970): 6-7.

102. Chailley, "La Musique," 95 (see note 52).

103. Martin Gerbert, *Scriptores ecclesiastici de musica sacra potissimum*, 3 vols. (St. Blasien, 1784); Charles-Edmond-Henri de Coussemaker, *Scriptorum de Musica Medii Aevi*, 4 vols. (Paris, 1864-76).

104. Charles-Edmond-Henri de Coussemaker, *Oeuvres complètes du trouvère Adam de la Halle, poésies et musique* (Paris, 1872). Jeanroy, B104, 45, remarks that the presentation of the texts is deplorable.

105. For the role of Coussemaker in "excavating" H 196, see Everist, B129, 111.

106. Jean Beck, *La Musique des troubadours* (Paris: Laurens, 1928), 122, so characterizes Restori's article.

107. Antonio Restori, "Per la storia musicale dei trovatori provenzali," *Rivista musicale italiana* 2 (1895): 1-22; 3 (1896): 231-60; 407-51.

108. "Per la storia," *Rivista* 2 (1895): 8.
109. 2 (1895): 17.
110. Carl Appel, B230; Van der Werf, B645; Stevens, B415.
111. Jacobsthal's dissertation was on *Die Mensural-notenschrift des 12. and 13. Jahrhunderts* (1871).
112. For a description of the *Repertorium*, see Hughes (B14) No. 1390, and the article on Ludwig in the *New Grove*. For the edition of Machaut, see B341.
113. *Music in the Middle Ages* (New York: Norton, 1940), 207. Emphasis added.
114. B230.
115. Jean-Baptiste Beck, *Die Melodien der Troubadours* (Straßburg: Trübner, 1908), *La Musique des troubadours* (Paris: Laurens, 1928). Pierre Aubry, *Trouvères et troubadours* (Paris: Alcan, 1909). Facsimiles: B112, B114, B117.
116. Aubry/Jeanroy, "Huit chansons de Berenger de Palazol" (B226), *Lais et descorts français* (B205), *Le Chansonnier de l'Arsenal* (B114); Aubry/Bédier, *Les Chansons de croisade* (B187); Beck/Bédier, *Les Chansons de Colin Muset* (B283). Pierre Aubry, *Le Roman de Fauvel* (Paris: SATF, 1908), *Cent motets* (B310).
117. For the paradoxical 19th-century re-evaluation of the Middle Ages, see Section IV on "Der Streit der Ideologien im 19. Jahrhundert," in *Mittelalter-Rezeption: Zur Rezeptionsgeschichte der romanischen Literaturen des Mittelalters in der Neuzeit*, ed. Reinhold R. Grimm (Begleitreihe zum GRLMA Bd. 2, Heidelberg: Winter, 1991).
118. Robert Guiette, "D'une poésie formelle en France au Moyen Age," *Revue des sciences humaines*, nouv. série, fasc. 54, avril-juin 1949, 61-9. Dragonetti, B492. Pierre Bec "La Douleur et son univers poétique chez Bernard de Ventadour" *Cahiers de civilisation médiévale* 11 (1968): 545-71; 12 (1969): 25-33; "L'Antithèse poétique chez Bernard de Ventadour," in *Mélanges de philologie romane dédiés à la mémoire de Jean Boutière* (Liège: Soledi, 1971), 107-37; Zumthor, B430.
119. Poirion, B765, 9.
120. Terry Eagleton, *Literary Theory: An Introduction* (Minneapolis: University of Minnesota Press, 1983), 74.
121. Joseph Kerman, *Contemplating Music: Challenges*

to Musicology (Cambridge: Harvard University Press, 1985), 12-3, 16-7, 113-54.
122. Cf. Terry Eagleton, *Literary Theory*, 46-53, 112. See Jonathan Culler, *On Deconstruction: Theory and Criticism after Structuralism* (Ithaca: Cornell University Press, 1982), 20, for contrasts between New Criticism and structuralism.
123. Cf. Kerman, *Contemplating Music*, 125.
124. Ian Bent, "Structuralism and Music," in the *New Grove*. Cf. Patricia Tunstall, "Structuralism and Musicology: An Overview," *Current Musicology* 27 (1979): 51.
125. Tunstall, "Structuralism," 56-7.
126. Arnold Whittall, "Analysis as Performance," in *Atti del XIV Congresso della Società Internazionale di Musicologia*, Bologna 27 agosto-1° settembre, Ferrara-Parma, 30 agosto, 1987, I Round Tables, ed. Angelo Pompilio, Lorenzo Bianconi, Donatella Restani, F. Alberto Gallo (Torino: Edizioni di Torino: 1990), 655.
127. Bent, "Structuralism and Music": "The main branch of this Structuralist analysis is termed the SEMIOLOGY of Music." See also Ian Bent, *Analysis*, with William Drabkin (London/New York: Macmillan/Norton, 1987), 58, 66, Ch. IV, Sect. 7.
128. Ruwet, B412; Nattiez, B404.
129. See Bent, *Analysis*, 41, and Leo Treitler "Structural and Critical Analysis" in *Musicology in the 1980s*, ed. D. Kern Holoman and Claude V. Palisca (New York: Da Capo Press, 1982), 67-8. Emphasis on style in musicology grows also out of musicology's relationship to art history.
130. See Guido Adler, "Style-Criticism," *Musical Quarterly* 20 (1934): 172-6 for a succinct statement of his goals.
131. Bent, *Analysis*, 6, 31-2; Kerman, *Contemplating Music*, 61-2; Treitler, "Structural," 72-3.
132. So argues Lee Patterson, "Literary History," in *Critical Terms for Literary Study*, ed. Frank Lentricchia and Thomas McLaughlin (Chicago: University of Chicago Press, 1990), 252-3.
133. John Carlos Rowe, "Structure," in *Critical Terms for Literary Study*, 25. Significantly for the comparison of music to literature, the term "Structure" finds no entry in the *New Grove*, although "Form" is amply discussed, as is "Style."

134. In the *New Grove* article on "Musicology" one may read: "Fundamental to the music historian is the concept of style ..." ("Musicology," II Disciplines, 1. Historical Method). Or again in his introduction to *Models of Musical Analysis* (B90), Mark Everist argues that individual medieval and early modern works are rarely analyzed for themselves but "as the individual links in a chain of style-critical observations" (vii).
135. Dominick LaCapra, *History and Criticism* (Ithaca: Cornell University Press, 1985), 95.
136. Raman Selden, *A Reader's Guide to Contemporary Literary Theory*, 2nd ed. (Lexington: University Press of Kentucky, 1989), 2.
137. Kerman, *Contemplating Music*, 37-8.
138. Andrew Bowie, "Music, Language and Modernity," in *The Problems of Modernity: Adorno and Benjamin*, ed. Andrew Benjamin (London: Routledge, 1989), 68.
139. See Lug, B551.
140. See the series of essays, from 1966 to 1988, in Leo Treitler, *Music and the Historical Imagination* (Cambridge: Harvard University Press, 1989) especially chapters 2-6.
141. Carl Dahlhaus, *Grundlagen der Musikgeschichte* (Cologne: Gerig, 1977), trans. as *Foundations of Music History* by J.B. Robinson (Cambridge: Cambridge University Press, 1983). Hans Georg Gadamer, *Wahrheit und Methode* (Tübingen: Mohr, 1960), trans. as *Truth and Method* (2nd rev. ed. New York: Crossroad, 1990).
142. Brook Thomas, *The New Historicism and Other Old-Fashioned Topics* (Princeton: Princeton University Press, 1991), 5.
143. Jean-François Lyotard, *The Postmodern Condition: A Report on Knowledge*, trans. Geoff Bennington and Brian Massumi, Theory and History of Literature 10 (Minneapolis: University of Minnesota Press, 1984), 27-37. For the use of "post" vs. "new," see Thomas, *The New Historicism*, 25.
144. *Foundations*, ch. 2. It is worth noting that the tension between the esthetic and the historical also figured importantly in Hans Robert Jauss's elaboration of Reception Theory.
145. *Foundations*, 35 and ch. 8.

146. Lydia Goehr, "Writing Music History," *History and Theory* 31 (1992): 182-99.
147. Kerman, *Contemplating Music*, 17.
148. Joseph Kerman, "American Musicology in the 1990s," *Journal of Musicology* 9 (1991): 141.
149. Goehr, "Writing," 182.
150. Kerman, *Contemplating Music*, 42.
151. Bernard Cerquiglini, *Eloge de la variante: Histoire critique de la philologie* (Paris: Seuil, 1989): Chapter on "Monsieur Procuste, philologue." The January 1990 issue of *Speculum* sparked vigorous debate on the meaning and uses of philology.
152. Margaret Bent, "Fact and Value in Contemporary Scholarship," *Musical Times* 127 (1986): 85.
153. Speer, B443, 25. This article gives an excellent summary of the debate over editing and critical theory.
154. Selden, *A Reader's Guide*, 2.
155. See Edward H. Roesner's review of Hans Tischler, *The Earliest Motets* in *Early Music History* 4 (1984): 363-4. The difficulty of distinguishing between different states of the "same" motet and different members of a "family" of motets presents major problems to the editor. Hence, Roesner points out, there is a tendency not to offer the motet repertory in critical editions but to edit motet collections in individual manuscripts "bearing witness to the state of a work at one particular point in its history."
156. See Earp, B726, 197, 203-7; Page, B764.
157. István Frank, "L'Art d'éditer les textes lyriques," in *Recueil de travaux offert à M. Clovis Brunel* (Paris: Société de l'Ecole des Chartes, 1955), 1:463-75. The Italian School has generally favored Lachmannian methods. See Mary B. Speer, "In Defense of Philology: Two New Guides to Textual Criticism," *Romance Philology* 32 (1979): 335-44; Maria Luisa Meneghetti, B567.
158. Caldwell, B439, 41. The points raised here are valid, but the facts concerning troubadour sources are incorrect. For example, northern French sources are not later but earlier than most southern sources, and there are more melodies in southern (G, R) than in northern (W, X) sources.
159. Pickens, B249, 35-9. For a critique of Pickens,

see Meneghetti, B567, and Kay, B532.

160. As Mary Speer has pointed out, with this kind of format "anyone genuinely interested in examining text and music simultaneously has to flip from the back of the book to the front to find the words to stanzas beyond the first--a maneuver requiring considerable manual dexterity and concentration" (B443), 40.

161. Caldwell, B439, 41.

162. Wulf Arlt, B450, 61.

163. Arlt, B450, 62.

164. Arlt, B450, 61.

165. Caldwell, B439, 41.

166. Charles Faulhaber, "Textual Criticism in the 21st Century," *Romance Philology* 45 (1991): 123-48. Cf. also B. Cerquiglini, *Eloge de la variante*, 112-6.

167. Van der Werf, B645, 35-45. Stevens, B415, 413-91; B625, 360-3. Switten, Review of Hendrik van der Werf, *The Extant Troubadour Melodies* in the *Journal of the American Musicological Society* 39 (1986): 382.

168. Van der Werf, B645-6; Review of John Stevens, *Words and Music in the Middle Ages* in the *Journal of Musicological Research* 8 (1989): 378-86.

169. See Stevens, B415, 457 for a summary.

170. Georges Lote, B433. Stevens speaks of his concept as "the isosyllabic hypothesis," B415, 8.

171. Stevens, B415, devotes a note (495n.10) to a refutation of Dragonetti's stance on rhythm, but since he claims as his own some rhythmic markings that come directly from Dragonetti, the note is unclear.

172. *Leys d'amors* (B181) 1, 46-8, 56-92. The discussion of accent in Latin (64-88) is much longer than the discussion of accent in Romance (88-92).

173. B181, 1, 58-60. The complete definition runs:
DE LA DIFFINITO DACCEN. Accens es regulars melodia. o tempramens de votz. lequals estay principalmens en una sillaba.
Melodia. so es cans melodios. o plazens sonoritatz. per loqual melodios can. o plazen sonoritat: tota dictios en quanque es votz: es segon dever pronunciada amb elevatio. oz am depressio. so es a dire haut. o bas.
Et entendatz can melodios. quom fay legen o pronuncian. non ges del can de musica. quar aquel regularmen no te. ni garda accen. segon que podetz vezer en lo res-

pos *benenicta* [sic] et *venerabilis*. quar mays trobaretz
deponhs en lo. *ta.* que es breus naturalmen. que en lo.
be. ni en lo. *dic.* quanque laccens principals sia en
aquela sillaba.
Aquo meteysh podetz vezer en lo vers daquel meteysh
respos. que comensa. *virgo.* quar en lo. *go.* trobaretz
gran re de ponhs: et en lo. *vir.* on es laccens principals. non trobaretz mas un.
Et aquest cans quom fay en accen. quan lieg o
pronuncia. es apelatz cans. per alcuna semblansa. quar
en ayssi co hom eleva la votz fortmen quan canta. ayssi
meteysh en la sillaba on cay le principals accens. eleva
hom la votz mays e plus fortmen. fazen major demora de
temps: que no fay en deguna de las autras sillabas.
Enquaras pot esser ditz cans. per alcuna autra semblansa. quar enaysi coma us cans melodios acordans. e ben
pauzatz: es plazens e gracios per auzir. en ayssi me-
teyhs es cauza agradabla. e plazens. auzir los motz. e
las paraulas. ben pauzadas. ben pronunciadas. et accen-
tuadas segon lor dever.
Cf. also Gonfroy, B508, 194.
174. But see the critique of Marshall by Madeleine
Tyssens, B642.
175. Cf. Chambers, B480, 10-5. It should be noted
that Eustache Deschamps, *Art de dictier*, does not use
the system of the *Leys* but rather counts all syllables.
The system described in the *Leys* will prevail.
176. B415, 36; B625, 368.
177. For word linkages in manuscripts, see Peter
Rickard, "Système ou arbitraire? Quelques réflexions sur
la soudure des mots dans les manuscrits français du moyen
âge," *Romania* 103 (1982): 270-512; Jacques Monfrin,
"Notes sur le chansonnier provençal C," in *Recueil de
travaux offert à M. Clovis Brunel* (Paris: Société de
l'Ecole des Chartes, 1955), 2:292-312; Switten, B631.
178. Don Ihde, *Listening and Voice: A Phenomenology
of Sound* (Athens: Ohio University Press, 1976), 6 and 15.
179. Cf. Ian Bent, *Analysis*, 63.
180. Thomas Clifton, *Music as Heard: A Study in Applied Phenomenology* (New Haven: Yale University Press,
1983), 143-55.
181. Yvonne Rokseth, B314, 4, 76; Sanders, B368,
531-7. Sanders cites and comments on Rokseth.

182. "The Function of Texts in French 13th-Century Motets," *Musical Quarterly* 28 (1942): 445-62. See also Page, B409, 99-110 for a discussion of *subtilitas* in the motet as a question of musical and verbal patterning rather than of meaning.

183. Beverly Jean Evans, "The Unity of Text and Music in The Late Thirteenth-Century French Motet: A Study of Selected Works from the Montpellier Manuscript, Fascicle VII" (Ph.D. diss., University of Pennsylvania, 1983); B667-8.

184. Cf. B95; Richard L. Crocker, "Rhythm in Early Polyphony," in B100, 147-77, examines the usefulness of the isosyllabic hypothesis for rhythm in early polyphony; Norman E. Smith, "The Earliest Motets: Music and Words," *Journal of the Royal Musical Association* 114 (1989): 141-63 and "The Notation of *Fractio Modi*," in B100, 283-304, investigates rhythmic differences between clausula and motet and nuances in methods of notating *fractio modi*.

185. "The Critical Reception of Machaut's *Voir-Dit* and the History of Literary History," *French Forum* 17 (1992): 143-8.

186. For lists of these romances, see B382, B663.

187. B731, 63; see further B736 and Hirshberg, B746.

188. *Foundations*, 17. Cf also for issues raised here Goehr, "Writing Music History" (note 146), 185-6.

189. *Style and Music: Theory, History, and Ideology* (Philadelphia: University of Pennsylvania Press, 1989). Meyer is primarily concerned with modern (especially 19th-century) music, but the general issues addressed could apply to the medieval period as well.

190. Meyer, *Style*, 99 and 101.

191. Cf. also B98, especially the introductions by Daniel Poirion and Nancy Regalado.

192. *Essai*, 240; quoted from the translation *Toward a Medieval Poetics* (B430), 183.

193. Paul Zumthor, "Style and Expressive Register in Medieval Poetry," in *Literary Style: A Symposium*, ed. Seymour Chatman (London: Oxford University Press, 1971), 274.

194. S.C. Aston, "The Troubadours and the Concept of Style," in *Stil-und Formprobleme in der Literatur*, ed. Paul Böckmann (Heidelberg: Winter, 1959), 142-7. Cf. also Nichols, B576.

195. These terms have received considerable critical attention. For a clear introduction, see Smith, B622, Ch. 1. Cf. also Paterson, B586; Taylor, B29, Nos. 202-207; Harvey and Gaunt, B520.

196. Cf. Tischler, B698.

197. For example, Gonfroy, B508. See also Robert H. Perrin, "Some Notes on the Troubadour Melodic Types," *Journal of the American Musicological Society* 9 (1956): 12-8.

198. Karp, B526, and article "Troubadours and Trouvères" in the *New Grove*. Dragonetti (B492, 433) designates "typical" courtly *versus* as either abab *or* abba.

199. Treitler, "Structural," 75 (see note 129).

200. For a similar type of analysis carried out on songs by Dufay, see Don Michael Randel, "Dufay the Reader," in *Studies in the History of Music*, Vol. 1: *Music and Language* (New York: Broude Brothers, 1983), 38-78; and B767.

201. Treitler, B641, 8-9, points out, for a troubadour song, that the first stanza sets the tone and "conditions the reception of the rest," without demonstrating how this "conditioning" takes place. For an approach to the issue see Switten, B627, 121-38.

202. Cf. Jean-Marie Schaeffer, *Qu'est-ce qu'un genre littéraire?* (Paris: Seuil, 1989), 10-1.

203. Alastair Fowler, *Kinds of Literature: An Introduction to the Theory of Genres and Modes* (Cambridge: Harvard University Press, 1982), 144. Cf also Cesare Segre with the collaboration of Tomaso Kemeny, *Introduction to the Analysis of the Literary Text*, trans. John Meddemmen (Bloomington: Indiana University Press, 1988), 202.

204. Pierre Bec, "Essai de synthèse et discussions," in *Actes du XVIIIe Congrès International de Linguistique et de Philologie Romanes*, Université de Trèves (Trier) 1986, vol. 6, ed. Dieter Kremer (Tübingen: Niemeyer, 1988), 264.

205. Ritva Jacobsson and Leo Treitler, "Tropes and the Concept of Genre," in *Pax et Sapientia: Studies in Text and Music of Liturgical Tropes and Sequences in Memory of Gordon Anderson*, ed. Ritva Jacobsson (Stockholm: Almquist & Wiksell, c.1986), 64.

206. B395. All quotations are from the 1982 English

translation and page numbers refer to that version.
207. B430. All page references are to the French
publication, 1972.
208. Cf. John M. Swales, *Genre Analysis--English in
Academic and Research Settings* (Cambridge: Cambridge
University Press, 1990), 38-42, "Genre in Linguistics."
209. The genres: "'Vers' und Kanzone, Descort und
Lai, Sirventes, Sirventes-Kanzone, Cobla, Kreuzzugslied,
Klagelied, Tenzone, Partimen, Pastorela, Tagelied,
Romanze, Tanzlied und Estampida, Religiöses Lied, Salut
d'amor."
210. Stevens's views coincide with the kind of typology proposed by Christopher Page (B407, 16). However,
Stevens also points out that rhythmic distinctions between dance and courtly song are only partly borne out
by manuscript evidence (B415, 187-8).
211. Evans, "The Unity," 2 (see note 183). Linda Jean
Speck, "Relationships between Music and Text in The Late
Thirteenth-Century French Motet" (Ph.D. diss., University
of Michigan, 1977) argues that the concept of tension
best reflects text/music relationships in the motet.
212. For the most complete lists, see Coldwell,
B663, and Boulton, B382.
213. Margaret Bent, "The Late-Medieval Motet," in
Companion to Medieval and Renaissance Music (B76), 114-8,
especially 118.
214. This point has recently been made by William D.
Paden in the introduction to a series of unpublished
papers on "Historicizing Genre in Medieval Lyric" from
conferences held at the Newberry Library in Chicago in
November of 1992 and at the Modern Language Association
in Toronto, December, 1993.
215. B85, Preface. See also the entire introduction.
216. B752, 9. The influence of Hans Georg Gadamer
(see note 141) is important to Leech-Wilkinson's arguments.
217. Kerman, *Contemplating Music*, 82 (see note 121);
Treitler "Structural," 75 (see note 129).
218. B752, 13. This assertion is based on Douglas
Kelly's analysis of "Music and Poetry" which forms an
appendix to his *Medieval Imagination: Rhetoric and the
Poetry of Courtly Love* (Madison: University of Wisconsin
Press, 1978). While the conclusions reached by Kelly are

suggestive, his arguments seem chiefly intended to justify the elimination of serious consideration of music-text relationships in his book.
219. Cf. Leech-Wilkinson's analysis of a Machaut virelai, B754; Pulido, B766; Günther, B741.
220. See B406, 59-74.
221. Everist, B413, 4. Gushee B391 and B743. Gushee was critical of Ruwet's methods, B391, 171.
222. "Proposition d'analyse pour une polyphonie vocale du XVIe siècle" *Revue de musicologie* 61 (1975): 35-58.
223. Cf. Eagleton, *Literary Theory*, 118 (see note 120).
224. J.L. Austin, *How to Do Things with Words* (Cambridge: Harvard University Press, 1962). John R. Searle, *Speech Acts: An Essay in the Philosophy of Language* (Cambridge: Cambridge University Press, 1969).
225. In *Report of the 11th International Musicological Society Congress* 1972 (Kassel: Bärenreiter, 1974), 67.
226. Lawrence Kramer, *Music as Cultural Practice, 1800-1900* (Berkeley: University of California Press, 1990), 9. The concept of "speech situation" is taken from Austin, *How to Do Things*, 139.
227. Kramer, *Music*, 10. Cf. also Lawrence Kramer, *Music and Poetry: The Nineteenth Century and After* (Berkeley: The University of California Press, 1984), Chapter 5: "Song."
228. Stanley Fish includes speech-act theory as a form of rhetoric because Austin's book ultimately re-places the "formal core of language" by a "world of utterances vulnerable to the sea change of every cir-cumstance--the world, in short, of rhetorical (situated) man" ("Rhetoric," in *Critical Terms for Literary Study*, ed. Frank Lentricchia and Thomas McLaughlin [Chicago: University of Chicago Press, 1990], 213).
229. B430, 52; quoted from the translation, 30.
230. Mary Carruthers, *The Book of Memory: A Study of Memory in Medieval Culture* (Cambridge: Cambridge University Press, 1990).
231. *De oratore*, ed. and trans. E.W. Sutton and H. Rockham, Loeb Classical Library (Cambridge: Harvard University Press, 1949), I, v. 18.

232. Jean-Claude Schmitt, *La Raison des gestes dans l'Occident médiéval* (Paris: Gallimard, 1990), 54.
233. Cf. Nichols, B578.
234. *The Dialogic Imagination: Four Essays by M.M. Bakhtin*, ed. Michael Holquist, trans. Caryl Emerson and Michael Holquist (Austin: University of Texas Press, 1981). *Rabelais and His World*, trans. Hélène Iswolsky (2nd ed. Bloomington: Indiana University Press, 1984).
235. The term was first used by Julia Kristeva in "Pour une sémiologie des paragrammes," *Tel Quel* 29 (1967): 57-73.
236. Hans Robert Jauss, *Toward an Aesthetic of Reception* and *Aesthetic Experience and Literary Hermeneutics* both published by the University of Minnesota Press, Minneapolis, in 1982. Robert C. Holub, *Reception Theory: A Critical Introduction* (London: Methuen, 1984) is an excellent discussion of the subject.
237. Cf. Mary B. Speer, B443; B567; William D. Paden, ed. *The Future of the Middle Ages: Medieval Literature in the 1990s* (Gainesville: University Press of Florida, 1994); Keith Busby, ed. *Towards a Synthesis? Essays on the New Philology* (Amsterdam: Rodopi, 1993).
238. John Shepherd, *Music as Social Text* (Cambridge: Polity Press and Blackwell, 1991), 164-73.
239. John Shepherd, *Music as Social Text*, 96-111. Susan McClary, "Narrative Agendas in 'Absolute' Music: Identity and Difference in Brahms's Third Symphony," in *Musicology and Difference: Gender and Sexuality in Music Scholarship*, ed. Ruth A. Solie (Berkeley: University of California Press, 1993), 326-44. But see Leo Treitler's comments in that same volume on the danger of falling into essentialism as a result of using gender as an interpretive practice: "Gender and Other Dualities" (23-45). Gender duality, Treitler points out, has guided musical discourse since at least Boethius.
240. Shepherd, *Music as Social Text*, 159-60.
241. Joseph Kerman, "American Musicology in the 1990s," *Journal of Musicology* 9 (1991): 138. For a rough chronology of the Historical Performance Movement see Kerman's *Contemplating Music*, 182-217 (see note 121).
242. *Contemplating Music*, 187.
243. Cited in Holub, *Reception Theory*, 42 (see note 236).

244. Dahlhaus, *Foundations*, 63 (see note 141).

245. Walter Benjamin, "The Work of Art in the Age of Mechanical Reproduction," in *Illuminations*, ed. Hannah Arendt, trans. Harry Zohn (New York: Shocken Books, 1969), 220. For a distinction between mechanical and electronic (digital) reproducibility, see John Mowitt, "The Sound of Music in the Era of its Electronic Reproducibility," in *Music and Society: The Politics of Composition, Performance and Reception*, ed. Richard Leppert and Susan McClary (Cambridge: Cambridge University Press, 1987), 173-97.

BIBLIOGRAPHY

BIBLIOGRAPHY AND REFERENCE

GENERAL BIBLIOGRAPHIES, REPERTORIES, DICTIONARIES AND ENCYCLOPEDIAS

1
Bossuat, Robert. *Manuel bibliographique de la littéra-
ture française du Moyen Age.* Melun: Argences, 1951.
Supplément 1 (1949-53). Paris: Argences, 1955.
Supplément 2 (1954-60). Paris: Argences, 1961. *Sup-
plément 3, pts 1 & 2* (1960-1980). Ed. François Viel-
liard and Jacques Monfrin. Paris: Centre National de
Recherche Scientifique, 1986, 1991.
2
Brogan, T.V.F. *Verseform: A Comparative Bibliography.*
Baltimore: The Johns Hopkins University Press, 1989.
3
*Bulletins de l'Association Internationale d'Etudes
Occitanes.* Royal Holloway and Bedford New College,
University of London. [Originally: Westfield College,
London.]
4
Cabeen, David C. *A Critical Bibliography of French
Literature.* Vol. 1: *The Mediaeval Period.* Ed. Urban T.
Holmes, Jr. Enlarged edition. Syracuse: Syracuse
University Press, 1952.
Dated but still useful.
5
Cahiers de civilisation médiévale.
There is a bibliography issue every year, including
all disciplines, for the 10th-12th centuries.
6
Chailley, Jacques. *Précis de musicologie.* Nouvelle
édition entièrement refondue. Paris: Presses
Universitaires de France, 1984. [1st ed. 1958]

7

Chambers, Frank. *Proper Names in the Lyrics of the Troubadours*. University of North Carolina Studies in the Romance Languages and Literatures, No. 113. Chapel Hill, 1971.
Bibliography includes all troubadour editions since the publication of István Frank, *Répertoire* (B12).
8

Dictionnaire des Lettres Françaises: Le Moyen Age. Sous la direction du Cardinal Georges Grente. Ouvrage préparé par Robert Bossuat, Louis Pichard, et Guy Raynaud de Lage. Edition entièrement revue et mise à jour sous la direction de Geneviève Hasenohr et Michel Zink. Paris: Fayard, 1992. [1st ed. 1964]
9

Doss-Quinby, Eglal. *The Lyrics of the Trouvères: A Research Guide (1970-1990)*. New York: Garland, 1994.

[Dyggve, Holger Petersen, see Petersen, B23, B24.]

10

Earp, Lawrence. *Guillaume de Machaut: A Guide to Research*. New York: Garland Press, forthcoming.
11

Encomia: Bibliographical Bulletin of the International Courtly Literature Society.
12

Frank, István. *Répertoire métrique de la poésie des troubadours*. 2 vols. Paris: Champion, 1953 and 1957.
Indispensable tool for troubadour research.
13

Gennrich, Friedrich. *Bibliographie der ältesten französischen und lateinischen Motetten*. Darmstadt: Summa Musicae Medii Aevi 2, 1957-8.
14

Hughes, Andrew. *Medieval Music: The Sixth Liberal Art*. Revised edition. Toronto: Toronto University Press, 1980. [1st ed. 1974]
Important reference bibliography.
15

Jackson, Roland. *Performance Practice, Medieval to Contemporary: A Bibliographic Guide*. New York: Garland, 1988.

16
Karp, Theodore. "Medieval Music in Perspective." In
Medieval Studies: An Introduction, second edition, ed.
James M. Powell, 401-31. Syracuse: Syracuse University
Press, 1992. [1st ed. 1976.]
For students beginning their study of the period.
Bibliography partially updated since the 1976 edition.
17
Kelly, Douglas. *The Arts of Poetry and Prose*. Typologie
des sources du moyen âge occidental, Fasc. 59.
Turnhout: Brepols, 1991.
18
Linker, Robert White. *A Bibliography of Old French
Lyrics*. University, Mississippi: Romance Monographs
31, 1979.
19
Modern Language Association International Bibliography.
Wide but not entirely dependable coverage of literary
matters pertinent to medieval song.
20
Mölk, Ulrich & Friedrich Wolfzettel. *Répertoire métrique
de la poésie lyrique française des origines à 1350*. 1
vol. with box of perforated cards. Munich: Fink, 1972.
Indispensable for research on formal structures.
21
Murphy, James J. *Medieval Rhetoric: A Select Bibliography*. Second Edition. Toronto: University of Toronto
Press, 1989.
22
The New Grove Dictionary of Music and Musicians. Ed.
Stanley Sadie. 20 vols. London: Macmillan, 1980.
Indispensable source of information about musical
matters.
23
Petersen Dyggve, Holger. *Onomastique des trouvères*.
Annales de l'Academiae Scientarum Fennicae, vol. 30,
1. Helsinki, 1934.
24
Petersen Dyggve, Holger. "Personnages historiques
figurant dans la poésie lyrique française des XIIe et
XIIIe siècles." *Neuphilologische Mitteilungen* 36
(1935): 1-29, 65-91; 37 (1936): 257-83; 41 (1941):
12-29, 46-60; 46 (1946): 157-80.

25
Pillet, Alfred and Henry Carstens. *Bibliographie der Troubadours*. Halle: Niemeyer, 1933.
Indispensable research tool for troubadour song.

26
Randel, Don Michael, ed. *The New Harvard Dictionary of Music*. Cambridge: Harvard University Press, 1986.
Excellent articles on medieval subjects.

27
Répertoire international de littérature musicale (RILM).
Yearly bibliography of musical materials (not only the Middle Ages). Useful summaries of many entries.

28
Spanke, Hans. *G. Raynauds Bibliographie des altfranzösischen Liedes*. Leiden: Brill, 1955. [Reprint 1980 with a discography and an alphabetical index of songs.]
Indispensable tool for study of the trouvères.

29
Taylor, Robert A. *La Littérature occitane du moyen âge: Bibliographie sélective et critique*. Toronto: University of Toronto Press, 1977.
Basic bibliography for troubadours. [Updates of this bibliography are published in the *Bulletins de l'Association Internationale d'Etudes Occitanes*. University of London, 1990, and following years.]

30
Van den Boogaard, Nico H.J. *Rondeaux et refrains du XIIe siècle au début du XIVe*. Paris: Klincksieck, 1969.

31
Van der Werf, Hendrik. *Integrated Directory of Organa, Clausulae, and Motets of the Thirteenth Century*. Rochester: published by the author, 1989.
Considerable useful information, concisely presented.

32
Wiacek, Wilhelmina M. *Lexique des noms géographiques et ethniques*. Paris: Nizet, 1968. [Les classiques d'oc]

GRAMMARS AND LANGUAGE DICTIONARIES

33
Andrieux, Nelly and Emmanuèle Baumgartner. *Systèmes morphologiques de l'ancien français: A. Le verbe*.

Vol. 3 of *Manuel du français du moyen âge*, ed. Yves Lefèvre. Bordeaux: Sobodi/Editions Bière, 1983.
34
Andrieux-Reix, Nelly and Emmanuèle Baumgartner. *Ancien français: Exercices de morphologie*. Paris: Presses Universitaires de France, 1990.
35
Anglade, Joseph. *Grammaire de l'ancien provençal*. Paris: Klincksieck, 1977. [1st ed. 1921]
36
Anglade, Joseph. *Grammaire élémentaire de l'ancien français*. Paris: Armand Colin, 1965.
37
Bec, Pierre. *Manuel pratique de philologie romane*. 2 vols. Paris: Picard, 1970-1.
Old Occitan, 1:395-458: detailed discussion of Bernard de Ventadour, "Quan vei la laudeta mover." Old French, 2:3-132.
38
Bonnard, Henri and Claude Régnier. *Petite grammaire de l'ancien français*. Paris: Magnard, 1989.
39
Einhorn, E. *Old French: A Concise Handbook*. Cambridge: Cambridge University Press, 1974.
40
Ewert, Alfred. *The French Language*. 2nd ed. London: Faber and Faber, 1943. [1st ed. 1933]
41
Foulet, Lucien. *Petite syntaxe de l'ancien français*. Classiques français du moyen âge 21. 3rd ed. rev. Paris: Champion, 1930.
42
Gardner, R. and M.A. Greene. *Brief Description of Middle French Syntax*. Chapel Hill: North Carolina University Press, 1958.
43
Godefroy, Frédéric. *Dictionnaire de l'ancienne langue française et de tous ses dialectes du IXe au XVe siècle*. 10 vols. Paris: Vieweg, 1880-1902.
44
Gossen, C.Th. *Grammaire de l'ancien picard*. Paris: Klincksieck, 1970.

45
Grandgent, C.H. *An Outline of the Phonology and Morphology of Old Provençal*. Boston: D.C. Heath, 1905. [Reprint: AMS Press, 1973.]
46
Greimas, A.J. *Dictionnaire de l'ancien français jusqu'au milieu du XIVe siècle*. Paris: Larousse, 1969.
47
Harris, M.R. *Index inverse du Petit dictionnaire provençal-français*. Heidelberg: Winter, 1981.
48
Hasenohr, Geneviève. *Introduction à l'ancien français de Guy Raynaud de Lage*. Paris: SEDES, 1990.
49
Kibler, William W. *An Introduction to Old French*. New York: Modern Language Association of America, 1984.
50
Lafont, Robert. *Eléments de phonétique de l'occitan*. Valderiès: "Vent Terral," 1983.
51
Levy, Emil. *Petit dictionnaire provençal-français*. 5th edition. Heidelberg: Winter, 1973. [1st ed. 1909]
52
Levy, Emil. *Provenzalisches Supplement-Wörterbuch*. 8 vols. Leipzig: Reisland, 1894-1924.
This dictionary completes Raynouard, *Lexique* (B60).
53
Marchello-Nizia, Christiane. *Histoire de la langue française aux XIVe et XVe siècles*. Paris: Bordas, 1979.
54
Martin, Robert and Marc Wilmet. *Syntaxe du moyen français*. Vol. 2 of *Manuel du français du moyen âge*, ed. Yves Lefèvre. Bordeaux: Sobodi, 1980.
55
Ménard, Philippe. *Syntaxe de l'ancien français*. Vol. 1 of *Manuel du français du moyen âge*, ed. Yves Lefèvre. Revised edition. Bordeaux: Sobodi, 1973.
56
Moignet, Gérard. *Grammaire de l'ancien français*. Paris: Klincksieck, 1973.
57
Mok, Q.I.M. *Manuel pratique de morphologie d'ancien occitan*. Muiderberg: Coutinho, 1977.

58
Paden, William D. *An Introduction to Old Occitan.* New
  York: The Modern Language Association of America,
  forthcoming.
59
Pope, Mildred K. *From Latin to Modern French.* Manchester:
  Manchester University Press, 1952. [1st ed. 1934]
60
Raynouard, François-Just-Marie. *Lexique roman, ou dic-
  tionnaire de la langue des troubadours.* 6 vols. Paris,
  1836-45. [Reprint: Heidelberg: Winter, n.d. (1928?)]
61
Rickard, Peter. *Chrestomathie de la langue française au
  quinzième siècle.* Cambridge: Cambridge University
  Press, 1976.
62
Smith, Nathaniel and Thomas G. Bergin. *An Old Provençal
  Primer.* New York: Garland, 1984.
63
Zink, Gaston. *Morphologie du français médiéval.* Paris:
  Presses Universitaires de France, 1989.
64
Zink, Gaston. *Phonétique historique du français.* Paris:
  Presses Universitaires de France, 1986.

COLLECTIVE WORKS AND CONFERENCE PAPERS

Individual articles given separate listing in this *Guide*
are indicated following the main entry.

65
1380-1430: An International Style? Conference Papers.
  Musica Disciplina 41 (1987).
66
*Actes du 5e Congrès international de langue et littéra-
  ture d'oc et d'études franco-provençales.* Ed. G.
  Moignet and R. Lasalle. Nice, 1974.
67
*Actes du premier Congrès International de l'Association
  Internationale d'Etudes Occitanes.* Ed. Peter Ricketts.
  London: AIEO/Westfield College, 1987. B452, B470,
  B563, B598.

68

Aktuelle Fragen der musikbezogenen Mittelalterforschung: Texte zu einem Basler Kolloquium des Jahres 1975. Forum musicologicum (*Basler Beiträge zur Musikgeschichte*) 3. Ed. Hans Oesch and Wulf Arlt. Winterthur: Amadeus, 1982. B391, B704, B723.

69

L'Amour et la musique: la chanson d'amour aux XIIe-XIIIe siècles, troubadours et trouvères. IIe Journées musicologiques de Poitiers, 7-8 mai 1982. *Cahiers de civilisation médiévale* 25 (1982): 171-238. B454, B508, B541, B555, B655.

70

Atti del Secondo Congresso Internazionale della "Association Internationale d'Etudes Occitanes," Torino, 31 agosto-5 settembre 1987. Ed. Giuliano Gasca-Queirazza. Torino: AIEO/Dipartimento di Scienze Letterarie e Filologiche, Università di Torino, 1993. B603.

71

Baltzer, Rebecca A., Thomas Cable and James I. Wimsatt, eds. *The Union of Words and Music in Medieval Poetry.* Austin: University of Texas Press, 1991. One accompanying cassette (D810). B640, B725, B744, B783.

72

Bellenger, Yvonne and Danielle Quéruel, eds. *Thibaut de Champagne: Prince et poète au XIIIe siècle.* Lyon: La Manufacture, 1987. B456, B498, B607.

73

Boorman, Stanley, ed. *Studies in the Performance of Late Medieval Music.* Cambridge: Cambridge University Press, 1984. B740, B770.

74

Chrétien de Troyes and the Troubadours: Essays in memory of the late Leslie Topsfield. Ed. Peter S. Noble and Linda M. Paterson. Cambridge: St. Catharine's College, 1984. B473, B579.

75

Comberiati, Carmelo P. and Matthew C. Steel, eds. *Music from the Middle Ages Through The Twentieth Century. Essays in Honor of Gwynn McPeek.* New York: Gordon and Breach, 1988. B693, B695, B699, B748.

76

Companion to Medieval and Renaissance Music. Ed. Tess

Knighton and David Fallows. New York: Schirmer, 1992.

77

Contacts de langues, de civilisations et intertextualité. Actes du IIIème Congrès International de l'Association Internationale d'Etudes Occitanes, Montpellier, 20-26 septembre [août] 1990. Ed. Gérard Gouiran. 3 vols. Montpellier: Université Paul Valéry, 1992. B482, B536, B545, B602, B629.

78

Ebin, Lois, ed. *Vernacular Poetics in the Middle Ages.* Kalamazoo: Western Michigan University, 1984. B377, B501, B762.

79

L'Enseignement de la musique au Moyen Age et à la Renaissance. Colloque organisé par La Fondation Royaumont, l'A.R.I.M.M. et le C.N.R.S. Royaumont: Fondation Royaumont, 1987.

80

Grundriss der romanischen Literaturen des Mittelalters. Ed. Hans Robert Jauss *et al.* Heidelberg: Carl Winter, 1969-. Thirteen volumes projected; three include medieval lyric:
Vol. 1: *Généralités.* Dir. Maurice Delbouille. 1972.
Vol. 2: *Les Genres lyriques* (to 1300). Dir. Erich Köhler, Ulrich Mölk, Dietmar Rieger. Tome 1 B *La Lyrique Occitane*: Fasc. 3, 1987; Fasc. 4, 1980; Fasc. 5, 1979; Fasc. 7, Documentation, 1990.
Vol. 8: *La Littérature en France aux XIVe et XVe siècles.* Tome 1. Dir. Daniel Poirion. 1988.

81

Guillaume de Machaut Poète et Compositeur. Actes et Colloques, N° 23. Paris: Klincksieck, 1982.

82

Günther, Ursula and Ludwig Finscher, eds. *Musik und Text in der Mehrstimmigkeit des 14. und 15. Jahrhunderts.* Basel: Kassel, 1984. B741, B760, B782.

83

A Handbook of the Troubadours. Ed. F.R.P. Akehurst and Judith M. Davis. Berkeley: University of California Press, forthcoming 1995.

84

Hommage à Jean-Charles Payen. Farai chansoneta novele. Caen: Centre de Publications de l'Université de Caen,

1989. B463, B643.
85
Jackson, W.T.H., ed. *The Interpretation of Medieval Lyric Poetry*. New York: Columbia University Press, 1980. B500.
86
Kenyon, Nicholas, ed. *Authenticity and Early Music: A Symposium*. New York: Oxford University Press, 1988.
87
Lyrique romane médiévale: La Tradition des chansonniers. Actes du Colloque de Liège, 1989. Ed. Madeleine Tyssens. Liège: Bibliothèque de la Faculté de Philosophie et Lettres de l'Université de Liège, 1991. B124, B125, B126, B144, B146.
88
Mélanges de langue et de littérature occitanes en hommage à Pierre Bec. Poitiers: Université de Poitiers C.E.S.C.M., 1991. B544, B574, B582, B628, B635, B652.
89
Miscellanea di studi in onore di Aurelio Roncaglia a cinquant'anni dalla sua laurea. 4 vols. Modena: Mucchi, 1989. B462, B600.
90
Models of Musical Analysis: Music before 1600. Ed. Mark Everist. Oxford: Blackwell, 1992. B641, B690, B735.
91
La Musica nel tempo di Dante. Ed. Luigi Pestalozza. Milan: Unicopli, 1988. B381, B535.
92
Musicologie Médiévale: Notations et Séquences. Actes de la Table Ronde du C.N.R.S., 6-7 Septembre 1982. Ed. Michel Huglo. Paris: Champion, 1987. B543.
93
Musique, Littérature et Société au Moyen Age. Actes du Colloque. Ed. Danielle Buschinger and André Crépin. Université de Picardie. Diffusion Paris: Champion, 1980. B540, B547, B554.
94
Nichols, Jr., Stephen G., ed. *The Troubadour Lyric: Texts and Contexts*. *L'Esprit Créateur*, XIX (1979).
95
La Notation des musiques polyphoniques aux XIe-XIIIe siècles. Actes des Journées musicologiques de Poitiers,

9-10 mai 1986. *Cahiers de civilisation médievale* 31 (1988): 93-181.
96
Paden, William D., ed. *The Voice of the Trobairitz: Perspectives on the Women Troubadours.* Philadelphia: University of Pennsylvania Press, 1989.
97
Poirion, Daniel, ed. *Styles et valeurs: Pour une histoire de l'art littéraire au moyen âge.* Paris: SEDES, 1990.
98
Poirion, Daniel and Nancy Freeman Regalado, eds. *Contexts: Style and Values in Medieval Art and Literature.* New Haven: Yale University Press, 1991. Special Issue of *Yale French Studies.* B668.
99
Studia Occitanica in memoriam Paul Remy. Ed. Hans-Erich Keller. 2 vols. Kalamazoo: The Medieval Institute, 1986. B261, B496, B507, B556, B573, B634.
100
Studies in Medieval Music: Festschrift for Ernest H. Sanders, ed. Peter M. Lefferts and Brian Seirup. *Current Musicology* 45-47 (1990). B733.
101
"Symposium: 'Peripherie' und 'Zentrum' in der Geschichte der ein-und mehrstimmigen Musik des 12. bis 14. Jahrhunderts." In *Bericht über den internationalen musikwissenschaftlichen Kongress Berlin 1974,* ed. Hellmut Kühn and Peter Nitsche, 15-170. Kassel: Bärenreiter, 1980. B743.

MANUSCRIPTS

BIBLIOGRAPHIES

102
Brunel, Clovis. *Bibliographie des manuscrits littéraires en ancien provençal.* Paris: Droz, 1935.
103
Gennrich, Friedrich. "Die beiden neuesten Bibliographien altfranzösischer und altprovenzalisher Lieder."

Zeitschrift für romanische Philologie 61 (1921):
289-346.
Discusses and completes the *Bibliographies sommaires*
by Alfred Jeanroy.
104
Jeanroy, Alfred. *Bibliographie sommaire des chansonniers
français du moyen âge.* Classiques français du moyen âge
18. New York: Burt Franklin, 1971. [Reprint of Paris,
1918 edition.]
105
Jeanroy, Alfred. *Bibliographie sommaire des chansonniers
provençaux.* Classiques français du moyen âge 16.
Paris: Champion, 1966. [Reprint of 1916 edition.]
106
The New Grove Dictionary of Music and Musicians.
"Sources: III, Secular monophony; V, Early motet; VII,
French polyphony 1300-1420." David Fallows (III),
Ernest H. Sanders (V), Ursula Günther and Gilbert
Reaney (VII).
107
Raynaud, Gaston. *Bibliographie des chansonniers français
des XIIIᵉ et XIVᵉ siècles.* 2 vols. Paris: Vieweg,
1884. [Reprint: New York, 1970]
108
Reaney, Gilbert. *Manuscripts of Polyphonic Music (11th
to early 14th century).* Répertoire international des
sources musicales, B IV^1. München: G. Henle, 1966.
Contains description, bibliography and thematic
incipits for all known manuscripts up to the Ars Nova
period.
109
Reaney, Gilbert. *Manuscripts of Polyphonic Music (c.
1320-1400).* Répertoire international des sources
musicales, B IV^2. München: Henle, 1969.
Contains description, bibliography and thematic
incipits for polyphonic manuscripts between c.1320 and
1400.
110
von Fischer, Kurt. *Handschriften mit mehrstimmiger Musik
des 14., 15. und 16. Jahrhunderts.* Répertoire international des sources musicales, Series B IV $^{3-4}$. 2 vols.
München: G. Henle, 1972. Volume B IV^3 covers France.

111
Werner, Ziltener. "Zur Bibliographie des altfranzösischen
Liedes." *Zeitschrift für romanische Philologie* 77
(1961): 70-74.

See also PC for troubadour mss; R, and Linker (B18), for
trouvère mss.

FACSIMILES

112
Beck, Jean. *Les Chansonniers des Troubadours et des Trouvères.* 1: *Reproduction phototypique du Chansonnier
Cangé (BN fr.846);* 2: *Transcriptions.* Paris: Champion,
1927.
113
Le Chansonnier d'Arras (B.N. d'Arras, MS. 657). Reproduction phototypique par Alfred Jeanroy. Paris: Société
des Anciens Textes Français/Champion, 1925. [Reprint:
New York 1968]
114
*Le Chansonnier de l'Arsenal (Trouvères du XIIe-XIIIe
siècle): Reproduction phototypique du manuscrit 5198
de la Bibliothèque de l'Arsenal.* Transcription du
texte musical en notation moderne par Pierre Aubry;
introduction par Alfred Jeanroy. Paris: Geuthner, n.d.
115
*Le Chansonnier français de Saint-Germain-des-Près (Bibl.
Nat. fr. 20050).* Reproduction phototypique avec
transcription par P. Meyer et G. Raynaud. Paris:
Société des Anciens Textes Français, 1892.
116
Everist, Mark. *French 13th-Century Polyphony in the Brit-
ish Library: A Facsimile Edition of the Manuscripts
Additional 30091 and Egerton 2615 (folios 79-94v).*
London: The Plainsong and Mediaeval Music Society,
1988.
117
Le Manuscrit du Roi. Fascimile. Published by Jean
Baptiste Beck. *Corpus Cantilenarum Medii Aevi,* 1st
ser. 2 vols. Philadelphia: University of Pennsylvania Press, 1938.

118
Le Roman de Fauvel in the Edition of Mesire Chaillou de Pesstain. A Reproduction in Facsimile of the Complete Manuscript Paris, Bibliothèque Nationale, Fonds Français 146. Intro. Edward H. Roesner, François Avril, and Nancy Freeman Regalado. New York: Broude Brothers Limited, 1990.

MANUSCRIPT STUDIES

119
Aubrey, Elizabeth. *A Study of the Origins, History and Notation of the Troubadour Chansonnier Paris, Bibliothèque Nationale, F.Fr. 22543.* Ph.D. dissertation, University of Maryland, 1982.
120
Aubrey, Elizabeth. "The Transmission of Troubadour Melodies: The Testimony of Paris, Bibliothèque Nationale, f.fr. 22543." *Text* 3 (1987): 211-50.
Description of R from the standpoint of the music. Finds that there must have been several scribes for the music and they probably used several music exemplars. The Guiraut Riquier section is an exception because it must have had its own unified model. It is possible that there existed a manuscript tradition for melodies separate from the poetic tradition.
121
Avalle, D'Arco S. *La letteratura medievale in lingua d'oc nella sua tradizione manoscritta: Problemi di critica testuale.* Turin: Giulio Einaudi, 1961.
122
Bent, Margaret. "Some Criteria For Establishing Relationships Between Sources of Late-Medieval Polyphony." In *Music in Medieval and Early Modern Europe*, ed. Iain Fenlon, 295-317. Cambridge: Cambridge University Press, 1981.
123
Bent, Margaret. "The Machaut Manuscripts Vg, B and E." *Musica Disciplina* 37 (1983): 53-82.
124
Bertolucci-Pizzorusso, Valeria. "Osservazioni e proposte per la ricerca sui canzonieri individuali." In *Lyrique*

*romane médiévale: La Tradition des chansonniers, Actes
du Colloque de Liège, 1989,* ed. Madeleine Tyssens, 273-
302. Liège: Bibliothèque de la Faculté de Philosophie
et Lettres de l'Université de Liège, 1991.
Addresses the concept of author's "book."
125
Brunel-Lobrichon, Geneviève. "L'Iconographie du chansonnier provençal R. Essai d'interprétation." In *Lyrique
romane médiévale: La Tradition des chansonniers, Actes
du Colloque de Liège, 1989,* ed. Madeleine Tyssens, 245-
272. Liège: Bibliothèque de la Faculté de Philosophie
et Lettres de l'Université de Liège, 1991.
126
Crespo, Roberto. "Il raggruppamento dei 'jeu-partis' nei
canzonieri A, a, E, b." In *Lyrique romane médiévale:
La Tradition des chansonniers, Actes du Colloque de
Liège, 1989,* ed. Madeleine Tyssens, 399-428. Liège:
Bibliothèque de la Faculté de Philosophie et Lettres
de l'Université de Liège, 1991.
The desire to group songs of prominent author/composers
has determined the organization of the manuscript.
Jehan Bretel and Guillaume le Vinier are the main
examples.
127
Earp, Lawrence. "Machaut's Role in the Production of
Manuscripts of His Works." *Journal of the American
Musicological Society* 42 (1989): 461-503.
Detailed discussion of the Machaut manuscripts, in a
chronological order spelled out in the article, and in
the light of recent literary and art-historical studies, in order to assess principles of organization
within the manuscripts and Machaut's evolving view of
manuscript organization. It is not possible to state
with certainty to what degree Machaut supervised his
manuscript production, but from indirect evidence, a
strong case can be made for C and A, with V_g and F-G
also likely based on authoritative materials.
128
Eusebi, Mario. "Singolarità del canzoniere provenzale R."
Romanische Forschungen 95 (1983): 111-16; "Tracce di
trasmissione orale nel canzoniere R." *Marche Romane* 33
(1983): 59-64.
Using examples from Arnaut Daniel, argues that at

least one source for MS R was oral.
129
Everist, Mark. *Polyphonic Music in Thirteenth-Century France: Aspects of Sources and Distribution.* New York: Garland, 1989.
130
Gomez, Mª Carmen. "El Manuscrito 823 de Montserrat (Biblioteca del Monasterio)." *Musica Disciplina* 36 (1982): 39-93.
Description and edition of a Spanish source of late 14th- and early 15th-century French polyphony, containing anonymous rondeaux, virelais, and ballades.
131
Günther, Ursula. "Unusual Phenomena in the Transmission of Late 14th Century Polyphonic Music." *Musica Disciplina* 38 (1984): 87-109.
Proposes that despite the many compositions originating in the South (Aragon, Foix, Avignon) which are included in it, the Codex Chantilly, Musée Condé 564, was copied in Florence from a source written in Paris.
132
Huot, Sylvia. "Visualization and Memory: The Illustration of Troubadour Lyric in a Thirteenth-Century Manuscript." *Gesta* 31 (1992): 3-14.
Discusses illustrations in troubadour chansonnier N (Pierpont Morgan 819).
133
Karp, Theodore. "The Trouvère Manuscript Tradition." In *Twenty-fifth Anniversary Festschrift (1937-1962)*, ed. Albert Mell, 25-52. New York: Queens College Press, 1964.
134
Marshall, J.H. "The Transmission of the Lyric *Lais* in Old French *Chansonnier T.*" In *The Editor and the Text*, ed. Philip E. Bennett and Graham A. Runnalls, 20-32. Edinburgh: Edinburgh University Press, 1990.
135
Norwood, Patricia P. "Performance Manuscripts from the Thirteenth Century?" *College Music Symposium* 26 (1986): 92-6.
Discussion of motet collections.
136
Norwood, Patricia P. "Evidence Concerning the Provenance

of the Bamberg Codex." *The Journal of Musicology* 8 (1990): 491-504.

137
Parker, Ian. "A Propos de la tradition manuscrite des chansons de trouvères." *Revue de musicologie* 64 (1978): 181-202.

138
Parker, Ian. "Notes on the Chansonnier Saint-Germain-des-Prés." *Music and Letters* 60 (1979): 261-80.

139
Schubert, Johann. *Die Handschrift Paris Bibl. Nat. Fr. 1591: Kritische Untersuchung der Trouvèrehandschrift R.* Frankfurt am Main, 1963.

140
Schwan, Eduard. *Die altfranzösische Liederhandschriften, ihre Verhältniss, ihre Entstehung, und ihre Bestimmung.* Berlin: Weidmann, 1886.
Basic description of chansonniers and discussion of their relationships.

141
Scully, Terence. "French Songs in Aragon: The Place of Origin of the *Chansonnier* Chantilly, Musée Condé 564." In *Courtly Literature: Culture and Context.* Selected Papers from the 5th Triennial Congress of the International Courtly Literature Society, Dalfsen, The Netherlands, 9-16 August, 1986, ed. Keith Busby and Erik Kooper, 509-21. Amsterdam/Philadelphia: Benjamins, 1990.
Argues that *Chantilly 564* was compiled at the court of John I of Aragon between 1392 and 1396.

142
Stevens, John. "The Manuscript Presentation and Notation of Adam de la Halle's Courtly Chansons." In *Source Materials and the Interpretation of Music: A Memorial Volume to Thurston Dart*, ed. Ian Bent, 29-64. London: Stainer & Bell, 1981.

143
Tavera, Antoine. "Le Chansonnier d'Urfé et les problèmes qu'il pose." *Cultura Neolatina* 38 (1978): 233-50.

144
Tyssens, Madeleine. "Les copistes du chansonnier français U." In *Lyrique romane médiévale: La Tradition des chansonniers, Actes du Colloque de Liège, 1989,* ed.

Madeleine Tyssens, 379-97. Liège: Bibliothèque de la
Faculté de Philosophie et Lettres de l'Université de
Liège, 1991.
Sees several hands at work in the chansonnier Saint-
Germain-des-Près, close in time and geographical
region (Lorraine script), and refutes the idea that
this was a "jongleur" manuscript.
145
Wolinski, Mary E. "The Compilation of the Montpellier
Codex." *Early Music History* 11 (1992): 263-301.
Proposes a new dating of the Montpellier codex that
invites re-thinking of the development of the motet in
the last half of the thirteenth century.
146
Ziino, Agostino. "Caratteri e significato della tradizione musicale trobadorica." In *Lyrique romane
médiévale: La Tradition des chansonniers*, Actes du
Colloque de Liège, 1989, ed. Madeleine Tyssens, 85-218.
Liège: Bibliothèque de la Faculté de Philosophie et
Lettres de l'Université de Liège, 1991.
Tabulation and discussion of transmission of troubadour
music, based on MSS R, G, W, X and including V which
has some staves but no music. Argues for independent
transmission of the music, probably more dependent on
oral transmission than the texts (written textual exemplars would have been mostly without music).
147
Zufferey, François. *Recherches linguistiques sur les
chansonniers provençaux*. Geneva: Droz, 1987.

MEDIEVAL DOCUMENTS AND THEORETICAL SOURCES

MUSIC

References to sources on musical theory may be
found in Andrew Hughes (B14); in Chailley (B6); in the
New Grove article "Theory, theorists"; in Michel Huglo,
"Bibliographie des éditions et études relatives à la
théorie musicale du Moyen Age (1972-1987)," *Acta Musicologia* 60 (1988): 229-72; in Karp (B16); and in Jackson

(B15), updated each year in *Performance Practice Review*.
For a discussion of medieval treatises "De rithmis," see
Fassler (B388). Listed here are collections of general
interest and some selected editions and translations.

148
Harrán, Don. *Word-Tone Relations in Musical Thought:
From Antiquity to the Seventeenth Century*. Musicological Studies and Documents 40. American Institute
of Musicology. Stuttgart: Hänssler-Verlag, 1986.
One chapter of this book treats the period covered by
the guide. There is an extensive bibliography.

149
Rowen, Ruth Halle. *Music Through Sources and Documents*.
Englewood Cliffs: Prentice Hall, 1979.
Chapters 4 and 5 concern the Middle Ages.

150
Schueller, Herbert M. *The Idea of Music: An Introduction
to Musical Aesthetics in Antiquity and the Middle
Ages*. Kalamazoo: Medieval Institute Publications, 1988.
Philosophically oriented discussion of sources and documents. The second part of the book is pertinent to the
subject of this guide. The main theoretical figures are
listed and their work summarized. The bibliography provides comprehensive reference to theorists accessible
in translation at the time of the book's publication.

151
Strunk, Oliver. *Source Readings in Music History*. New
York: Norton, 1950. Standard collection of excerpts
from theoretical sources in translation (no Latin
originals given). Sections II-IV concern the Middle
Ages.

152
Weiss, Piero and Richard Taruskin, eds. *Music in the
Western World: A History in Documents*. New York:
Schirmer, 1984.
Part II contains documents from the Middle Ages. Excel-
lent presentation, with useful glossary for the non
specialist.

Anonymous IV
153
Yudkin, Jeremy, ed. *The Music Treatise of Anonymous IV:*

A New Translation. Musicological Studies and Documents, 41. American Institute of Musicology, 1985.

Anonymous of St. Emmeram
154
Yudkin, Jeremy, ed. *De musica mensurata: The Anonymous of St. Emmeram.* Bloomington: Indiana University Press, 1990.

Augustine, Bishop of Hippo
155
Augustine, St., *De Musica libri sex (Oeuvres de Saint Augustin, VII).* Ed. Guy Finaert and F.J. Ronard. Bruges/Paris: Desclée De Brouwer, 1947. *On Music.* Trans. Robert Catesby Taliaferro. In *The Fathers of the Church New Translation,* 4. Washington D.C.: The Catholic University of America Press, c.1947. [Reprint 1977] Translation also published as *Saint Augustine On Music,* Annapolis: The Saint John's Bookstore, 1939.

Berkeley Manuscript
156
Ellsworth, Oliver B. *The Berkeley Manuscript: A New Critical Text and Translation.* Lincoln: University of Nebraska Press, 1984.

Boethius
157
Bower, Calvin M., ed. and trans. *Fundamentals of Music. Anicius Manlius Severinus Boethius.* Music Theory Translation Series, ed. Claude V. Palisca. New Haven: Yale University Press, 1989.

Franco of Cologne
158
Franconis de Colonia. *Ars cantus mensurabilis.* Ed. Gilbert Reaney and André Gilles. *Corpus Scriptorum de Musica,* vol 18. American Institute of Musicology, 1974.

Guido of Arezzo
159
Hucbald, Guido, and John on Music: Three Medieval

Treatises. Trans. Warren Babb. Ed., with introductions, by Claude V. Palisca. New Haven: Yale University Press, 1978. Translation of the *Micrologus* with an introduction by Claude Palisca.

Hucbald
160
Hucbald, Guido, and John on Music: Three Medieval Treatises. Trans. Warren Babb. Ed., with introductions, by Claude V. Palisca. New Haven: Yale University Press, 1978. Translation of the *De harmonica institutione* with introduction by Claude Palisca.

Jacobus of Liège
161
Jacobi Leodiensis (Jacob of Liège). *Speculum musicae*, ed. Roger Bragard. 7 vols. Rome: American Institute of Musicology, 1955-73.

Jean de Muris
162
Johannes de Muris. *Notitia artis musicae; Compendium musicae practicae*, ed. Ulrich Michels. In *Corpus Scriptorum de Musica*, vol. 17. American Institute of Musicology, 1972. [See also for Muris: Martin Gerbert, *Scriptores ecclesiastici de musica sacra*, Vol. III. St. Blasien, 1784 and C.E.H. Coussemaker, *Scriptorum de Musica Medii Aevi*, Paris, 1864-76. Vol. III.]

Johannes Ciconia
163
Ciconia, Johannes. *Nova Musica and De Proportionibus.* Ed. Oliver B. Ellsworth. Lincoln: University of Nebraska Press, 1993.

Johannes de Grocheio
164
Grocheo, Johannes de. *De Musica.* Trans. Albert Seay. Colorado Springs: Colorado College Music Press, 1974.
165
Page, Christopher. "Johannes de Grocheio on Secular Music: A Corrected Text and A New Translation." *Plainsong and Medieval Music* 2 (1993): 17-41.

John of Afflighem (John Cotton)
166
Hucbald, Guido, and John on Music: Three Medieval Treatises. Trans. Warren Babb. Ed., with introductions, by
Claude V. Palisca. New Haven: Yale University Press,
1978. Translation of De Musica with introduction by
Claude Palisca.

John of Garland
167
Johannes de Garlandia. Concerning Measured Music (De
mensurabili musica). Trans. Stanley H. Birnbaum.
Colorado Springs: Colorado College Music Press, 1978.

Musica Enchiriadis
168
Rosenstiel, Leonie. Music Handbook (Musica Enchiriadis).
Colorado Springs: Colorado College Music Press, 1976.
Defective translation.
169
Schmid, Hans. Musica et Scolica enchiriadis. Veröffent-
lichungen der musikhistorischen Kommission 3. Munich:
Bayerische Akademie der Wissenschaften, 1981. Critical
edition based on all manuscripts.
170
Musica enchiriadis and Scolica enchiriadis. Trans.
Raymond Erickson. Ed. Claude Palisca, forthcoming,
Yale University Press.

Philippe de Vitry
171
Philippi de Vitriaco, Ars Nova. Ed. Gilbert Reaney,
André Gilles and Jean Maillard. Corpus Scriptorum de
Musica, Vol. 8. American Institute of Musicology, 1964.
172
Philippe de Vitry. "Ars Nova." Trans. Leon Plantinga.
Journal of Music Theory 5 (1961): 204-33.

Summa musice
173
Page, Christopher, ed. The Summa musice: A Thirteenth-
Century Manual for Singers. Cambridge: Cambridge
University Press, 1991.

POETRY

References to works on rhetoric and poetic theory may
be found in Kelly (B17) and in Murphy (B21). A brief list
of relevant publications appears as the Preface to the
paperback edition of *Three Medieval Rhetorical Arts*, ed.
James J. Murphy, listed below. Charles Sears Baldwin's
Medieval Rhetoric and Poetic (to 1400) (New York, 1928,
Reprint: Gloucester, MA, 1959), though dated, can still
yield useful information. Listings here emphasize treatises that could be useful for vernacular works.

Arts poétiques
174
Faral, Edmond. *Les Arts Poétiques du XIIe et du XIIIe
siècle*. Paris: Champion, 1958. Standard collection of
texts of important *artes poetriae*.

Dante Alighieri
175
Dante Alighieri. *De vulgari eloquentia*. Ed. Aristide
Marigo. Florence: Le Monnier, 1968.

Eustache Deschamps
176
Deschamps, Eustache. *L'Art de dictier et de fere
chançons*. *Oeuvres complètes d'Eustache Deschamps*, ed.
A. Queux de Saint-Hilaire and Gaston Raynaud. 11 vols.
Société des Anciens Textes Français. Paris: Firmin
Didot, 1878-1903. 7:266-93.

Geoffrey of Vinsauf
177
Gallo, Ernest A. *The Poetria Nova and Its Sources in
Early Rhetorical Doctrine*. The Hague: Mouton, 1971.
Translation with Latin facing.
178
Geoffrey of Vinsauf. *Poetria Nova*. Trans. Margaret F.
Nims. Toronto: Pontifical Institute of Mediaeval
Studies, 1967.
179
Murphy, James J., ed. *Three Medieval Rhetorical Arts*.

Berkeley: University of California Press, 1985
(paperback edition; 1st ed 1971). Contains Anonymous
of Bologna, and Robert of Basevorn in translation, in
addition to Vinsauf.

John of Garland
180
Lawler, Traugott, ed. and trans. *Parisiana Poetria of
John of Garland*. New Haven: Yale University Press,
1974.

Leys d'amors
181
Leys d'amors. (Molinier, Guilhem.) *Las Flors del Gay
Saber, estier dichas Las Leys d'Amors*. Trans. d'Aguilar
and d'Escouloubre, revised and completed by Adolphe-F.
Gatien-Arnoult. Monumens de la littérature romane 1-3.
Toulouse: Privat, 1841-43. [Reprint: Slatkine 1977]
Toulouse Version A.
182
Leys d'amors. Anglade, Joseph. *Las Leys d'amors*. 4 vols.
Toulouse: Privat, 1919-20. [Reprint: New York: Johnson,
1971] Manuscript of the Académie des Jeux Floraux.
Toulouse Version B, with excerpts of Barcelona Version
b in Part IV.

Matthew of Vendôme
183
Galyon, Aubrey E. *Matthew of Vendôme: The Art of Versification*. Ames: Iowa State University Press, 1980.
184
Paar, Roger P. *Matthew of Vendôme: Ars versificatoria*.
Milwaukee: Marquette University Press, 1981.

Raimon Vidal de Besalù
185
Marshall, John H. *The Razos de trobar of Raimon Vidal
and Associated Texts*. London: Oxford University Press,
1972. The associated texts include Terramagnino da
Pisa, *Doctrina d'Acort*; Jofre de Foixà, *Regles de
Trobar*; *Doctrina de compondre dictats*; Two anonymous
treatises from MS. Ripoll 129.

Uc Faidit

186
Marshall, John H. *The* Donatz Proensals *of Uc Faidit.*
London and New York: Oxford University Press, 1969.

In addition to treatises, vernacular works themselves yield important information about medieval song.
Christopher Page, *Voices and Instruments* (B407), furnishes a "selective typology of musical references
in French narrative fiction to 1300" in Appendices, 151-
209. Two articles may be cited as examples of how to
exploit literary references: Elizabeth Aubrey, "References to Music in Old Occitan Literature" (B453); and
Sylvia Huot, "Voices and Instruments in Medieval French
Secular Music" (B393).

MODERN ANTHOLOGIES AND EDITIONS

ANTHOLOGIES

187
Aubry, Pierre and Joseph Bédier. *Les Chansons de Croi-
sade.* Paris: Champion, 1909. [Reprint: Slatkine, 1974]
Transcriptions of melodies in an Appendix.
188
Bartsch, Karl. *Altfranzösische Romanzen und Pastourellen.*
Leipzig: Vogel, 1870.
189
Bartsch, Karl. *Chrestomathie de l'ancien français.* 12th
edition revised by Leo Wiese. New York: Hafner, 1958.
Accompanying grammar and glossary still useful.
190
Bartsch, Karl and E. Koschwitz. *Chrestomathie provençale.*
Revised edition. Hildesheim/New York, 1971.
Glossary still useful.
191
Baumgartner, Emmanuèle and Françoise Ferrand. *Poèmes
d'amour des XIIe et XIIIe siècles.* Paris: 10/18, 1983.

192
Bec, Pierre. *Nouvelle anthologie de la lyrique occitane du moyen âge*. Avignon: Aubanel, 1970.
193
Bec, Pierre. *Anthologie des troubadours*. Paris: 10/18, 1979.
194
Bec, Pierre. *La Lyrique française* (B458), vol. 2.
195
Boutière, Jean and A.H. Schutz. *Biographies des troubadours*. 2nd revised edition. Paris: Nizet, 1964.
196
Bruckner, Matilda Tomaryn, Laurie Shepard and Sarah White. *The Songs of the Women Troubadours*. New York: Garland, forthcoming.
197
Cluzel, Irenée-Marcel and Léon Pressouyre. *La Poésie lyrique d'oïl*. 2nd edition revised by I.-M. Cluzel and Jean Mouzat. Paris: Nizet, 1969.
198
Dufournet, Jean. *Anthologie de la poésie lyrique française des XIIe et XIIIe siècles*. Paris: Gallimard, 1989.
199
Egan, Margarita. *The Vidas of the Troubadours*. New York: Garland, 1974. English translation based on Boutière and Schutz (B195).
200
Ferrand, Françoise and François Suard. *Quatre siècles de poésie: La lyrique médiévale au nord de la France du XIIe au XVe siècle*. Corps 9. Troesnes: Limonaire, 1993.
201
Gennrich, Friedrich. *Rondeaux, Virelais und Balladen aus dem Ende des XII., dem XIII. und dem ersten den über Drittel des XIV. Jh., mit überlieferten Melodien*. 3 vols. Vols. 1 and 2: Gesellschaft für Romanische Literatur 43, 47. Dresden, 1921; Göttingen, 1927. Vol. 3: *Das altfranzösische Rondeau und Virelai im 12. und 13. Jahrhundert*. Summa Musicae Medii Aevi 10, Langen bei Frankfurt, 1963.
202
Goldin, Frederick. *Lyrics of the Troubadours and Trouvères*. New York: Anchor, 1973.

203
Hamlin, Frank R., Peter T. Ricketts, and John Hathaway.
*Introduction à l'étude de l'ancien provençal: Textes
d'étude*. 2nd ed. Geneva: Droz, 1985. [1st ed. 1967]
204
Hill, Raymond Thompson, and Thomas Goddard Bergin. *An-
thology of the Provençal Troubadours*. New Haven: Yale
University Press, 1941. 2d ed. rev. by Thomas G.
Bergin with the collaboration of Susan Olson, William D.
Paden, Jr., Nathaniel Smith. 2 vols. New Haven: Yale
University Press, 1973.
205
Jeanroy, Alfred, Louis Brandin and Pierre Aubry. *Lais et
descorts français du 13e siècle*. Paris: H. Welter,
1901.
206
Paden, William D. *The Medieval Pastourelle*. 2 vols. New
York: Garland, 1987.
207
Press, Alan R. *Anthology of Troubadour Lyric Poetry*.
Edinburgh Bilingual Library, 3, Edinburgh University.
Austin: University of Texas Press, 1971.
208
Riquer, Martín de. *Los trovadores: historia literaria y
textos*. 3 vols. Letras e Ideas. Barcelona: Ariel, 1983.
209
Rivière, Jean-Claude. *Pastourelles. Introduction à
l'étude formelle des pastourelles anonymes françaises
des XIIe et XIIIe siècles*. 3 vols. Geneva: Droz, 1974,
1975, 1976.
210
Rosenberg, Samuel N. and Hans Tischler. *Chantar m'estuet:
Songs of the Trouvères*. Bloomington: Indiana University
Press, 1981. [To appear in French translation in the
series "Lettres Gothiques," Livre de Poche.]
211
Switten, Margaret and Howell Chickering, eds. *The Medieval Lyric: Anthologies and Cassettes for Teaching. A
Project Supported by the National Endowment for the
Humanities and Mount Holyoke College*. 3 Anthologies;
Commentary volume; 5 audio cassettes. South Hadley,
MA: Mount Holyoke College, 1988-9. Troubadour and
trouvère songs and Machaut's *Remede de Fortune*. See
also B419, D807.

212
Wilkins, Nigel. *One Hundred Ballades, Rondeaux and Vire-lais from the Late Middle Ages*. Cambridge: Cambridge University Press, 1969.
213
Wilkins, Nigel. *Armes, Amours, Dames, Chevalerie: An Anthology of French Song from the Fourteenth Century*. A performing edition. Cambridge: The New Press, 1987.
214
Zink, Michel. *Belle: Essai sur les chansons de toile suivi d'une édition et d'une traduction* (B654). Edition of the *chansons de toile* with music transcribed by Gérard Le Vot.

TROUBADOURS (12th and 13th centuries)

Listed here are editions of those named troubadours for whom we have a significant number of melodies or whose importance is such as to justify inclusion. If an edition of a specific troubadour includes music, that fact is indicated. Editions of the troubadour melodic corpus are given separately. Anonymous songs are not listed. Many can be found in the general anthologies. For editions of anonymous songs, the bibliography section of Frank Chambers's *Proper Names in the Lyrics of the Troubadours* (B7) can be consulted; it supplements the listing of editions of anonymous songs furnished by István Frank (*Répertoire métrique* [B12], Vol. II). Additional information on troubadour editions is furnished by Taylor *La Littérature occitane* (B29), supplemented by issues of the *Bulletins de l'Association Internationale d'Etudes Occitanes* (Royal Holloway and Bedford New College, University of London). One may consult also the *Dictionnaire des lettres françaises: Le Moyen Age* (B8).

Troubadour Corpus: Melodies Only

215
Sesini, Ugo. *Le Melodie trobadoriche nel canzoniere provenzale della Biblioteca Ambrosiana R71 Sup*. Torino, 1942. [Also *Studi medievali*, n.s. 12 (1939): 1-101; 13 (1940): 1-107; 14 (1941): 31-105; 15 (1942): 189-90, plus 24 pp. of facsimiles.]

216
Gennrich, Friedrich. *Der musikalische Nachlass der Trou-badours*. 3 vols. Summa musicae medii aevi 3, 4, and 15. Darmstadt, 1958, 1960, 1965.
217
Fernandez de la Cuesta, Ismael. *Las cançons dels troba-dors*. Toulouse: Institut d'estudis occitans, 1979.
218
Van der Werf, Hendrik. *The Extant Troubadour Melodies*. Rochester, 1984. Texts (the first stanza only for each song) edited by Gerald A. Bond.

Aimeric de Peguillan
219
Shepard, William P. and Frank M. Chambers. *The Poems of Aimeric de Peguilhan*. Evanston: Northwestern University Press, 1950.

Arnaut Daniel
220
Toja, Gianluigi. *Arnaut Daniel: Canzoni*. Florence: Sansoni, 1960.
Melodies in facsimile and transcribed.
221
Perugi, Maurizio. *Le canzoni di Arnaut Daniel*. 2 vols. Milan/Naples: Ricciardi, 1978.
222
Wilhelm, James J. *The Poetry of Arnaut Daniel*. New York: Garland, 1981.
Melodies in an appendix, facsimiles and transcriptions.
223
Eusebi, Mario. *Arnaut Daniel: Il sirventese e le canzoni*. Milan: Vanni Scheiwiller, 1984.

Arnaut de Maroill
224
Johnston, Ronald C. *Les Poésies lyriques du troubadour Arnaut de Mareuil*. Paris: Droz, 1935.

Beatritz de Dia (La Comtessa de Dia)
225
Kussler-Ratyé, Gabrielle. "Les Chansons de la comtesse

Béatrix de Dia." *Archivum Romanicum* 1 (1917): 161-82.

See Rieger, *Trobairitz* (B268).
The songs of the Comtessa de Dia occupy pp. 585-626.

Berenguier de Palazol
226
Jeanroy, Alfred and Pierre Aubry. "Huit chansons de Berenger de Palazol." In *Annuari de l'Institut d'Estudis Catalans* II (1908): 520-40.
227
Newcombe, Terence H. "The Troubadour Berenger de Palazol: A Critical Edition of his Poems." *Nottingham Medieval Studies* 15 (1971): 54-95.
228
Beretta Spampinato, M. *Berenguer de Palol, Poesie.* Modena: Mucchi, 1978.

Bernart de Ventadorn
229
Appel, Carl. *Bernart von Ventadorn, Seine Lieder.* Halle: Niemeyer, 1915. Melodies appended in facsimile.
230
Appel, Carl. "Die Singweisen Bernarts von Ventadorn nach dem Handschriften mitgeteilt." Heft 81 in *Beihefte zur Zeitschrift für romanische Philologie.* Halle: Niemeyer, 1934.
231
Nichols, Stephen G. Jr. et al. *The Songs of Bernart de Ventadorn.* University of North Carolina Studies in the Romance Languages and Literatures, No. 39. Chapel Hill: University of North Carolina Press, 1965.
232
Lazar, Moshé. *Bernard de Ventadorn, troubadour du XIIe siècle: Chansons d'amour.* Paris: Klincksieck, 1966.

Bertran de Born
233
Gouiran, Gérard. *L'Amour et la Guerre: l'oeuvre de Bertran de Born.* 2 vols. Aix-en-Provence: Université de Provence, 1985.
234
Gouiran, Gérard. *Le Seigneur-Troubadour d'Hautefort:*

l'oeuvre de Bertran de Born. 2nd edition. Aix-en-
Provence: Université de Provence, 1987.
235
Paden, William D. Jr., Tilde Sankovitch and Patricia H.
Stäblein. *The Poems of the Troubadour Bertran de Born*.
Berkeley: University of California Press, 1986.
Melodies transcribed in Appendix.

Cadenet
236
Appel, Carl. *Der Trobador Cadenet*. Halle: Niemeyer, 1920.
[Reprint: Slatkine, 1974]
237
Zemp, Josef. *Les Poésies du troubadour Cadenet*. Berne:
Lang, 1978.

Daude de Pradas
238
Schutz, A.H. *Poésies de Daude de Pradas*. Paris: Didier,
1933. [Reprint: 1971]

Folquet de Marseilla
239
Stronski, Stanislaw. *Le Troubadour Folquet de Marseille*.
Cracow: Spolka Widawnicza Polska, 1910.

Gaucelm Faidit
240
Mouzat, Jean. *Les Poèmes de Gaucelm Faidit*. Paris: Nizet,
1965.

Gui d'Ussel
241
Audiau, Jean. *Les Poésies des quatre troubadours d'Ussel*.
Paris: Delagrave, 1922.
2 facsimiles of music.

Guilhem de Peitieu (Guillaume IX / William IX)
242
Pasero, Nicolò. *Guglielmo IX d'Aquitania: Poesie*.
Modena: Mucchi, 1973.
243
Bond, Gerald A. *The Poetry of William VII, Count of*

Poitiers, IX Duke of Aquitaine. New York: Garland, 1982.
Excellent supporting material with the melody fragment from the *Jeu de Sainte Agnès* in facsimile and transcribed.

Guiraut de Borneill
244
Sharman, Ruth Verity. *The 'Cansos' and 'Sirventes' of the Troubadour Giraut de Borneil: A Critical Edition.* Cambridge: Cambridge University Press, 1989.
Melodies in an appendix, but in Gennrich's rhythmic transcriptions only, long outdated at the time of this edition.

Guiraut Riquier
245
Anglés, Higinio. "Les Mélodies del trobador Guiraut Riquier." *Estudis Universitaris Catalans* 2 (1926): 1-78.
246
Mölk, Ulrich. *Guiraut Riquier. Las Cansos.* Heidelberg: Winter, 1962.
247
Longobardi, Monica. "I *vers* del trovatore Guiraut Riquier." *Studi mediolatini e volgari* 29 (1982-3): 17-163.

Jaufre Rudel
248
Jeanroy, Alfred. *Les Chansons de Jaufré Rudel.* 2e ed. revue. Classiques français du moyen âge 15. Paris: Champion, 1965. [1st ed. 1915]
249
Pickens, Rupert T. *The Songs of Jaufré Rudel.* Toronto: Pontifical Institute, 1978.
250
Wolf, George and Roy Rosenstein. *The Poetry of Cercamon and Jaufre Rudel.* New York: Garland, 1983.
Melodies in an appendix, facsimiles and transcriptions by Hendrik van der Werf.
251
Chiarini, Georgio. *Il canzoniere di Jaufre Rudel.*

L'Aquila: Lapadre, c.1985.

Marcabru
252
Dejeanne, J.M.L. *Poésies complètes du troubadour
Marcabru.* Toulouse: Privat, 1909. [Reprint: New York:
Johnson, 1971]

Monge de Montaudon
253
Routledge, Michael J. *Les Poésies du Moine de Montaudon.*
Montpellier: Centre d'Etudes Occitanes, 1977.
Melodies appended in modern rhythmic transcriptions.

Peire d'Alvergne
254
Del Monte, Alberto. *Peire d'Alvernha: Liriche; testo,
traduzione, e note.* Turin: Loescher-Chiantore, 1955.

Peire Cardenal
255
Lavaud, René. *Poésies complètes du troubadour Peire
Cardenal (1180-1278).* Toulouse: Privat, 1957.
Appendix on music with facsimiles and rhythmic tran-
scriptions into modern notation.

Peire Vidal
256
Anglade, Joseph. *Les Poésies de Peire Vidal.* 2nd ed.
Classiques français du moyen âge 11. Paris: Champion,
1923. [1st ed. 1913]
257
Avalle, D'Arco S. *Peire Vidal, Poésie.* 2 vols. Milan:
Napoli, 1960.

Peirol
258
Aston, S.C. *Peirol, Troubadour of Auvergne.* Cambridge:
Cambridge University Press, 1953.
Facsimiles of the melodies appended.

Perdigon
259
Chaytor, Henry J. *Les Chansons de Perdigon.* Classiques

français du moyen âge 53. Paris: Champion, 1926.

Pons de Capdoill
260
Napolski, Max von. *Leben und Werke des Trobadors Ponz de Capduoill*. Halle: Niemeyer, 1879.
261
Rivière, Jean-Claude. "En prélude à une nouvelle édition de Pons de Capdoill. La chanson 'Us gais conortz me fai gajamen far' (PC 375,27)." In *Studia Occitanica in memoriam Paul Remy*, ed. Hans-Erich Keller, 1:241-51. Kalamazoo: The Medieval Institute, 1986.
New edition of one of the songs with music, but music is not mentioned.

Raimbaut d'Aurenga
262
Pattison, Walter T. *The Life and Works of the Troubadour Raimbaut d'Orange*. Minneapolis: University of Minnesota Press, 1952.

Raimbaut de Vaqueiras
263
Linskill, Joseph. *The Poems of the Troubadour Raimbaut de Vaqueiras*. The Hague: Mouton, 1964.

Raimon de Miraval
264
Topsfield, Leslie. *Les poésies du Troubadour Raimon de Miraval*. Paris: Nizet, 1971.

See Switten, *The Cansos of Raimon de Miraval* (B627).
Part II is an edition of the 22 *cansos* with melodies, music and texts.

Rigaut (Richart) de Berbezilh
265
Braccini, Mauro. *Rigaut de Barbezieux: Le canzoni, testo e commento*. Florence: L.S. Olschki, 1960.
266
Varvaro, Alberto. *Rigaut de Berbezilh*. Bari: Adriatica, 1960.

Uc de Saint Circ
267
Jeanroy, Alfred and J.-J. Salverda de Grave. *Poésies de Uc de Saint-Circ*. Toulouse: Privat, 1913.

Trobairitz corpus
268
Rieger, Angelica. *Trobairitz: Der Beitrag der Frau in der altokzitanischen höfischen Lyrik. Edition des Gesamtkorpus*. Beihefte zur Zeitschrift für romanische Philologie, 233. Tübingen: Niemeyer, 1991.

269
Bond, Gerald A. "The Last Unpublished Troubadour Songs." *Speculum* 60 (1985): 827-49.
Four songs, possibly refrain songs, discovered by Higinio Anglés but whose texts had never previously been edited. Given with music.

TROUVÈRES (12th and 13th centuries)

    Listed here are editions of works by named trouvères for whom we have a substantial number of melodies (roughly 10 or more). If the edition of a specific trouvère includes music, that fact is indicated. Anonymous works are not listed; many can be found in the anthologies listed above and in the collective editions of motets below. The *Bibliography of Old French Lyrics* by Robert White Linker (B18) gives full references for editions up to 1979, both of individual songs and composers, and of anonymous songs. For editions of named trouvères published 1970-90, see Eglal Doss-Quinby, *The Lyrics of the Trouvères* (B9). References for most named trouvères can also be found in the *Dictionnaire des Lettres Françaises: Le Moyen Age* (B8).

Trouvère Corpus: Melodies Only
270
Van der Werf, Hendrik. *Trouvères-Melodien*. 2 vols.

Monumenta Monodica Medii Aevi, 11 and 12. Kassel:
Bärenreiter, 1977-79. Vol. I contains songs by Blondel
de Nesles; Gautier de Dargies; the Châtelain de Couci;
Conon de Béthune; Gace Brulé. Vol. II contains the
works of Thibaut de Navarre; Moniot d'Arras; Moniot de
Paris; Audefroid le Bâtard; Adam de la Halle.

Adam de la Halle
271
Wilkins, Nigel. *The Lyric Works of Adam de la Hale.*
Corpus Mensurabilis Musicae, 44. Rome/Dallas: American
Institute of Musicology, 1967. [Revised ed., 1984]
Scholarly edition of texts and music of *rondeaux,*
jeux-partis, chansons and motets. Monophonic music
transcribed in mensural notation, matching "in spirit
and convention the rhythms found in Adam's polyphonic
works."
272
Marshall, John H. *The Chansons of Adam de la Halle.*
Manchester: Manchester University Press, 1971.
273
Maillard, Jean. *Adam de la Halle: Perspective musicale.*
Paris: Champion, 1982.
274
Nelson, Deborah Hubbard and Hendrik van der Werf. *The*
Lyrics and Melodies of Adam de la Halle. New York:
Garland, 1985.
Edition of the 36 *chansons.*
275
Adam de la Halle. *Le Jeu de Robin et Marion.* Edited and
translated by Jean Dufournet. Paris: Flammarion, 1989.
Musical transcriptions from the Ernest Langlois edition
of 1896.
276
Adam de la Halle. *Le Jeu de Robin et Marion.* Edited and
translated by Shira I. Schwam-Baird. Music edited by
Milton G. Scheuermann, Jr. New York: Garland, 1994.

Andrieu Contredit
277
Nelson, Deborah Hubbard and Hendrik van der Werf. *The*
Songs Attributed to Andrieu Contredit d'Arras with a

Translation into English and the Extant Melodies.
Amsterdam: Rodopi, 1992.

Audefroi le Bastart
278
Cullmann, Arthur. *Die Lieder und Romanzen des Audefroi le Bastart*. Halle: Niemeyer, 1914.

See Zink, *Les Chansons de toile* (B214).
Contains the five *chansons de toile* attributed to Audefroi.

Blondel de Nesle
279
Wiese, Leo. *Die Lieder des Blondel de Nesles*. Dresden: Gesellschaft für romanische Literatur, 1904.
280
L'Oeuvre lyrique de Blondel de Nesle. 2 vols. 1: Textes. Ed. Yvan G. Lepage. 2: Mélodies. Ed. Avner Bahat and Gérard Le Vot. Paris: Champion, forthcoming.

Chastelain de Coucy
281
Lerond, Alain. *Chansons attribuées au Chastelain de Couci (fin du XIIe-début du XIIIe siècle)*. Paris: Presses Universitaires de France, 1964.

Colart le Boutellier
282
Petersen-Dyggve, Holger. "Chansons françaises du XIIIe siècle," *Neuphilologische Mitteilungen* 30 (1929), 177-81 and 188-214.

Colin Muset
283
Bédier, Joseph. *Les Chansons de Colin Muset*. 2d ed. Classiques français du moyen âge 7. Paris: Champion, 1938. [Original edition 1912, with transcriptions of melodies by Jean Beck.]

Conon de Béthune
284
Wallensköld, Axel. *Les Chansons de Conon de Béthune.*

Classiques français du moyen âge 24 (revision of 1891 edition). Paris: Champion, 1921. [Reprint: 1968.]

Gace Brulé
285
Rosenberg, Samuel N. and Samuel Danon. *The Lyrics and Melodies of Gace Brulé*. Music edited by Hendrik van der Werf. New York: Garland, 1985.

Gautier de Coinci
286
Koenig, Frederic. *Les Miracles de Notre Dame par Gautier de Coinci*. 4 vols. Geneva: Droz, Lille: Girard, 1955-70.
287
Chailley, Jacques. *Les Chansons à la Vierge de Gautier de Coinci*. Paris: Heugel et Cie, 1959.
Critical musical edition of the songs contained in the *Miracles de Notre Dame*, plus four other songs that can be ascribed to Gautier de Coinci.

Gautier de Dargies
288
Raugei, Anna-Maria. *Gautier de Dargies. Poesie*. Florence: Nuova Italia, 1981.

Gautier d'Espinal
289
Lindelöf, Uno and Axel Wallensköld. *Les Chansons de Gautier d'Epinal. Mémoires de la Société néophilologique de Helsinki*, vol. 3, 205-318. Helsinki: Société Néophilologique, 1902.

Gillebert de Berneville
290
Fresco, Karen, ed. *Gillebert de Berneville: Les Poésies*. Geneva: Droz, 1988.

Gontier de Soignies
291
Formisano, Luciano. *Gontier de Soignies: Il Canzoniere*. Milan: Ricciardi, 1980.

Guillaume Le Paigneur d'Amiens (or *Guillaume d'Amiens*)
292
Petersen-Dyggve, Holger. "Chansons françaises du XIIIe siècle." *Neuphilologische Mitteilungen* 30 (1929): 184-5, 31 (1930): 21-62.

Guillaume le Vinier
293
Ménard, Philippe. *Les Poésies de Guillaume le Vinier.* Geneva: Droz, 1983.

Guiot de Dijon
294
Nissen, Elizabeth. *Les Chansons attribuées à Guiot de Dijon et à Jocelin.* Classiques français du moyen âge 59. Paris: Champion, 1929.

Jehan Bretel

There is no edition of the complete works. Partial editions:
295
Raynaud, Gaston. "Les Chansons de Jean Bretel." *Bibliothèque de l'Ecole des Chartes* 41 (1880); 195-214; reproduced in *Mélanges de philologie romane*, Paris: Champion, 1913, pp. 315-31. Edition of six *chansons*.
296
Langfors, Arthur. "*Mélanges de poésie lyrique française.*" *Romania* 52 (1926): 420-2. Edition of the seventh *chanson*.
297
Langfors, Arthur, Alfred Jeanroy and Louis Brandin. *Recueil général des jeux-partis français.* 2 vols. Paris: Société des Anciens Textes Français, 1926. Vol. I, 87-355.
Edition of most of the *jeux-partis.*

Jehan Erart
298
Newcombe, Terence. *Les Poésies du trouvère Jehan Erart.* Geneva: Droz, 1972.
299
Newcombe, Terence. *The Songs of Jehan Erart, 13th-Century*

Trouvère. American Institute of Musicology, 1975.
Edition of 25 songs, 3 of uncertain authorship. Sum-
maries of content but no translations of texts. With
Les Poésies, makes a complete edition.

Jehannot de Lescurel (or L'Escurel)
300
Wilkins, Nigel. *The Works of Jehan de Lescurel. Edited
from the manuscript B.N. fr. 146. Corpus Mensurabilis
Musicae*, 30. Rome/Dallas: American Institute of
Musicology, 1966. Both music and poetry included.

Moniot d'Arras and *Moniot de Paris*
301
Petersen-Dyggve, Holger. *Moniot d'Arras et Moniot de
Paris, trouvères du XIIIe siècle. Edition des chansons
et étude historique. Mémoires de la Société néophilologique de Helsinki*, vol. 12. Helsinki: Société Néophilologique, 1938.

Perrin d'Angicourt
302
Steffens, George. *Die Lieder des Troveors Perrin von
Angicourt.* Halle: Niemeyer, 1905.

Richart de Fournival
303
Lepage, Yvan G. *L'Oeuvre lyrique de Richart de Fournival.*
Ottawa: Editions de l'Université d'Ottawa, 1981.

Richart de Semilli
304
Johnson, Susan M. *The Lyrics of Richard de Semilli: A
Critical Edition and Musical Transcription.* Binghamton:
Center for Medieval and Early Renaissance Studies,
1992.

Thibaut de Champagne (Roi de Navarre)
305
Anglés, Higinio. *Las Canciones del rey Teobaldo* (Obra
póstuma). Pamplona: Excma, Diputacion Floral de
Navarra, 1973. Edition reconstructed by Aurelio
Sagaseta.

306

Brahney, Kathleen J. *Lyrics of Thibaut de Champagne.* New
  York: Garland, 1989.
307

Wallensköld, Axel. *Les Chansons de Thibaut de Champagne.*
  Société des Anciens Textes Français. Paris: Champion,
  1925.

THIRTEENTH-CENTURY MOTET

308

Anderson, Gordon A. *Compositions of the Bamberg Manu-
  script: Bamberg, Staatsbibliothek, Lit. 115 (olim Ed.
  IV. 6.).* Corpus Mensurabilis Musicae, 75. Dallas/Rome:
  American Institute of Musicology, 1977.
  Renews Aubry's *Cent motets* (see below) by conforming
  to modern standards of editing. A. Stimming's edition
  of French texts used (*Die altfranzösische Motette der
  Bamberger Handschrift,* Gesellschaft für romanische
  Literatur 13, Dresden, 1906), with translation by
  Robyn E. Smith.
309

Anderson, Gordon A. *Motets of the Manuscript La Clayette,
  Paris, Bibliothèque Nationale, nouv. acq. f. fr. 13521.*
  Corpus Mensurabilis Musicae, 68. Dallas/Rome: American
  Institute of Musicology, 1975.
  French texts edited and translated by Elizabeth A.
  Close.
310

Aubry, Pierre. *Cent motets du XIIIe siècle.* 3 vols.
  Paris: A. Rouart, Lerolle, 1908. [Reprint, 1964]
311

Auda, Antoine. *Les "Motets Wallons" du Manuscrit de
  Turin: Vari 42.* 2 vols. Brussels: Chez l'auteur [Cen-
  trale Don Bosco, 90, avenue du Val d'Or], 1953. Texts
  edited by Rita Lejeune.
  Facsimile and edition of the motets in this MS.
312

Haub, Rita. *Die Motetten in der Notre-Dame-Handschrift
  MüA (Bayer. Staatsbibl., Cod. Gall. 42).* Tutzing: H.
  Schneider, 1986.
  Critical edition of the 28 motets of the first quire
  of MüA.

313
Raynaud, Gaston. *Recueil de motets français des XIIe et XIIIe siècles*. 2 vols. Paris: Vieweg, 1881-83. Texts only, no music. But Vol. 2 is followed by a lengthy (some 200 pages) discussion of music by Henri Lavoix, fils, entitled *La Musique au siècle de Saint Louis*, and including a list of identifiable "musiciens, chanteurs, compositeurs, théoriciens, faiseurs et joueurs d'instruments des XIIe et XIIIe siècles," an index, a bibliography, and an appendix with a few transcribed musical examples.

314
Rokseth, Yvonne. *Polyphonies du XIIIe siècle: Le Manuscrit H 196 de la Faculté de Médecine de Montpellier*. 4 vols. Paris: Editions de l'Oiseau Lyre, 1935-39.

315
Tischler, Hans. *The Earliest Motets (to circa 1270): A Complete Comparative Edition*. New Haven: Yale University Press, 1982.

316
Tischler, Hans. *The Montpellier Codex*. 4 vols. Madison [Wis]: A-R Editions, 1978-85. Translations by Susan Stakel and Joel C. Relihan.

ROMANCES WITH LYRIC INSERTIONS

Only a few major 13th-century romances are listed here. See Maureen Boulton (B382) for a complete list. Transcriptions and reconstructions of the music for these romances may be found in Friedrich Gennrich, *Rondeaux, Virelais und Balladen* (B201) and in the Ph.D. dissertation of Maria Vedder Fowler, "Musical Interpolations in Thirteenth- and Fourteenth-Century French Narratives," 2 vols, Yale University, 1979.

317
Aucassin et Nicolette. Chantefable du XIIIe siècle. Ed. Mario Roques. Classiques français du moyen âge 41. 2nd edition. Paris: Champion, 1965. Musical transcriptions by Théodore Gérold. (Technically not a lyric-insertion romance because the musical interpolations are not songs but *laisses*, and singing and speaking recur in

strict alternation.)
318
Baudoin de Condé. *Li Prisons d'amours que Bauduins de Condé fist.* In *Dits et contes de Baudouin de Condé et de son fils Jean de Condé,* ed. August Scheler, Vol. I, 267-377. Brussels: Victor Devaux, 1866-67. Music in B.N. fr.25532. (See Gennrich.)
319
La Court de Paradis. Ed. E. Vilamo-Pentti. Helsinki: Société de la Littérature Finnoise, 1953. Music in B.N. fr.25532. (See Gennrich and Fowler.)
320
Gerbert de Montreuil. *Le Roman de la Violette ou de Gerard de Nevers.* Ed. Douglas L. Buffum. Paris: Société des Anciens Textes Français/Champion, 1928. (No music in the manuscripts. For reconstructions, see Fowler and Gennrich.)
321
Jacquemart Gielée. *Renart le Nouvel.* Ed. Henri Roussel. Paris: Société des Anciens Textes Français/Picard, 1961. Music in B.N. fr.372, 1593, 25566. (See Fowler and Gennrich.)
322
Jacques Bretel. *Tournoi de Chauvency.* Ed. Maurice Delbouille. Paris: Droz/Liège: Vaillant/Carmanne, 1932. (No music in the manuscripts. For reconstructions, see Fowler and Gennrich.)
323
Jakemès. *Roman du Castelain de Couci et de la Dame de Fayel.* Ed. Maurice Delbouille and John E. Matzke. Paris: Société des Anciens Textes Français/Paillart, 1936. (No music in the manuscripts. For reconstructions, see Fowler and Gennrich.)
324
Jean le Court. *Le Restor du paon.* Ed. E. Donkin. Modern Humanities Research Association Texts and Dissertations, 15. London, 1980. Music for one rondeau in Bodl. 264. (See Gennrich.)
325
Jean Renart. *Le Roman de la Rose ou de Guillaume de Dole.* Ed. Félix Lecoy. Classiques français du moyen âge 91. Paris: Champion, 1979. [1st ed. 1962] (No music in the manuscript. Some reconstructions are proposed by

Fowler and Gennrich.)
326
Nicole de Margival. *Le Dit de la Panthère d'Amours*. Ed.
Henry A. Todd. Paris: Société des Anciens Textes
Français/Firmin Didot, 1883. (No music in the manu-
scripts. See Fowler, Gennrich, and Lawrence Earp
[B725, 13-31.])
327
Thibaut. *Le Roman de la Poire par Tibaut*. Ed. Christiane
Marchello-Nizia. Paris: Société des Anciens Textes
Français/Picard, 1984. Music in B.N. fr.24431 given in
the edition. (See also Fowler and Gennrich.)
328
Le Roman de Tristan en Prose
The beginning was edited by Renée L. Curtius (3 vols.:
1, Munich, 1963; 2, Leyde, 1973; 3, Cambridge, 1985).
Philippe Ménard is directing further publication (Vol.
1, ed. Philippe Ménard, Geneva, 1987, Textes Littéraires Français 353; Vol. 2, ed. Marie-Luce Chênerie
and Thierry Delcourt, Geneva, 1990, TLF 387; Vol. 3,
ed. Giles Roussineau, Geneva, 1991, TLF 398; Vol. 4,
ed. Jean-Claude Faucon, Geneva, 1991, TLF 408; Vol. 5,
ed. Denis Lalande and Thierry Delcourt, Geneva, 1992;
9 volumes projected).
For the lais, see: *Les Lais du Roman de Tristan en
prose*, ed. Tatiana Fotitch and Ruth Steiner. Munich:
Fink, 1974.

FOURTEENTH CENTURY

Collective editions
329
Apel, Willi. *French Secular Music of the Late Fourteenth
Century*. Cambridge, Mass: Mediaeval Academy of America,
1950. Texts edited by Robert W. Linker and Urban T.
Holmes, Jr.
330
Apel, Willi. *French Secular Compositions of the Four-
teenth Century*. 3 vols. *Corpus Mensurabilis Musicae* 53.
Rome/Dallas: American Institute of Musicology, 1970-72.
Texts edited by Samuel N. Rosenberg.

331
Greene, Gordon K. *French Secular Music. Polyphonic Music of the Fourteenth Century*, Vols. 18-22. Monaco: Editions de l'Oiseau-Lyre, 1981-89. 18-19: *Manuscript Chantilly, Musée Condé 564* (1981-82); 20: *Ballades and Canons* (1982); 21: *Virelais* (1987); 22: *Rondeaux and Miscellaneous Pieces* (1989). Texts edited by Terence Scully. Underlaid texts not printed separately.
332
Günther, Ursula. *The Motets of the Manuscripts Chantilly, Musée Condé, 564 (olim 1047) and Modena, Biblioteca estense, M. 5 α 24 (olim lat. 568). Corpus Mensurabilis Musicae*, 39. Rome/Dallas: American Institute of Musicology, 1965. French and Latin texts given separately with commentary and variants.
333
Hoppin, Richard H. *The Cypriot-French Repertory of the Manuscript Torino, Biblioteca Nazionale J. II. 9.* 4 vols. Corpus Mensurabilis Musicae, 21. Dallas/Rome: American Institute of Musicology, 1960-63. Underlaid texts not printed separately.
334
Lefferts, Peter M., music ed. and Sylvia Huot, text ed. and trans. *Five Ballades for the House of Foix*. Devon: Antico Edition, 1989.

Le Roman de Fauvel and *Philippe de Vitry*
335
Langfors, Arthur. *Le Roman de Fauvel par Gervais du Bus, publié d'après tous les manuscrits connus*. Paris: Société des Anciens Textes Français, 1914-19. Standard critical edition.
336
Schrade, Leo. *The* Roman de Fauvel, *The Works of Philippe de Vitry, French Cycles of the* Ordinarium Missae. *Polyphonic Music of the Fourteenth Century*, 1. Monaco: Editions de l'Oiseau-Lyre, 1956. [Reprint: 1984, with Introduction by Edward H. Roesner.]
337
Rosenberg, Samuel N. and Hans Tischler. *The Monophonic Songs in the Roman de Fauvel*. Lincoln: University of Nebraska Press, 1991.

Guillaume de Machaut
338
Machaut, Guillaume de. Le Livre du Voir-Dit. Ed. Paulin
    Paris. Paris: Société des Bibliophiles François, 1875.
    [Reprint Slatkine, 1969.]
339
Hoepffner, Ernest. Oeuvres de Guillaume de Machaut. 3
    vols. Société des Anciens Textes Français. Paris:
    Firmin Didot, 1908-21.
340
Machaut, Guillaume de. Poésies lyriques. Ed. Vladimir
    Chichmaref. 2 vols. Paris: Champion, 1909. [Reprint
    Slatkine, 1973.]
341
Ludwig, Friedrich. Guillaume de Machaut: Musikalische
    Werke. 4 vols. Leipzig: Breitkopf and Härtel, 1928.
342
Schrade, Leo. The Works of Guillaume de Machaut, Poly-
    phonic Music of the Fourteenth Century, vols. 2 and 3.
    Monaco: L'Oiseau Lyre, 1956.
343
Machaut, Guillaume de. La Louange des dames. Ed. Nigel
    Wilkins. Edinburgh: Scottish Academic Press, 1972.
344
Guillaume de Machaut: Le Jugement du roy de Behaigne and
    Remede de Fortune. Ed. James I. Wimsatt and William W.
    Kibler. Music edited by Rebecca A. Baltzer. The Chaucer
    Library. Athens, Georgia: University of Georgia Press,
    1988.
345
Machaut, Guillaume de. Le Livre du Voir Dit. Ed. Paul
    Imbs, continued by Jacqueline Cerquiglini. Forthcoming
    in the series Société des Anciens Textes Français.
346
Palmer, R. Barton and Daniel Leech-Wilkinson. Guillaume
    de Machaut: Le Voir-Dit (The True Poem). New York:
    Garland Press, forthcoming.

Johannes Ciconia
347
Bent, Margaret and Anne Hallmark. The Works of Johannes
    Ciconia. Polyphonic Music of the Fourteenth Century,
    Vol. 24. Monaco: Editions de l'Oiseau-Lyre, 1985.

GENERAL STUDIES

HISTORY

348
Baumgartner, Emmanuèle. *Moyen Age: 1050-1486*. Paris: Bordas, 1988.
Brief history of French literature with introductory sections on historical and intellectual contexts, bibliographies, a chronology, and an index of authors indicating periods when they flourished.
349
Beltrando-Patier, Marie-Claire, ed. *Histoire de la musique: la musique occidentale du moyen âge à nos jours*. Part I, *Le Monde médiéval*. Paris: Bordas, 1982.
Articles on "Le Chant Grégorien" by Jean-Yves Hameline; "Troubadours et trouvères" by Gérard Le Vot; "La Musique de l'époque gothique; le siècle de Saint Louis" by Marie-Claire Beltrando-Patier; "XIVe et XVe siècle" by Claude Petillot. For a general public.
350
Bergner, Heinz, ed. *Lyrik des Mittelalters: Probleme und Interpretationen*. 2 vols. Stuttgart: Philipp Reclam, 1983.
Vol. 1 has essays with examples on Latin lyric by Paul Klopsch (19-196), on Old Provençal lyric by Dietmar Rieger (197-390), on Old French lyric by Friedrich Wolfzettel (391-578). Vol. 2 treats German (Ulrich Müller) and Middle English (Heinz Bergner).
351
Caldwell, John. *Medieval Music*. Bloomington: Indiana University Press, 1978.
A history intended for undergraduates and others "who require a straightforward account of medieval music above all in its technical aspects" (9). Covers Western music during the period to 1500. Ample sections on chant; slim treatment of vernacular monophonic song; full treatment of polyphony. Considerable emphasis on notation.
352
Cattin, Giulio. *Music of the Middle Ages I*. Translated by Steven Botterill. Cambridge: Cambridge University

Press, 1984. English translation of the Italian *Il Medioevo I* published in 1979.
Concise general history of music with one chapter in which vernacular monody is treated. A selection of theoretical readings, a glossary and bibliography conclude the work. See Gallo, B355.

[Davenson, Henri. See Marrou, Henri-Irénée, B362.]

353
Diehl, Patrick. *The Medieval European Religious Lyric.* Berkeley: University of California Press, 1985.
Intended as an *ars poetica*, not a literary history, the book adopts a broad comparative approach to functions; genres, forms, structures; and rhetoric, based on study of Latin, Greek, and nine vernaculars. A few passing references to music.
354
Dronke, Peter. *The Medieval Lyric.* 2d ed., Cambridge: Cambridge University Press, 1977.
One of the best introductions to European lyric poetry covering the period 850-1300.
355
Gallo, F. Alberto. *Music of the Middle Ages II.* Trans. Karen Eales. Cambridge: Cambridge University Press, 1985. English translation of Italian *Il Medioevo II* published in 1977.
A concise general history of music. The first chapter on the 13th century treats the motet in French; the second chapter is entirely devoted to 14th-century France. A selection of theoretical readings and a bibliography conclude the volume. See Cattin, B352, for the companion volume.
356
Gallo, F. Alberto. *Musica nel castello: Trovatori, libri, oratori nelle corti italiane dal XIII al XV secolo.* Bologna: Mulino, 1992.
Substantial chapter on troubadours in Italy with numerous musical examples. Discusses Peirol, Arnaut de Maroill, Peire Vidal, Gaucelm Faidit, Guiraut Riquier, Aimeric de Peguilhan, among others.
357
Histoire de la musique occidentale. Sous la direction

de Brigitte et Jean Massin. Vol. 1, Chapter 1: "Des origines chrétiennes au quatorzième siècle." Paris: Messidor/Temps Actuels, 1983.
Contains articles by Françoise Ferrand and Michel Huglo on Chant, vernacular monody, early polyphony, and Ars nova. For the general public.

358
Hölzle, Peter. *Die Kreuzzüge in der okzitanischen und deutschen Lyrik des 12. Jahrhunderts.* 2 vols. Gröppingen: Kümmerle, 1980.
Exhaustive study of crusade texts, proposing a strict definition that includes chiefly exhortations to join a crusade to the Holy Land.

359
Hoppin, Richard H. *Medieval Music.* Accompanied by an *Anthology of Medieval Music.* New York: Norton, 1978.
One of the best general histories available. It contains substantial chapters on secular monophonic song, on 13th-century polyphony, and on the Ars nova in France.

360
Jammers, Ewald. "Aufzeichnungsweisen der einstimmigen außerliturgischen Musik des Mittelalters." In *Palaeographie der Musik. Band I: Die Einstimmige Musik des Mittelalters*, ed. Wulf Arlt, 4.1-4.146, with plates. Cologne: Volk, 1979.
Extensive general discussion including list of sources (now superseded by the article "Sources" in the *New Grove*), types of verse and rhythmic modes, modal and mensural notation. Troubadours and trouvères treated under "Die vormodale Musik." Little close reading of manuscripts, but the cautiously modal transcriptions raise some questions that can still be examined with profit.

361
Janik, Dieter, ed. *Die Französische Lyrik.* Grundriss der Literaturgeschichten nach Gattungen. Darmstadt: Wissenschaftliche Buchgesellschaft, 1987.
This general history of French lyric includes substantial chapters on the troubadours by Kurt Ringger, on the trouvères by Michel Zink, and on 14th- and 15th-century lyric by Manfred Tietz.

362
Marrou, Henri-Irénée. 2d edition. *Les Troubadours*.
Paris: Seuil, 1971. [First edition under the name of
Henri Davenson, Paris, 1961]
Still the best compact non-specialist introduction to
troubadour song.
363
McKinnon, James, ed. *Antiquity and the Middle Ages: From
Ancient Greece to the 15th Century*. New York: Prentice
Hall, 1991. [First published in the United Kingdom,
1990]
Part of the *Music and Society* series accompanying the
television program *Man and Music*. Contains chapters on
"The Polyphonic Music of the Medieval Monastery, Cathe-
dral and University" by Marion S. Gushee; "Court and
City in France, 1100-1300" by Christopher Page; "Ars
Antiqua - Ars Nova - Ars Subtilior" by Daniel Leech-
Wilkinson. The approach of viewing musical history in
its response to social circumstances makes the book
useful for the general reader.
364
Möller, Hartmut and Rudolf Stephan, eds. *Die Musik des
Mittelalters*. Vol. 2 of *Neues Handbuch der Musikwissen-
schaft*, ed. Carl Dalhaus, continued by Hermann Danuser.
Laaber: Laaber Verlag, 1991.
General introduction to medieval music. Sections on the
motet by Wolf Frobenius and on secular song by Robert
Lug in the second chapter: "Music of the 12th and 13th
Centuries." A section on France and French influence by
Karl Kuegle in the third chapter: "Music of the 14th
Century."
365
*The New Oxford History of Music. II: The Early Middle
Ages to 1300*. Rev. ed. Ed. Richard Crocker and David
Hiley. Oxford: Oxford University Press, 1990.
Covers Chant of Eastern and Western Churches, Medieval
Monophony and Medieval Polyphony in Western Europe.
Substantial articles by John Stevens (B625) and
Richard Crocker (B664) on vernacular song and the
French motet.
366
Payen, Jean Charles. *Littérature française. I. Le Moyen
Age*. Paris: Arthaud, 1984.

Manual of French literature from the origins to 1430.
Organized around issues rather than works or authors.
Contains a useful *Dictionnaire des auteurs et des
oeuvres*, a chronology, and a bibliography.
367
Poirion, Daniel, ed. *Précis de littérature française du
moyen âge*. Paris: Presses Universitaires de France,
1983.
History of medieval French literature by a group of
French specialists under the direction of Daniel
Poirion. Chapters on troubadours and trouvères (by
Michel Zink) and on 14th and 15th-century lyric (by
Jacqueline Cerquiglini).
368
Sanders, Ernest H. "The Medieval Motet." In *Gattungen
der Musik in Einzeldarstellungen: Gedenkschrift Leo
Schrade*, ed. Wulf Arlt et al, 497-575 (article written
in 1967). Bern: Francke, 1973.
Basic and comprehensive summary of the history of the
motet from its beginnings to the early 15th century.
369
Sanders, Ernest. "Motet." In the *New Grove*.
Brief sketch of the history of the medieval motet in
the first section of the article.
370
Wagner, David L. *The Seven Liberal Arts in the Middle
Ages*. Bloomington: Indiana University Press, 1983.
Chapter 7 by Theodore Karp treats music as a liberal
art.
371
Wilkins, Nigel. *The Lyric Art of Medieval France*.
Cambridge: The New Press, 1988.
This is a study of the art of French song over the
entire medieval period. Included are songs with French
texts, composed within or outside the boundaries of
France. Concluding chapters list the chansonniers,
with illustrative facsimiles, and discuss theoretical
sources as well as other sources of information about
the songs. A substantial bibliography, a list of the
opening lines of the songs cited, and an index complete the work.
372
Wilson, David Fenwick. *Music of the Middle Ages: Style*

and *Structure*. With *An Anthology for Performance and Study*, translation of Latin and Italian texts by Robert Crouse and of French and Provençal by Hans T. Runte, and *Recording to Accompany Music of the Middle Ages* by the Hilliard Ensemble and the Western Wind, Paul Hillier, director. New York: Schirmer, 1990.
A history and manual designed for undergraduate or graduate courses. The practical orientation makes it a useful source of information for the non-specialist, although it is not an introductory text. The Anthology provides three examples of vernacular monophony, several examples of French motets, while polyphonic song is chiefly represented by Machaut, with one Ars subtilior ballade. All of the styles are expertly represented on the two accompanying cassettes (D808).
373
Winn, James. *Unsuspected Eloquence: A History of the Relations between Poetry and Music*. New Haven: Yale University Press, 1981.
Only one chapter of this general study is devoted to the Middle Ages: "Polyphonists and Troubadours." Treatment of the repertories involved is brief and mostly derivative, but some useful issues are raised by placing monophonic and polyphonic music together and both in larger contexts.
374
Yudkin, Jeremy. *Music in Medieval Europe*. Englewood Cliffs: Prentice Hall, 1989.
The presentation is clear and logical, useful for non-specialists, with numerous musical examples. A substantial chapter on "The Vernacular Tradition" analyzes a generous selection of troubadour and trouvère songs (where it would however have been preferable to take texts and translations from reliable editions); the vernacular motet is treated in a chapter on "The New Music of Paris"; and a chapter is devoted to "Fourteenth-Century France." Each chapter closes with a brief bibliography and a discography. Two cassettes were prepared by Thomas Binkley to accompany the volume (D809).
375
Zink, Michel. *Le Moyen Age: Littérature française*. Nancy: Presses Universitaires de Nancy, 1990. Translated by

Jeff Rider as: *Medieval French Literature: An Introduction*. Binghamton: Medieval & Renaissance Texts &
Studies, 1994.
General history of medieval French literature with
short but lucid chapters on "Troubadours and Trouvères"
and "La Poésie au XIVe et au XVe siècle." A brief bibliography and a useful "chronologie sommaire" complete
the work.
376
Zink, Michel. *Littérature française du Moyen Age*. Paris:
Presses Universitaires de France, 1992.
A richer and more detailed version of the 1990 book,
for university students.

CRITICISM AND ANALYSIS

377
Allen, Judson Boyce. "Grammar, Poetic Form, and the Lyric
Ego." In *Vernacular Poetics in the Middle Ages*, ed.
Lois Ebin, 199-226. Kalamazoo: Western Michigan
University, 1984.
Argues that the medieval lyric ego is in the grammati-
cal sense a substance seeking qualification; that one
qualifies it by entering it and experiencing its form
as linear process. Examples from Occitan include
Bernart de Ventadorn and William IX. Discusses perform-
ance and audience.
378
Arlt, Wulf. "Aspekte des Gattungsbegriffs in der Musik-
geschichtsschreibung." In *Gattungen der Musik in
Einzeldarstellungen: Gedenkschrift Leo Schrade*, ed.
Wulf Arlt et al, 11-93. Bern: Francke, 1973.
Introductory historical discussion of aspects of and
problems inherent in the concept of genre, as well as
its relations to the concepts of form and style.
379
Arlt, Wulf. "Musik und Text." *Die Musikforschung* 37
(1984): 272-80.
Argues for more subtle relationships between music and
text in medieval song than usually assumed. Uses examples from Machaut and Ciconia, pertinent to monophonic
as well as polyphonic repertories. One of the keys to

all such relationships is the Chant, and close connections between "singing" and "saying."
380
Arlt, Wulf. "*Nova Cantica:* Grundsätzliches und Spezielles
zur Interpretation musikalischer Texte des Mittelalters." *Basler Jahrbuch für Historische Musikpraxis*
10 (1986): 13-62.
Argues that in the Middle Ages music is closely related
to texts and to text meanings. Arguments based on Latin
song are also useful for the vernacular.
381
Arlt, Wulf. "Musica e testo nel canto francese: dai primi
trovatori al mutamento stilistico intorno al 1300." In
La Musica nel tempo di Dante, ed. Luigi Pestalozza,
175-97 and 306-21. Milan: Unicopli, 1988.
Reacting against the notion that text-music relations
reside chiefly in formal coordinations, or can be lo-
cated only in the domain of performance, Arlt argues
that musical composition even in earliest songs should
be related to various textual semantic levels. Discusses troubadour songs by Marcabru, Jaufre Rudel, Folquet de Marseille, Guiraut de Bornelh; and Jehannot
Lescurel.
382
Boulton, Maureen Barry McCann. *The Song in the Story:
Lyric Insertions in French Narrative Fiction, 1200-
1400*. Philadelphia: University of Pennsylvania Press,
1993.
The most complete discussion of lyric insertion romances to date, with some references to music.
383
Cerquiglini, Jacqueline. "Pour une typologie de l'insertion." *Perspectives médiévales* 3 (1977): 9-14.
Proposes three types of lyric insertion for 13th- and
14th-century narratives: *collage* (The "I" of the songs
is not the "I" of the narration); *montage* (songs are
the source of the narration); *collage-montage* (juxtaposition of songs to narrative). For further discussion
see below, Taylor B422.
384
Dragonetti, Roger. "*La Musique et les lettres*": Etudes de
littérature médiévale. Geneva: Droz, 1986.
Selected essays dating from 1959 to 1985. Section II,

"La Musique et la langue," contains an article on the meaning of "musique naturele" in the *Art de dictier* by Deschamps and another on "Le mariage des Arts au Moyen âge," first published in *Littérature et musique*, ed. Raphaël Célis, Bruxelles, 1982. Section III, "Le Gai Savoir," includes several articles on courtly lyric, notably on troubadours.

385
Dronke, Peter. "Profane elements in literature." *Renaissance and Renewal in the Twelfth Century*, ed. Robert Benson and Giles Constable, 569-92. Cambridge, MA: Harvard University Press, 1982.
Discussion of profane (defined as irreverent, blasphemous, ribald) elements based chiefly on examples drawn from lyric poetry, Latin and vernacular. Brief bibliography.

386
Dronke, Peter. *Women Writers of the Middle Ages: A Critical Study of Texts from Perpetua (d. 203) to Marguerite Porete (d. 1310)*. Cambridge: Cambridge University Press, 1984.
Contains an important discussion of the *trobairitz* and especially of "A chantar m'er de so q'ieu no volria" by the Comtessa de Dia.

387
Duby, Georges. "The Culture of the Knightly Class: Audience and Patronage." In *Renaissance and Renewal in the Twelfth Century*, ed. Robert L. Benson and Giles Constable, 248-62. Cambridge: Harvard University Press, 1982.
Concise summary of characteristics of aristocratic patronage and audience for 12th-century artistic productions.

388
Fassler, Margot E. "Accent, Meter, and Rhythm in Medieval Treatises 'De rithmis.'" *The Journal of Musicology* 5 (1987): 164-90.
Discusses several 12th- and 13th-century treatises on rhythmic poetry, placed in historical context. Argues that the importance of certain accentual patterns in Latin poetry, and the constant musical setting of these patterns, contributed to the invention of ways to create such patterns by musical means alone. Although the

vernacular is not discussed, the article opens new perspectives on vernacular monophony and on the early motet.

389
Fernandez, Marie-Henriette. "Notes sur les origines du rondeau: Le 'répons bref' - les 'preces' du Graduel de Saint-Yrieix." *Cahiers de civilisation médiévale* 29 (1976): 265-75.
Argues for liturgical origins of the rondeau with close comparative analyses of formal structures, poetic and musical, between the rondeau and two other types: "répons bref" and "preces."

390
Gonfroy, Gérard. "L'Ecriture poétique et ses modèles dans les *Leys d'Amors*." *Littérales* 4: *Théories et pratiques de l'écriture au moyen âge* (1988): 213-26.
Description of the *Leys d'Amors* that places the work accurately in its 14th-century context as a rhetorical treatise and a manual of composition for poets and judges of poetic contests. Rigorously systematic on a general level, the *Leys* are riddled with contradictions on practical levels such as the place of music. Proposes that study of the *Leys* can open new perspectives on the mentality of the scribes who compiled troubadour manuscripts.

391
Gushee, Lawrence. "Analytical Method and Compositional Process in some Thirteenth and Fourteenth-Century Music." In *Aktuelle Fragen der musikbezogenen Mittelalterforschung. Forum musicologicum (Basler Beiträge zur Musikgeschichte)* 3: 165-91. Winterthur: Amadeus, 1982.
Addresses the difficult question of whether or not compositional process can be understood by means of musical analysis, given how little we can know about how medieval composers worked. Argues that paradigmatic analysis of some songs by Adam de la Halle shows musical and textual patterns out of phase whereas we think of their connectedness as a feature of composition. The argument would be more persuasive if the poetic texts were analysed in detail.

392
Huot, Sylvia. *From Song to Book*. Ithaca: Cornell University Press, 1987.

Excellent discussion of 13th and 14th-century French
lyric and lyrical narrative poetry in relation to
their manuscript traditions. The method adopted,
which combines iconographic, codicological and poetic
analyses is intended to chart the emergence of a culture of the book in which the poet becomes a writer.
Music as such is not treated.

393
Huot, Sylvia. "Voices and Instruments in Medieval French
Secular Music: On the Use of Literary Texts as Evidence for Performance Practice." *Musica Disciplina* 43
(1989): 63-113.
Although literary texts are an important source for
medieval performance practices, extracting sure information from these texts is neither an easy nor a
straightforward task. By discussing exemplary passages
drawn from Old and Middle French literary works, Huot
demonstrates how literary texts can be used to study
performance practice.

394
Jammers, Ewald. "Die Rolle der Musik in Rahmen der romanischen Dichtung." *Grundriss der romanischen Literaturen des Mittelalters,* Vol. 1, 483-537. Heidelberg:
Carl Winter, 1972.
Discusses relations between text and music in general
terms, with specific reference to questions of rhythm
and stanza structures. Examples mainly drawn from troubadour and trouvère monophonic repertories.

395
Jauss, Hans Robert. "Littérature médiévale et théorie des
genres." *Poétique* 1 (1970): 79-101. This is a French
translation of "Theorie der Gattungen und Literature
des Mittelalters," In *Grundriss der romanischen
Literaturen des Mittelalters,* ed. Hans Robert Jauss
and Erich Köhler, vol. 1, 107-38. Heidelberg: Winter,
1972. An English translation has also been published.
"Theory of Genres and Medieval Literature," in Hans
Robert Jauss *Toward an Aesthetic of Reception,* trans.
Timothy Bahti, 76-109. Minneapolis: University of
Minnesota Press, 1982.
Seminal discussion of genre theory applied to medieval
works.

396
Kelly, Henry Ansgar. "The Varieties of Love in Medieval
   Literature According to Gaston Paris." *Romance
   Philology* 40 (1987): 301-27.
   Reviewing Gaston Paris's ideas on "courtly" love, Kelly
   argues that these ideas were more varied and subtle
   than generally recognized and deplores the oversimpli-
   fications of Duby's treatment of adultery as a central
   component of courtly love. We should not allow the term
   "amour courtois" to mask the complexities of medieval
   thinking.
397
Le Vot, Gérard. "Considérations sur le temps et la
   musique au Moyen Age." In *Le Nombre du temps: en
   hommage à Paul Zumthor*, 137-52. Paris: Champion, 1988.
   In answer to the question "Quelle(s) sorte(s) de temps
   la musique médiévale façonne-t-elle?" (p. 137), discusses different ways of organizing musical time from
   the troubadours to Ars nova.
398
Le Vot, Gérard. "Apprentissage coutumier, processus de
   création et technique vocale au Moyen Age." *Analyse
   musicale* 19 (1990): 62-71.
   Discusses the education of singers first for the chant
   repertory then for the troubadour/trouvère repertory,
   recognizing that about the latter very little is known.
   Slightly shorter version published as "Apprentissage
   coutumier et technique vocale au Moyen-Age," *Le Français aujourd'hui* 88 (1989): 14-21.
399
Lemaire, Ria. *Passions et Positions: Contribution à une
   sémiotique du sujet dans la poésie lyrique médiévale
   en langues romanes*. Amsterdam: Rodopi, 1988.
   Comparative study of the feminine and masculine lyric
   subject in the *cantigas de amigo* and 38 trouvère
   cansos taken from *La poésie lyrique d'oïl* by Cluzel,
   Pressouyre, and Mouzat (B197). Given the restrictions
   placed on the *cansos*, especially the elimination of
   the *trobairitz*, the scope is considerably narrower
   than the title suggests.
400
Lidov, David. "Musical Phrase Structure in the Theories
   of Riemann, Cooper and Meyer, and Ruwet." In *On Musical*

Phrase, 35-77. Montreal: University of Montreal, 1975. The part of this article devoted to Ruwet's theories addresses medieval examples ("Kalenda maya" and "Molt me mervoilt") discussed by Ruwet in his controversial but seminal essay on "Méthodes d'analyse en musicologie" (B412).

401
Maillard, Jean. *Evolution et esthétique du lai lyrique des origines à la fin du XIVe siècle*. Paris: Centre de Documentation Universitaire et SEDES, 1963. This doctoral thesis is a comprehensive study of the *lai* in its musical and, to a degree, textual components. Dated but still useful due to the breadth of the approach.

402
[Maillard, Jean] *Jean Maillard, Médiéviste, Musicologue, Professeur: Reflets de son oeuvre*. Béziers: Société de Musicologie de Languedoc, 1987. Collection of articles published by Jean Maillard before his untimely death in 1985. See B553, B555, B678, B758.

403
McGee, Timothy J. "Medieval Dances: Matching the Repertory with Grocheio's Descriptions." *The Journal of Musicology* 7 (Fall 1989): 498-517. Argues that on close examination, extant medieval dances can be found to correspond to Grocheio's descriptions. Among vocal dances, discusses "Kalenda maya."

404
Nattiez, Jean-Jacques. *Fondements d'une sémiologie de la musique*. Paris: 10/18, 1975. First important development by Nattiez of the theories of musical semiology which have since become the focus of sometimes heated theoretical debates. For the third division of the book, Ruwet is his point of departure, and he takes up again some of Ruwet's examples from medieval song.

405
Nattiez, Jean-Jacques. *Musicologie générale et sémiologie*. Paris: Christian Bourgois, 1987. Translated by Carolyn Abbate as *Music and Discourse: Toward a Semiology of Music*. Princeton: Princeton University

Press, 1990.
The first of a projected two volumes, this book attempts to widen the approach of the earlier *Fondements* by situating a semiology of music within the larger context of "musicologie générale." The English translation omits sections on melody and rhythm and makes other revisions in the text. The second volume will treat semiology and musical analysis.

406

Nattiez, Jean-Jacques. "Reflections on the Development of Semiology in Music." Trans. Katharine Ellis. *Music Analysis* 8 (1989): 21-75.
Argues that there is no single semiological science and describes the causes, main orientations, and nature of the activity of musical semiology. Extensive bibliography.

407

Page, Christopher. *Voices and Instruments of the Middle Ages: Instrumental Practice and Songs in France 1100-1300*. Berkeley: University of California Press, 1986.
Argues that certain genres, especially the *grand chant courtois* (belonging to the "high style") were less appropriate for instrumental participation, while others, such as dancing songs (belonging to the "lower style") were more suitable for performance with instruments. A second part of the book addresses performance practice. The appendix contains the literary sources that undergird most of the arguments and a typology of these sources.

408

Page, Christopher. *The Owl and the Nightingale: Musical Life and Ideas in France 1100-1300*. Berkeley: University of California Press, 1990. [First published, London, 1989.]
Stimulating discussion of musical activities based on contemporaneous writings such as sermons, romances, and theological treatises, and placed in the context of the emergence of the French state with its new laws and controls. A conspectus of the major types of sources and a bibliography complete the study.

409

Page, Christopher. *Discarding Images: Reflections on Music and Culture in Medieval France*. Oxford: Clarendon

Press, 1993.
A series of essays questioning some "received generalizations . . . habitually used to constitute the 'medieval' period in our minds" (xx). Two framing chapters
examine the concept of "Cathedralism" and Huizinga's
Waning of the Middle Ages. Three middle chapters examine aspects of the medieval motet: Ars antiqua and Ars
nova.
410
Powers, Harold S. "Language Models and Musical Analysis."
Ethnomusicology 24 (1980): 1-60.
Wide-ranging discussion of the use of language models
for analysis of different types of music. Substantial
critique of Ruwet, "Méthodes d'analyse en musicologie,"
and other structuralist approaches. Argues that language models can be useful for music analysis if applied circumspectly and with attention to a full spectrum of analytical traditions in music, medieval and
modern, western and non-western.
411
Rouse, Richard. "Roll and Codex: The Transmission of the
Works of Reinmar von Zweter." *Paläographie 1981: Colloquium des Comité International de Paléographie*.
München, 15.-18. September 1981, ed. Gabriel Silagi,
107-23. München: Arbeo-Gesellschaft, 1982.
Argues that vernacular song first circulated on rolls.
Refers to illustrations of Folquet de Marseille,
Pierpont Morgan 819, Jehan Bodel, Arsenal 3142, and
Guillaume de Machaut BN Fr.1586.
412
Ruwet, Nicolas. *Langage, musique, poésie*. Paris: Seuil,
1972.
Collection of essays by Ruwet containing his seminal
article "Méthodes d'analyse en musicologie," first
published in 1966. "Méthodes" furnished a basis for
the development of musical semiotics, and it concen-
trates on monophonic music from the 12th to the 14th
centuries.
413
Ruwet, Nicolas. "Methods of Analysis in Musicology."
Translated and introduced by Mark Everist. *Music
Analysis* 6 (1987): 3-36.
Translation of "Méthodes d'analyse en musicologie."
The introduction situates the article in the contexts

of preceding and following scholarship, arguing that despite the criticism the article has received, Ruwet's "Methods" should figure more importantly in the analysis of early music.

414
Shapiro, Marianne. *De Vulgari Eloquentia: Dante's Book of Exile*. Lincoln: University of Nebraska, 1990.
Detailed discussion of *De Vulgari Eloquentia* with a new translation. Dante's treatise is set in historical and political contexts and related to earlier vernacular treatises. There are also new translations of Raimon Vidal's *Razos de trobar* as well as *De la doctrina de compondre dictatz*.

415
Stevens, John. *Words and Music in the Middle Ages: Song, Narrative, Dance and Drama, 1050-1350*. Cambridge: Cambridge University Press, 1986.
Magisterial treatment of monophonic song repertories. Argues that the overriding esthetic concept is number: straight counting of syllables on the one hand; doctrines of proportion and harmony on the other. The view that music reflects the form, not the meaning, of the words leads to the rhythmic concept of isosyllabism (melodic units of approximately equal length correspond to single text syllables). The arguments about rhythm are set forth in rich scholarly detail.

416
Storey, H. Wayne. "Transferring Visual Ambiguity from Manuscript to Modern Edition." *Romance Philology* 43 (1989-90): 154-80.
Although this study focusses on an Italian poem, it raises excellent general questions concerning the transfer of medieval works from manuscript to edition.

417
Supičić, Ivo. "Les Approches socio-historiques de l'oeuvre musicale." *International Review of the Aesthetics and Sociology of Music* 17 (1986): 223-38.
Basic discussion of methodology useful for the study of the sociology of music defined as the study of music as a social phenomenon (as opposed to a formal or esthetic entity). Argues for a widening of the musicological enterprise. Does not directly address the medieval period, but raises issues pertinent to that period.

418
Supičić, Ivo. "Les Fonctions sociales de la musique." In
Musique et Société: Hommages à Robert Wangermée, ed.
Henri Vanhulst and Malou Haine, 173-182. Bruxelles:
Editions de l'Université de Bruxelles, 1988.
Argues that social functions of music should be separated from practical utilization. The latter is a mere
statement of fact (what and how); the former explores
reasons and goals of such utilization and identifies
the social significance of a work of music for differ-
ent social groups (thus answering the question "why").
419
Switten, Margaret and Howell Chickering, eds. *The Medieval Lyric* (B211). *Commentary Volume*.
Essays on music and poetics covering troubadours, trouvères and Machaut.
420
Tarasti, Eero. "Music as Sign and Process." In *Analytica:
Studies in the Description and Analysis of Music*, ed.
Anders Lönn and Erik Kjellberg, 97-115. Uppsala:
Almqvist and Wiksell, 1985.
Raises general issues of musical semiotics. The treatment of time and memory, and the argument that schemas
such as ABAB are inadequate to the description of music
as process, offer approaches applicable to the medieval
period.
421
Taruskin, Richard et al. "The Limits of Authenticity: A
Discussion." *Early Music* 12 (1984): 3-25.
Seminal discussion of the problematics of the term
"authenticity" applied to early music.
422
Taylor, Jane. "The Lyric Insertion: Towards a Functional
Model." In *Courtly Literature: Culture and Context*,
ed. Keith Busby and Erik Kooper, 539-48. Amsterdam/
Philadelphia: Benjamins, 1990.
Taylor's model recognizes but moves beyond Cerquiglini
(1977 above). The model places lyric interpolations
along a continuum going from total integration into
the diegesis to total structural separation from the
diegesis. Concluding application of the model to
Froissart's *Roman de Meliador*.

423
Treitler, Leo. "Musical Syntax in the Middle Ages: Background to an Aesthetic Problem." *Perspectives of New
Music* 4 (1965-66): 75-85.
Argues that there developed in the Middle Ages, and in
conjunction with poetic developments, a music new in
its logical arrangement of structural units, in its
sense of order and symmetry, and that in principle
these same features are observable through the eighteenth and nineteenth centuries. Arguments based on
examples of monastic song drawn from Saint Martial
manuscripts ca 1100-1200, but the arguments set forth
can illuminate subsequent vernacular song as well.
424
Treitler, Leo. "Oral, Written, and Literate Process in
the Transmission of Medieval Music." *Speculum* 56
(1981): 471-91.
Analyzes concepts of oral and written transmission,
the continuity from oral to written tradition, and the
implications of a distinction between written and literate traditions. "Literate" writing must be explicit
and autonomous, not just an aid to memory.
425
Treitler, Leo and Ritva Jonsson. "Medieval Music and Language: A Reconsideration of the Relationship." *Studies
in the History of Music*, Vol. 1: *Music and Language*, 1-
23. New York: Broude Brothers, 1983.
Refutes the argument that only in the Renaissance did
reflection of word meaning in music become important.
The medieval musician's response to language's meaning
was through syntax and structure, not through the imitation and expressiveness that would later dominate
Renaissance thinking. The conception of music as "sung
language" has important ramifications for vernacular
song.
426
Wimsatt, James I. *Chaucer and His French Contemporaries:
Natural Music in the Fourteenth Century*. Toronto: University of Toronto Press, 1991.
An exposition of the "main facts of Chaucer's relationships to his French contemporaries" (xiii) that contains substantial treatment of Middle French lyric,
including Jean de Le Mote, Machaut, Froissart, Oton de

Granson, and Deschamps. A fresh evaluation of "natural music" and middle French lyric modes.

428
Zink, Michel. *La Pastourelle*. Paris: Bordas, 1972.
Argues that the function of the pastourelle is to express carnal desire "à l'état pur," as free of ideology as of spirituality. One chapter treats briefly the role of music, and an appendix offers a transcription by Solange Corbin of the pastourelles with musical notation in BN Fr.20050.

428
Zink, Michel. "Le Lyrisme en rond. Esthétique et séduction des poèmes à forme fixe au Moyen Age." *Cahiers de l'Association Internationale des Études Françaises* 32 (1980): 71-90.
Discusses the fixed forms both chronologically and oppositionally, with emphasis on the rondeau. Early fixed forms stand in opposition to the *canso*; later fixed forms to the *dit*. Judicious remarks on the esthetic of the refrain, with some references to the role of music, monophonic and polyphonic, in relation to *canso* and rondeau.

429
Zink, Michel. *La Subjectivité littéraire*. Paris: Presses Universitaires de France, 1985.
Argues that the 13th century sees the appearance of a literary subjectivity, which can be defined as the focussing on individual experiences (as opposed to exterior authority) as the essential vehicle of meaning, and as the featuring of a subject which situates itself with respect to the circumstances and contingencies of real life. Although the primary focus of the book is on texts, a brief contrastive discussion of song and text raises issues central to an understanding of vernacular song.

430
Zumthor, Paul. *Essai de poétique médiévale*. Paris: Seuil, 1972. Translated by Philip Bennett as *Toward a Medieval Poetics*, Minneapolis: University of Minnesota Press, 1992.
Comprehensive and influential study of medieval poetry and poetics, primarily structuralist in approach. The concept of "mouvance" is elaborated, and the widely

utilized chapter on the "grand chant courtois" fixes
properties of song in ways that are restrictive but
penetrating.
431
Zumthor, Paul. *Introduction à la poésie orale*. Paris:
Seuil, 1983. Translated by Kathryn Murphy-Judy as *Oral
Poetry: An Introduction*. Minneapolis: University of
Minnesota Press, 1990. *La Poésie et la voix dans la
civilisation médiévale*. Paris: Presses Universitaires
de France, 1984. *La Lettre et la voix: de la "littérature" médiévale*. Paris: Seuil, 1987.
These three books develop the concept of the essential
"orality" even "theatricality" of medieval literature
understood as the work of the "voice," in all of its
physical density, and not of the "letter." The first
book, *Introduction*, sets forth a theory of the nature
of "vocal" poetry of all types, not merely medieval
European; the second is a briefer discussion of the
central issues applied to medieval civilization for a
series of lectures presented at the Collège de France;
the third, *La Lettre et la voix*, draws on the *Introduction* to focus on medieval literature and explores
with theoretical sophistication and exuberance the
vocal dimension of this "literature."

VERSIFICATION

432
Elwert, Theodor. *Traité de versification française des
origines à nos jours*. Paris: Klincksieck, 1965.
Basic manual of French versification for beginners and
non-specialists. Although the orientation is chiefly
modern, each section--la versification, la rime, les
vers, la strophe, poèmes à forme fixe--contains remarks
on medieval versification.
433
Lote, Georges. *Histoire du vers français*. 3 vols. Paris:
Boivin, 1949-55.
The first part of an ambitious work on French verse,
published posthumously. The three published volumes
treat the Middle Ages exclusively, making them the
most comprehensive and detailed study of medieval

versification and poetics available to scholars.
434
Mazaleyrat, Jean. *Elements de métrique française.* Paris:
Armand Colin, 1974.
Thorough discussion of principles of modern French
verse. The medieval period is not treated as such because the ordering of the material is analytical and
not historical; but the definitions of important terms
and concepts can be useful for study of medieval lyric.
435
Meschonnic, Henri. *La Rime et la vie.* Paris: Verdier,
1989.
Treats poetry and rhythm, with a substantial discussion of orality and literature and the "poétique de
la voix."
436
Scott, Clive. *French Verse-art: A Study.* Cambridge:
Cambridge University Press, 1980.
An introduction for English-speaking students to fundamental principles and terminology of French verse.
Although the focus is on modern verse, the principles
and terminology can be useful for medievalists.
437
Verrier, Paul. *Le Vers français.* 2 vols. Paris: Didier,
1931-32.
Comprehensive study of the structure and evolution of
French verse forms.

EDITING AND NOTATION

438
Arlt, Wulf. "Aspekte der musikalischen Paläographie." In
*Palaeographie der Musik. Band I: Die Einstimmige Musik
des Mittelalters,* ed. Wulf Arlt. Cologne: Volk, 1979,
1.1-1.48.
General discussion of issues involved in the study of
medieval notations.
439
Caldwell, John. *Editing Early Music.* Oxford: Clarendon
Press, 1985.
Contains a chapter on medieval and early Renaissance
music chiefly addressing technical musical problems

but also raising useful editorial issues of text/music relations. Good bibliography.
440
Foulet, Alfred L. and Mary Blakely Speer. On *Editing Old French Texts*. Lawrence: The Regents Press of Kansas, 1979.
Handbook of editorial practices for both general and specialized public, preceded by a substantial historical orientation. Covers the period 1150-1300, emphasizing the "Francien literary Koine" (xv). Lyric editing is not discussed. Good bibliography.
441
Parrish, Carl. *The Notation of Medieval Music*. New York: Norton, 1957. [Reprint: New York: Pendragon, 1978]
Standard work on medieval notation.
442
Rastall, Richard. *The Notation of Western Music: An Introduction*. New York: St. Martin's Press, 1982.
A general discussion of the underlying principles of notation. Useful bibliography.
443
Speer, Mary B. "Editing Old French Texts in the Eighties. Theory and Practice." *Romance Philology* 45 (1991): 7-43.
Review of the theory and practice of editing, including a brief section on "Texts with Music."

PERFORMANCE AND PRONUNCIATION

444
Alton, Jeannine and Brian Jeffrey. *Bele Bouche e Bele Parleure*. London: Tecla Editions, 1976. With cassette.
Succinct and useful guide to medieval and Renaissance French pronunciation, including a brief section on Old Provençal. Troubadour and trouvère courtly song is scarcely represented.
445
Brown, Howard Mayer and Stanley Sadie. *Performance Practice: Music before 1600*. Norton/Grove Handbooks in Music. New York: Norton, 1989.
Part One covers the Middle Ages and includes an excellent introduction by Howard Brown. See B450, B763.

446
Mcgee, Timothy J. *Medieval and Renaissance Music: A Performer's Guide.* Toronto: University of Toronto Press, 1985.
The intention of this book is to furnish practical information that will permit historically accurate performance of repertories of Western music before about 1600, with the exception of Chant. Monophonic courtly song and early secular polyphony are more briefly treated than later repertories.

SPECIFIC STUDIES

TROUBADOUR AND TROUVÈRE: MONOPHONIC, 12th AND 13th CENTURIES

447
Abramowicz, Maciej. "Le lieu commun et l'imaginaire; exordes des pastourelles et des chansons de toile." *Romania* 109 (1988): 472-501.
Arguing that the exordium is a poem in miniature, analyzes the formulae used therein to characterize the poem and set the stage for the action to come.
448
Agustín, Javier de. "Apuntes tematológicos acerca de las canciones de Jaufré Rudel." *Revista de filología románica* 2 (1984): 269-75.
Argues for motival analysis of troubadour song, using songs of Jaufre Rudel as examples.
449
Arens, Arnold. "Traditionelles und Originelles bei Thibaut IV. von Champagne: die Kanzone 'Por conforter ma pesance.'" In *Romania Cantat. Gerhard Rohlfs zum 85. Geburtstag Gewidmet*, ed. Francisco J. Oroz Arizcuren with Gio Batta Bucciol and Irene Monreal-Wickert, 2: 435-47. Tübingen: Gunter Narr, 1980.
Finds traditional thematic elements combined with formal originality.
450
Arlt, Wulf. "Secular Monophony." In *Performance*

Practice: Music before 1600, ed. Howard Mayer Brown and Stanley Sadie, 55-78. New York: Norton, 1989. Full discussion of general principles. The section on "songs" covers editions and manuscript sources, music and text, questions of rhythm, instrumental participation, with specific examples from the Occitan repertory, as well as one from Jehannot Lescurel. Some contradictions in detail and repetition of material previously published, but the general approach provides a guide to future research on performance practices.

451
Asperti, Stefano. "Contrafacta provenzali di modelli francesi." *Messana* 8 (1991): 5-49.
Examination of Occitan contrafacta of French models enables Asperti to establish a more precise chronology than hitherto available and locate centers of activity both for French imitation of Occitan models and for Occitan imitation of French models.

452
Aubrey, Elizabeth. "Forme et formule dans les mélodies des troubadours." In *Actes du premier Congrès International de l'Association Internationale d'Etudes Occitanes*, ed. Peter T. Ricketts, 69-83. London: AIEO/ Westfield College, 1987.
Argues that study of repetitions of motifs or of formulae can lead to a better understanding of troubadour melodies, which must have been largely products of oral tradition. Examples given from songs of Jaufre Rudel.

453
Aubrey, Elizabeth. "References to Music in Old Occitan Literature." *Acta Musicologica* 61 (1989): 110-49.
Collection of quotations, with translations, from a) lyric poems; b) *vidas* and *razos*; c) epic, narrative, hagiographic, dramatic, and historical works; d) *ensenhamens*, encyclopedias, and other didactic works. Discussion of terms and expressions to ascertain their possible musical significance.

454
Baumgartner, Emmanuèle. "Trouvères et 'Losengiers.'" *Cahiers de civilisation médiévale* 25 (1982): 171-8.
Examines the function of the *losengiers*, starting with the question of whether Köhler's sociological analyses

are valid for the *lyrique d'oïl*. Argues that in the *lyrique d'oïl* the theme of the *losengiers* symbolizes resistance encountered by the poet attempting to cultivate and impose an "écriture poétique" that is elitist and sophisticated.

455
Baumgartner, Emmanuèle. "Remarques sur la poésie de Gace Brulé." *Revue des langues romanes* 88 (1984): 1-13. Reacting against exclusively formalistic analysis of trouvère song, argues for the existence of individual and personal voices among the poets, using Gace Brulé as an example. Studies initial stanzas and envois in the attempt to discern how Gace reorients thematics from the troubadours. Sees this reorientation chiefly as an emphasis on writing, on "écriture," which marginalizes the usual inspirations of nature or the lady.

456
Baumgartner, Emmanuèle. "Présentation des chansons de Thibaut de Champagne dans les manuscrits de Paris." In *Thibaut de Champagne: Prince et poète au XIIIe siècle*, ed. Yvonne Bellenger and Danielle Quéruel, 35-44. Lyon: La Manufacture, 1987. Examination of the manuscripts shows how they place value on the songs of Thibaut by putting them first in the collection; how the illustrations interpret the songs and propose performing contexts; and how the manuscripts might have served commercial interests by contributing as much to the fame of Champagne as did the fairs.

457
Baumgartner, Emmanuèle. "La Terre estrange: variations sur un motif." *Perspectives médiévales* 16 (1990): 7-14. Argues that trouvères differ from troubadours in their treatment of two ideas of space: the horizontal (or geographic) and the vertical (or structured by feudal hierarchy), both capable of generating obstacles essential to the perpetuation of desire and hence of song.

458
Bec, Pierre. *La Lyrique française au moyen âge (XIIe-XIIIe siècles). Contribution à une typologie des genres poétiques médiévaux.* Vol. 1: *Etudes*; Vol. 2: *Textes.* Paris: Picard, 1977 and 1978. Vol. 1 contains a rich and fundamental discussion of

Old French lyric genres. Emphasis is placed on anonymous pieces. Complete bibliography through date of
publication. Vol. 2 contains texts to illustrate the
various genres, without translation but with brief
notes and glossary.

459
Bec, Pierre. "'Trobairitz' et chansons de femme. Contribution à la connaissance du lyrisme féminin au moyen
âge." *Cahiers de civilisation médiévale* 22 (1979):
235-62.
Important early discussion of the trobairitz corpus
and of the forms of discourse that define it.

460
Bec, Pierre. "Le problème des genres chez les premiers
troubadours." *Cahiers de civilisation médiévale* 25
(1982): 31-47.
Discusses generic distinctions with respect to Guilhem
de Peiteus, Jaufre Rudel, Marcabru and Cercamon, taking
into consideration what the terms used by these troubadours can tell us about the "genres" they cultivated.
Analyzes three terms in particular: *vers* which refers
to the text or to the entire song; *chant* which refers
to the sung text, possibly also to melody; *son* which
refers to the melody or to the sung text. Neither *chant*
nor *son* can designate a genre. The *vers* is not a genre
either; but it prefigures the *canso*, and remains
throughout the troubadour lyric as a paradigmatic
reference.

461
Bec, Pierre. "Du son poétique médiéval à la lettre du
pseudo-exégète." *Cahiers de civilisation médiévale* 29
(1986): 243-55.
Sharp and witty criticism of psychoanalytic approaches
to medieval lyric based on the "letter" without consideration of sounds, of real linguistic specificity,
or of socio-cultural contexts.

462
Bec, Pierre. "'Amour de loin' et 'dame jamais vue.' Pour
une lecture plurielle de la chanson VI de Jaufré
Rudel." In *Miscellanea di Studi in onore di Aurelio
Roncaglia: a cinquant'anni dalla sua laurea*, 101-18.
Modena: Mucchi, 1989.
Close analysis of "No sap chantar" in all its variant

versions to demonstrate how it embodies main themes of the rudelian universe. Compared to the more famous "Lanquan li jorn," which is specifically the song of "amor de lonh," "No sap chantar" is specifically the song of "La dame jamais vue."

463
Bec, Pierre. "Pour une typologie de la *balada* occitane: à propos de la pièce 'Quant lo gilos er fora.'" In *Hommage à Jean-Charles Payen. Farai chansoneta novele: Essais sur la liberté créatrice au Moyen Age*, 53-65. Caen: Centre de Publications de l'Université de Caen, 1989.
Proposes a more complete definition of the Occitan *balada* based on a review of the corpus and close analysis of "Quant lo gilos er fora." Brief mention of two songs with music, "A l'entrade del tens clar" and the motet "Tuit cil," which are not considered true examples of the type.

464
Beech, George T. "Contemporary Views of William the Troubadour, IXth Duke of Aquitaine, 1086-1126." In *Medieval Lives and the Historian: Studies in Medieval Prosopography*, ed. Neithard Bulst and Jean-Philippe Genet, 73-89. Kalamazoo: Medieval Institute Publications, 1986.
Argues that William IX was practically unknown in his own time as political figure or poet, outside a select group of aristocracy at his own court, and raises the question of how the poems survived at all.

465
Bertolucci, Valeria. *Morfologie del testo medievale.* Bologna: Mulino, 1989. Collection of articles previously published. Two of these concern Old Occitan lyric: "Il canzoniere di un trovatore: il 'libro' di Guiraut Riquier," first published in *Medioevo romanzo* 5 (1978): 216-59, and "Libri e canzonieri d'autore nel Medioevo: prospettive di ricerca," first published in *Studi mediolatini e volgari* 30 (1984): 91-116.
The first article is an edition of the rubrics in C and R that accompany Guiraut Riquier's songs. A discussion of the differences between the two manuscripts leads, among other things, to the hypothesis that C's exemplar must have had music, since, although melodies are absent in C, it nonetheless retains rubrics refer-

ring specifically to the absent music. The second article compares several poets' "collections": Guiraut
Riquier, Alfonso X el Sabio, Gautier de Coinci to study
the significance and applicability of the terms "chansonnier" and author's "book."

466
Billy, Dominique. "Le Descort occitan: Réexamen critique
du corpus." *Revue des langues romanes* 87 (1983): 1-28.
In a new effort to define the *descort*, Billy conducts
a review of the entire corpus, leading to the conclusion that the *descort* may be considered a genre with
diverse structures based chiefly on the principle of
the *versicle* (defined as "strophe composée de membres
identiques des *descorts* hétérostrophiques") and drawn
from para-liturgical models. The *descort* would then be
the result of integrating these models into the ideologies of the *canso*.

467
Billy, Dominique. "La *Canso redonda* ou les déconvenues
d'un genre." *Medioevo romanzo* 11 (1986): 369-78.
Argues that the two songs so designated by Guiraut
Riquier are united by a concept of circularity realized by rhyme sounds in PC 248,85 and by repetition of
final stanza verses in PC 248,66.

468
Billy, Dominique. *"L'altrier cuidai aber druda*: pièce
lyrique en langue mixte." *Revue des langues romanes* 91
(1987): 109-20.
Discusses Gérard-Zai (B507), Taylor (B634), and Billy
(B659).

469
Billy, Dominique. "Les Empreintes métriques de la musique
dans l'estampie lyrique." *Romania* 108 (1987): 207-29.
Supplements Cummins (1982 below) on specific points of
strophic form and relations between music and poetry.

470
Billy, Dominique. *"Lai* et *descort*: la théorie des genres
comme volonté et comme représentation." In *Actes du
premier Congrès International de l'Association Internationale d'Etudes Occitanes*, ed. Peter Ricketts, 95-
117. London: Westfield College, 1987.
Discusses the generic reality of lai and *descort*, arguing that the two can be separated and that if they have

not been clearly distinguished this is in part due to a faulty theory of genres.

471

Billy, Dominique. *L'Architecture lyrique médiévale: Analyse métrique et modélisation des structures inter- strophiques dans la poésie lyrique des troubadours et des trouvères.* Montpellier: Section Française de l'Association Internationale d'Etudes Occitanes, 1989. Reaffirming the central importance of metrics for an understanding of troubadour and trouvère lyric, Billy presents a detailed analysis of formal structures. An index helps to explain the difficult terminology. Complete bibliography.

472

Bossy, Michel-André. "Cyclical Composition in Guiraut Riquier's Book of Poems." *Speculum* 66 (1991): 277-93. Argues persuasively that Riquier's "book" reveals an organization at once numerical and chronological, on the basis of binary opposition of genres (*vers* and *canso*), and that it simultaneously creates artistic symmetries and a narrative of the poet's career. The enterprise can be compared to the *Cantigas* of Alfonso the Wise (Riquier's patron) and especially to Dante's *Vita Nuova* (intriguing connections between Dante and Narbonne are outlined). Riquier thus becomes a valuable link in the larger cultural transition from court per- formance to book.

473

Braet, Herman. "*Non es meravelha s'eu chan*: le même et l'autre." In *Chrétien de Troyes and the Troubadours: Essays in memory of the late Leslie Topsfield*, ed. Peter S. Noble and Linda M. Paterson, 44-51. Cam- bridge: Saint Catharine's College, 1984. Close analysis of this song to show how it announces and then embodies the relationship between love and artistic creation.

474

Brucker, Charles. "Conventions, variations et innovations stylistiques dans la poésie lyrique du XIIIe siècle: *Thibaut de Champagne.*" In *Le Génie de la forme: Mélan- ges de langue et de littérature offerts à Jean Mourot*, 27-40. Nancy: Presses Universitaires de Nancy, 1982. Seeks to discern Thibaut de Champagne's originality in the use of adjectives, in comparisons, and in music-text relations.

475
Bruckner, Matilda Tomaryn. "Jaufré Rudel and Lyric Reception: The Problem of Abusive Generalization." *Style* 20 (1986): 203-19.
Argues it is important not to read the poems as manifestations of later generalizations but to consider a variety of possible reader receptions and hence interpretations of individual songs.
476
Bruckner, Matilda Tomaryn. "Fictions of the Female Voice: The Women Troubadours." *Speculum* 67 (1992): 865-91.
Argues that the trobairitz were able to invent their own unique voices "at the crossroads of a lyric system . . . already mapped out by several generations of male poets" (890). Includes an analysis of "A chantar m'er de so q'ieu no volria" by the Comtessa de Dia, the only remaining trobairitz song with music.
477
Calin, William. "Singer's Voice and Audience Response: On the Originality of the Courtly Lyric, or How 'Other' was the Middle Ages and What Should We Do About It?" *L'Esprit Créateur* 23 (Spring, 1983): 75-90.
Analysis of lyric performance and audience response in order to question the view that medieval lyric is only a construct of rhetorical commonplaces.
478
Carrara, Antonio F. "Il linguaggio poetico di Gace Brulé e la tradizione lirica occitanica." *Spicilegio moderno* 9 (1978): 90-120.
Points out specific textual relationships between Gace Brulé and a number of troubadours, from William IX to the beginning of the 13th century.
479
Chambers, Frank M. "Some Deviations from Rhyme Patterns in Troubadour Verse." *Modern Philology* 80 (1983): 343-55.
Examines a small number of Old Provençal poems with masculine and feminine rhymes occurring in successive stanzas that would seem to cause problems in fitting each stanza to the same melody. None of the pieces actually has a melody; but several hypotheses

concerning possible relations between melody and text
are offered.
480
Chambers, Frank M. *An Introduction to Old Provençal Versification*. Philadelphia: American Philosophical Society, 1985.
  Chronological presentation of Old Provençal versification. Indispensable guide to basic concepts and techniques, accessible to a general audience as well as to
  specialists.
481
Cholakian, Rouben. "Marcabru and the Art of Courtly
Misogyny." *Neuphilologische Mitteilungen* 90 (1989):
195-206.
  Concentrates on Marcabru's *pastorela* "L'autrier jost'
  una sebissa" as a seemingly "feminist" poem to show
  that Marcabru is fundamentally a misogynist. Interesting perceptions, but the treatment of Marcabru
  lacks subtlety.
482
Cirlot, Victoria. "Discussion troubadouresque sur l'*amor
de lonh*." In *Contacts de langues, de civilisations et
intertextualité, Actes du IIIème Congrès International
de l'Association Internationale d'Etudes Occitanes*, ed.
Gérard Gouiran, 3: 855-64. Montpellier: Université Paul
Valéry, 1992.
  Argues that Jaufre Rudel's concept of "l'amor de lonh"
  provoked during the 12th century an often polemical
  discussion engaging other troubadours such as Marcabru,
  Bernart Marti, Cercamon, Peire d'Alvernha, Giraut de
  Bornelh, Raimbaut d'Aurenga and then during the 13th
  century settled into a more stable meaning, fixed by
  the authority accorded Jaufre Rudel and codified by
  the *vida*.
483
Cohen, Joel. "Peirol's Vielle: Instrumental Participation in the Troubadour Repertory." *Historical Performance* 3 (1990): 73-7.
  Argues that two lines in a song by Albertet de
  Sestairon (PC 16, 8, *tornada*), overlooked by other
  scholars, provide clear indication that troubadour
  songs were sometimes accompanied by instruments.

484
Coldwell, Maria V. "'Jongleresses' and 'Trobaritz':
Secular Musicians in Medieval France." In *Women Making
Music: The Western Art Tradition, 1150-1950*, ed. Jane
Bowers and Judith Tick, 39-61. Urbana: University of
Illinois Press, 1986.
Presents evidence of women's musical activity from ro-
mances, archival records, and manuscript illustrations,
with transcriptions of the four songs in the troubadour
and trouvère tradition that can be ascribed to women.
485
Crist, Larry. "Dieu ou ma dame: The Polysemic Object of
Love in Jaufré Rudel's 'Lanquan li jorn.'" *Marche
Romane* 29 (1979): 61-75.
Argues for multiple interpretations of the song. Review
of previous critical positions followed by a structural
analysis of "Lanquan li jorn."
486
Cropp, Glynnis M. *Le Vocabulaire courtois des troubadours
de l'époque classique.* Geneva: Droz, 1975.
Important classification and discussion of key terms
used by 12th-century troubadours.
487
Cummins, Patricia W. "Le Problème de la musique et de la
poésie dans l'estampie." *Romania* 103 (1982): 259-77.
Starting from an observation by Jacques Handschin that
the *estampie* is essentially defined by its music,
Cummins reviews in detail structural aspects of the
corpus of *estampies*, along with medieval definitions
of the genre, with a view toward tracing its development, both sung and instrumental, from the 12th to the
14th centuries.
488
Cyrus, Cynthia J. "Musical Distinctions Between Descorts
and Lais: Non-Strophic Genres in the Troubadour and
Trouvère Repertory." *Ars Musica Denver* 4 (1991): 3-19.
Takes up from the standpoints of musical notation,
style, and structure the much-vexed question of what
distinctions can be made between the *descort* and the
lai. Concludes that the forms were loosely interpreted
by the troubadours, showed codification of structures
with the trouvères, moved then to the transitional
treatment in the *Roman de Fauvel* which prefigured the

establishment of one standard type.

489

Dolly, Martha Rowe and Raymond J. Cormier. "Aimer, souvenir, souffrir: Les chansons d'amour de Thibaut de Champagne." *Romania* 99 (1978): 311-46.
Analysis of structure, subjects, themes, motifs, *topiques*, and vocabulary. Memory (*souvenir*) is a unifying and original theme throughout.

490

Doss-Quinby, Eglal. *Les Refrains chez les trouvères du XIIe siècle au début du XIVe*. New York/Berne/Frankfort: Peter Lang, 1984.
Detailed study of refrains from the literary standpoint, with a view toward characterizing them as a "genre," describing their different stylistic and thematic traits, situating them within their contexts, and underscoring their poetic function.

491

Doss-Quinby, Eglal. "*D'Esquern las razos*: contribution à la définition de la pastourelle médiévale." *Romance Quarterly* 36 (1989): 131-9.
Uses two infrequently cited descriptions from medieval theorists, the verse description of Guillaume Molinier and the brief reference in *Le Doctrinal de trobar* by Ramons de Cornet, to refine the definition of the pastourelle. *Esquern* (mockery) emerges as a key characteristic of the genre.

492

Dragonetti, Roger. *La Technique poétique des trouvères dans la chanson courtoise*. Bruges: De Tempel, 1960.
Fundamental and still indispensable general study of themes and versification in trouvère courtly song.

493

Falvy, Zoltán. "Manuskripte, Herkunft und Verzierung in der Troubadour-Musik." *Studia Musicologica* 27 (1985): 193-202.
Examines problems surrounding the composition of troubadour music by tabulating most (though not all, for reasons not stated) of the songs in at least 3 of the 4 main manuscripts (G R W X) and discussing 2 of these songs: Gaucelm Faidit's "Chant e deport" and "Fortz causa."

494
Falvy, Zoltán. *Mediterranean Culture and Troubadour Music*. Trans. María Steiner, revised by Brian McLean. Budapest: Akadémiai Kiadó, 1986.
Relates the origins of troubadour music to Mediterranean influences, of which Arab poetry is but one. Discusses the court of Alfonso the Wise. Argues, but not convincingly, for close links between troubadours and Catharism. After a substantial chapter on troubadours in Hungary, the melodies of two troubadours who visited Hungary, Peire Vidal and Gaucelm Faidit, are presented. The idea is advanced, though not clearly substantiated, that musical forms take no account of textual forms. Awkward translation.
495
Fernandez, Marie-Henriette. "Le Génie ondoyant et divers du trouvère Guillaume le Vinier (Essai d'analyse littéraire et musicale)." *Marche Romane* 30 (1980): 93-103.
By describing the various aspects of Guillaume le Vinier's music, seeks to demonstrate that for richness and variety of melodic invention the music is clearly the equal of the words.
496
Fernandez, Marie-Henriette. "Une réminiscence hébraïque dans la musique du troubadour Guillaume IX." In *Studia Occitanica in memoriam Paul Remy*, ed. Hans-Erich Keller, 1, 81-6. Kalamazoo: The Medieval Institute, 1986.
Cites evidence to suggest that the surviving melodic fragment quoted in the *Jeu de Sainte Agnès* as composed by Guillaume IX bears traces of Hebraic song and that this, in turn, could raise the possibility that Arabic influence on troubadour song was in large part Jewish influence.
497
Ferrand, Françoise. "*Ut musica poesis*: la relation de la lyrique profane des XIIe et XIIIe siècles à un modèle sacré." In *L'Imitation: aliénation ou source de liberté*, 107-28. Paris: La Documentation française, 1985.
Argues that the courtly lyric adopted the model of sacred music for secular purposes. Courtly lyric, like its sacred model, is a science of proportions. The theme of the desire of woman parallels the notion of

the desire for God, and, especially in the 13th century, the Lady is frequently replaced by the Virgin. But the sacred model cannot entirely explain secular song.

498
Ferrand, Françoise. "Thibaut de Champagne, de l'obsession du mal à la mort du chant." In *Thibaut de Champagne: Prince et poéte au XIIIe siècle*, ed. Yvonne Bellenger and Danielle Quéruel, 77-89. Lyon: La Manufacture, 1987.
Thibaut's obsession with evil and death is examined in the light of a cultural mutation that would lead to the death of courtly song.

499
Ferrand, Françoise. "Les Nombres dans l'espace-temps poétique des trouvères." In *Le Nombre du temps: en hommage à Paul Zumthor*, 73-85. Paris: Champion, 1988.
Examines the role of numbers and number symbolism in the *grand chant courtois* and in the *Chansons à la Vierge* by Gautier de Coinci.

500
Ferrante, Joan M. "'Ab joi mou lo vers e'l comens.'" In *The Interpretation of Medieval Lyric Poetry*, ed. W.T.H. Jackson, 113-41. New York: Columbia University Press, 1980.
Close analysis of the sound structures of Bernart de Ventadorn's poem, including music.

501
Ferrante, Joan M. "*Farai un vers de dreyt nien:* The Craft of the Early Trobadors." In *Vernacular Poetics in the Middle Ages,* ed. Lois Ebin, 93-128. Kalamazoo: Western Michigan University, 1984.
Examines poems by Guillem IX, Marcabru, Jaufré Rudel, Bernart de Ventadorn, Raimbaut d'Aurenga, Arnaut Daniel, and, as an epilogue, Dante to show how the troubadours created a new literary language and a new secular poetic tradition.

502
Gally, Michèle. "Disputer d'amour: Les Arrageois et le jeu-parti." *Romania* 107 (1986): 55-76.
Finds in the vocabulary and language of the *jeu-parti* ambivalent relationships to courtly song that help define this urban genre.

503
Gally, Michèle. "Jehan Bretel, poète et mécène." In
Figures de l'écrivain au moyen âge. Actes du Colloque
du Centre d'Etudes Médiévales de l'Université de
Picardie, Amiens 18-20 mars 1988, ed. Danielle
Buschinger, 125-38. Göppinger: Kümmerle, 1991.
Argues that the jeu-parti allows the participation of
a poetic community in the creation of songs and that
Jehan Bretel is a "figure emblématique" (135) of the
community.
504
Gaunt, Simon B. Troubadours and Irony. Cambridge:
Cambridge University Press, 1989.
After an introductory discussion of definitions of
irony, medieval and modern, Gaunt analyzes irony in
poems of Marcabru, Bernart Marti, Peire d'Alvernha,
Raimbaut d'Aurenga, and Giraut de Borneil. There is no
reference to music per se, but the importance of performance to an understanding of irony is discussed.
505
Gaunt, Simon B. "Poetry of Exclusion: A Feminist Reading
of Some Troubadour Lyrics." Modern Language Review 85
(1990): 310-29.
Takes up the argument that troubadour poetry was a
poetry "between men" from which women were excluded.
The troubadour lyric does not exalt women but explores
men's emotions and sets up masculine poetic rivalries.
Discusses poems by Guilhem IX, Marcabru, Bernart de
Ventadorn and Arnaut de Mareuil.
506
Gérard-Zai, Marie-Claire. "Approche typologique de la
pastourelle médiévale." Revista de istorie si teorie
literarǎ 31 (1982): 193-7.
Proposes a stricter definition of the pastourelle than
is usually adopted, eliminating pieces closer to the
romance or to the sirventès (such as Marcabru's
pastorela "L'autrier jost'una sebissa" which she
considers entirely a sirventès).
507
Gérard-Zai, Marie-Claire. "Edition d'une romance
parodique occitane: 'L'altrier cuidai aber druda,'"
in Studia Occitanica in memoriam Paul Remy, ed.
Hans-Erich Keller, Vol. II, 53-63. Kalamazoo: The

Medieval Institute, 1986.
Edition of a problematic text, preserved in its
entirety in BN fr.844 as a monophonic song, but
entering into the composition of 13th-century motets
as well. See Taylor (B634); Billy (B468, B659).
508
Gonfroy, Gérard. "Le Reflet de la *canso* dans le *De
Vulgari Eloquentia* et dans les *Leys d'Amors*." *Cahiers
de civilisation médiévale* 25 (1982): 187-96.
Argues that neither the *Leys d'Amors* nor the *De Vulgari
Eloquentia* can constitute an entirely reliable guide to
understanding the Old Occitan *canso*: both are useful,
but they must be used with caution.
509
Gonfroy, Gérard. "Les genres lyriques occitans et les
traités de poétique: de la classification médiévale à
la typologie moderne." In *Actes du XVIIIe Congrès
International de Linguistique et de Philologie
Romanes*, Vol. 6, ed. Dieter Kremer, 121-35. Tubingen:
Max Niemeyer, 1988.
Indicates the usefulness of medieval poetic treatises
dealing with the vernacular for developing a clearer
modern classification of lyric genres.
510
Gossen, Nicoletta. "Musik und Text in Liedern des
Trobadors Bernart de Ventadorn." *Schweizer Jahrbuch
für Musikwissenschaft* 4-5 (1988): 9-40.
Argues that troubadour melodies can be related to
texts on several levels: form, genre, content, syntax,
with syntax playing a central role. As demonstration,
conducts a close analysis of the first stanzas of four
songs by Bernart de Ventadorn: "Can vei la lauzeta,"
"Be m'an perdut," "Ab ioi mou lo vers," "Eras no vei
luzir," with briefer discussion of "Tan m'abelis" by
Folquet de Marselha. Since analysis is limited to one
stanza, the question of how relationships play themselves out over a complete song is not raised. Curiously unaware of much previous research in the field.
511
Gravdal, Kathryn. "Camouflaging Rape: The Rhetoric of
Sexual Violence in the Medieval Pastourelle." *Romanic
Review* 76 (1985): 361-73.
A vigorous feminist interpretation of the Old French

pastourelle as chiefly a celebration of rape, arguing that even the songs in which rape does not occur (four-fifths of the corpus, in fact) prepare and justify sexual violence in the others. See Paden (B581).

512
Gruber, Jörn. *Die Dialektik des Trobar.* Tübingen: Niemeyer, 1983.
Seminal discussion of troubadour song, with implications for the trouvères. Reacting against formalist approaches, Gruber utilizes techniques from reception theory to show that troubadour song is a continuing debate, a "dialectic," in which poets take up textual and musical materials from their predecessors in order to acknowledge, refute, and surpass previous achievements. Detailed model analyses trace this process of intertextual "Aufhebung" (term borrowed from Hegelian dialectic, central to Gruber's thinking).

513
Gruber, Jörn. "La Dialectique du trobar: essai de poétique troubadouresque." *Marche romane* 33 (1983): 123-25.
Gives a model analysis of the process of intertextual borrowing and re-forging elaborated in *Die Dialektik* using songs by Guilhem de Peitieu ("Pus vezem"), Marcabru ("Lo vers comens"), Cercamon ("Assatz es ora oimai"), Jaufre Rudel ("No sap chantar"), and Bernart de Ventadorn ("Chantars non pot").

514
Gruber, Jörn. "Singen und Schreiben, Hören und Lesen als Parameter der (Re-)Produktion und Rezeption des Occitanischen Minnesangs des 12. Jahrhunderts." *Zeitschrift für Literaturwissenschaft und Linguistik* 15 (1985): 35-51.
Argues that troubadour songs were neither composed in writing nor received through the written word, but rather conceived for performance and received by listening or singing, especially through the 12th century. Only in the 13th century do writing and reading acquire primary importance.

515
Gruber, Jörn. "L'Art poétique de Jaufre Rudel. Analyse philologique, musicologique et herméneutique de la chanson *No sap chantar qui so non di* (262,3)." In *La*

Chanson française et son histoire, ed. Dietmar Rieger,
15-25. Tübingen: Gunter Narr, 1988.
Using techniques of intertextual analysis, argues that
this song takes up and transforms by inverting them
elements from songs of William IX.
516
Halperin, David. "Distributional Structure in Troubadour
Music." *Orbis Musicae: Studies in Musicology* 7 (1979-
80): 15-26.
Computer analysis of the structure of musical phrases
(taken as defined by textual rhymes) based on the linguistic method of Zellig Harris. The analysis produced
statistics on melodic intervals used and isolated 56
initial melodic formulas, 41 final formulas and 33
internal formulas. No consideration of larger issues
raised by applying linguistic methods to music, or of
the work of Ruwet or Nattiez.
517
Harvey, Ruth E. "The Troubadour Marcabru and His Public."
*Reading Medieval Studies: Annual Proceedings of the
Graduate Centre for Medieval Studies in the University
of Reading* 14 (1988): 47-76.
In an attempt to answer the question of why the works
of so acrimonious a troubadour should have possessed
such enduring appeal, Harvey argues that Marcabru might
have associated himself with the *soudadiers*, or aspir-
ing members of the seigneurial household, that he might
consequently have expressed their frustrations, that he
might further have created a poetic *persona*, with a
personal style of performance, that permitted him to
distance himself from the harsh moralizing of his works
so that he pleased an audience of fellow *soudadiers*,
poets, and even the lords of at least some courts.
518
Harvey, Ruth E. *The Troubadour Marcabru and Love*. London:
Westfield Publications in Medieval Studies, 1989.
A detailed and rich examination of Marcabru as a
satirical and moralizing poet.
519
Harvey, Ruth E. "*Joglars* and the Professional Status of
The Early Troubadours." *Medium Aevum* 62 (1993): 221-41.
Re-examination of the evidence on which a sharp distinction between troubadour and joglar has been drawn

shows that the distinction, as it contrasts, say,
William IX or Jaufre Rudel to Cercamon or Marcabru,
needs careful nuancing.

520
Harvey, Ruth E. and Simon Gaunt. "Bibliographie commentée
du troubadour Marcabru (mise à jour)." *Le Moyen Age* 94
(1988): 425-55.
This bibliography is a useful update on Marcabru
scholarship; it does not include music, however.

521
Hatcher, Anna Granville and Mark Musa. "Rhyme Schemes and
Provençal Poetry." *Romance Philology* 38 (1984-85): 171-
99.
The authors select three basic criteria of rhyme
change: nature, extent, and frequency of occurrence of
the change; claim that the nature of change is always
either rhyme renewal, rhyme shift, or a combination of
the two; then list and briefly describe examples of
troubadour poetry to explain and illustrate their
criteria.

522
Hiley, David. "The Plica and Liquescence." In *Gordon
Athol Anderson (1929-1981) In Memoriam von seinen
Studenten, Freunden und Kollegen,* ed. Luther Dittmer,
2: 379-91. Henryville, Ottawa: Institute of Medieval
Music, 1984.
Discusses use of the plica in 13th-century polyphonic
music; includes table of plicas in vernacular songs in
BN 844 with the suggestion that these should be studied
more carefully.

523
Johnson, Susan. "The Role of the Refrain in the Pastourelles *à refrain.*" In *Literary and Historical Perspectives of the Middle Ages, Proceedings of the 1981 SEMA
Meeting,* ed. Patricia W. Cummins, Patrick W. Conner and
Charles W. Connell, 78-92. Morgantown: West Virginia
University Press, 1982.
Examination of the role of the refrain in the corpus
of Old French single-refrain *pastourelles* reveals that
definite conventions governed the use of the refrain
and its integration into the text.

524
Jung, Marc-René. "A propos de la poésie lyrique courtoise

d'oc et d'oïl." *Romanica vulgaria. Quaderni 8/9. Studi francesi e provenzali* 84/85 (1986): 5-36.
Shows how relationships between poems and poets engage form as well as content. Multiple examples, emphasizing texts but with some references to music.
525
Kaehne, Michael. *Studien zur Dichtung Bernarts von Ventadorn.* 2 vols. München: Wilhelm Fink, 1983.
The first volume contains a general review of critical interpretations of Bernart de Ventadorn's poetry which serves as background to the close analysis of each poem in the second volume. Only passing reference to the music.
526
Karp, Theodore. "Interrelationships between Poetic and Musical Form in Trouvère Song." In *A Musical Offering: Essays in Honor of Martin Bernstein,* ed. Edward H. Clinkscale and Claire Brook, 137-61. New York: Pendragon Press, 1977.
Investigates ways of classifying and discussing poetico-musical formal structures in the trouvère repertory based on rhyme patterns and meters for the poetry, melodic repetitions and other aspects of melodic composition for the music. Syntax and meaning are not included. Broad classifications do not differ from those to which we are accustomed. Detailed discussion of a few cases where poetic and musical patterns apparently conflict demonstrates unsuspected complexities and points the way to further research.
527
Karp, Theodore. "Three Trouvère Chansons in Mensural Notation." In *Gordon Athol Anderson (1929-1981) In Memoriam von seinen Studenten, Freunden und Kollegen,* ed. Luther Dittmer, 2: 474-94. Henryville, Ottawa: Institute of Medieval Music, 1984.
Discusses the theory of the rhythmic modes in relation to three trouvère songs from MSS Fr 844 and 846, newly transcribed for the article: "Ki de bons est, souëf flaire" (844, f° 215 r° and v°); "La plus noble emprise (844, f° 44); and Blondel de Nesle, "Amour dont sui espris" (846, f° 79). The first song, the focal point of the discussion, seems to display a quasi-didactic exposition of modal theory from the end of the 13th

century; the second demonstrates familiarity with
Franconian notation; the third seems to reveal techniques used in certain 13th-century polyphonic compositions.

528
Kasten, Ingrid. *Frauendienst bei Trobadors und Minne-
sängern im 12. Jahrhundert: Zur Entwicklung und
Adaption eines literarischen Konzepts.* Heidelberg:
Winter, 1986.
The first part of this comparative study treats the
troubadours. Kasten argues that "Frauendienst" in poet-
ry is directly related to social milieu, using William
IX, Jaufre Rudel, Cercamon, Marcabru, and Bernart de
Ventadorn as examples. The theories of Erich Köhler,
notably, are reviewed and rectified in useful ways.
529
Kasten, Ingrid. "Weibliches Rollenverständnis in den
Frauenliedern Reinmars und der Comtessa de Dia."
Germanisch-Romanische Monatsschrift 38 (1987): 131-46.
Brief examination of the songs of the Comtessa de Dia
to discern how she defines herself and establishes a
sense of self, compared to the way Reinmars establishes
a feminine voice.
530
Kay, Sarah. "Love in a Mirror: An Aspect of the Imagery
of Bernart de Ventadorn." *Medium Aevum* 52 (1983): 272-
85.
Relates Bernart de Ventadorn's use of the story of
Narcissus to the anonymous *Lai de Narcisse*, the *Romance
of the Rose*, and medieval conceptions of the mirror in
order to arrive at a fresh interpretation of "Can vei
la lauzeta mover."
531
Kay, Sarah. "La Notion de personnalité chez les troubadours: encore la question de la sincérité." In
Mittelalterbilder aus neuer Perspektive, ed. E. Ruhe
and R. Behrens, 166-82. München: Wilhelm Fink, 1985.
Reacting against romantic, sociological and structural
approaches, argues for a concept of troubadour personality, and with it sincerity, that allows historical
identification of an author but at the same time recognizes the rhetorical sophistication that produces a
poetic "I" whose sentiments are both shared by and

distanced from the historically identified poet.
532
Kay, Sarah. "Continuation as Criticism: The Case of
   Jaufre Rudel." *Medium Aevum* 56 (1987): 46-64.
   Assuming, unlike Pickens in his edition, that Jaufre
   Rudel did not "authorize" all the versions of his
   songs, that some versions contain the work of "continuators," Kay concentrates on "Quan lo rius de la
   fontana" to show how such "continuators" may have
   understood and interpreted Rudel's songs. Analysis of
   the different versions in a^1, M, C, U, and e shows that
   the mystical or crusading interpretations of *amor de
   lonh* are absent. Continuators tend to associate Jaufre
   with clerical or courtly moralistic traditions.
533
Kay, Sarah. "Rhetoric and Subjectivity in the Troubadour
   Lyric." In *The Troubadours and the Epic*, ed. L.M.
   Paterson and S.B. Gaunt, 102-42. Coventry: University
   of Warwick, 1987.
   Argues (against the structuralists) that it is reason-
   able to associate the "I" of troubadour song with an
   individual historical figure, but that this autobiographical assumption must consider the rhetorical techniques used in the representation of the self, the most
   explicit being allegory.
534
Kay, Sarah. *Subjectivity in Troubadour Poetry*. Cambridge:
   Cambridge University Press, 1990.
   Argues, against Zumthor, that subjectivity, however
   difficult it may be to define, is a central issue in
   troubadour poetry. The subject can be read as a grammatical position whose interpretation is complicated
   by the use of irony, hyperbole, and other forms of
   "difficult" ornament. The subject can ally itself with
   an allegorized self; it has gender and status in society; it is a "performer"; it can be identified in some
   cases with an historical author. Kay raises the issue
   of a "self" vs. a "character." A concluding chapter
   briefly examines romance reception of troubadour subjectivity in Guillaume de Lorris, *Romance of the Rose*,
   Jean Renart, *Guillaume de Dole*, and *Flamenca*.
535
Kropfinger, Klaus. "Dante e l'arte dei trovatori." In *La

Musica nel tempo di Dante, ed. Luigi Pestalozza, 130-74. Milan: Unicopli, 1988.
Discussion of Dante's views of troubadour art with a detailed analysis of the poetry and music of Arnaut Daniel's sestina, to show why Dante admired it.

536
Krülls-Hepermann, Claudia. "Contextes de transmission médiévaux: manuscrits et notations musicales." In *Contacts de langues, de civilisations et intertextualité, Actes du IIIème Congrès International de l'Association Internationale d'Etudes Occitanes*, ed. Gérard Gouiran, 2: 627-36. Montpellier: Université Paul Valéry, 1992.
Argues that transmission and preservation of troubadour song should be studied in historical and "communicative" contexts in order to bring out the importance of diverse concretizations--oral and written--through which the song passes.

537
Lavis, Georges. *L'Expression de l'affectivité dans la poésie lyrique française du moyen âge (XIIe-XIIIe s.)*. *Etude sémantique et stylistique du réseau lexical* joie-dolor. Paris: Les Belles Lettres, 1972.
Exhaustive study of the two central lyric terms, based on the study of twenty-four troubadours and the trouvère corpus.

538
Lepage, Yvan G. "Blondel de Nesle et Richard Coeur de Lion: Histoire d'une légende." *Florilegium* 7 (1985): 109-28.
Reviews evidence concerning Blondel de Nesle; would identify him as Jehan Ier de Nesle rather than Jehan II.

539
Lepage, Yvan G. "L'Edition des textes lyriques: le cas de Blondel de Nesle." In *Actes du XVIIIe Congrès International de Linguistique et de Philologie Romanes*, Vol. 6, ed. Dieter Kremer, 88-99. Tübingen: Max Niemeyer, 1988.
Analysis of the manuscript tradition of one song of Blondel de Nesle shows that the methods of the neo-Lachmannians cannot be applied to it.

540
Le Vot, Gérard. "Sur l'interprétation musicale de la
chanson des troubadours: pour une 'musicologie' ap-
pliquée." In *Musique, Littérature et Société au Moyen
Age*, ed. Danielle Buschinger and André Crépin, 99-121.
Paris: Champion, 1980.
Delineation of an approach to performance that invites
study of manuscript sources, of songs' cultural matrix,
and of characteristics of melody and text in order to
arrive at imaginative reconstruction and interpretation.
541
Le Vot, Gérard. "Notation, mesure, et rythme dans la
canso troubadouresque." *Cahiers de civilisation médiévale* 25 (1982): 205-17.
Approaches problems of rhythm by rapidly reviewing
previous theories, attempting to propose a new definition of rhythm, examining the chansonniers in themselves and in the light of medieval conceptions of
time, and, finally, proposing different practical solutions. Uses four troubadour songs: Pons d'Ortafa, "Si
ai perdut mon saber"; Jaufre Rudel, "Non sap chantar";
Aimeric de Peguilhan, "En greu pantais"; and Marcabru,
"Bel m'es quan son li fruich madur."
542
Le Vot, Gérard. "Chanter les troubadours et les trouvères." *Perspectives médiévales* 9 (1983): 59-70.
Discusses various possible responses to the question
of how troubadour and trouvère song can reach a modern
audience through modern performances.
543
Le Vot, Gérard. "Pour une épistémologie de l'édition
musicale du texte lyrique français médiéval." In
Musicologie Médiévale: Notations et Séquences (Actes
de la Table Ronde du CNRS 6-7 septembre 1982), ed.
Michel Huglo, 187-207. Paris: Champion, 1987.
Raises some of the fundamental issues involved in editing trouvère song, with several examples to illustrate
cases of one or multiple manuscript traditions.
544
Le Vot, Gérard. "Quelques indices du silence dans la
canso des troubadours." In *Mélanges de langue et de
littérature occitanes en hommage à Pierre Bec*, 295-306.

Poitiers: Université de Poitiers C.E.S.C.M., 1991.
Silence is here interpreted as a pause or an abrupt
shift in melodic continuity that helps shape a song.
The article discusses marks of "melodic discontinuity"
such as large intervals, melodic inflections mid-line
or at cadence points, and vertical bars or textual
punctuation in the manuscripts. Reference is made also
to the *Leys d'amors*.
545
Le Vot, Gérard. "Intertextualité, métrique et composition
mélodique dans les *cansos* du troubadour Folquet de
Marseille." In *Contacts de langues, de civilisations
et intertextualité, Actes du IIIème Congrès International de l'Association Internationale d'Etudes Occitanes*, ed. Gérard Gouiran, 2: 637-67. Montpellier:
Université Paul Valéry, 1992.
Argues that due to the extreme fluidity of the melodies, it is difficult if not impossible to speak of
melodic intertextuality in the sense of conscious
borrowing.
546
Le Vot, Gérard, Pierre Lusson and Jacques Roubaud. "La
Chanson de 'l'amour de loin' de Jaufre Rudel: Essai de
lecture rythmique." *Mesura* 3 (1979): 1-92.
Exhaustive analysis of "Lanquan li jorn son lonc en
mai" according to formal analytical procedures that
are "précises, régulières et falsifiables." The authors
argue that different elements of troubadour song are
united by an overarching, abstract coherence that makes
them amenable to analysis based on a common theoretical
approach. They adopt an approach qualified as rhythmic,
breaking down musical and poetic elements into "divisions minimales" (such as note or syllable). The interplay of these minimal divisions creates dynamic movement. Their procedures are intended to reveal the
song's multi-layered architecture.
547
Le Vot, Gérard, Pierre Lusson and Jacques Roubaud. "La
Sextine d'Arnaut Daniel: Essai de lecture rythmique."
In *Musique, Littérature et Société au Moyen Age*, ed.
Danielle Buschinger and André Crépin, 123-57. Paris:
Champion, 1980.
Analysis of Arnaut Daniel's sestina according to their

method for Jaufre Rudel's "Lanquan li jorn" (B546).
The results show more subtle correlations between
different elements for the sestina than for Rudel's
canso.

548
Le Vot, Gérard, Pierre Lusson and Jacques Roubaud. "La
Conveniencia del texto y de la melodía en la canción
de los trovadores: Estudio ritmico de la *canso Bel
m'es qu'ieu chant e coindei* de Raimon de Miraval."
Revista de Musicología 7 (1984): 1-28.
Detailed analysis of words and melody in Miraval's
canso.

549
Locher, Caroline. "Folquet de Marseille and the Structure
of the Canso." *Neophilologus* 64 (1980): 192-207.
Discussion of formal characteristics of Folquet's
songs, including some that have music, although music
is not mentioned in the article.

550
Longobardi, Monica. "Osservazioni metrico-retoriche sui
vers di Guiraut Riquier." *Studi mediolatini et volgari*
31 (1985): 247-57.
Description of formal structures in the *vers* of
Guiraut Riquier with a table based on I. Frank's
Répertoire.

551
Lug, Robert. "Zwischen objektiver Historizität, oraler
Authentizität und postmoderner Komposition. Zwölf
Bermerkungen zur Seinsweise des mittelalterlichen
Liedes im 20. Jahrhundert." *Studia musicologica* 31
(1989): 45-55. The main points of this paper were
discussed at a study session on "Troubadour Research
and Performing Practice Today" at the XIV Congress of
the International Musicological Society in Bologna in
1987. A summary of the study session is published in
the Acts of the Congress (Torino, 1990).
What is the ontology of a medieval song performed in
the 20th century? Neither a medieval "object," although the performer may seek both historical objectivity and what Lug calls "oral authenticity," nor a
modern composition, the 20th-century performance might
be termed "post modern," to accentuate the way in which
any performance is but one realization among many

possible realizations undertaken in the effort to give
a song renewed existence.

552
Magnussen, E.B. "Elements of the Morphological and Syn-
tactic Structure of Jaufre Rudel's Poems." *Revue
Frontenac* 2 (1984): 19-36.
Argues that Jaufre Rudel's style is not simplistic.
Examines the entire corpus preserved in MS C to demon-
strate the refinement and complexity of morphological
and syntactic structures.

553
Maillard, Jean. "Approche musicologique du Trobar." *Revue
Internationale de Musique Française* 2 (1980). [Reprint-
ed in B402, 133-45]
General advice on how to go about studying troubadour
and trouvère music. Somewhat dated, but many of the
problems raised have not yet been resolved.

554
Maillard, Jean. "Variantes mélodiques dans les chansons
des trouvères." In *Musique, Littérature et Société au
Moyen Age*, ed. Danielle Buschinger and André Crépin,
159-70. Paris: Champion, 1980.
Calls attention of future researchers to the importance
of studying melodic variants. Using the example of Adam
de la Halle, Maillard discerns two types: (a) totally
different melodies for the same text; (b) variants in
details. The latter do not necessarily affect the melodic structure and can be explained by various factors
including transmission "par audition" or scribal error.
The former are more perplexing and may require an approach that departs from notions of the song as symbi-
otic of word and sound according to "rules" of the
grand chant courtois.

555
Maillard, Jean. "'Descort, que me veux-tu?'" *Cahiers de
civilisation médiévale* 25 (1982): 219-23. [Reprinted
in B402, 273-77.]
Discusses musical features of the *descort* of Aimeric
de Peguilhan, "Qui la ve en ditz": a melody strangely
distorted in MS W; an esthetically pleasing melody in
MS R, reflecting typical features of the *descort*. A
formal analysis and edition of the R version are included.

556
Maillard, Jean. "A propos de deux mélodies de Raimon
 Jordan." In *Studia Occitanica in memoriam Paul Remy*,
 ed. Hans-Erich Keller, 1: 121-30 Kalamazoo: The
 Medieval Institute, 1986.
 Discussion and edition of Raimon Jordan's "Lo clar
 temps vei brunezir" and "Vas vos soplei, domna,
 premeiramen."
557
Marshall, John H. *The Transmission of Troubadour Poetry*.
 London, 1975.
 This Inaugural Lecture at Westfield College remains
 the clearest and most succinct introduction to the
 multiple problems of the written transmission of
 troubadour poetic texts.
558
Marshall, John H. "The *descort* of Albertet and its Old
 French Imitations." *Zeitschrift für romanische Philologie* 95 (1979): 290-306.
 Argues that the study of *contrafacta* can lead to a
 better understanding of medieval versification, help
 define literary genres (in this case lai and *descort*)
 and restore lost tunes. The tune of Albertet's *descort*
 is reconstructed.
559
Marshall, John H. "Pour l'étude des *contrafacta* dans la
 poésie des troubadours." *Romania* 403 (1980): 289-335.
 Rich and important discussion of the principles of the
 study of *contrafacta* and the application of those principles to a substantial number of songs. Argues that
 since there are few cases in the Provençal repertory of
 contrafacta clearly attested by the preservation of two
 different texts with the same melody, we are obliged to
 use textual criteria, including the duplication of a
 metrical structure alone; duplication of metrical
 structure plus rhyme scheme, to which may be added
 copying of rhyme sounds; or other aspects of composition such as *coblas doblas*. The metrical structure remains fundamental. The discussion reveals a diversity
 of practices in both troubadour and trouvère repertories. Concluding remarks focus on the use of *contrafacta* to reconstruct lost melodies, especially on the
 sixteen recuperated melodies in Gennrich's *Nachlass*,

of which Marshall would retain eight.

560
Marshall, John H. "The Isostrophic *descort* in the Poetry of the Troubadours." *Romance Philology* 35 (1981): 130-57.
Since the *descort* was heterostrophic, an isostrophic *descort* would seem to be a contradiction in terms. However, Marshall argues that the isostrophic *descort* did exist (he adduces five pieces plus some *contrafacta*) and that its existence can show one way in which troubadours incorporated "irregular" forms into a system dominated by the isostrophic *canso*.

561
Marshall, John H. "Un prétendu *descort* fragmentaire et ses congénères." *Romania* 105 (1984): 341-51.
Presents another case for which normalizing versification obscures the nature of the song and the relationships between words and music.

562
Marshall, John H. "Textual Transmission and Complex Musico-metrical Form in the Old French Lyric." In *Medieval French Textual Studies in Memory of T.B.W. Reid*, ed. Ian Short, 119-48. London: Anglo-Norman Text Society, 1984.
By the close examination of musico-metrical form in an anonymous *pastourelle*, "Quant voi nee" (R 534), Marshall argues that it is incorrect to normalize all songs when editing: some songs, which he terms "heteromorphic," do not follow the rigorously isosyllabic and isostrophic patterns of the courtly *chanson* and should not be made to do so.

563
Marshall, John H. "Une versification lyrique popularisante en ancien provençal." In *Actes du premier Congrès International de l'Association Internationale d'Etudes Occitanes*, ed. Peter Ricketts, 35-66. London: AIEO/Westfield College, 1987.
Using mostly textual examples but with some references to music, argues that alongside the versification "rigoureuse, rigoureusement mise en musique" of the *canso*, there existed a freer kind of "popularisante" versification that editors should not normalize. Placing this "irregular" versification beside the *canso*

leads to the hypothesis that different lyric systems
may have been in conflict, with the *canso* type dominat-
ing in the south. The "popularizing" type would, in
Marshall's view, better fit a melody with definite
rhythms, while the *canso* suits freer rhythmic treatment.

564

Mayer-Martin, Donna. "The *Chansons* of Gace Brulé. A
Stylistic Study of the Melodies." In *Literary and
Historical Perspectives of the Middle Ages: Proceedings of the 1981 SEMA Meeting*, ed. Patricia W.
Cummins, Patrick W. Conner and Charles W. Connell,
93-103. Morgantown: West Virginia University Press,
1982.

Discusses elements of style and form in the melodies
of Gace Brulé. Argues that Gace followed many of the
trends of his generation of trouvères but demonstrated
originality in melodic variation and in subtle structural interrelationships between text and melody.

565

Meneghetti, Maria Luisa. "Una *vida* pericolosa. La
'mediazione' biografica e l'interpretazione della
poesia di Jaufre Rudel." *Cultura Neolatina* 40 (1980):
145-63.

Detailed discussion of the songs of Jaufre Rudel to
show that the *vida's* interpretations do not reflect
the richness of Jaufre's slim corpus and consequently
should not be allowed to act as our chief guide to that
corpus.

566

Meneghetti, Maria Luisa. *Il pubblico dei trovatori*.
Modena: Mucchi, 1984.

Based on modern reception theory, this important book
examines the reception of early troubadour song by a
contemporaneous public, initally quite small; the formation of dialogue genres; the intertextual development
of the "canto per amore" motif in changing conditions
of reception; mediated reception through *vidas* and
razos; and the interpretations offered by the illustrations in the *chansonniers*.

567

Meneghetti, Maria Luisa. "De l'art d'éditer Jaufré
Rudel." *Cahiers de civilisation médiévale* 34 (1991):

167-75.
Discusses the approaches of two recent editors, Rupert
Pickens (1978, B249) and Giorgio Chiarini (1985, B251).
Although the neo-Lachmannian method adopted by Chiarini
is judged preferable, both editors emphasize the need
to consider the specificity of individual manuscript
traditions in order to understand not only the texts
presumed to be "authentic" but also their cultural
resonance.

568
Menocal, María Rosa. "Close Encounters in Medieval Provence: Spain's Rôle in the Birth of Troubadour Poetry."
Hispanic Review 49 (1981): 43-64.
Essentially a review of Roger Boase, *The Origin and
Meaning of Courtly Love* (Manchester, 1977), this
article, after summarizing the contents of Boase's
book, lucidly examines the prejudices and ideological
blind spots that have prevented scholars from justly
evaluating the role of Hispanic-Arabic poets. A full
bibliography of works not mentioned by Boase is extremely useful.

569
Menocal, María Rosa. "The Etymology of Old Provençal
trobar: trobador: A Return to the 'Third Solution.'"
Romance Philology 36 (1982); 137-48. With an Editorial
Post-Script by Yakov Malkiel: "Old Provençal *trobar*,
Old Spanish *fallar*."
After briefly reviewing the difficulties involved in
the two main solutions to the etymology of *trobar*: (1)
turbare, (2) *tropare*, Menocal argues that a third solution proposed by Julián Ribera in 1928, *tarab* ("song"),
is more completely viable phonetically, morphological-
ly and semantically than the others. The major problem
this "third solution" leaves unresolved is the prove-
nience of *trobar* "to find" and its links to *trobar/
trobador*. The Post-Script contains reflections on the
question of *trobar* "to find," and the entire notion of
"finding."

570
Mölk, Ulrich. "Troubadour Versification as Literary
Craftsmanship." *L'Esprit Créateur* 19 (1979): 3-16.
Discussion of several troubadours' use of versifica-
tion, focussed on subtleties of rhyme in relation to

line and stanza, in order to demonstrate the troubadours' self-conscious artistry.

571
Mölk, Ulrich. "Zur Metrik der Trobadors." In *Grundriss
der romanischen Literaturen des Mittelalters*, Vol. 2:
Les genres lyriques, tome 1, fasc. 3: B, *La lyrique
occitane*, dir. Erich Köhler, 29-44. Heidelberg: Winter,
1987.
Elaboration of material in preceding article.

572
Monson, Don Alfred. "Jaufré Rudel et l'amour lointain:
les origines d'une légende." *Romania* 106 (1985): 36-56.
Argues that the elements of Rudel's *vida* come from one
song, "Lanquan li jorn," and the organization of the
elements into a narrative whole could have been modeled
on saints' lives. This encounter between lyricism and
hagiography explains how the theme of distant love was
transformed into a legend.

573
Monson, Don Alfred. "Lyrisme et sincérité: sur une chanson de Bernart de Ventadorn." In *Studia Occitanica in
memoriam Paul Remy*, ed. Hans-Erich Keller, 1: 143-59.
Kalamazoo: The Medieval Institute, 1986.
Argues that "sincerity" is best understood as a poetic
theme, and that it determines both the text and texture
(with a brief note on the music) of "Non es meravelha
s'eu chan."

574
Monson, Don Alfred. "Bernart de Ventadorn et Tristan." In
*Mélanges de langue et de littérature occitanes en hom-
mage à Pierre Bec*, 385-400. Poitiers: Université de
Poitiers C.E.S.C.M., 1991.
Argues that the designation "Tristan" in Bernart's
poems alludes in different ways to the legend of
Tristan and Iseut or to the meaning of Tristan's name.
Detailed discussion of "Tant ai mo cor ple de joya"
and of "Can vei la lauzeta mover."

575
Monterosso, Raffaello. *Musica e ritmica dei trovatori*.
Milan: Giuffrè, 1956.
Reviews the manuscript transmission of troubadour song
and argues for rhythmic flexibility, concluding with a
transcription of the first three stanzas of Marcabru

"L'autrier jost'una sebissa" from MS R to show how
espousal of text rhythms by the melody might be indicated in modern musical notation. Old but still useful.
576
Nichols, Stephen G. Jr. "Toward an Aesthetic of the
Provençal Lyric II: Marcabru's *Dire vos vuoill ses
doptansa* (BdT 293, 18)." In *Italian Literature, Roots
and Branches*, ed. Giose Rimanelli and Kenneth John
Atchity, 15-37. New Haven: Yale University Press, 1976.
Argues against Zumthorian formalism, for the importance
of individual creative imagination in the making of
troubadour poetry.
577
Nichols, Stephen G. Jr. "The Promise of Performance:
Discourse and Desire in Early Troubadour Lyric." In
The Dialectic of Discovery, ed. John Lyons and Nancy
Vickers, 93-108. Lexington: French Forum, 1984.
Manipulation of different voices in Marcabru's "Al
departir del brau tempier" reveals criticism of a
fallen world, the gap between promise and performance,
the "representing" of potential distance between
founders and successors. This early poetry is aware
that its models will be surpassed. Such complexity
reveals a richness of subjective dimension analysed
here in Marcabru but evident in different ways in all
the early troubadours.
578
Nichols, Stephen G. "Voice and Writing in Augustine and
in the Troubadour Lyric." In *Vox Intexta: Orality and
Textuality in the Middle Ages*, ed. A.N. Doane and
Carol Braun Pasternack, 137-61. Madison: University of
Wisconsin Press, 1991.
Voicing a poetic song demonstrates the multiple complexities of the act as a transgressive gesture and as
the continual coming into being of language.
579
Paden, William D. Jr. "The Role of the Joglar in Troubadour Lyric Poetry." In *Chrétien de Troyes and the Troubadours: Essays in memory of the late Leslie Topsfield*,
ed. Peter S. Noble and Linda M. Paterson, 90-111.
Cambridge: Saint Catharine's College, 1984.
Study of the role of the joglar as it can be deduced
from references in troubadour poetry. Some 56 poets

named 81 joglars; the activities of the joglars are tabulated and discussed. Paden argues that the joglar gradually disappeared from the lyric texts and that this disappearance corresponded to a shift from initially more significant oral transmission to later predominantly written transmission.

580
Paden, William D. "Reading Pastourelles." *Tenso* 4 (1988): 1-21.
Argues that we should be careful not to read *pastourelles* through inappropriate generic expectations: generic expectations themselves develop over time. Since no system of genres functioned among the early troubadours, one cannot understand Marcabru's "L'autrier jost'una sebissa" as a "conventional" dialogue between a knight and a shepherdess satirizing courtly society. We should rather read it on its own terms as advocating clarity in definition of social classes (*mesura*). To develop the concept of evolving generic expectations, the article examines two other poems, one from a period when the *pastourelle* as genre was at its height, another from the late period of relative decline.

581
Paden, William D. "Rape in the Pastourelle." *Romanic Review* 80 (1989): 331-49.
Challenges Gravdal's 1985 (B511) interpretation of the Old French *pastourelle* as a celebration of rape on the grounds that arbitrary isolation of a single group of songs produces a false picture of the genre. Consideration of the entire range of *pastourelles* in several languages reveals a much more complex genre containing many songs that do not have rape as a theme. Neither innocent fun nor brutal violence, the *pastourelle* is animated by conflicting drives felt by both women and men.

582
Paden, William D. "Bernart de Ventadour le troubadour devint-il abbé de Tulle?" In *Mélanges de langue et de littérature occitanes en hommage à Pierre Bec,* 401-13. Poitiers: Université de Poitiers C.E.S.C.M., 1991.
Reviews the seductive hypothesis that Bernart de Ventadorn was of noble birth and became Abbot of Tulle,

finding the hypothesis not altogether implausible. Were the hypothesis exact, Bernart de Ventadorn would have to be placed a generation later in the history of Occitan lyric.

583
Parker, Ian R. "Troubadour and Trouvère Song: Problems in Modal Analysis." *Revue Belge de Musicologie* 31 (1977): 20-37.
Discusses the drawbacks of the medieval modal system as an analytical system for the secular repertory, but finds it difficult not to use it as a constant term of reference. Assesses also the methods of Curt Sachs which, though not without problems, can provide useful tools. Numerous analyses of troubadour songs.

584
Pasero, Nicolò. "Sulla collocazione socioletteraria della 'pastorela' de Marcabruno." *L'Immagine riflessa* IV (1980): 347-64.
Early statement and grounding of ideas more fully developed in the article following. Interesting reading of the *pastorela* against the notion of tripartite class structure, leading to the idea that Marcabru criticizes the transgression of divinely ordained social order in the works of William IX.

585
Pasero, Nicolò. "Pastora contro cavaliere, Marcabruno contro Guglielmo IX - Fenomeni di intertestualità in *L'autrier jost'una sebissa* (BdT 293,30)." *Cultura Neolatina* 43 (1983): 9-25.
Argues that Marcabru's *pastorela* alludes to William IX's poetry in order to criticize the earlier poet's attitude toward love. The *toza* of "L'autrier" would thus represent Marcabru while the knight represents William IX. Important article for intertextual approaches and reception theory, along with Gruber 1983a and Meneghetti 1984 above.

586
Paterson, Linda. *Troubadours and Eloquence*. Oxford: Oxford University Press, 1975.
Fundamental study of troubadour poetics and stylistics, based on careful readings of five poets: Marcabru, Peire d'Alvernhe, Giraut de Bornelh, Raimbaut d'Aurenga, and Arnaut Daniel.

587
Paterson, Linda. "Great Court Festivals in the South of France and Catalonia in the Twelfth and Thirteenth Centuries." *Medium Aevum* 51 (1982): 213-24.
Demonstrates that large festivals were not typical of courtly life in the Midi which was characterized above all by its intimate scale. What the troubadours found at court was *solatz*: the pleasure of good conversation.

588
Pensom, Roger. "On the Prosody of the Decasyllabic Lyrics of the Roi de Navarre." *French Studies* 39 (1985): 257-75.
Based on research on the *Song of Roland*, argues for the possibility of an accentual prosody for Old French decasyllabic lines in general. Extremely detailed analysis, but results not entirely convincing because some of the principles (e.g. that epic and lyric obeyed similar constraints, or that musical notation has explicitly rhythmic significance) are questionable.

589
Pensom, Roger. "Thibaut de Champagne and the Art of the Trouvère." *Medium Aevum* 57 (1988): 1-26.
Effort to discover rules for accentuation of poetic texts, particularly for the accenting of monosyllables, that would lead to a better understanding of sung rhythms, based on research on the *Song of Roland*. Argues against completely free or random accentuation and for a distribution of accented and unaccented tones and syllables that would be varied but ordered. Critique of Van der Werf's theories. Analysis and transcription of two strophes of "Bons rois Thiebaut." Provocative but inconclusive.

590
Phan, Chantal. "Le Style poético-musical de Guiraut Riquier." *Romania* 108 (1987): 66-78.
Analysis of relationships between rhyme schemes and melodic structure, ways of highlighting key words and of relating melodic gestures to significant poetic notions, and the use of refrains. Far from being merely artificial, Riquier's melodies are highly artistic. Moreover, the apparent desire to stabilize each melodic detail, reducing the factor of improvisation, distinguishes Riquier's work from that of previous troubadours.

591
Phan, Chantal. "La tornada et l'envoi: fonctions struc-
turelles et poïétiques," *Cahiers de civilisation
médiévale* 34 (1991): 57-61.
Brief analysis of the function of the *tornada* deriving
from its placement and structure.
592
Poe, Elizabeth Wilson. *From Poetry to Prose in Old Provençal. The Emergence of the* Vidas, *the* Razos, *and the*
Razos de trobar. Birmingham, AL: Summa Publications,
1984.
Analysis of the *vidas*, the *razos*, and the grammatical
treatise the *Razos de trobar*. These texts preserved
the lyric universe of the troubadours while transforming it and redefining its terms. A final chapter moves
into Dante's *Vita Nuova* and the *De Vulgari Eloquentia*.
593
Poe, Elizabeth Wilson. "New Light on the Alba: A Genre
Redefined." *Viator* 15 (1984): 139-50.
After a general discussion of the *alba* and of the
principles according to which it may be considered a
genre, proposes a new and more flexible definition.
594
Poe, Elizabeth Wilson. "The Three Modalities of the Old
Provençal Dawn Song." *Romance Philology* 37 (1984): 259-
72.
Enlarges the descriptive schemes of Pierre Bec (*La
Lyrique française*, B458) to include two subgenres within the *alba*: the counter-*alba* and the religious *alba*.
595
Poe, Elizabeth Wilson. "The Lighter Side of the *Alba: Ab
la genser que sia*." *Romanistisches Jahrbuch* 36 (1985):
87-103.
Study of "Ab la genser que sia" as a parody of the
alba genre and as a comic response to Guiraut de
Borneill's "Reis glorios."
596
Poe, Elizabeth Wilson. "La Transmission de l'*alba* en
ancien provençal." *Cahiers de civilisation médiévale*
31 (1988): 323-45.
MSS C and R contain a high concentration of *albas*; few
are found in MSS copied in Italy. These observations
and others lead to the hypothesis that the scribes of

C and R drew most of their *albas* from a single collection that must, among other things, have provided musical notation for "Reis glorios" and "S'anc fui belha."

597
Pollina, Vincent. "Troubadours dans le Nord: Observations sur la transmission des mélodies occitanes dans les manuscrits septentrionaux." *Romanistische Zeitschrift für Literaturgeschichte/Cahiers d'histoire des littératures romanes* 9 (1985): 263-78.
Analysis of reactions of northern French scribes to Occitan texts and melodies. Based on "A chantar m'er de so qu'eu no volria" by the Comtessa de Dia and "Fortz chausa es" of Gaucelm Faidit, the former preserved with its melody only in a northern manuscript, the latter with text and melody in both northern and southern manuscripts. Argues that the textual and musical alterations in the song by the Comtessa de Dia suggest the existence of a southern model and that the three northern versions of Gaucelm Faidit's *planh* suggest exceptional northern influence on the repertory.

598
Pollina, Vincent. "*Canso* mélodique et *canso* métrique: *Era.m cosselhatz, Senhor* de Bernart de Ventadorn." *Actes du premier Congrès International de l'Association Internationale d'Etudes Occitanes,* ed. Peter T. Ricketts, 409-22. London: A.I.E.O./Westfield College, 1987.
Close analysis of relations between melodic and metric schemas in Bernart de Ventadorn's *canso*, with comparative discussion of the two manuscript versions of the song in R and G. Concludes that the two versions show different ways of manifesting through melody the nature of the poetic schemas.

599
Pollina, Vincent. "Melodic Continuity and Discontinuity in *A chantar m'er* of the Comtessa de Dia." *Miscellanea di studi romanzi offerta a Giuliano Gasca-Quierazza* 2: 887-96. Alessandria: Edizioni dell' Orso, 1988.
Study of the melody of "A chantar m'er," complementing an earlier discussion of the music and the "Frenchified" text (B597), showing that the melody embodies both discontinuity and continuity, ultimately affirming the principle of continuity.

600
Pollina, Vincent. "Word/Music Relations in the Work of
the Troubadour Gaucelm Faidit: Some Preliminary Observations on the Planh." In *Miscellanea di studi in
onore di Aurelio Roncaglia* 2: 1075-90. Modena: Mucchi,
1989. [First published in *Cultura Neolatina* 47 (1987):
263-78.]
Close analysis of "Fortz chausa es." Argues that the
four melodic versions, although differing among themselves, all display refined and subtle relationships
between words and music, particularly in the first
stanza.
601
Pollina, Vincent. *Si cum Marcabrus declina: Studies in
the Poetics of the Troubadour Marcabru.* Modena:
Mucchi, 1991.
Rich discussion of two poems (PC 31 and 32). Although
neither poem discussed has music, attention is given
to conditions of performance. Useful general remarks
about Marcabru's music in the introduction.
602
Pollina, Vincent. "Structure verbale et expression
mélodique dans *Mon cor e mi* du troubadour Gaucelm
Faidit." In *Contacts de langues, de civilisations et
intertextualité, Actes du IIIème Congrès International
de l'Association d'Etudes Occitanes*, ed. Gérard
Gouiran, 2: 669-78. Montpellier: Université Paul
Valéry, 1992.
Close analysis of the first stanza of Gaucelm Faidit's
canso to demonstrate not only structural relationships
but also melodic effects that illustrate the text and
thus constitute a kind of "madrigalism."
603
Pollina, Vincent. "Les Mélodies du troubadour Marcabru:
Questions de style et de genre." In *Atti del Secondo
Congresso Internazionale della "Association Internationale d'Etudes Occitanes,"* Torino, 31 agosto-5
settembre 1987, ed. Giuliano Gasca-Queirazza, 1:
289-306. Torino: AIEO/Dipartimento di Scienze
Letterarie e Filologiche, Università di Torino, 1993.
Discussion of Marcabru's four extant melodies. Argues
that stylistic and generic differences are reflected
in melodies as well as in texts.

604
Pulega, Andrea. "Modelli trobadorici della sestina dantesca: esercizi di lettura." *ACME* 31 (1978): 261-328.
Analysis of themes and function of rhyme words in Dante's sestina "Al poco giorno e al gran cerchio d'ombra" leads to a discussion of models, including Raimbaut d'Aurenga "Er resplan la flors inversa," Peire d'Alvernha "Deiosta·ls breus iorn e·ls loncs sers," and especially Arnaut Daniel, whose "Lo ferm voler" is given detailed treatment including remarks about the music.

605
Räkel, Hans-Herbert S. *Die musikalische Erscheinungsform der Trouvèrepoesie.* Bern and Stuttgart: Paul Haupt, 1977.
Discussion of transmission and stylistic features of trouvère song based on a study of *contrafacta.* Argues for early oral transmission, followed in the later 13th century by the use of written models growing out of a "writerly" and "bourgeois" milieu.

606
Räkel, Hans-Herbert S. "Höfische Strophenkunst." *Zeitschrift für deutsches Altertum und deutsche Literatur* 111 (1982): 193-219.
Discussion of formal structures primarily in trouvère song, for which the point of departure is Silvia Ranawake's book of the same title.

607
Räkel, Hans-Herbert S. "Le Chant du roi, le roi du chant. L'Invention mélodique chez Thibaut de Champagne." In *Thibaut de Champagne: Prince et poète au XIIIe siècle,* ed. Yvonne Bellenger and Danielle Quéruel, 57-64. Lyon: La Manufacture, 1987.
Compares "Tant ai amours servie longuement" by Thibaut to "Quant je plus sui en paor de ma vie" by Blondel de Nesles to show how Thibaut renewed the art of trouvère melodic invention.

608
Ranawake, Silvia. *Höfische Strophenkunst: Vergleichende Untersuchungen zur Formentypologie von Minnesang und Trouvèrelied.* München: Beck, 1976.
Comprehensive comparative study of the songs of the

trouvères and the Minnesinger on the basis of formal structures.

609
Rea, John A. "The Pilgrim Figure in Jaufré Rudel."
Neophilologus 55 (1981): 518-23.
Discussion of the erotic overtones of the pilgrim figure in "Lanquan li jorn son lonc en mai."

610
Rieger, Angelica. "*En conselh no deu hom voler femna*: Les dialogues mixtes dans la lyrique troubadouresque."
Perspectives médiévales 16 (1990):47-57.
Inventories and characterizes the "dialogues mixtes," between men and women, in the troubadour repertory. Argues that, although it cannot be proved that these are real women's voices, it also cannot be proved that they are not, and that feminine performances, the female singing voice, was surely an important facet of troubadour song.

611
Rieger, Angelica. "Beruf: *Joglaressa*. Die Spielfrau im okzitanischen Mittelalter." In *Feste und Feiern im Mittelalter*, ed. Detlef Altenburg, Jörg Jarnut and Hans-Hugo Steinhoff, 229-42. Sigmaringen: Thorbecke, 1991.
Investigates the role of the *joglaressa* compared to the *soldadeira* and the *trobairitz*.

612
Rieger, Dietmar. "Audition et lecture dans le domaine de la poésie troubadouresque." *Revue des langues romanes* 87 (1983): 69-85.
Argues that a particular lack in troubadour studies is work on conditions of production and reception of the songs. To begin to fill that lack, the article attempts to offer proof of reading as a type of reception beside the "normal" mode of listening.

613
Rieger, Dietmar. "'Par devant lui chantent li jugleor': Mittelalterliche Dichtung im Kontext des 'Gesamtkunstwerks' der höfischen Mahlzeit." In *Essen und Trinken in Mittelalter und Neuzeit. Vorträge eines interdisziplinären Symposions vom 10.-13. Juni 1987 an der Justus-Liebig-Universität Gießen*, ed. Irmgard Bitsch, Trude Ehlert, Xenja von Ertzdorff and Rudolf Schulz,

27-44. Sigmaringen: Thorbecke, 1987.
Underscoring the importance of mealtimes to courtly
society for establishing conviviality and forging social bonds, this article examines the essential role
of musical and poetic performance at meals. Although
supporting evidence is chiefly drawn from romances, the
arguments developed can shed light on performance of
lyric as well.
614
Rieger, Dietmar. "'Senes breu de parguamina'? Zum Problem
des 'gelesenen Lieds' im Mittelalter." *Romanische
Forschungen* 99 (1987): 1-18.
Argues for the reception of troubadour song by reading.
615
Rieger, Dietmar. "'Chantar' und 'faire.' Zum Problem
der trobadoresken Improvisation." *Zeitschrift für
romanische Philologie* 106 (1990):423-35.
After a review of scholarly discussion of this problem,
argues against improvisation.
616
Rosenstein, Roy. "Latent Dialogue and Manifest Role-
Playing in Bernart de Ventadorn." *Neuphilologische
Mitteilungen* 91 (1990): 357-68.
A discussion of "Non es mervelha s'eu chan."
617
Rosenstein, Roy. "New Perspectives on Distant Love:
Jaufre Rudel, Uc Bru, and Sarrazina." *Modern Philology*
87 (1990): 225-38.
Argues that some of the problems surrounding "Qan lo
rius de la fontana" can be resolved by examination of
the life of Hugh VII of Lusignan, the recipient of the
song. Claims that Jaufre redirects Hugh from the profane love of Sarrazina, his late wife, to the infinite
love of the Spouse.
618
Roubaud, Jacques. *La Fleur inverse: Essai sur l'art
formel des troubadours*. Paris: Ramsay, 1986.
Study of troubadour poetry by a modern poet and math-
ematician. Poetry seen as formal art but also as pas-
sion.
619
Scherner-Van Ortmerssen, Gisela. *Die Text-Melodiestruktur
in den Liedern des Bernart de Ventadorn*. Münster:

Aschendorff, 1973.
Rigorous analysis of Bernart de Ventadorn's songs, but overly schematic since no account is taken of variants or of nuances of performance.
620
Schlager, Karlheinz. "Annäherung an ein Troubadour-Lied. 'Tant m'abellis l'amoros pessamens' von Folquet de Marseille." In *Analysen: Beiträge zu einer Problemgeschichte des Komponierens. Festschrift für Hans Heinrich Eggebrecht zum 65. Geburtstag*, ed. Werner Breig, Reinhold Brinkmann and Elmar Budde, 1-13. Stuttgart: Steiner, 1984.
Discussion of the formal properties of Folquet's song, focussed on the melody.
621
Segarra, Marta. "*Can vei la lauzeta mover*: une analyse rhythmique." *Revue des langues romanes* 95 (1991): 136-46.
Analysis based on the theories of Henri Meschonnic (*Critique du rythme: anthropologie historique du langage* [Paris: Verdier, 1982]) comparing rhythm in music and language.
622
Smith, Nathaniel. *Figures of Repetition in the Old Provençal Lyric*. University of North Carolina Studies in the Romance Languages and Literatures, No. 176. Chapel Hill, 1976.
Analysis of repetition drawing on medieval rhetoric and modern criticism to demonstrate its central importance to troubadour song. Some reference to music.
623
Städtler, Katharina. *Altprovenzalische Frauendichtung (1150-1250): Historisch-soziologische Untersuchungen und Interpretationen*. Heidelberg: Winter, 1990.
Identifies the trobairitz corpus; attempts to situate the female poets in southern French society; and discusses selected poems, among them "A chantar m'er" by the Comtessa de Dia, the only trobairitz text for which we have a melody.
624
Steel, Matthew C. "A Case for the Predominance of Melody over Text in Troubadour Lyric: Bernart de Ventadorn's 'Can vei la lauzeta mover.'" *Michigan Academician* 14

(1982): 259-71.
Argues that the music in R reflects the specific text
in R in ways that are obscured if an edited composite
text is substituted for R's text.
625
Stevens, John. "Medieval Song." In *The New Oxford History
of Music*, Vol. II: *The Early Middle Ages to 1300*, ed.
Richard Crocker and David Hiley, 357-451. Oxford:
Oxford University Press, 1990.
General survey of sources, questions of rhythm and
notation, and genres, each of which is given separate
treatment. Includes Latin as well as the various vernaculars. Numerous musical examples.
626
Suchla, Beate Regina. "Zu Notation, Metrum und Rhythmus
des altfranzösischen Liedes. Dargestellt an einem
Melodienachtrag zu dem Lied *Pour le tens qui verdoie* im
Chansonnier de Saint-Germain, Paris, BN, f.fr.20050."
Archiv für Musikwissenschaft 36 (1979): 159-84.
After a study of the notation of this song, different
from the normal messine neumes of 20050, and of general
issues of meter and rhythm, dates the added melody to
the late 13th or early 14th century.
627
Switten, Margaret Louise. *The Cansos of Raimon de
Miraval: A Study of Poems and Melodies*. Cambridge, MA:
The Medieval Academy, 1985.
The first part constitutes an analysis of music/text
relationships in the songs of Raimon de Miraval, treating separate parameters of the song, then the weaving
of separate elements into a complex, multi-layered
whole. The stanza is the richest locus for music/text
analysis and has been the most studied; this book also
moves beyond the stanza to examine the song as a whole.
The second part of the book is an edition of melodies
of the 22 extant *cansos* with music.
628
Switten, Margaret. "De la Sextine: amour et musique chez
Arnaut Daniel." In *Mélanges de langue et de littérature
occitanes en hommage à Pierre Bec*, 549-65. Poitiers:
Université de Poitiers C.E.S.C.M., 1991.
A reading of the sestina of Arnaut Daniel in the light
of passages from Plato's *Timaeus* on the creation of the

universe and the world soul, focussing on musical and
poetic structures in the sestina and analogies between
Plato's creator and the fabricating poet.

629
Switten, Margaret. "Modèle et variations: Saint Martial
de Limoges et les troubadours." In *Contacts de langues,
de civilisations et intertextualité, Actes du IIIème
Congrès International de l'Association Internationale
d'Etudes Occitanes*, ed. Gérard Gouiran, 2: 679-96.
Montpellier: Université Paul Valéry, 1992.
Analysis of the probable use of the "Ave maris stella"
melody by several troubadours as an intertextual phenomenon. Argues that the use of this melody by Guiraut
de Bornelh in "Reis glorios" brings a feminine
presence--specifically the Virgin/Eve complex carried
by the melody--to the *alba* from the outset, enriching
the tensions between religious and secular topoi dis-
played by the text.

630
Switten, Margaret. "Singing the Second Crusade." In *The
Second Crusade and the Cistercians*, ed. Michael
Gervers, 67-76. New York: St. Martin's Press, 1992.
Discussion of Jaufre Rudel's "Lanquan li jorn," music
and words, in the context of the Second Crusade, arguing that the song may be richly interpreted in the
light of the love and desire as well as the frustration
and failure that characterized St. Bernard's experience
of crusade.

631
Switten, Margaret. "The Voice and the Letter: On Singing
in the Vernacular." In *Acta 17: Words and Music*, ed.
Paul R. Laird, 51-73. Binghamton: CEMERS, 1993.
Examination of the first examples of Old Occitan song
with both words and music in the Saint Martial source
BN 1139 and projection of the findings onto the troubadour manuscript tradition. Argues that reading troubadour manuscripts, all from the 13th and 14th centuries,
in the light of the earlier image from the period during which the troubadours began to compose, reinforces
the concept of troubadour song as a close union of melodic motion with the natural idiom of the vernacular.
When music later attained a rhythmic life of its own
and the notational techniques to express it, the

earlier union was altered because the conceptual framework undergirding the union of words and music had
shifted.

632
Szabics, Imre. "Structure et sens poétiques dans les
anciennes chansons d'amour occitanes." *Acta Litteraria
Academiae Scientiarum Hungaricae* 25 (1983): 237-47.
Literary analysis of the *alba* of Guiraut de Bornelh
and "Can l'erba fresch'e·lh folha par" by Bernart de
Ventadorn.

633
Tavera, Antoine. "Lanquan li jorn: l'inépuisable texte."
In *Hommage à Pierre Nardin*, 67-81. Annales de la Faculté des Lettres de Nice, Nº 29. [Paris]: "Les Belles
Lettres," 1977.
Argues that it is the absence of narration, of progression in the text, whose formal perfection holds in
perfect equilibrium the underlying tensions of love,
that enables one to read different stanza orders as so
many different but equally valid expressions of these
tensions: the song's meanings are thus inexhaustible.

634
Taylor, Robert A. "'L'altrier cuidai aber druda' (PC
461, 146): Edition and Study of a Hybrid-Language
Parody Lyric." In *Studia Occitanica in memoriam Paul
Remy*, ed. Hans-Erich Keller, 2: 189-201. Kalamazoo:
The Medieval Institute, 1986.
Argues that "L'altrier cuidai," preserved in BN fr.
844, was composed in northern France rather than in
Occitania and that it is a pastiche of a troubadour
poem. Includes an edition of the poem and a transcrip-
tion of the melody from BN 844. See Gerard-Zai (B507);
Billy (B468, B659).

635
Taylor, Robert. "Pons d'Ortaffa: Images of Exile and
Love." In *Mélanges de langue et de littérature occitanes en hommage à Pierre Bec*, 567-73. Poitiers: Université de Poitiers, C.E.S.C.M., 1991.
Discussion and edition based on MS C of Pons's two
poems, one of which has music, although the melody is
not mentioned here.

636
Thomas, Patrick A. "La Voyelle en miroir: la tapisserie

vocalique de 'Can vei la lauzeta mover.'" *Neuphilologische Mitteilungen* 92 (1990): 363-70.
Detailed analysis of intralinear vowel sounds ("voyelles accentuées intraversiculaires") to show how these sounds reflect the mirror imagery characteristic of the poem as a whole.

637
Tischler, Hans. "Trouvère Songs: The Evolution of Their Poetic and Musical Styles." *Musical Quarterly* 72 (1986): 329-40.
Analysis of Gace Brulé, Thibaut de Navarre, Adam de la Halle. Argues that these songs show increasingly greater variety of formal structures with a decreasing emphasis on church modes and a change from "minor" to "major." Findings illustrated by several pages of tables.

638
Tischler, Hans. "The Performance of Medieval Songs." *Revue Belge de Musicologie* 43 (1989): 225-42.
Continues the argument for metric-rhythmic interpretation of medieval song, with illustrative transcriptions from the troubadour and trouvère repertory.

639
Topsfield, L.T. *Troubadours and Love.* Cambridge: Cambridge University Press, 1975.
Study of themes of love in eleven troubadours, presented chronologically, including Jaufre Rudel, Marcabru, Bernart de Ventadorn, Peire d'Alvernha, Arnaut Daniel, Raimon de Miraval, Peire Cardenal, and Guiraut Riquier for whom music has been preserved although the music is not discussed. One of the best available general introductions to troubadour poetry.

640
Treitler, Leo. "The Troubadours Singing Their Poems." In *The Union of Words and Music in Medieval Poetry,* ed. Rebecca A. Baltzer, Thomas Cable and James I. Wimsatt, 15-48. Austin: University of Texas Press, 1991.
Argues that in the troubadour tradition, music interprets language by responding to verse structures, to syntax, to semantic and poetic nuance. After a short exposition of some pertinent features of melodic grammar underlying medieval melody, illustrates the main argument with Jaufre Rudel, "Lanquand li jorn"; Bernart

de Ventadorn, "Can vei la lauzeta mover"; and Raimon de Miraval "Aissi cum es genser pascors" (texts and melodies furnished with article and performed on the cassette accompanying the volume).

641
Treitler, Leo. "Medieval Lyric." In *Models of Musical Analysis: Music before 1600*, ed. Mark Everist, 1-19. Oxford: Blackwell, 1992.
Proposes techniques of musical analysis for two Aquitanian *versus*, one troubadour song (Jaufre Rudel "Lanquand li jorn"), and one German song, considering them representative of medieval lyric in general.

642
Tyssens, Madeleine. "Chansons hétéromorphiques?" *Cultura Neolatina* 48 (1988): 113-41.
Vigorously refutes the arguments advanced by Marshall (1984 above) to define a category of song called "heteromorphic." Finds Marshall's "irregularities" can most satisfactorily be explained as errors.

643
Tyssens, Madeleine. "Colin Muset et la liberté formelle." In *Hommage à Jean-Charles Payen. Farai chansoneta novele: Essais sur la liberté créatrice au Moyen Age*, 403-17. Caen: Centre de Publications de l'Université de Caen, 1989.
Considers strophic irregularity in four songs by Colin Muset and finds the irregularities neither so numerous nor so certain as has been thought. The "liberty" of Colin Muset's poetry resides not in negligence but in skillful manipulation of theme and form.

644
Van Os, J.A. "Structures mélodiques et rythme déclamatoire dans la chanson de trouvère." In *Langue et Littérature Françaises du Moyen Age*, ed. R.E.V. Stuip, 51-62. Amsterdam: Van Gorcum, 1978.
Using as a point of departure Zumthor's *Essai de poétique médiévale* and an article by Ruwet, "Fonction de la parole dans la musique vocale" (in *Langage, musique, poésie*, ch. 2), and taking methodology from Dragonetti (*La Technique poétique des trouvères*) for the texts and Smits Van Waesberghe (*Melodieleer*, Amsterdam, 1950) for the music, Van Os proposes an analysis of text and melody, each having its own

identity, leading to a synthesis that shows the dialectical relationships between them. The analysis is carried out on "Tant m'a mené force de signorage" by Gace Brulé, in the version of the *Chansonnier de l'Arsenal*.

645
Van der Werf, Hendrik. *The Chansons of the Troubadours and Trouvères*. Utrecht: Oosthoek, 1972.
The impact of this study, partly because of the controversy it aroused over the question of rhythm, and partly because it is one of the few studies in English, has been considerable. The first part examines the major musical questions of the repertories; the second part presents 15 songs with variant melody versions by important troubadours and trouvères.

646
Van der Werf, Hendrik. "The 'Not-so-precisely Measured' Music of the Middle Ages." *Performance Practice Review* 1 (1988): 42-60.
Presents arguments in favor of performing monophonic repertories by making pitches of more or less equal duration.

647
Van Vleck, Amelia E. *Memory and Re-Creation in Troubadour Lyric*. Berkeley: University of California Press, 1991.
Examines the troubadour corpus (texts, with only brief passing reference to music) from the standpoint of influences brought to bear upon it by modes of transmission. Inspired by Zumthor's theory of *mouvance*, the analysis seeks to demonstrate the troubadours' attitudes towards their texts and then describes what can be deduced about transmission from extant manuscripts. Finally, in a concluding section, troubadour controversies about poetics are reviewed in the light of the deductions about transmission.

648
Van Vleck, Amelia E. "Rigaut de Berbezilh and the Wild Sound: Implications of a Lyric Bestiary." *Romanic Review* 84 (1993): 223-40.
Argues that Rigaut is specifically concerned with the "dimension of sound implicit in the visual images he invokes" (224). Songs with melodies are treated but without specific reference to music.

649
Venturi, Mariacristina. "Ancora un caso d'intertestualità

fra trovieri e trovatori." *Medioevo Romanzo* 13 (1988):
321-29.
Compares incipits from texts by Jaufre Rudel, Conon de
Béthune, Guiraut de Bornelh, Raoul de Soissons, and Uc
de Saint Circ to show how poets individualize compositions by diversely developing similar motifs. The motif
selected for emphasis is the requirement that a song be
readily understood by the audience ("Chançon legiere a
entendre . . .").
650
Warning, Rainer. "Moi lyrique et société chez les troubadours." In *Archéologie du Signe*, ed. Lucie Brind'Amour
and Eugene Vance, 63-100. Toronto: Pontifical Institute, 1983.
Argues that one of the chief components of courtly poetry is its public nature: it is eminently social. It
is also institutional in that it depends for its reception on public understanding and recognition of its
ideals, while it, in turn, becomes part of an historical process institutionalizing those ideals. The critic
must therefore approach texts as acts of institutionalized language (although we cannot know completely
the institutional reality behind the language). Music
is not studied; but several suggestions in the notes
underline the importance of the concept of singing,
and how connotative dimensions of music might be taken
into consideration.
651
Winter-Hosman, Mieke de. "La Naissance d'une terminologie
des genres chez les premiers troubadours." *Amsterdamer
Beiträge zur älteren Germanistik* 30 (1990): 139-49.
Argues for a consideration of troubadour genres as historical phenomena rather than as timeless categories.
652
Wunderli, Peter. "Réflexions sur le système des genres
lyriques en ancien français." In *Mélanges de langue et
de littérature occitanes en hommage à Pierre Bec*, 599-
615. Poitiers: Université de Poitiers C.E.S.C.M., 1991.
Proposes several revisions to the system of genres
elaborated chiefly by Köhler in the *Grundriss der
romanïschen Literaturen des Mittelalters*, Vol. II.
653
Zaganelli, Gioia. *Aimer, sofrir, joïr: i paradigmi della*

soggettività nella lirica francese dei secoli XII et XIII. Firenze: La Nuova Italia, 1982.
Discussion of various thematic developments of fin'amor in trouvère poetry, from Chrétien de Troyes to Adam de la Halle and Guillaume le Vinier. Complete chapters devoted to Gace Brulé and Thibaut de Champagne.

654
Zink, Michel. *Belle. Essai sur les chansons de toile, suivi d'une édition et d'une traduction.* Transcriptions musicales de Gérard Le Vot. Paris: Champion, 1978.
The introductory essay reviews the problems posed by the *chansons de toile,* addressing the question of their "archaic" quality and underlining relations to the *chanson de geste.*

655
Zink, Michel. "Musique et subjectivité: Le passage de la chanson d'amour à la poésie personnelle au XIIIe siècle." *Cahiers de civilisation médiévale* 25 (1982): 225-32.
Argues that the 13th century witnesses the development of a new poetry that is subjective in the sense that it presents an anecdotal self anchored in real space and time, rather than the generalized subject of troubadour and trouvère lyric. The paradigm of this new poetry is the *dit.* It renounces music and strophic construction, which characterized the earlier esthetic, thus bringing about a divorce between poetry and music that is the inevitable result of the discovery by poetry of its own power and its own truth.

THIRTEENTH-CENTURY INTERACTIONS: MONOPHONIC AND POLYPHONIC STYLES; LYRIC AND NARRATIVE

656
Anderson, Gordon A. "Motets of the Thirteenth-Century Manuscript La Clayette." *Musica Disciplina* 27 (1973): 11-40 "The Repertory and its Historical Significance"; 28 (1974): 5-37 "A Stylistic Study of the Repertory."
The first article lists and discusses the contents of the manuscript, arguing that the MS belongs to the middle period of the early motet tradition and that its greatest claim to historical importance is its

collection of 13 bilingual motets. The second article
describes stylistic features: rhythm, melody, and
vertical alignment (or "harmony").

657
Barth-Wehrenalp, Renate. *Studien zu Adan de la Hale.*
Tutzing: Schneider, 1982.
Studies the melodies, and text-melody relationships,
in Adam de la Halle's works in their sociological
context and in comparison to songs of trouvères and
troubadours, using computer methodology.

658
Baumgartner, Emmanuèle. "Les Citations lyriques dans le
Roman de la Rose de Jean Renart." *Romance Philology* 35
(1981-2): 260-66.
Argues that courtly songs and dance refrains function
as a metaphor for the couple Conrad-Lïenor. Their marriage is the union of two conceptions of love: the
imaginary courtly conception transformed by the carole.
Thus the lyric quotations give the love story its exem-
plarity and meaning.

659
Billy, Dominique. "Une Imitation indirecte de *L'Altrier
cuidai aber druda:* le motet *Quant froidure trait a fin/
Encontre la saison d'esté.*" *Neophilologus* 74 (1990):
536-44.
An edition of the motet text as it appears in Cl (BN
nouv. acq. fr.13521, "La Clayette") and in W2
(Wolfenbüttel 1099). The melody is also transcribed.
The edition serves to rectify some erroneous listings
of the text and also to propose, based on comparative
examination of versification, that *L'Altrier cuidai*
served as a model for a series of motets on the tenor
Agmina milicie. See Billy (B468); Gérard-Zai (B507);
Taylor (B634).

660
Bonifacio, Mariella Vianello. "Temi e motivi nelle
'chansons' di Gautier de Coinci." *Studi francesi* 27
(1983): 458-70.
Argues from close analysis of vocabulary and key concepts in Gautier's songs that the blending there of
liturgical and courtly traditions constitutes a new
and original art of love.

661
Butterfield, Ardis. "Repetition and Variation in the Thirteenth-Century Refrain." *Journal of the Royal Musical Association* 116 (1991): 1-23.
Examines problems of identifying refrains, taking into account their melodies. Analyzes formulae to discern minimal structural units and describe their functioning. Focusses on the refrain "Hareu, li maus d'amer m'ochist." Argues for the perception of some refrains as groups possessing certain shared fundamental syntactic structures.

662
Butterfield, Ardis. "The Language of Medieval Music: Two Thirteenth-Century Motets." *Plainsong and Medieval Music* 2 (1993): 1-16.
Examines the motets "E non Dieu/Quant voi/NOBIS" and "Pour escouter/L'autrier joer/SECULORUM AMEN" to demonstrate that because relationships between lines of text are ordered by music, the syntactic function of music acquires semantic significance.

663
Coldwell, Maria V. "*Guillaume de Dole* and Medieval Romances with Musical Interpolations." *Musica Disciplina* 35 (1981): 55-85.
General overview of 13th- and 14th-century romances with musical interpolations, including several tables listing romances, manuscripts, number and types of interpolation, presence or absence of musical notation. Gives detail for *Guillaume de Dole* with song concordances where they exist. Analyzes for *Guillaume de Dole* how the interpolated songs function in the narrative, and describes the different performance situations.

664
Crocker, Richard. "French Polyphony of the Thirteenth Century." In *The New Oxford History of Music*, Vol. II: *The Early Middle Ages to 1300*, ed. Richard Crocker and David Hiley, 636-78. Oxford: Oxford University Press, 1990.
Excellent overview, focussing primarily on polyphony with French texts in order to begin to discern their specific nature (compared to polyphony with Latin texts). Discussion organized by manuscript sources: motets in "Munich MüA"; in the Chansonniers; in W$_2$; in

the Codex Montpellier.

665
Dömling, Wolfgang. "Eine Motette der ars antiqua: *Quant flourist - Non orphanum - Et gaudebit.*" In *Chormusik und Analyse: Beiträge zur Formanalyse und Interpretation mehrstimmiger Vokalmusik*, ed. Heinrich Poos, 2 vols., 1: 21-27. Mainz: Schott, 1983.
Analysis of an exemplary Ars antiqua motet, texts and music. Complete piece in Vol. 2 which contains all examples.

666
Drzewicka, Anna. "La Fonction des emprunts à la poésie profane dans les chansons mariales de Gautier de Coinci." *Le Moyen Age* 91 (1985): 33-51; 179-200.
Reacting against the idea that the religious lyric is merely a parasite genre, borrowing themes from secular lyric, Drzewicka argues that religious song can be seen, on the one hand, as a "conversion" of secular songs and on the other as possessing its own "register" which draws as much on Latin as on vernacular sources.

667
Evans, Beverly. "The Textual Function of the Refrain Cento in a Thirteenth-Century French Motet." *Music and Letters* 71 (1990): 187-97.
Argues the case for textual unity in the motet "Qui amours veut maintenir/Li dous pensers/Cis, a cui" from the Montpellier Codex, on the basis of chains of associations of phonetic patterns and lexical repetitions, with the refrain acting to balance and unify the entire structure.

668
Evans, Beverly. "Music, Text, and Social Context: Reexamining Thirteenth-Century Styles." In *Contexts: Style and Values in Medieval Art and Literature*, ed. Daniel Poirion and Nancy Freeman Regalado, 183-95. Special Issue, *Yale French Studies*, 1991.
Examines 13th-century plurilingual motets (French and Latin) from the Montpellier Codex to argue that the motet is a skillful blending of simultaneous but different voices that can be situated in the 13th-century contexts described by Zumthor as "dynamismes conflictuels": encounters and interactions between old and new styles.

669
Everist, Mark. "The Rondeau Motet: Paris and Artois in the Thirteenth Century." *Music and Letters* 69 (1988): 1-22.
Discussion of the rondeau motet as a genre, arguing that of the 13 works previously identified as rondeau motets only eight have sufficient common characteristics to constitute a genre, and these eight may have been composed away from mainstream Parisian musical practices, possibly in Arras.

670
Everist, Mark. "The Refrain Cento: Myth or Motet?" *Journal of the Royal Musical Association* 114 (1989): 164-88.
Argues that of the 19 works that have been proposed as examples of a "refrain cento" genre, only three fit the description of refrain cento, and those three are so diverse that refrain cento needs to be considered a technique and not a genre.

671
Everist, Mark. "Anglo-French Interaction in Music, C1170-C1300." *Revue Belge de Musicologie* 46 (1992): 5-22.
Investigates the presence of "French" music in "English" manuscripts as an antidote to the more usual practice of seeking "English" compositions in "French" sources.

672
Everist, Mark. *French Motets in the Thirteenth Century: Music, Poetry and Genre.* Cambridge: Cambridge University Press, 1994.
Discusses the origins of the vernacular motet focussing specifically on the French motet, the processes of texting and creating structures, and the ways of understanding genre as a tool for classification.

673
Gally, Michèle. "Disputer d'Amour: Les Arrageois et le jeu-parti." *Romania* 107 (1986): 55-76.
Discussion of the language of the *jeu-parti*, emphasizing metaphors and proverbs as a way of diversifying, deconstructing and re-constructing the discourse of the *canso*. Argues, by a brief comparison to Thibaut de Champagne, that the school of Arras moves further toward transforming the genre than does Thibaut, a

move possibly due to the desire to reflect urban tastes.

674

Huot, Sylvia. "Transformations of Lyric Voice in the Songs, Motets and Plays of Adam de la Halle." *Romanic Review* 78 (1987): 148-64.

Argues that through experimentation with lyric con-structs, Adam explores relationships between private and public identities, between personal experience and poetic topos, and thus creates a complex lyric persona that functions as author and as protagonist, imparting to his corpus a high degree of poetic unity.

675

Huot, Sylvia. "Polyphonic Poetry: The Old French Motet and Its Literary Context." *French Forum* 14 (1989): 261-78.

Discusses 13th-century motets in the Montpellier Codex (H 196). Relates the motet to other poetic innovations of the 13th century, emphasizing affinities with such phenomena as debate poems, lyric-insertion romances, or first-person narratives.

676

Jung, Marc-René. "L'Empereur Conrad, chanteur de poésie lyrique: Fiction et vérité dans le *Roman de la Rose* de Jean Renart." *Romania* 101 (1980): 35-50.

Argues that the courtly songs performed by Conrad de-fine both his character and a fictional discourse that leads to an impasse. The impasse is resolved when Conrad sings a concluding refrain that allows him to find the truth of his love for Lïenor.

677

Le Vot, Gérard. "La Notation musicale et le chant dans les chansonniers et les recueils de motets français au XIIIe siècle." In *Littérales 4: Théories et pratiques de l'écriture au moyen âge* (1988): 155-89.

Comparative study of 13th-century musical notation in trouvère chansonniers and in motet collections, and of the different relations between notation and perform-ance that characterize the two repertories.

678

Maillard, Jean. "Les Refrains de carole dans Renart le Nouvel." In B402, 205-21.

Brief overview of the number and function of refrains

in *Renart le Nouvel*. Numerous examples transcribed.
679
Malizia, Uberto. "Gautier de Coinci: la volontà di rinnovare la musica lirica ne 'Les Miracles de Nostre Dame.'" In *La Lengua y la literatura en tiempos de Alfonso X*, *Actas del Congreso Internacional*, Murcia 5-10 marzo 1984, ed. Fernando Carmona and Francisco J. Flores, 319-32. Murcia: Universidad de Murcia, 1985.
Argues that Gautier de Coinci participated knowledgeably in the development of a new kind of religious song, in "un' evoluzione dalla musica gregoriana a quella profana e popolare."
680
Malizia, Uberto. "Gautier de Coinci e la *chanson* medievale." In *Quaderni di filologia e lingue romanze*, 3rd Series, 2 (1987): 63-75.
Pursues the examination of technical terms begun at the Trèves conference (see below) by setting them in their cultural contexts in order to draw conclusions about Gautier's understanding of *chanson*.
681
Malizia, Uberto. "Intorno al lessico tecnico-musicale ne *Les Miracles de Nostre Dame* di Gautier de Coinci." In *Actes du XVIIIe Congrès International de Linguistique et Philologie Romanes*, *Université de Trèves (Trier)*, *1986*, 405-17. Tübingen: Niemeyer, 1988.
Philological examination of technical musical terms.
682
Malizia, Uberto. "Note sull'atto musicale: Gonzalo de Berceo e Gautier de Coinci." *Quaderni di filologia e lingue romanze*, 3rd Series, 5 (1990): 21-39.
Studies specific terms that qualify and describe music and the act of singing.
683
Mullally, Robert. "Cançon de Carole." *Acta Musicologica* 58 (1986): 224-31.
Argues that the carole, which first appeared (but with text alone) in Jean Renart's *Romance of the Rose* in the early 13th century, was typically performed to the singing of the dancers themselves, often solo singers, without instruments. The song, typically in the form of a rondeau or rondeau refrain, was initially designated *chançon*; specific terms such as rondeau or

virelai came only in the 14th century. Although refrains are discussed, no reference is made to Van Den
Boogaard.

684

Page, Christopher. "The Performance of Ars Antiqua
motets." *Early Music* 16 (1988): 147-64.
Discussion of important technical aspects of motet
performance: types and number of voices, instrumental
participation, performing pitch, handling of wordless
tenor parts, pronunciation and manner of articulation,
tempo.

685

Pesce, Dolores. "The Significance of the Text in
Thirteenth-Century Latin Motets." *Acta Musicologica* 58
(1986): 91-117.
Argues that motet poetry reveals a manipulation of
sounds, rhetorical expressions, and rhythmic patterns
that can be enhanced by skillful polyphonic musical
presentation. Text likely played a more significant
role in motet design than has usually been recognized.
Emphasizes Latin double motets from the Bamberg Codex
with some reference to the French or bilingual versions of which they may have been *contrafacta*.

686

Pesce, Dolores. "A Case for Coherent Pitch Organization
in the Thirteenth-Century Double Motet." *Music Analysis* 9 (1990): 287-318.
Argues persuasively, using examples of Latin double
motets from Mo H 196, that a number of techniques con-
verge to create a high degree of pitch coherence in
these motets despite the absence of a system of tonality or modality.

687

Rahn, John. "Teorie sur alcuni mottetti dell'*ars antiqua*,
con relative considerazioni metodologiche." In *Musical
Grammars and Computer Analysis*, ed. M. Baroni and L.
Callegari, 39-58. Florence: Olschki, 1984.
Analyzes the motet "Je cuidoie bien metre jus/Se j'ai
folement amé/SOLEM."

688

Sciacca, Brunella. "Analisi delle strutture musicali e
testuali nel motetto del XIII sec." *Nuova Rivista
Musicale Italiana* 1 (1993): 69-86.

Using a sampling of 10 motets, Sciacca analyzes relationships of language sounds and melodic "cellules" in
tenor and upper parts, first separately then together.

689
Smith, Norman E. "The Earliest Motets: Music and Words."
Journal of the Royal Musical Association 114 (1989):
141-63.
Reviews hypotheses about the origins of the motet; ac-
cepts the traditional assumption that Latin texts were
added to the duplum voice of pre-existent clausulae;
emphasizes features of notation to support his views.
690
Smith, Norman E. "An Early Thirteenth-Century Motet." In
Models of Musical Analysis: Music before 1600, ed. Mark
Everist, 20-40. Oxford: Blackwell, 1992.
Excellent model analysis of "Hodie Marie concurrant/
REGNAT," with an introduction succinctly defining the
motet and summarizing the main features of its origins.
691
Smith, Robyn E. "Music or Literary Text? Two Ways of
Looking at the Thirteenth-Century French Motet."
Parergon 4 (1986): 35-47.
A persuasive argument that study of the music is important to establish motet text divisions, despite a misunderstanding of the syllabic nature of French verse
that vitiates a portion of the argument. [See B771]
692
Smith, Robyn E. "Gennrich's *Bibliographisches Verzeichnis
der französischen Refrains*: Tiger or Fat Cat?" *Parergon*
8 (1990): 73-101.
Prolegomenon to renewed examination of what constitutes
a refrain in the 13th-century motet, discussing criteria and categories for classification; definition of
the refrain; use of evidence such as position of refrains, or manuscript punctuation.
693
Speck, Linda. "The Lives and Loves of Robin and Marion:
Subjects Juxtaposed in the Late Thirteenth-Century
French Motet." In *Music from the Middle Ages Through
The Twentieth Century. Essays in Honor of Gwynn McPeek*,
ed. Carmelo P. Comberiati and Matthew C. Steel, 34-39.
New York: Gordon and Breach Science Publishers, 1988.
Of the 188 late 13th-century French motets, 13 contain

a reference to Robin, to Marion, or to both, in one or
more of their texts. Describes how the treatment of
these stock characters provides a glimpse of motet compositional process as a whole.
694
Spottswood, Louisa. "The Influence of Old French on Latin
Text-Setting in Early Measured Polyphony." In *Beyond
the Moon: Festschrift Luther Dittmer*, ed. Bryan
Gillingham and Paul Merkley, 163-82. Ottawa: The
Institute of Medieval Music, 1990.
Argues that composers of early measured polyphony heard
and spoke Old French and hence likely understood Latin
with the rhythmic patterns of the vernacular. Illustra-
tive examples are taken from the Montpellier Codex.
695
Steel, Matthew. "A Reappraisal of the Role of Music in
Adam de la Halle's *Jeu de Robin et de Marion.*" In *Music
from the Middle Ages Through The Twentieth Century.
Essays in Honor of Gwynn McPeek,* ed. Carmelo P.
Comberiati and Matthew C. Steel, 40-55. New York:
Gordon and Breach Science Publishers, 1988.
Discusses the contribution of the musical refrains or
rondets de carole to the dramatic complexity of Adam's
play.
696
Stevens, John. "The Manuscript Presentation and Notation
of Adam de la Halle's Courtly Chansons." In *Source
Materials and the Interpretation of Music: A Memorial
Volume to Thurston Dart,* ed. Ian Bent, 29-64. London:
Stainer and Bell, 1981.
Describes all the manuscript sources of Adam's songs
and analyses briefly one song, "Je n'ai autre re-
tenanche," from the standpoint of notation. Argues for
the existence of a genuinely diversified notational
tradition for monophonic song; sees, for example, a
carefully planned juxtaposition of mensurally notated
monophonic music (refrains of *Robin et Marion* and of
Renart nouvel), polyphonic pieces, and non-mensural
courtly chansons (where scribes seem to avoid clear
mensural patterns) in the chansonnier Pn 25566(W) containing Adams's "complete works." A series of notational charts supports the reasonings.

697
Stewart, Michelle F. "The Melodic Structure of
Thirteenth-Century 'Jeux-Partis.'" *Acta Musicologica*
51 (1979): 86-107.
Examines stylistic traits in the melodies of 105 *jeux-
partis*, including formal textual and musical structures, tonality, melodic design, repetition of melodic
motifs, opening and cadential motions. Argues that the
melodies exhibit the art of variation within traditional forms developed to a high degree by performers.
698
Tischler, Hans. *The Style and Evolution of the Earliest
Motets (to circa 1270)*. Musicological Studies 40. 3
vols. Henryville/Ottawa/Binningen: Institute of Medieval Music, 1985.
Designed as a companion volume to the edition of *The
Earliest Motets* (B315). Volume 1 is a study of the repertory's historic evolution and musical and textual
styles; Volume 2 provides in tabular form information
about tenor sources, names and dates of poets and musicians, quotations and "refrains," poetic form and content, manuscript contents; Volumes 3a and b constitute
a *catalogue raisonné* of bibliographic, formal, and
stylistic information about each work or work family.
699
Tischler, Hans. "The Lyric Lai before Machaut." In *Music
from the Middle Ages Through The Twentieth Century.
Essays in Honor of Gwynn McPeek*, ed. Carmelo P.
Comberiati and Matthew C. Steel, 56-63. New York:
Gordon and Breach Science Publishers, 1988.
The lai is characterized by two features: stanzas of
differing length and versification; musical repetition
in most or all sections. There are three groups of
pre-Machaut lais: those edited by Jeanroy, Brandin and
Aubry (B205); remaining 13th-century lais; 10 pieces
from the *Roman de Fauvel*. Tischler reviews questions
of terminology (seeing, for example, no discernible
difference in this repertory between "lai" and
"descort"), musical rhythm, modality, structural
features, and, briefly, performance.
700
Tischler, Hans. "A Unique and Remarkable Trouvère Song."
The Journal of Musicology 10 (1992): 106-12.

Calls attention to and transcribes "Quant je voi plus
felon rire" in MS M, where the five stanzas of the poem
are notated throughout in consistent mensural notation,
contrary to usual practice for trouvère songs.

701
Van den Boogard, Nico H.J. *Autour de 1300: Etudes de
philologie et de littérature médiévales*. Ed. Sorin
Alexandrescu, Fernand Drijkoningen and Willem Noomen.
Amsterdam: Rodopi, 1985.
Collection of 15 of Van den Boogard's essays in a
memorial volume. Some essays had been previously
published in French; others are translated for this
volume. Several articles are relevant to research on
13th- and 14th-century poetry and music, such as
"Français, Arithmétique, Histoire: Observations sur
les textes des motets français du moyen âge" 3-17
(first given as an inaugural lecture at the University
of Amsterdam, 1973); or "La Forme des polémiques et
les formes poétiques: dits et motets du XIIIe siècle"
19-40 (published in *Miscellanea Mediaevalia* 10 [1976]:
220-39).

702
Walker, Thomas. "Sui *Tenor* Francesi nei mottetti del
'200." *Schede medievali* 3 (1982): 309-36.
Repertory of 22 motets with French tenors. The tenors
are identified and described. Musical examples.

703
Zaganelli, Gioia. "Sul canzoniere di Adam de la Halle:
sistema lessicale e itinerario ideologico." *Medioevo
Romanzo* 6 (1979): 247-70.
Argues that not only the *congés* but also Adam's courtly
songs reveal a "new art." Bases the argument on com-
parisons to the songs of Gace Brulé and Thibaut de
Navarre.

FOURTEENTH CENTURY

704
Arlt, Wulf. "Aspekte der Chronologie und des Stilwandels
im französischen Lied des 14. Jahrhunderts." In
*Aktuelle Fragen der musikbezogenen Mittelalter-
forschung*. Forum musicologicum 3: 193-280. Winterthur:

Amadeus, 1982.
After a review of research on 14th-century French song,
Arlt examines the songs of Lescurel, early Machaut bal-
lades, and Machaut's monophonic virelais, addressing
problems of chronology and stylistic change in the 14th
century.
705
Arlt, Wulf. "*Donnez signeurs*-Zum Brückenschlag zwischen
Ästhetik und Analyse bei Guillaume de Machaut." In
*Tradition und Innovation in der Musik. Festschrift für
Ernst Lichtenhahn zum 60. Geburtstag*, ed. Christopher
Ballmer and Thomas Gartmann, 39-64. Winterthur:
Amadeus, 1993.
Argues that the concepts elaborated in Machaut's *Pro-
logue* ("scens," "retorique," "musique") are useful for
analysis of his music. The argument is developed
through careful analysis of compositional process
revealed by the two versions of "Donnez signeurs,"
where the second version can be considered a reworking
of the first.
706
Bent, Margaret. "Manuscripts as Répertoires, Scribal
Performance and the Performing Scribe." In *Atti del
XIV Congresso della Società Internazionale di
Musicologia: Trasmissione e recezione delle forme di
cultura musicale*, ed. Angelo Pompilio, Donatella
Restani, Lorenzo Bianconi and F. Alberto Gallo, 1:
Round Tables, 138-47. Torino: E.D.T., 1990.
Addresses the question of in what sense manuscripts
can be considered "living" repertories of polyphonic
music. Based on discussion of four different cases:
Machaut manuscripts; Old Hall and related manuscripts;
Bologna Q15; and parts of the Trent codices. Argues
that Machaut manuscripts constitute a living repertory
reflecting movement and change. For all four cases,
the conclusions raise the question of how manuscripts
relate to composition and performance.
707
Bent, Margaret. "Deception, Exegesis and Sounding Number
in Machaut's Motet 15." *Early Music History* 10 (1991):
15-27.
The second of two articles on this motet (see Kevin
Brownlee B715). Precise and rich analysis of the

overlapping numerical structures of the motet which reveals that the composer's carefully crafted duplicitous and ambivalent musical strategies reflect the duplicities of the texts. Perceptive analysis of the role of the tenor.

708
Berger, Christian. "Die melodische Floskel im Liedsatz des 14. Jahrhunderts: Magister Franciscus' Ballade 'Phiton.'" In *Atti del XIV Congresso della Società Internazionale di Musicologia: Trasmissione e recezione delle forme di cultura musicale*, ed. Angelo Pompilio, Donatella Restani, Lorenzo Biancioni and F. Alberto Gallo, 3: *Free Papers*, 673-79. Torino: E.D.T., 1990.
Points out the implications of melodic flourishes not only for musical structure *per se* but also for transcription, and for the elaboration of musical rhetoric independent of texts.

709
Berger, Christian. *Hexachord, Mensur und Textstruktur: Studien zum französischen Lied des 14. Jahrhunderts*. Beihefte zum *Archiv für Musikwissenschaft*, vol. 35. Stuttgart: Steiner, 1992.
Emphasizing Ars subtilior, and the Codex Reina, demonstrates analytic techniques that can reveal how 14th-century music works. Edition and close analysis of the ballade "L'escu d'amors."

710
Boogaart, Jacques. "Love's Unstable Balance. Part I: Analogy of Ideas in Text and Music of Machaut's Motet 6" and "Love's Unstable Balance. Part II: More Balance Problems and the Order of Machaut's Motets." *Muziek & Wetenschap* 3 (1993): 1-23; 24-33.
Analyses of motets 6 and 10 to show that text and isorythmic plan are related (motet 6) and that number symbolism presides in part over the ordering of the motets.

711
Boulton, Maureen. "Guillaume de Machaut's *Voir Dit*: The Ideology of Form." In *Courtly Literature: Culture and Context*, selected papers from the 5th Triennial Congress of the International Courtly Literature Society, Dalfsen, The Netherlands, 9-16 August, 1986, ed. Keith

Busby and Erik Kooper, 39-47. Amsterdam/Philadelphia:
Benjamins, 1990.
Argues that form represents truth in the sense that
distinct forms (prose, octosyllabic verse, lyric
pieces) reflect simultaneous narrative strategies
pertaining both to the narrator/poet and to the lady.
712
Brown, Howard Mayer. "A Ballade for Mathieu de Foix:
Style and Structure in a Composition by Trebor." *Musica
Disciplina* 41 (1987): 75-107.
Arguing that it is now time to begin discussion about
ways of analyzing and understanding late 14th-century
music, Brown conducts an analysis of Trebor's "Se
Alixandre" that can serve as a model. The analysis is
based on an emended version of Willi Apel's edition of
the song, given as Example 1 at the conclusion of the
article.
713
Brownlee, Kevin. *Poetic Identity in Guillaume de Machaut.*
Madison: University of Wisconsin Press, 1984.
Study of Machaut's *dits amoureux* to examine the new
range of poetic stances Machaut opens up. Argues that
Machaut's concept of poetic identity approaches our
modern notion of "poet." Substantial essays on the
Remede de Fortune and the *Voir-Dit*. No discussion of
music.
714
Brownlee, Kevin. "Guillaume de Machaut's *Remede de
Fortune:* The Lyric Anthology as Narrative Progres-
sion." In *The Ladder of High Design,* ed. Doranne
Fenoaltea and David Rubin, 1-25. Charlottesville:
University of Virginia Press, 1989.
Discussion of the structure and function of lyric
insertions in the *Remede.*
715
Brownlee, Kevin. "Machaut's Motet 15 and the *Roman de la
Rose:* The Literary Context of *Amours qui a le pouvoir/
Faus Semblant m'a deceü/Vidi Dominum.*" *Early Music His-
tory* 10 (1991): 1-14.
The first of two articles on this motet (see Margaret
Bent B707). Summary description of the passage in the
Romance of the Rose by Jean de Meun where Amours con-
fronts Faux Semblant provides a literary context for

the opposition articulated in the motet's triplum and
motetus. This apparent opposition turns out on closer
examination to be false because both Amours and Faux
Semblant belong to the fallen linguistic world of appearances. Against this world is placed the Latin tenor
and God's transcendent word.

716
Calin, William C. "Medieval Intertextuality: Lyric In-
serts and Narrative in Guillaume de Machaut." *French
Review* 62 (1988), 1-20.
Study of the *Remede de Fortune* from the standpoint of
literary techniques.

717
Campbell, Thomas P. "Machaut and Chaucer: *Ars Nova* and
the Art of Narrative." *The Chaucer Review* 24 (1990):
275-89.
A discussion of the text and music of Machaut's three-
part ballade "Je puis trop bien" forms the basis of a
comparison between the two authors that leads to a concluding characterization of Chaucer's style, by analogy
to medieval music, as "'simultaneous' or 'parallel,'
rather than 'vertical' or 'organic'" (287).

718
Cerquiglini, Jacqueline. "Le Clerc et l'écriture: le *Voir
Dit* de Guillaume de Machaut et la définition du *dit*."
In *Literatur in der Gesellschaft des Spätmittelalters*.
*Begleitreihe zum Grundriss der romanischen Literaturen
des Mittelalters, 1*, ed. Hans Ulrich Gumbrecht, 151-68.
Heidelberg: Winter, 1980.
Discussion of generic characteristics of the *dit* as
they can be discerned by analysis of Machaut's *Voir
Dit*: the *dit* has as a principal feature discontinuity;
it constantly presents, or represents, an "I"; and this
I is a *clerc*. Distinguishes between *dit* and *roman*, romances of Chrétien de Troyes as well as romances with
lyric interpolations such as Jean Renart's *Guillaume
de Dole*; sees the *Roman de Fauvel* (where the designation *roman* is from the 19th century) as a *dit*, and
points to the somewhat ambiguous position of the *Roman
de la Rose*.

719
Cerquiglini, Jacqueline. "Le Lyrisme en mouvement."
Perspectives médiévales 6 (1980): 75-86.

Seeks to show how 14th- and 15th-century poetry is not
"fixed" but mobile by comparing it to the *grand chant
courtois*: whereas the latter is composed of discontinu-
ous pieces, the former tends to link pieces together
to form an almost narrative movement through time; to
the latter's single "je," the former opposes the multiple voices of a polyphonic art; and the lyricism of
song is replaced by a lyricism divorced from music
seeking its authenticity in the act of writing.
720
Cerquiglini, Jacqueline. *"Un engin si soutil"*: *Guillaume
de Machaut et l'écriture du XIVe siècle*. Paris:
Champion, 1985.
Important examination of the theory of poetic creation
(or *écriture*) elaborated by Guillaume de Machaut, based
on detailed analysis of the *Voir Dit*, its lyric forms,
poetic voices, and representations of the act of writing.
721
Cerquiglini, Jacqueline. "Le Rondeau." In *Gundriss der
Romanischen Literaturen des Mittelalters*, Vol. VIII/1,
La Littérature française aux XIVe et XVe siècles, ed.
Daniel Poirion, 45-58. Heidelberg: Winter, 1988.
Discusses the structure, evolution, esthetic and social
values of the rondeau, from the standpoint of the text.
722
Cerquiglini-Toulet, Jacqueline. *"Le Voir Dit* mis à nu par
ses éditeurs, même. Etude de la réception d'un texte à
travers ses éditions." In *Mittelalter-Rezeption. Zur
Rezeptionsgeschichte der romanischen Literaturen des
Mittelalters in der Neuzeit*, ed. Reinhold R. Grimm,
337-80. *Grundriss der romanischen Literaturen des
Mittelalters*, ed. Hans Robert Jauss et al. Begleitreihe zum GRLMA, 2. Heidelberg: Winter, 1991.
Shows how the *Voir Dit* has been understood and misunderstood by its several editors.
723
Dahlhaus, Carl. "'Zentrale' und 'periphere' Züge in der
Dissonanztechnik Machauts." In *Aktuelle Fragen der
musikbezogenen Mittelalterforschung. Forum musicologicum* 3: 281-305. Winterthur: Amadeus, 1982.
Discusses syncopated dissonances in Machaut's Ballade 1
to propose the hypothesis (needing further study) that

they constitute a "central" phenomenon however exceptional they may have been when first used by Machaut.
724
Doss-Quinby, Eglal. "*Chix refrains fu bien respondus*: Les
refrains dans la *Suite anonyme de la 'Court d'Amours'*
de Mahieu le Poirier." *Romance Notes* 28 (1987): 125-35.
Argues that the refrains appear in narrative contexts
of courtly entertainment and as expressions of amorous
sentiments.
725
Earp, Lawrence. "Lyrics for Reading and Lyrics for Singing in Late Medieval France: The Development of the
Dance Lyric from Adam de la Halle to Guillaume de
Machaut." In *The Union of Words and Music in Medieval
Poetry*, ed. Rebecca A. Baltzer, Thomas Cable and James
I. Wimsatt, 101-31. Austin: University of Texas Press,
1991.
Argues that in the 14th-century the *grand chant
courtois* virtually disappeared to be supplanted by
dance songs with refrains. Charting this development
is not easy due to the paucity of musical sources.
Tries to account not only for the elevation of the
previously "popular" poetic forms but also for the
conjoined appearance of a new musical style. Machaut's
position is seen as central in both musical and, eventually separate, poetic traditions.
726
Earp, Lawrence. "Texting in 15th-Century French Chansons:
A Look Ahead from the 14th Century." *Early Music* 19
(1991): 195-210.
Argues that starting from 14th-century texting practices can provide a better understanding of 15th-
century practices. In the 14th century, text was
copied first and the music *overlaid*, a sometimes
cumbersome technique that nevertheless when carefully
practiced could produce unambiguous text settings,
although correlations between text and music might be
corrupted by repeated copying. By the mid 15th century,
scribes began to copy the music first, relinquishing
efforts to correlate text and music. This presumes
norms of performance practice that took care of text
setting. Argues further that text should not be applied

to untexted parts of the 14th-century *chanson*.
727
Enders, Jody. "Music, Delivery, and the Rhetoric of
Memory in Guillaume de Machaut's *Remede de Fortune*."
PMLA 107 (1992): 450-64.
Argues that because seeing, saying and singing co-exist
in the memory, mnemonics provides a framework for reviewing and revitalizing concepts of invention and
performance of lyric poetry. In the case of Machaut's
Remede, memory theory can help us understand specific
features such as the "performance" of a polyphonic
song by one performer, as well as the entire conceptual
matrix undergirding the composition of the work.
728
Ferrand, Françoise. "Aux frontières de l'écriture de la
narration et du lyrisme: la Complainte." In *Mélanges de
littérature médiévale . . . offerts à Wolfgang Spiewok*,
ed. Danielle Buschinger, 101-17. Université de Picardie: Centre d'études médiévales, 1988.
Brief discussion of Rutebeuf, fuller analysis of
Machaut, including the music of the *Remede de Fortune*.
729
Frobenius, Wolf. "Petrue de Cruces Motette *Aucun ont
trouvé chant par usage/Lonc tans me sui tenu de
chanter/ANNUNTIANTES:* Französische Motettenkomposition
um 1300." In *Analysen: Beiträge zu einer Problemgeschichte des Komponierens. Festschrift für Hans
Heinrich Eggebrecht zum 65. Begurtstag*, ed. Werner
Breig, Reinhold Brinkmann and Elmer Budde, 29-39.
Wiesbaden: Steiner, 1984.
Study of priorities in compositional decisions for
Petrus's motet. Describes seven steps in the compositional process. This compositional process differs
from that of earlier motets and leads to the 14th-
century isorhythmic motet.
730
Fuller, Sarah. "A Phantom Treatise of the Fourteenth
Century? The *Ars Nova*." *The Journal of Musicology* 4
(1985): 23-50.
Argues that Philippe de Vitry is unlikely to have
written a treatise entitled *Ars nova*. Rather, various
writings with that title were transmitted anonymously.
These treatises seem chiefly to provide knowledge

necessary for performing contemporaneous compositions. *Ars nova* was presented in a complementary (rather than immediately confrontational) relationship to the *ars vetus*: mastery of both older and newer idioms was important to the performer.

731

Fuller, Sarah. "On Sonority in Fourteenth-Century Polyphony: Some Preliminary Reflections." *Journal of Music Theory* 30 (1986): 35-70.
Argues that further study of sonority in 14th-century polyphony is needed. Explores two approaches: examination of *contrapunctus* manuals for information about matters such as nomenclature and classification of sonorities; and analysis of two Machaut motets, "Bone Pastor" and "Faus Samblant m'a deçu," to study syntactical issues such as prolongation, progression, cadence.

732

Fuller, Sarah. "Line, *Contrapunctus* and Structure in a Machaut Song." *Music Analysis* 6 (1987): 37-58.
Close analysis of Machaut's two-part ballade "J'aim miex languir." Brief analysis of the poetic structure seen as basic to an understanding of the music. Approaches the music first from the standpoint of the single line, then the framework of consonances, the *contrapunctus*. Concludes that the ballade should be viewed as a "complex of intersecting planes that do not naturally align themselves hierarchically to form a one-track linear core" (55).

733

Fuller, Sarah. "Modal Tenors and Tonal Orientation in Motets of Guillaume de Machaut." *Studies in Medieval Music: Festschrift for Ernest H. Sanders*, ed. Peter M. Lefferts and Brian Seirup. *Current Musicology* 45-47 (1990): 199-245.
Argues that pitch features of motet tenors, as well as rhythmic patterns, conditioned motet composition, illustrating the argument by numerous examples from Machaut's motets.

734

Fuller, Sarah. "Machaut and the Definition of Musical Space." *Sonus* 12 (1991): 1-15.
Discusses the virelai "Mors sui" in its monophonic and

polyphonic settings and the polyphonic ballade "Donnez seigneurs" to examine their musical space, defined as the initial contexts of a mode of motion and a pitch realm. Definition of musical space is never perfunctory in Machaut's works. How textual contexts might relate to musical contexts is mentioned in a note but not treated in the essay.

735
Fuller, Sarah. "Guillaume de Machaut: *De toutes flours*." In *Models of Musical Analysis: Music before 1600*, ed. Mark Everist, 41-65. Oxford: Blackwell, 1992.
Superb edition and model analysis of Machaut's ballade, expertly linking text and music.

736
Fuller, Sarah. "Tendencies and Resolutions: The Directed Progression in *Ars Nova* Music." *Journal of Music Theory* 36 (1992): 229-58.
Carrying on her previous analysis of 14th-century sonority (1986), Fuller here gives a careful definition of the concept of "directed progression," drawing examples from Machaut. Argues that as Machaut uses it, the directed progression is a significant artistic resource; it can be integrated with text; and it enables diverse and striking tonal effects.

737
Gieber, Robert L. "Poetic Elements of Rhythm in the Ballades, Rondeaux, and Virelais of Guillaume de Machaut." *Romanic Review* 73 (1982): 1-12.
Analyzes use of caesura, rhyme, poetic rhythms. Shows structural importance of rhyme and caesura particularly in ballades and rondeaux. Argues that poetic structure is reflected in musical lines.

738
Göllner, Marie Louise. "Musical and Poetic Structure in the Refrain Forms of Machaut." In *Liedstudien Wolfgang Osthoff zum 60. Geburtstag*, ed. Martin Just and Reinhard Wiesend, 61-76. Tutzing: Hans Schneider, 1989.
Discusses coordinations of text and music in several virelais and ballades to show how Machaut has invented new ways of combining the two. By considering poetic line and musical phrase as independent yet always coordinated elements, Machaut is able to develop unexpected and original interpretations of both.

739

Greckel, Wilbert C. "The *Ballades notées* of Guillaume de Machaut." *The Music Review* 42 (1981): 91-102.
Analysis of the ballades to demonstrate musical innovation and personal expression. Relates texts to musical features. Discusses performance practice.

740

Günther, Ursula. "Fourteenth-century Music with Texts Revealing Performance Practice." In *Studies in the Performance of Late Medieval Music*, ed. Stanley Boorman, 253-70. Cambridge: Cambridge University Press, 1984.
Adduces several 14th-century examples, including "Il vient bien sans appeler" from the Reina Codex, here edited, to demonstrate the importance of manuscript layout and text structure and meanings for performance practice.

741

Günther, Ursula. "Sinnbezüge zwischen Text und Musik in ars nova und ars subtilior." In *Musik und Text in der Mehrstimmigkeit des 14. und 15. Jahrhunderts*, ed. Ursula Günther and Ludwig Finscher, 229-68. Kassel: Bährenreiter, 1984.
Argues that relationships of meaning must be considered to complement formal relationships if deeper understanding of the songs in these repertories is to be achieved. Demonstrates with numerous examples various ways text meanings can be expressed musically on different levels.

742

Günther, Ursula. "Citazione e modello nella musica del XIV secolo." In *Musica e storia tra Medio Evo e Età moderna*, ed. F. Alberto Gallo, 143-8. Bologna: Mulino, 1986.
Traces the development of textual and musical citations across the 14th century. No longer were there motets *entés*, but the technique of refrain citation was transferred to the ballade and subsequently to the virelai. Although the position and function of the quotation remained the same as with the motet *enté*, progressively popular refrains were abandoned in favor of quotations from works of known masters. The culmination, which includes Machaut and several late 14th-century composers,

is reached by Ciconia in "Sus une fontayne" which by
its references to Filippo da Caserta became the first
hommage piece in European music.
743
Gushee, Lawrence. "Two Central Places: Paris and The
French Court in the Early Fourteenth Century." In
*Bericht über den internationalen musikwissenschaft-
lichen Kongress Berlin, 1974*, ed. Hellmut Kühn and
Peter Nitsche, 135-57. Kassel: Bärenreiter, 1980.
Asks whether there might not have been interaction
between Machaut and Parisian minstrelsy in the 14th
century as one factor leading to the development of
the polyphonic chanson. After a discussion of musicians in Paris, Gushee proposes that the polyphonic
chansons of Machaut could perhaps be understood as the
synthesis of monophonic song (in the Cantus) with the
ensemble practices of urban minstrelsy (in Tenor and
Contratenor) rather than as a product of continuous
historical development for which manuscript evidence
would have disappeared. The thesis rests on the idea
that the lower voices of the polyphonic chanson were
instrumental; this and other implications of the proposal were questioned during the Berlin Congress discussions.
744
Guthrie, Steven. "Meter and Performance in Machaut and
Chaucer." In *The Union of Words and Music in Medieval
Poetry*, ed. Rebecca A. Baltzer, Thomas Cable and James
I. Wimsatt, 72-100. Austin: University of Texas Press,
1991.
Examination of the rhythmic structure of octosyllabic
and decasyllabic lines--epic, lyric, and narrative--in
Old Provençal, Old French, Middle French and Middle
English, utilizing linguistic methods. The aim is to
provide background for closer examination of Machaut
and Chaucer and to explore the possibility of different patterns in lyrics with music and those without.
His versification categories do not allow distinctions
such as between a caesura and a break, and outdated or
unreliable editions are used for the earlier period.
745
Higgins, Paula. "Parisian Nobles, A Scottish Princess,
and the Woman's Voice in Late Medieval Song." *Early*

Music History 10 (1991): 145-200.
Although the subject of this article is Antoine
Busnoys, Higgins touches on Machaut's "Toute Belle"
and the *trobairitz* to bolster her very persuasive
argument that much more work needs to be done on the
"role of women as active agents in the creation and
propagation of musical culture in the late Middle
Ages" (194).

746
Hirshberg, Jehoash. "Hexachordal and Modal Structure in
Machaut's Polyphonic Chansons." In *Studies in Musicology in Honor of Otto E. Albrecht*, ed. John Walter Hill,
19-42. Kassel: Bärenreiter, 1980.
Offers a systematic description of the pitch-
structuring process in Machaut's polyphonic chansons,
leading to the conclusions that the repertory of
Machaut's chansons shows gradual formation of a unified harmonic technique, and that the hexachord system
provides a framework for the organization of the chansons. On the basis of his analysis, Hirshberg sets up a
division of Machaut's songs into three groups, and reviews questions of the use of accidentals and the evolution and distribution of cadences.

747
Josephson, Nors S. "Intersectional Relationships in the
French *grande ballade*." *Musica Disciplina* 40 (1986):
79-97.
Examines stylistic features of the *grande ballade*
(1380-1410) to show how composers became more and more
preoccupied with large-scale structural interrelationships and climactic formal devices. Distinguishes
three basic chronological subdivisions: (1) post-
Machaut composers (Hasprois, Cuvelier, Olivier, and
Goscalch); (2) Solage and Senleches; and (3) later
pieces from Chantilly, Modena, and Turin collections.

748
Karp, Theodore. "Compositional Process in Machaut's
Ballades." In *Music from the Middle Ages Through The
Twentieth Century. Essays in Honor of Gwynn McPeek*,
ed. Carmelo P. Comberiati and Matthew C. Steel, 64-78.
New York: Gordon and Breach Science Publishers, 1988.
Raises the question of in what order the diverse parts
of a piece were composed for Machaut's ballades.

Proposes that if voice parts differ in tonal stability, the more stable part was likely composed first; and that if voice parts differ in the degree of medium-scale thematic interrelationship, the part possessing the greater thematic unity was likely composed first. Illustrates these criteria with a group of ballades in which the tenor was likely composed first, followed by a contrasting group in which the cantus was probably conceived first.

749

Koehler, Laurie. "Subtilitas in Musica: A Reexamination of Johannes Olivier's 'Si con cy gist.'" *Musica Disciplina* 36 (1982): 95-118.
Close analysis of Olivier's song, text and music, to bring out the subtlety of its details.

750

Kühn, Hellmut. "Guillaume de Machaut, Motette Nr. 22." In *Chormusik und Analyse: Beiträge zur Formanalyse und Interpretation mehrstimmiger Vokalmusik*, ed. Heinrich Poos, 2 vols, 1, 29-41. Mainz: Schott, 1983.
Analysis of a Latin motet exemplifying isorhythmic techniques. The entire piece is in Volume 2 which contains all musical examples.

751

Leech-Wilkinson, Daniel. "Related Motets from Fourteenth-Century France." *Proceedings of the Royal Musical Association* 109 (1982-83): 1-22.
Because many of the surviving Ars nova motets from before about 1365 are closely related in certain compositional details, they appear to be the work of a small group of composers working together in the same area as part of a continuous tradition, following Philippe de Vitry.

752

Leech-Wilkinson, Daniel. "Machaut's *Rose, lis* and the Problem of Early Music Analysis." *Music Analysis* 3 (1984): 9-28.
Argues against the conception of 14th-century polyphony as exclusively created by "successive composition" and for the validity of applying modern analytical techniques knowledgeably to medieval music. Gives an analysis of Machaut's "Rose, lis" using approaches derived from Schenker. This type of analysis implies that

musical form could operate, to a large extent, independently of textual associations.

753
Leech-Wilkinson, Daniel. *Compositional Techniques in the Four-Part Isorhythmic Motets of Philippe de Vitry and His Contemporaries*. 2 vols. New York: Garland, 1989.
Arguing that a major task now confronting musicologists interested in early music is to formulate questions about the music itself, Leech-Wilkinson studies four-part isorhythmic motets from France c.1315-c.1365. In Vol. 1 he analyzes exhaustively, including the texts but focussing chiefly on the music, three motets of Philippe de Vitry, four motets of Guillaume de Machaut, and six motets from the Ivrea Codex. The conclusion rapidly summarizes the musical processes essential to the form. Examples, charts, and editions to support his analyses are placed together in Vol. 2.

754
Leech-Wilkinson, Daniel. "Not Just A Pretty Tune: Structuring Devices in Four Machaut Virelais." *Sonus* 12 (1991): 16-31.
Argues that the monophonic virelais are far more complex than generally assumed, full of musical subtleties, and that in them there is a consistently appropriate match of music, text, and function.

755
Leech-Wilkinson, Daniel. "*Le Voir Dit* and *La Messe de Nostre Dame*: Aspects of Genre and Style in Late Works of Machaut." *Plainsong and Medieval Music* 2 (1993): 43-73. "*Le Voir Dit*: A Reconstruction and Guide for Musicians." *Plainsong and Medieval Music* 2 (1993): 103-40.
A re-evaluation of the *Voir Dit* songs. Argues that reconstructing the chronology of the songs and comparing them to the Gloria and Credo of the Mass allows a fuller understanding of Machaut's compositional techniques.

756
Lefferts, Peter M. "*Subtilitas* in the Tonal Language of *Fumeux fume*." *Early Music* 16 (1988): 176-83.
Discussion of how *subtilitas* is achieved in tonal language, matching the effects of textual language, with a new edition of the song.

757
Little, Patrick. "Three Ballades in Machaut's *Livre du Voir-Dit*." *Studies in Music* [Australia] 14 (1980): 45-60.
Discusses Machaut's comments about his music and possible application of these ideas to "Ploures, dames," "Nes que on porroit," and "Se pour ce muir" from the *Voir-Dit*. The notion that only a lover can compose music properly and that the composing comes from, or leads to happiness pervades Machaut's work. Argues that in each of the three ballades discussed, Machaut intended emotional tone and significance to be reflected in the music.
758
Maillard, Jean. "Un dyptique marial chez Guillaume de Machaut: Les lais XV et XVI." In *Mélanges . . . offerts à Alice Planche*, 2: 327-37. Nice: Centre d'études médiévales, 1984. [Reprinted in B402, 289-99.]
Analyzes text and music of the two lais to indicate their relationship and how Machaut exploits the resources of textual image and musical technique, both monophony and implied polyphony ("cryptopolyphonie").
759
Malizia, Uberto. "Guillaume de Machaut: Le sette *chansons* del *Remede de Fortune*." *Quaderni di filologia e lingue romanze* 6 (1984): 11-48.
Demonstrates by analysis of each of the songs in the *Remede* that text and melody (for the polyphonic songs, he emphasizes primarily the cantus part) are tightly linked and that melodic language and poetic language are consequently not subordinated to each other but are everywhere in complete harmony.
760
Newes, Virginia. "The Relationship of Text to Imitative Technique in 14th-Century Polyphony." In *Musik und Text in der Mehrstimmigkeit des 14. and 15. Jahrhunderts*, ed. Ursula Günther and Ludwig Finscher, 121-54. Kassel: Bährenreiter, 1984.
Argues that, despite evidence of lack of concern on the part of scribes and composers for text underlay and expression in this repertory, some examples of text-related imitation reveal a desire to bring text structures and meanings into focus, representing a

counter-current to the rhythmic and textural obscurity of the Ars subtilior.

761
Newes, Virginia. "Dialogue and Dispute in Some Polytextual Songs by Machaut and his Successors." *Sonus* 12 (1991): 66-86.

The argument that the polytextual *chanson* is a separate genre, different from polytextual motet or single-texted *chanson,* is developed by reference to dialogue songs and paired texts going back to the Provençal and Old French *tenso* and by close analysis of seven polytextual *chansons* by Machaut and his successors. Shows that the composer's decision to prepare a simultaneous setting of multiple texts led to musical structures having equal and coordinated parts.

762
Olson, Glending. "Toward a Poetics of the Late Medieval Court Lyric." In *Vernacular Poetics in the Middle Ages,* ed. Lois Ebin, 227-48. Kalamazoo: Western Michigan University, 1984.

Discusses ballades, virelais, rondeaux by Machaut, Froissart, Senleches and others (poetry and music) in the context of ethical, educational, and recreational ideas of the late medieval court. Relates lyric production in its social dimension to Aristotelian ideas of social amusement, and shows how, on the personal level, the making of songs can be considered a kind of therapy, a constructive outlet for feeling.

763
Page, Christopher. "Polyphony before 1400." In *Performance Practice: Music before 1600,* ed. Howard Mayer Brown and Stanley Sadie, 79-104. New York: Norton, 1989.

Addresses basic problems of performing this repertory, such as tuning and voice quality, rhythm, instrumentation, subjects discussed in his previous articles but here drawn together and refined. Theories are generously and judiciously illustrated by practical examples.

764
Page, Christopher. "Going beyond the limits: experiments with vocalization in the French chanson, 1340-1400." *Early Music* 20 (1992): 447-59.

Review of evidence for and theoretical and practical

reflections on the question of vocalization of textless parts.
765
Poirion, Daniel. *Le Poète et le Prince: L'évolution du lyrisme courtois de Guillaume de Machaut à Charles d'Orleans*. Paris: Presses Universitaires de France, 1965. [Reprint: Slatkine, 1978]
Fundamental and landmark study of late medieval French poetry.
766
Pulido, Alejandro. "Machaut's Ballade *Tres douce dame*: An Interdisciplinary Approach." *Sonus* 12 (1991): 45-65.
Close analysis of the ballade, taking both textual and musical structures into consideration.
767
Randel, Don Michael. "Reading Composers Reading." In *Acta* 17: *Words and Music*, ed. Paul R. Laird, 89-107. Binghamton: CEMERS, 1993.
Although the subject of this article is Dufay, the excellent analyses of words and music in the *formes fixes* suggest approaches valid for earlier repertories.
768
Reaney, Gilbert. "The Chronology and Structure of the *Roman de Fauvel*." In *La Musique et le rite sacré et profane. Actes du XIIIe Congrès de la Société Internationale de Musicologie. 2: Communications libres*, ed. Marc Honegger and Paul Prevost, 85-104. Strasbourg: Association des Publications près les Universités de Strasbourg, 1986.
Discusses the dating of the manuscript Fr.146 on the basis of the musical interpolations, confirming the accepted chronology (part 1, 1310; part 2, 1314) and arguing that the placing of pieces is closely connected with the action of the *roman*.
769
Regalado, Nancy Freeman. "Masques réels dans le monde de l'imaginaire. Le rite et l'écrit dans le charivari du *Roman de Fauvel*, MS. B.N.fr. 146." In *Masques et déguisements dans la littérature médiévale*, ed. Marie-Louise Ollier, 111-26. Montréal: Les Presses de l'Université de Montréal, 1988.
Discusses the structure (textual and musical) and meaning of the *chalivali* in *Fauvel* fr.146, arguing

that the *Lai des Hellequines* holds the key to the
function of the charivari as moral lesson for the king.

770
Seebass, Tilman. "The Visualization of Music through
Pictorial Imagery and Notation in Late Medieval
France." In *Studies in the Performance of Late Medie-
val Music*, ed. Stanley Boorman, 19-33. Cambridge:
Cambridge University Press, 1984.
Uses pictorial imagery and notation to explore, among
other things, aspects of performance practice in the
Ars subtilior repertory.

771
Smith, Robyn E. "Towards a New Edition of the French
Double and Triple Motets in Fascicles II, V, and VII
of the Manuscript Montpellier, Bibliothèque de l'Ecole
de Médecine, H 196: Some Comments on Editorial Method
and the Motet 'Qui la vaudroit'/'Qui d'amors velt bien
joïr'/'Qui longuement porroit joïr'/Nostrum (Mo ff.
23v-25r)." In *Gordon Athol Anderson (1929-1981) In
Memoriam von seinen Studenten, Freunden und Kollegen*,
ed. Luther Dittmer, 2:544-54. Henryville, PA: Institute of Medieval Music, Ltd., 1984.
Argues that a new edition of the literary texts of the
motets of the Montpellier manuscript is needed and discusses some of the problems these texts pose. Gives a
proposed resolution of the problems using the example
found on folios 23v-25r in the Montpellier codex. Particular attention is given to coordination of musical
and textual structures which can help clarify each
other.

772
Stevens, John. "The 'Music' of the Lyric: Machaut,
Deschamps, Chaucer." In *Medieval and Pseudo-Medieval
Literature*, ed. Piero Boitani and Anna Torti, 109-29.
Cambridge: D.S. Brewer and Tübingen: Gunter Narr, 1984.
Asks how three poets conceived of the relationship between music and poetry. Bases discussion of Machaut on
the *Remede de Fortune*. Finds that for Machaut the relationship is based on "numerical" harmoniousness. Finds
also that Deschamps' conception of music parallels the
medieval notion of *armonia*. Sees Chaucer's relationship
to the French tradition as ambiguous.

773
Strohm, Reinhard. "'La Harpe de mélodie' oder das Kunst-
werk als Akt der Zueignung." In *Das musikalische Kunst-
werk. Festchrift Carl Dahlhaus zum 60. Geburtstag*, ed.
H. Danuser, H. de la Motte-Haber, S. Leopold and N.
Miller, 305-16. Laaber: Laaber-Verlag, 1988.
Demonstrates how "La harpe de mélodie," and other songs
of Senleches, can be seen in their social context as
dedicatory works. In the case of this song, the harp
itself can be interpreted as part of the work's meaning
and the composer's intention.
774
Sturges, Robert S. "The Critical Reception of Machaut's
Voir-Dit and the History of Literary History." *French
Forum* 17 (1992): 133-51.
Argues that the critical reception of Machaut's work
reflects the preoccupations of the critics as much as
or perhaps more than the innate characteristics of the
work itself. The analysis of critical reception of the
Voir-Dit covers the last hundred years. Music is not
included.
775
Switten, Margaret. "Guillaume de Machaut: Le *Remede de
Fortune* au carrefour d'un art nouveau." *Cahiers de
l'Association Internationale des Etudes Françaises*
(1989): 101-16.
Sees the *Remede* not only as an *ars poetica* but also as
an embodiment of the transformation in lyric art usually designated Ars nova. The transformation is expressed
most clearly through the musical notation as visual
representation: a shift in notational technique marks
the passage from old to new at about the mid-point of
the work.
776
Tischler, Hans. "A Lai from the *Roman de Fauvel*." In
*Essays on the Music of J.S. Bach and Other Divers
Subjects: A Tribute to Gerhard Herz*, ed. Robert L.
Weaver, 145-55. New York: Pendragon Press, 1981.
Discussion and transcription of "En ce dous temps."
777
Tischler, Hans. "Die Lais im *Roman de Fauvel*." *Die
Musikforschung* 34 (1981): 161-79.
There are nine lais, four in French, five in Latin.

Describes the lais from the standpoints of performance practice, notation and rhythm, melody and modality, formal structures.

778
Tischler, Hans. "The Two-part Motets of the *Roman de Fauvel*. A Document of Transition." *The Music Review* 41 (1981): 1-8.
The specific "transitional" character of the musical insertions in the *Fauvel* can be seen in microcosm in the two-part motets; a new transcription of "Quare fremuerent" is compared to Schrade's transcription.

779
Uhl, Patrice. "Les 'sotes chançons' du *Roman de Fauvel* (MS E): La symptomatique indécision du rubricateur." *French Studies* 45 (1991): 385-402.
Describes the nature and importance of the "sotes chançons" ("foolish songs") in themselves and as fore-runners of the *fatras*. Further, these "sotes chançons" can provide a glimpse of how the *fatras* might have been presented to an audience since they contain the only examples of music for any songs of that type.

780
Van Nevel, Paul. *Johannes Ciconia (ca. 1370-1411): Een muzikaal-historische situering*. Bierbeek: W. Vergaelen, c.1981.
This study is intended to be a practical approach to issues of interpretation in Ciconia's works. The dis-cussion of interpretation and stylistic features is preceded by a brief review of chronology, manuscripts, Ciconia's compositions and theoretical works, and char-acteristics of musical notation systems used in the manuscripts. Mentions Ciconia's influence on later composers.

781
Weber-Bockholdt, Petra. "Beobachtungen zu den Virelais von Guillaume de Machaut." *Archiv für Musikwissenschaft* 49 (1992): 263-81.
Analyzes poetic and musical structures, emphasizing textual and melodic coordinations of rhythm and versi-fication. Relationships between strophe and refrain are a particular focus.

782
Wilkins, Nigel. "The Late medieval French Lyric: With

Music and Without." In *Musik und Text in der Mehrstimmigkeit des 14. und 15. Jahrhunderts*, ed. Ursula Günther and Ludwig Finscher, 155-73. Basel: Kassel, 1984.
Brief survey of all types of late medieval lyric as a context for those songs with music.

783
Wimsatt, James I. "Chaucer and Deschamps' 'Natural Music.'" In *The Union of Words and Music in Medieval Poetry*, ed. Rebecca A. Baltzer, Thomas Cable and James I. Wimsatt, 132-50. Austin: University of Texas Press, 1991.
Discussion of the concept of "natural music" as Deschamps used it and its influence on Chaucer. Chaucer's works in the fixed forms are contrasted with English alliterative lyric to bring out relationships between Chaucer's verse and the prosodic characteristics of the French lyric.

784
Wright, Lawrence. "Verbal Counterpoint in Machaut's Motet 'Trop plus est belle - Biauté paree de valour - Je ne sui mie.'" *Romance Studies* 7 (1985-86): 1-12.
Analysis of the Machaut motet intended to show, on an introductory level, how one can listen to several poems at once and draw meaning from the experience.

785
Zaslaw, Neal. "Music in Provence in the 14th Century." *Current Musicology* 25 (1978): 99-120.
Discusses the sole remaining Provençal motet within the context of Provençal musical culture in the Middle Ages.

DISCOGRAPHY

GENERAL

786
"A chantar" Lieder der Frauen-Minne im Mittelalter
(Songs of Women--Courtly Love in the Middle Ages).
Estampie: Münchner Ensemble für frühe Musik: Michael
Popp, Sigrid Hausen, Ernst Schwindl. CD DDD,
Christophorus 74583, recorded 1989, issued 1990.

Beatritz de Dia: A chantar. Thibaut de Navarra: Dame
Merci. Audefroi li Bastars: Bele Ysabiauz (9 of 13
stanzas). Anonymous: Por coi me bait mes maris.
Guillaume de Machaut: Lasse, comme oublieray/Se j'aim
mon loyal ami/Pour quoy me bat mes maris; Moult sui de
bonne heure nee.

Instruments used for all songs. The two upper voices
of the Machaut motet are instrumental. Original texts
with summaries in English.

787
L'Anthologie Sonore. <u>Pro Musica Antiqua</u> (Brussels),
Safford Cape and Guillaume de Van, directors. Vol. I.
Gregorian Chant to the 16th Century. LP, The Haydn
Society, Boston, AS 1-5, issued 1954.

Record 1: Gregorian Chant to the 13th Century.
Blondel de Nesles: A l'entrant d'esté. Perrin
d'Angicourt: Quant voi an la fin d'estey. Richard
Coeur de Lion: Ja nuns hons pris. Anonymous: A la
clarté/[Surge] et illuminare [Jerusalem] (instrumental); Au tens pascour/L'autre jour par un matin.
Adam de la Halle: Li dous regars de ma dame.

Record 2: The 13th and 14th centuries. *Anonymous*: En
mai la rosée; Se je chant mains que me suel (chace).
From the *Roman de Fauvel*: Fauvel nous a fait present/
Je voi douleur a venir/Fauvel autant. *Matheus de
Perusio*: Plus onques dame n'a mercy. *Pierre des Mou-
lins*: De ce que fol pense.
Record 3: The 14th and 15th centuries (Machault and
Dufay). *Guillaume de Machault*: Je puis trop bien;
Quant Theseus/Ne quier veoir; De tout sui si confortee.

Chiefly useful as an indication of 1950s performing
styles and approaches to interpretation.

788
*Camino de Santiago: Musik auf dem Pilgerweg zum Hl.
Jacobus*. Ensemble für frühe Musik Augsburg: Wolfgang
Zahn, Pommer, Schlagwerk; Hans Ganser, Sänger,
Blockflöten, Schlagwerk; Sabine Lutzenberger,
Sängerin, Blockflöten; Heinz Schwamm, Fidel, Lira,
Blockflöte, Dulcimer, Drehleier; Rainer Herpichböhm,
Sänger, Chitarra sarazenica, Mittelalter-Laute,
arabischer Ud. LP, Christophorus SCGLX 74032,
recorded 1986.

Anonymous: El mois d'avril/Al cor ai une alegrance/Et
gaudebit. *Guillaume d'Amiens*: Prendés i garde.
Wilhelm IX von Aquitanien: Pos de chantar m'es pres
talenz (6 stanzas and tornada); Farai un vers pos mi
sonelh.

Melodies for the songs of William IX taken from the
14th-century *Jeu de Sainte Agnès* (Pos de chantar) and
from a Saint Martial versus (Farai un vers). Texts and
German translation provided, with helpful notes. All
songs performed with instruments.

789
A Dictionary of Medieval Music. LP, Harmonia Mundi HMF
440 (3). See *History of European Music* (D795), and
separate entries: *Monks and Troubadours* (D798); *The
Heritage of the Troubadours* (D793); *Adam de la Halle
and the 13th Century* (D860).

790

L'Europe Médiévale. La Camerata de Paris: Elena
Polonska, harpes, percussions; Nicole Maison, chants,
percussions; Isabelle Quellier, vièle à archet, cro-
morne, flûtes, percussions; Jean Mac Lean, flûtes,
cromorne, cor de chamois, chalmie. LP, Elyon 35024,
issued 1985.

Marcabru: L'autrier just'una sebissa. *Guiraut de
Riquier*: Fis e verays (instrumental only). *Guiraut de
Bornelh*: Rei glorios. *Thibaut IV de Champagne*: Chanson
(instrumental only). *Richard de Semilli*: Aubade (instrumental only). *Adam de la Halle*: Rondeau. *Guillaume
de Machaut*: Douce dame jolie; Quand j'ay liespart (both
instrumental only).

One or two stanzas of each song; no accompanying texts.
Excessive use of instruments: only three of the songs
listed are actually sung.

791

French Music of the Middle Ages and Renaissance. Studio
für alte Musik, Düsseldorf: Helga Eicke, soprano and
recorder; Doris Slembeck, viola and recorder; Maritta
Kersting, Renaissance lute; Josef Jörres, Renaissance
lute, theorbo, percussion; Birgit Abele, treble viol;
Horst Hedler, tenor viol. LP, MHS 1442, (no date
given).

Gui II, chastelain de Couci: Quant voi esté et le tens
revenir (2 stanzas). *Adam de la Halle*: Robins m'aime,
Robins m'a. *Moniot d'Arras*: Ce fu en mai. *Guillaume
de Machaut*: Ballade, Virelai: Plus dure que (instruments only); Virelai: De tout sui confortee.

Texts and translations provided. Use of instruments
and, frequently, dance-like rhythms characterize the
performances.

792

*Guinevere Yseut Melusine: The Heritage of Celtic Woman-
hood in the Middle Ages*. Ensemble La Reverdie: Ella
de' Mircovich, Elisabetta de' Mircovich, Claudia

Caffagni, Livia Caffagni, with Doron David Sherwin. CD DDD, Musica Antiqua GS 201007, issued 1991.

Cunelier: Se Geneive, Tristan (1 stanza). *Richard I Lionheart*: Ja nus hons pris (12 stanzas and envoi). *Anonymous French*: Pucelete/Je langui/Domino. *Anonymous Provençal*: A l'entrada del tens clar.

Original texts provided with separate translations (not facing). All songs performed with voice(s) and instruments.

793
The Heritage of the Troubadours. L'Héritage des Troubadours. (Trouvères; Minnesänger; chants italiens, ibériques, anglais, Meistersinger; polyphonie précoce: organum, motet). Schola Cantorum of London, Denis Stevens, Musical Director. LP, Harmonia Mundi France HM 442, Musique d'abord, issued 1974. [Also issued as Volume 2 of *A Dictionary of Medieval Music*, HMF 440, and Vol. 2 of the *History of European Music*, MHS OR 350.]

Guillaume le Vinier: Espris d'ire (one section omitted). *Anonymous motet*: Pucelete bele et avenant/Je languis des maus d'amours.

Texts but no translations. Trouvère song with voice alone.

794
Historical Anthology of Music. Early Medieval Music, Pt. 1. University of Chicago Collegium Musicum, Howard Brown, director. LP, Pleiades P 247, issued 1976. [See also *History of European Music,* Vol. 1.]

Marcabru: Pax in nomine. *Bernart de Ventadorn*: Be m'an perdut. *Guiraut de Bornelh*: Reis Glorios. *Raimbaut de Vaqueiras*: Kalenda maya (instrumental). *Richard Coeur de Lion*: Ja nuns hons pris. *Perrin d'Agincourt*: Quant voi en la fin d'estey. *Anonymous*: Douce Dame; En ma Dame.

Texts, transcriptions, and translations (usually 1 or
2 stanzas sung) taken from Archibald T. Davison and
Willi Apel, *Historical Anthology of Music* (Cambridge,
MA, 1946), ch. 2. Instruments used for all songs.

795
History of European Music. Musical Heritage Society collection based on the *Historical Anthology of Music* by
Archibald T. Davison and Willi Apel (Cambridge, MA,
1946). Part One, *Music of the Early Middle Ages*, includes the first three volumes, issued as three recordings, c.1970: OR 349/350/351. These three volumes were
reissued by Harmonia Mundi as *A Dictionary of Medieval
Music*, HMF 440(3). They were also issued separately
as: I, *Monks and Troubadours*, HMF 441 (D798); II, *The
Heritage of the Troubadours*, HMF 442 (D793); III. *Adam
de la Halle and the 13th Century*, HMF 443 (D860). The
volumes are described under their separate headings in
the appropriate section of this discography. Part Two,
Music of the Late Middle Ages and Early Renaissance,
includes Vols. IV-VI issued c.1970 as OR 437/438/439.
These volumes were not reissued by Harmonia Mundi. For
Vol. IV see D899. Vols. V and VI lie outside the purview of this book.

796
Masterpieces of Music Before 1750. 1: *Gregorian Chant to
the 16th Century*. Mogens Wöldike, Musical Director.
LP, Haydn Society HS 7-9038, recorded 1953. CD HSCD-
9038 (no issue date given).

Anonymous trouvère song: Or la truix. *Anonymous motet*:
En non Diu! Quant voi/Eius in Oriente.

Texts in Carl Parrish and John F. Ohl, *Masterpieces of
Music Before 1750* (New York: Norton, 1951). The trouvère song is in modal rhythm. Voice(s) only for both
songs.

797
Medieval Music and Songs of the Troubadours. Musica Reservata, John Beckett, director. Jantina Noorman,
mezzo-soprano; Grayston Burgess, counter-tenor; Nigel

Rogers, tenor; Edgar Fleet, tenor; Geoffrey Shaw, baritone; Ruth David, treble rebec; Daphne Webb, treble
rebec; Desmond Dupré, viol; Michael Morrow, crumhorn,
bagpipe; David Munrow, crumhorn, shawm; Tess Miller,
crumhorn; John Sothcott, recorder, citole; Brian
Wilson, harp; John Beckett, citole, drum, organetto;
Jeremy Montagu, nakers, large tabor. LP, Everest 3270,
issued 1973.

Raimbaut de Vaqueiras: Kalenda maya (3 stanzas). *Adam
de la Halle*: Tant can je vivrai; Amours et ma dame
aussi; Robin m'aime; Li dous regars. *Gace Brulles*: De
bone amor (5 stanzas). *Anonymous*: Prisoner's song;
Mout me fu grief/Robin m'aime/Portare; Pucelete/Je
langui/Domino; Jolietement; Au cuer ai un mal/Je ne
m'en repentirai/Jolietement; J'ai un cuer/Docebit;
Flor de lis/Je ne puis/Douce dame; On parole/A
Paris/Frese nouvele.

No texts or translations provided. Instruments used
with all songs. Contains some attempts, particularly
by Jantina Noorman, to represent medieval vocal
qualities.

798
Monks and Troubadours. Moines et Troubadours. Denis
Stevens, Musical Director. Schola Cantorum of London,
Edgar Fleet, director. LP, Harmonia Mundi 441, Musique
d'abord, issued c.1974. [Also issued as Vol. 1 of
History of European Music OR 349 (D795), and as Vol. 1
of *Dictionary of Medieval Music*, HMF 440 (D789).]

Marcabru: Pax in nomine Domini. *Bernart de Ventadorn*:
Be m'an perdut. *Guiraut de Bornelh*: Reis glorios.
Raimbault de Vaqueiras: Kalenda maya. *Richard Coeur
de Lion*: Ja nuns hons pris. *Perrin d'Angicourt*: Quant
voi en la fin d'estey. *Guillaume d'Amiens*: Vos n'alez
mie. *Anonymous*: Douce dame debonnaire; En ma dame ai
mis mon cuer; C'est la fin; E, dame jolie; Pour mon
cuer.

Texts of stanzas sung (usually 1 or 2) in Archibald T.
Davison and Willi Apel, *Historical Anthology of Music*

(Cambridge, MA, 1946). No instruments used. The first stanza of "Reis glorios" is performed in the three rhythmic interpretations given in the anthology.

799
Music at the Time of the Crusades. Vocal and Instrumental Music of the 13th Century. The Florilegium Musicum of Paris. LP, Vanguard Everyman SRV 317 SD, issued 1973.

Roman de Fauvel: Je vois douleur/Fauvel nous a fait présent; Quant je le voi/Bon vin doit/Ci chans veult boire. *Jehannot de l'Escurel*: Ballade (instrumental). *Anonymous*: Quant define la verdour/Quant repaire la dolçor; L'autre jour par un matin/Au tens pascour/In seculum; Chançonnete, va t'en tost/A la cheminée/Veritatem; Hé, Marotelle/En la prairie. *Guiraut de Bornelh*: Reis glorios.

Summaries and descriptions in English, but no original texts. A variety of instruments used.

800
Music of the Crusades. The Early Music Consort of London, David Munrow, director. Christina Clarke, soprano; James Bowman, counter tenor; Charles Brett, counter tenor; Nigel Rogers, tenor; Geoffrey Shaw, baritone; Eleanor Sloan, treble rebec; Oliver Brookes, bass rebec; James Tyler, lute, citole; Christopher Hogwood, harp, organ, nakers, tabor; Gillian Reid, bells; James Blades, nakers, tabor; David Munrow, recorder, flute, shawm. LP Argo ZRG 673, issued 1971. CD ADD, London 430 264-2, recorded 1970, issued 1991.

Marcabru: Pax in nomine Domini! (3 stanzas). *Guiot de Dijon*: Chanterai por mon corage (3 stanzas). *Le Châtelain de Coucy*: Li noviaus tens (3 stanzas). *Gaucelm Faidit*: Fortz chausa es (1 stanza and tornada). *Conon de Béthune*: Ahi! Amours (3 stanzas and envoi). *Richard Coeur-de-Lion*: Ja nus hons pris (2 stanzas). *Thibaut de Champagne*: Au tens plain de felonnie (2 stanzas and envoi). *Anonymous French*: Je ne puis/Amors me tienent/Veritatem; Chevalier, mult estes guariz (3 stanzas); Parti de mal (2 stanzas and envoi).

All songs are accompanied. Performances are suave and polished. Excellent example of styles cultivated in the 1970s. Texts and translations provided.

801
Music of the Gothic Era. 3 vols. <u>Early Music Consort of London</u>, David Munrow, director. James Bowman, Charles Breet, David James (counter tenors), Rogers Covey-Crump, Paul Elliot, Martyn Hill, John Nixon, John Potter (tenors), Geoffrey Shaw (bass). LP, Archiv Production 2723045 (3), recorded 1975, issued 1976.

[Volume I: The Notre Dame Period: Leonin and Perotin]. Volume II: Ars Antiqua Motets. *Petrus de Cruce*: Aucun ont trouvé/Lonc tans. *Adam de la Halle*: De ma dame vient/Dieux; J'os bien a m'amie parler. *Roman de Fauvel*: La mesnie fauveline/J'ai fait nouveletement; Quant je le voi/Bon vin doit/Cis chans. *Anonymous*: On parole de batre/A Paris/Frese nouvelle; Quant voi/Virgo virginum; S'on me regarde/Prennes i garde; En mai/ L'autre jour/Hé! resvelle toi; El mois de mai/De sedebant bigami.
Volume III: Ars Nova Motets. *Guillaume de Machaut*: Lasse! comment oublieray/Se j'aim mon loyal ami/ Pourquoi me bat; Qui est promesses/Ha Fortune trop suis/Et non est. *Anonymous* (Ivrea Codex): Clap, Clap par un matin/Sur Robin; Les l'ormel a la turelle/Mayn se leva/Je n'y saindai.

Reissued in CD ADD format, CD 415 292-2, abridged (re-issue date not given). The CD contains [Notre Dame Period]; Ars antiqua motets: *Anonymous*: S'on me regarde. *Petrus de Cruce*: Aucun ont trouvé. *Adam de la Halle*: De ma dame vient; J'os bien a m'amie parler. Ars nova: La mesnie fauveline. *Anonymous*: Clap, clap par un matin. *Guillaume de Machaut*: Qui est promesses; Lasse! comment oublieray.

No texts included for the CD. Abridged notes by David Munrow from the earlier set. Instruments generally used in performance; "La mesnie fauveline" and "Lasse, comment oublieray" performed with voices only.

802

Music of the Middle Ages. Collegium Musicum Krefeld,
Robert Haass, director. LP, Vox Pl 8110, issued 1953.
[Also Lyrichord, LLST 897, issued 1961].

Raimbaut de Vaqueiras: Kalenda maya (3 stanzas).
Bernart de Ventadorn: Lancan vei la folha (2 stanzas
plus tornada). *Adam de la Halle*: Dieu soit en cheste
maison.

No texts or translations provided. Instruments used
with all songs.

803

Music of the 12th and 13th Centuries. Pro Musica Antiqua
(Brussels), Safford Cape, director. LP, EMS 201,
c.1950.

Anonymous: Bele Doette (2 stanzas); En mai la rousée
(instrumental); A la clarté; Entre Copin et Bourgois
Bernard de Ventadorn: Can vei la lauzeta mover (1 stanza). *Moniot d'Arras*: Ce fut en mai (3 stanzas). *Adam
de la Halle*: Amours et ma dame aussi; Li dous regars.

Very discreet use of instruments, none with "Can vei
la lauzeta." No texts or translations provided.

804

Songs and Dances of the Middle Ages. Sonus: James
Carrier, shawms, recorder, harp, saz, oud, psaltery,
gemshorn, lute, chitarra, percussion; Hazel Ketchum,
voice, saz, lute, percussion; John Holenko, chitarra,
saz, psaltery, oud, recorder, percussion. CD DDD,
Dorian DIS-80109, issued 1993.

Bernard de Ventadorn: Can vei la lauzeta mover (instrumental). *Colin Muset*: Quant je voi yver (instrumental). *Guillaume de Machaut*: Comment qu'a moy; Dame ne
regardez pas (instrumental). *Guiraut de Bornelh*: Reis
glorios (1 stanza sung twice).

The introduction to this disc warns the listener that
the performers "explore a broad spectrum of improvisa-

tional and timboral aspects" in their interpretations.
This is indeed what happens, to the degree that songs
are quite unrecognizable as such. Several errors mar
the booklet and the disc cover.

805
A *Treasury of Early Music*. 1: *Music of the Middle Ages*.
Compiled and edited by Carl Parrish. Mogens Wöldike,
Musical Director. LP, Haydn Society HSE 7-9100, is-
sued c.1958. CD 7-9100 (no issue date given).

Bernart de Ventadorn: Be m'an perdut (2 stanzas et tornada). *Anonymous Motet*: Je n'amerai autre/In seculum.

Texts in Carl Parrish, *A Treasury of Early Music* (New
York: Norton, 1958).
"Be m'an perdut" is performed in modal rhythm without
instruments. Instruments are used for the motet.

806
Vox Humana: Vokalmusik aus dem Mittelalter. Studio der
frühen Musik: Andrea von Ramm, singer; Sterling Jones,
string instruments; Richard Levitt, singer; Thomas
Binkley, plucked instruments; Candy Smith, singer;
Barbara Thornton, singer; Benjamin Bagby, singer;
Harlan B. Hokin, singer; Alice Robbins, string instruments. LP, Reflexe EMI Electrola 1C 069-46401, issued
1976.

Arnaut Daniel: Lo ferm voler. *Raimbaut d'Aurenga*: Pos
tals sabers (3 stanzas and 1st tornada). *Petrus de
Cruce*: Aucun ont trouvé/Lonc tans sui tenu de chanter;
Mout m'a fait cruieus/He Diex! tant sui de joie es-
loignez; A vous, douce, debonnaire.

Instruments generously used. Texts and translations
provided.

CASSETTES ONLY

807
The Medieval Lyric (B211). Five audio cassettes. Per-

formers: Peter Becker, baritone; Marke Bleeke, tenor; Paul Hillier, baritone; Laurie Monahan, soprano; William Sharp, baritone. The Folger Consort: Robert Eisenstein, vielle; Christopher Kendall, lute, mandora; Scott Reiss, recorders; with Tina Chancey, rebec. Recorded 1987 and 1988, Stereo/Dolby.

Troubadour and Trouvère Songs: *William IX*: Pos de chantar. *Marcabru*: Dirai vos senes duptansa; L'autrier jost'una sebissa. *Jaufre Rudel, vida*; Lanquand li jorn son lonc en mai. *Bernart de Ventadorn*: Can vei la lauzeta; Amics Bernartz de Ventadorn. *Guiraut de Bornelh*: Reis glorios. *Arnaut Daniel*: Lo ferm voler. *Gaucelm Faidit*: Fortz chausa es. *La Comtessa di Dia*: A chantar m'er. *Peire Vidal*: Pus tornatz sui. *Raimon de Miraval*: Aissi cum es genser pascors. *Raimbaut de Vaqueiras*: Kalenda maia, *razo*; Eissamen ai gerreiat. *Guiraut Riquier*: Pus sabers no·m val. *Gace Brulé*: Quant flors et glaiz. *Thibaut de Champagne*: Ausi conme unicorne sui; Chançon ferai; Sire loëz-moi a choisir; Deus est ensi conme li pellicanz. *Etienne de Meaux*: Trop est mes maris jalos. *Colin Muset*: En mai quant li rossignolet. *Anonymous*: O Maria Deu maire; Ben deu hoi mais; In hoc anni circulo; Volez-vous que je vous chant; Bele Doette. *Guillaume de Machaut, Remede de Fortune:* Qui n'auroit (lai); Tels rit au main (complainte, here abridged); Joie, plaisance (chanson roial); En amer (baladelle); Dame de qui (ballade); Dame a vous (virelai); Dame mon cuer (rondelet).

Available: The Medieval Lyric, Margaret Switten, Director, Mount Holyoke College, South Hadley, MA 01075. All songs performed are complete. Texts and translations in separate Anthologies. Voices alone except that instruments are used for one version of "Lo ferm voler," "Kalenda maia" *razo*, "Eissamen ai gerriat," "Deus est ensi," "En mai quant li rossignolet," and for the baladelle and one version of the ballade from the *Remede de Fortune*. Variant melody versions given for some songs.

808
Music of the Middle Ages, David Fenwick Wilson. The

Western Wind and The Hilliard Ensemble, Paul Hillier, director. Recorded 1990. Illustrates examples from the book of the same title (B372). 2 cassettes.

Cassette 1: *Arnaut Daniel*: Lo ferm voler. Cassette 2: *Anonymous*: Quant je parti/Tuo; En non Diu/Quant voi/Eius in Oriente; Trop sovent/Brunete/In seculum; J'ai mis/Je n'en puis/Puerorum. *Petrus de Cruce*: Amours qui/Solem justicie/Solem. *Guillaume de Machaut*: Quant en moy/Amour et biaute; De bon espoir/Puis que la douce; Dame, vostre doulze viaire; Se je souspir; Puis qu'en oubli; Quant je ne voy; Amours me fait desirer; De toutes flours. *Jacob Senleches*: Fuions de ci.

Available from: Schirmer Books, A Division of Macmillan, Inc., 866 Third Avenue, New York, NY 10022. Extensive notes on performance by Paul Hillier and David Fenwick Wilson accompany the cassettes. Voices alone and different combinations of voices and instruments expertly illustrate different performance styles.

809
Music of Medieval Europe I, Jeremy Yudkin. 1 cassette (of 2 in complete set). Studio der Frühen Musik, Thomas Binkley, director, Early Music Institute, Indiana University School of Music. Focus 883-45, stereo. These recordings accompany the book of the same title (B374).

Bernart de Ventadorn: Can vei la lauzeta mover. *Gaucelm Faidit*: Fortz chausa es.

Available from: Focus Recordings, Indiana University Press, 10th and Morton, Bloomington, Indiana 47401, or Prentice Hall, Order Department, 200 Old Tappan Road, Old Tappan, NJ 07675. These examples are taken from previous recordings by the Studio der Frühen Musik.

810
The Union of Words and Music in Medieval Poetry, ed. Rebecca Balzer, Thomas Cable and James I. Wimsatt. Sequentia: Barbara Thornton, voice; Benjamin Bagby,

voice, harp, symphonia; with Eric Mentzel, voice; Patrice Ann Neely, fiddle. Recorded 1988, issued 1991. This cassette accompanies a collection of essays of the same title (B71), originally a colloquium held at the University of Texas.

Jaufre Rudel: Lanquand li jorn son lonc en mai. *Bernard de Ventadorn*: Can vei la lauzeta mover. *Raimon de Miraval*: Aissi cum es genser pascors (2 manuscript versions). *Guillaume de Machaut*: Je sui aussi; Esperance qui m'asseüre. *Adam de la Halle*: Bonne amourette. *Jehan de Lescurel*: A vous douce debonnaire (2 versions: monophonic and three-voice). *Nicole de Margival* (text; music anonymous): Soiez liez, et menez joie. *Anonymous*: E Dex, or ne voi je mie.

Available from: University of Texas Press, Austin, TX 78713. Notes on performance, texts, transcriptions and discussion of the pieces are part of the essay collection.

MONOPHONIC MUSIC OF THE TROUBADOURS AND TROUVÈRES

811
L'Agonie du Languedoc. Studio der frühen Musik, Thomas Binkley, director. Andrea von Ramm, sängerin, organetto; Richard Levitt, sänger, schlaginstrumente; Sterling Jones, streichinstrumente; Thomas Binkley, zupfinstrumente; Claude Marti, chanteur, rezitation; Banjamin Bagby, sänger; Harlan Hokin, sänger; Alice Robbins, streichinstrumente; Paul O'Dette, zupfinstrumente. LP, Reflexe EMI Electrola 1C 063-30 132, issued 1976.

Peire Cardenal: Tartarassa ni voutor; Ben volgra; Razos es qu'ieu m'esbaudei; L'afar del comte Guió. *Guilhem Figueira*: D'un sirventes far. *Tomier et Palazi*: Si col flacs molins torneja. *Peire Bremon Ricas Novas*: Ab marrimen. *Bernart Sicart Marjevols*: Ab greu cossire.

As the introduction points out, "this recording is not

a song recital; it is an attempt to portray the art
and the feelings of a civilization about to die."
Snatches of songs, sometimes read, sometimes sung, are
interspersed with readings from the *Chanson de la croisade albigeoise*. Introduction in English with descriptions and summaries of the different sections. Texts in
Old Occitan with German translations.

812
Amours & Desirs: Songs of the Trouvères. Ensemble für
frühe Musik Augsburg: Sabine Lutzenberger, Sängerin,
Blockflöten, Schalmei, Gotische Harfe; Hans Ganser,
Sänger 2, Psalterium, Schlagwerk; Rainer Herpichböhm,
Sänger 1, Mittelalter-Laute, Chitarra sarazenica,
Gotische Harfe; Heinz Schwamm, Fideln, 5-saitig,
4-saitig, 3-saitig, Schalmei. CD DDD, Christophorus
CHR 77117, recorded 1991, issued 1992.

Moniot d'Arras: Ce fu en mai. *Anonymous*: En un vergier lez une fontenele; Por coi me bait mes maris.
Blondel de Nesle: L'amours dont sui espris. *Jehan
Bodel*: Contre le dous tans novel. *Anonymous*: Jheru-
salem, grant damage me fais. *Colin Muset*: Volez oïr
la muse Muset. *Jean Erart*: Par un tres bel jour de
mai. *Thibaut de Champagne*: L'autrier par la matinee.
Chanson de toile: Bele Yolanz en ses chambres se seoit.

Over a steady and frequently rapid instrumental beat
and framed by sometimes lengthy instrumental preludes,
different vocal combinations are employed, with some
recitation. Texts and German translation, with summaries in English.

813
*Bella Domna. The Medieval Woman: Lover, Poet, Patroness
and Saint.* Sinfonye, Stevie Wishart, director. Mara
Kiek, voice; Stevie Wishart, medieval fiddle, symphony; Andrew Lawrence-King, harps; Jim Denley, percussion (pandeiro, bendir). LP, Hyperion A66283, recorded 1987, issued 1988. CD DDD, CDA66283, issued 1988.

Richart de Fournival: Onques n'amai tant que jou fui
amee. *La Comtesse de Die*: A chantar m'er de so qu'ieu

non volria. *Anonymous*: Domna, pos vos ay chausida;
Lasse, pour quoi refusai.

Useful introduction in English; original texts with
English translation provided. Studied use of instruments, except for "A chantar m'er" which features the
voice alone.

814
*Bernart de Ventadorn, Chansons d'amour: Martim Codax,
Canciones de amigo.* Studio der frühen Musik, Thomas
Binkley, director. Andrea von Ramm, sängerin;
Sterling Jones, streichinstrumente; Richard Levitt,
sänger; Thomas Binkley, zupfinstrumente. LP, Reflexe
EMI Electrola C063-30118, issued 1973.

Bernart de Ventadorn: Ab joi mou lo vers e·l comens;
Pois preyatz me, senhor.

Introduction in English. Original texts with German
translation only. Generous use of instrumental preludes, interludes and accompaniments. Two voices al-
ternate stanzas.

815
Cansós de Trobairitz (Lyrik der Trobairitz um 1200).
Hespèrion XX: Jordi Savall, vielle und lira; Mont-
serrat Figueras, gesang; Josep Benet, gesang; Pilar
Figueras, gesang; Hopkinson Smith, laute und guitarra
moresca; Lorenzo Alpert, flöte und schlaginstrumente;
Gabriel Garrido, guitarra moresca, flöte und schlag-
instrumente; Christopher Coin, vielle und rebab. LP,
Reflexe EMI Electrola 1C 065-30 941 Q, issued 1978.
CD ADD, Reflexe EMI CDM 7 63417 2, digital remastering
1990.

Condesa de Provensa und Gui de Cavaillon, text,
Gaucelm Faidit, music: Vos que'm semblatz dels corals
amadors. *Condesa de Dia*, text, *Raimon de Miraval*, music: Estat ai en greu cossirier. *Alais, Na Yselda i
Na Carenza*, text, *Arnaut de Mareulh*, music: Na Carenza
al bel cors avinen. *Guiraut de Bornelh*, text and music: Si·us quer conselh, bel'ami'Alamanda. *Condesa de*

Dia, text, *Bernart de Ventadorn*, music: Ab joi et ab joven m'apais. *Condesa de Dia*, text and music: A chantar m'er de so q'ieu no voldria. *Cadenet*, text and music: S'anc fui belha ni prezada.

Introduction in English; texts with translation into German. Songs are complete; melodies borrowed as indicated in the booklet; instruments used for all songs.

816
Chansons des Rois et des Princes du Moyen Age. <u>Ensemble Perceval</u>, Guy Robert, director. Katia Caré, voix, flûtes à bec médiévales; Emmanuelle Huret, voix; Alain Serve, voix, luth oriental, percussions; Jean Pierlot, vièle à arc, percussions; Guy Robert, luth médiéval, guitare sarassine, orgue portatif, hautbois à capsule; with Alain Barré, flûtes traversières et flûtes à bec médiévales. CD DDD, Arion ARN 68031, recorded 1987, issued 1987.

Thibaut IV, comte de Champagne et roi de Navarre: J'aloie l'autrier errant (5 stanzas); Du tres douz non a la Virge Marie; Dame, merci; Seigneur, sachiez qui ore ne s'en ira (3 stanzas). *Charles d'Anjou*, roi de Naples: La plus noble emprise qui soit. *Guillaume VII de Poitiers*, duc d'Aquitaine: Pos de chantar (5 stanzas, melody from the Miracle of Sainte-Agnès). *Conon de Béthune*, régent de l'Empire de Constantinople: L'autrier avint en cel autre païs. *Richard Coeur-de-Lion*, roi d'Angleterre: Ja nul hons pris ne dira sa raison (4 stanzas).

Introductory notes in English. Original texts of stanzas sung with English summaries. Generous use of instruments. This recording was produced to celebrate the thousandth anniversary of the Capetian kings.

817
Chansons de Toile au temps du Roman de la rose. Esther Lamandier. LP, Aliénor AL 11, issued 1983. CD ADD, AL 1011, issued 1987.

Manuscrit de St. Germain (Anonymes): Bele Yolanz; Bele

Doette; Oriolanz. *Manuscrit du Roi (Audefroi le Bâtard)*: Bele Isabiauz; Bele Ydoine; Au novel tans.

Original texts with French translations, except that in the CD booklet, no texts or translations are given for the last two songs. No instruments used. Rhythms freely reflecting texts.

818
Chansons der Troubadours: Lieder und Spielmusik aus dem 12. Jahrhundert. Studio der frühen Musik, Thomas Binkley, director. Andrea von Ramm, mezzosopran; Richard Levitt, tenor; Sterling Jones, lira, fidel und rebec; Thomas Binkley, laute und chitarra saracenica; with Nigel Rogers, tenor; Johannes Fink, fidel; Max Hecker, flöte; Robert Eliscu, schalmei; David Fellow, schlagzeug. LP, Telefunken 6.41126 AS (SAWT 9567-B), issued 1970. Reissued in sets 26.35519 and 46.35412, and Musical Heritage Society 847442W.

Peire Vidal: Baron de mon dan covit. *Guiraut de Bornelh*: Leu chansonet'e vil. *Anonymous*: A l'entrada del temps clar. *Bernart de Ventadorn*: Can vei la lauzeta mover. *Raimbaut de Vaqueiras*: Kalenda maia (5 stanzas). *Comtessa de Dia*: A chanter m'er de so qu'eu no volria.

Original texts with English translations provided. Substantial and sometimes disruptive (as in "A chantar") instrumental accompaniments, with the exception of "Can vei la lauzeta" which is performed with voice alone.

819
Chansons der Trouvères: Lieder des 13. Jahrhunderts aus Nordfrankreich. Studio der frühen Musik, Thomas Binkley, director. Andrea von Ramm, mezzosopran, organetto, psalterium, harfe; Richard Levitt, tenor; Thomas Binkley, flöte, dulzian, laute, tambourin, chitarra saracenica, psalterium; Sterling Jones, vielle, lyra, rabel, rebec; with Alice Robbins, vielle, lyra; Hopkinson Smith, chitarra saracenica, laute, tambourin. LP, Telefunken 6.41275 (SAWT-9630), issued 1974. Reissued in sets 26.35519 and 46.35412, and

Musical Heritage Society 847442W.

Jacques de Cambrai: Retrowange novelle. *Guiot de Dijon*: Chanterai por mon coraige. *Anonymous*: Lasse, pour quoi refusai; Li joliz temps d'estey. *Gillebert de Berneville*: De moi doleros vos chant. *Gace Brulé*: Biaus m'est estez. *Etienne de Meaux*: Trop est mes maris jalos.

Original texts provided. Generous use of instruments.

820
Chansons des troubadours: La lyrique occitane au moyen âge XII-XIIe siècles. Gérard Le Vot, direction. Dominique Ferran, orgue portatif; Paul Fustier, vielle à roue; Salah A. Mohammed, luth arabe; Elisabeth Renault, chant; Julien Skowron, vièle à archet, rebec; Jean-Claude Trichard, luth médiéval; Dominique Vellard, chant; Patrick Verdié, cabrette, flûte en canne à trois trous, tabourin à cordes; Gérard Le Vot, chant, tambour de basque. LP, Studio SM 30 1043 [SM37], recorded 1980, issued 1981. Partially reissued in *Troubadours and Trouvères* CD, SM 12 21.75, 1993 (D855). [Also issued in English in 1982 as Medieval and Renaissance Sounds, vol. 7. LP, Desto DC 7217.]

Aimeric de Peguilhan: En greu pantais m'a tengut longamen. *Bertrand de Born*: Rassa, tan creis e monta e poja. *Marcabru*: L'autrier, a l'issida d'abriu. *Rigaud de Barbezieux*: Atressi com Persavaus. *Guiraud Riquier*: Pus astres no m'es donatz. *Gaucelm Faidit*: S'om pogués partir son voler. *Bernard de Ventadour*: Estat ai com om esperdutz. *Raimon de Miraval*: Bel m'es qu'ieu chant e coindei. *Berenguer de Palou*: Domna, si totz temps vivia.

Texts furnished for stanzas (usually 2 or 3) sung. French translations in SM 30 1043; English translations for Desto DC 7217. All songs accompanied except "Bel m'est." Manuscript sources for melodies given in the French but not in the English version.

821

Chansons des Trouvères: La Lyrique française au moyen âge XIIe-XIIIe siècles. Gérard Le Vot, direction. Marcelo Ardizzone, vièle à archet, rebec; Marion Chauvineau, vielle à roue; Paul Fustier, vielle à roue, flûte; Anne-Marie Lablaude, chant; Eric Montbel, chabretou en roseau, cornemuses limousines, chabra et chabrette; Jean-Blaise Roch, chant; Jean-Claude Trichard, luth médiéval; Gérard Le Vot, chant, petite harpe. LP, Studio SM 3011.51 [SM 37], recorded 1981, issued 1982. Partially reissued in *Troubadours and Trouvères*, CD, SM 12 21.75, 1993 (D855).

Gace Brulé: Ire d'amors qui en mon cuer repaire. *Thibaut de Champagne*: Deus est ensi conme le pellicanz. *Blondel de Nesle*: A la dolçor d'esté qui renverdoie. *Hue de Saint-Quentin*: Jerusalem se plaint et li païs. *Joffroi de Chastillon*: Molt ai esté long tens en esperance. *Anonymous*: A vous, Tristan, amis verai (lai arthurien); Chevauchoie lez un bruel; Bele Yolanz en ses chambres seoit; Bien m'ont amors entrepris (motet); A l'entrant dou temps novel.

Original Texts with French translation furnished for stanzas (usually 2 or 3) sung. All songs have instrumental accompaniment. Manuscript sources of melodies provided.

822

Chansons et Danses au Temps des Cathédrales: "La Fête sur le Parvis Nostre-Dame." La Maurache (Mediaeval instruments and voices). CD ADD, Arion ARN 68181, recorded 1981, issued LP 1982, issued CD 1991.

Gautier de Coincy: Entendez tuit ensemble; Puisque voi la fleur novele. *Guiraut Riquier*: Jhesu Crist.

Brief notes but no texts provided. The songs are arranged in different ways, using varied vocal and instrumental forces, with rhythms for Gautier de Coincy adapted from Jacques Chailley's edition. A stanza of "De la Sainte Léocade" is inserted into "Entendez tuit ensemble" following the first two stanzas, followed in turn by a repeat of the first stanza. Preceding "Puis-que voi" one hears a stanza of Gautier de Dargies' "Au tens gent que reverdoie," which has an identical melo-dy. For the Guiraut Riquier song, the first stanza only is performed, followed by a mixture of the final *torna-das*.

823

Le Chant des troubadours. Ensemble Guillaume de Machaut de Paris: Jean Belliard, contre-ténor, percussions; Julien Skowron, crwth gallois, rebecs, vièles à arc; Guy Robert, luth médiéval, guitare mauresque; Bernard Huneau, flûtes à bec, flûte traversière ancienne, cro-morne, flûte de roseau. LP, Arion ARN 38503, recorded 1978, issued 1979.

Guiraut d'Espanha de Toloso: Ben volgra (instruments only). *Jaufré Rudel*: Lan quan li jorn. *Raimbaut de Vaqueiras*: Kalenda Maya. *Bernard de Ventadour*: Quan vei l'alauzeta mover; Quan l'erba fresq'. *Marcabru*: L'autrier just'una sebissa. *Anonymous*: A l'entrada del tens clar; Tuit cil qui sunt enamourat.

Introduction in English. No original texts; modern French translation only. 3-5 stanzas sung; no song complete. Generous use of instruments.

824

The Courts of Love: Music from the time of Eleanor of Aquitaine. Sinfonye, Stevie Wishart, director. Mara Kiek, voice; Jim Denley, bendirs and pandeiro; Paula Chateauneuf, medieval lute; Bonnie Shaljean, medieval harp; Stevie Wishart, medieval fiddles, symphony. CD DDD, Hyperion CDA66367, recorded 1989, issued 1990.

Gui d'Ussel: Se be·m partetz, mala dompna, de vos. *Raimbaut de Vaqueiras*: Kalenda Maia ni fueills de faia (second time instrumental). *Anonymous*: L'on dit q'a-mors est dolce chose. *Bernart de Ventadorn*: Era·m cosselhatz, senhor; Conortz, era sai ben (instruments only); Can vei la lauzeta mover (instruments only). *Cadenet*: S'anc fuy belha ni prezada (second time in-strumental). *Giraut de Bornelh*: S'i·us quer conselh, bel'ami'Alamanda. *Gace Brulé*: Quant je voi la noif remise; Quant voi le tens bel et cler; Quant flours et glais; Quant voi renverdir (all Gace Brulé instrumental only).

Texts and English translations furnished for songs that are sung. A surprising number of songs are turned into instrumental pieces; only "Era·m cosselhatz" is performed without instruments.

825

Danse Royal: French, Anglo-Norman and Latin songs and dances from the 13th century. Ensemble Alcatraz: Susan Rode Morris, soprano; Cheryl Ann Fulton, medieval harps; Kit Higginson, recorders and psaltery; Shira Kammen, vielle and rebec; Peter Maund, percussion; with Roy Whelden, vielle. CD DDD, Elektra Nonesuch 79240-2, recorded 1989, issued 1990.

Anonymous: En Avril au tens pascour; El tens d'iver. *Anglo-Norman Crusade Song*: S'onques nuls hoem (2 stanzas). *Renault de Hoilande*; Si tost c'amis (2 stanzas). *Guillaume Le Vinier*: Espris d'ire et d'amour. *Etienne de Meaux*: Trop es mes maris jalos.

Introduction in English. Original texts for stanzas sung, with English translation (but the Guillaume Le Vinier text is garbled in the booklet). Generous use of instruments.

826

The Dante Troubadours. Martin Best Mediaeval Ensemble: Martin Best, Jeremy Barlow, David Corkhill, Alastair McLachlan. LP (45 rpm), Nimbus 45017, recorded 1982, issued 1982. CD, NI 5002, issued 1983.

Guiraut de Bornelh: Leu chansoneta; Si·us quer conselh. *Bertran de Born*: Ges de disnar; Chasutz sui; Ai, Lemozi. *Arnaut Daniel*: Chanson do-lh mot; Lo ferm voler (melody only). *Bernart de Ventadorn*: Can vei la lauzeta. *Peire Vidal*: Pois tornaz sui. *Raimbaut de Vaqueiras*: Kalenda maya. *Gaucelm Faichit*: Non alegra. *Aimeric de Belenoi*: Nuls om en ren (melody only).

Folquet de Marselha: Ben an mort.

1-4 stanzas of each song are performed with instruments and sometimes zippy rhythms. Original texts with English translations. The Bertran de Born songs have no melodies in the manuscripts. No information on the source of the melodies is provided.

827
Domna. Esther Lamandier. LP, Aliénor AL 19, recorded 1987, issued 1987. CD DDD, AL 1019, 1987.

Guillaume de Machaut: Dame vostre doulz viaire; J'aim la flour de valour. *Peire Vidal*: Pos tornatz sui. *Bernart de Ventadour*: Can l'herba. *Guiraut Riquier*: Jhesu Crist (3 stanzas). Also on the CD: *Machaut*: Dou mal qui m'a longuement; Foy porter, honneur garder; and *Folquet de Marseille*: En chantan.

Presentation of texts is incomplete. For the LP, we have, in original and French translation, Machaut "Dame, vostre" and "J'aim la flour"; Vidal "Pos tornatz"; Riquier "Jhesu Crist." For the CD, Machaut "Dame vostre", "Dou mal"; Ventadorn "Can l'erba"; Riquier "Jhesu Crist." Discreet use of instruments.

828
Le Fou sur le pont. Bernatz de Ventadorn: Troubadour Songs. Camerata Mediterranea, Joel Cohen, director. Anne Azéma, voice; Jean-Luc Madier, voice; François Harismendy, voice; Margriet Tindemans, vièle; Cheryl Ann Fulton, harp; Joel Cohen, voice, oriental lute. CD DDD, Erato 4509-94825-2, issued 1994.

Can vei la lauzeta mover (instrumental and sung versions); Non es meravelha s'eu chan; Cantarai d'aquest trobadors (text: Peire d'Alvernhe; music: Gautier de Coincy); Lo gens temps de pascor (text: Ventadorn; music: Guiraut de Riquer); Can l'herba fresch'e·l folha par; Pois preyatz me, senhor; Tant ai mo cor ple de joya (text: Ventadorn; music: Anonymous, Chansonnier Cangé); Per melhs cobrir lo mal pes (text: Ventadorn; music: Uc Brunenc); Bel m'es can eu vei la brolha;

Lancan vei per mei la landa (text: Ventadorn; music:
Anonymous, Chansonnier Cangé); En cossirer et en
esmai; Era·m cosselhatz, senhor; Lancan vei la folha
(instrumental); Tuit cil que·m preyon qu'eu chan;
Amics Bernart de Ventadorn.

Attractive tribute to a famous troubadour by performers
with excellent knowledge of Occitan. Most songs have
been abridged. Narration from *vidas* and *razos*.

829
Lo Gai Saber: Troubadours et jongleurs 1100-1300. Camerata Mediterranea, Joël Cohen, director. Anne Azéma,
chant; Cheryl Ann Fulton, harpes; François Harismendy,
chant; Shira Kammen, vielle, rebec, harpe; Jean-Luc
Madier, chant; Joël Cohen, luth, cistre, percussion,
chant. CD DDD, Erato 2292-45647-2, recorded 1990,
issued 1991.

Gaucelm Faidit: Del grand golfe de mar (2 stanzas, recited). *Peire Vidal*: Pos tornatz sui en Proenza (1
stanza); Ab l'alen tir vas me l'aire (4 stanzas, melody from Conon de Béthune). *Sordello di Mantova*: Er,
quan renovella e gensa (4 stanzas, anonymous melody).
Bertrand de Born: Bel m'es, quan vei chamjar lo sen-
horatge (3 stanzas, source of melody not given). *Comtessa de Dia*: Ab joi et ab joven (4 stanzas, anonymous
melody). *Raimon d'Avignon*: Sirvens sui avutz et arlotz
(3 stanzas recited). *Raimbaut de Vaqueiras*; Dona, tant
vos ai preiada (6 stanzas, melody from Adam de la
Halle). *Anonymous*: Domna, pos vos ai chausida (cobla).
Guillaume IX de Poitiers: Ab la dolchor del temps novel
(5 stanzas, borrowed melody). *Rogeret de Cambrai*:
French text with melody, 2 stanzas, Nouvele Amor qui si
m'agrée; Anonymous Occitan imitation (13ème siècle), 2
stanzas, Novel'amour que tant m'agreia. *Bernard de
Ventadorn*: Lancan vei la folha (3 stanzas). *Marcabru*:
Dirai vos senes duptansa (6 stanzas). *Peire Cardenal*:
Ar mi puesc ieu lauzar d'amor (4 stanzas); Un sirventes
novel vueill comensar (5 stanzas and tornada). *Azalais
de Porcairagues*: Ar em al freg temps vengut (1 stanza
recited with lengthy instrumental prelude). *Guiraut
Riquier*: Be'm degra de chantar tener (4 stanzas,

melody Bernart de Ventadorn, "Can vei"). *Anonymous*:
O Maria Deu maire (4 stanzas). *Guillaume d'Autpol*:
Esperanza de totz ferms esperans (3 stanzas, melody
from Martim Codax).

The aim is to provide a sampling of the *gai saber*.
Texts are given priority; where there is no extant
melody for a given text, one is borrowed from elsewhere. Instrumental accompaniments are freely devised.
Care was given to pronunciation by the choice of native
speakers of modern Occitan as singers and recitants.
Songs are rarely complete, creating a sense of fragmentation. Detailed information on texts, translations,
and music provided, with a brief rationale for the approach.

830
*Gaucelm Faidit: Songs, Troubadour Music from the 12th-
13th Centuries.* Kecskés Ensemble, Andras L. Kecskés,
director. István Szabó, jingle, zurna, kobsa, recorder, tambourine, psaltery; István Tóth, recorder, drum,
kobsa; Lilla Várhelyi, lyre, rebec, bass rebec; with
Tamás Csányi, voice, tambourine, tabor, pot drum, jingle, drum, hurdy-gurdy; Tamás K. Kiss, hurdy-gurdy, cog
rattle, voice, saz, whistle, kobsa, lyre; Gérard Le
Vot, voice; Miquèu Montanaro, galoubet, Jew's harp,
tabor, bass galoubet; Andras L. Kecskés, tambur, ud,
tambourine, crotales, Irish harp. LP, Hungaroton SLPD
12584 (distribution Harmonia Mundi HM 63), issued 1986.
CD DDD, HCD 12584-2.

Gaucelm Faidit: Al semblan del rei thyes; Chant e
deport; Fortz chausa es que tot lo major dan; Gen
fora, contra l'afan; Ja mais, nuill temps; Lo gens
cors honratz; Lo rossignolet salvatge; Mon cor e mi e
mas bonas chanssos; No m'alegra chans ni critz; Coras
qe'm des benananssa; Si anc nuills hom, per aver fin
coratge; Si tot m'ai tarzat mon chan; S'om pogues
partir son voler; Tant ai sofert longamen greu afan.

Emphasis placed on presenting the melodies; texts are
all incomplete, usually 2 or 3 stanzas. English introduction; original texts with translation into French.

Use of instruments and different rhythmic interpretations.

831

Gérard Zuchetto chante les troubadours XIIe et XIIIe siècles. Patrice Brient, vièle à archet, citole, tympanon; Jaques Khoudir, bendir, derboukas, percussions; Gérard Zuchetto, chant. CD, Gallo CD-529, recorded 1985, issued 1988.

Raimbaud d'Orange: Ar resplan la flors enversa. *Peire Vidal*: Mos cors s'alegr'e s'esjau. *Arnaut Daniel*: En cest sonet coind'e leri; Lo ferm voler qu'el cor m'intra. *Raimon de Miraval*: Chans, quan non es qui l'entenda; Un sonet m'es belh qu'espanda; Bel m'es qu'ieu cant e coindei; Cel que no vol auzir chansos; D'Amor es totz mos cossiriers.

The first stanza only of each text is provided, with translations into English for Arnaut Daniel and Raimon de Miraval. All stanzas are sung. Where melodies have not been preserved, they are invented, and even extant melodies are freely altered. Modern Occitan pronunciation vivifies the language but often distorts medieval sound effects. Instrumental accompaniments and varied vocal forces are employed, though generally the single voice projecting the text is featured.

832

Gérard Zuchetto chante les troubadours XIIe et XIIIe siècles, vol. 2. Trobar et Cantar. Gérard Zuchetto: chant, flûtes de corne et de roseau, guimbardes; Dominique Regef: rebecs, israj, vielle à roue; Jacques Khoudir: Derbourkas, bendirs, percussions. CD DDD, Gallo CD-684, recorded 1991, issued 1992.

Raimon de Miraval: Cel que no vol auzir chansos; Ar'ab la forsa del freis; Apenas sai don m'apreing. *Peire Vidal*: Pos tornatz sui en Proensa. *Peire Raimon de Tolosa*: Pessamen ai e cossir (source of melody not indicated). *Peirol*: Mainta gens mi malrasona.

Original texts with English translations provided.

Free treatment of melodies and rhythms; generous use
of instruments in performance. Modern Occitan pronunciation.

833

Guiraut Riquier et la Cour d'Alphonse X Le Sage. La
Compagnie Médiévale, Hervé Berteaux, director. CD
DDD, Pierre Verany PV.789011, recorded 1989, issued.
1989.

Instrumental "suites" drawn from music associated with
Alfonso's court. No texts.

834

*History of Spanish Music vol. II: Medieval Courtly
Monody, Arabian-Andalusian Music*. Chorus and Atrium
Musicae, José-Lui Ochoa de Alza, director. Carmen
Orihuela, soprano; Maria-Aragón, mezzo-soprano; Lola
Quijano, contralto; Jens-Uwe Eggers, tenor. LP, Musi-
cal Heritage Society MHS 1573, recorded by Hispavox (no
date given).

Marcabru: Pax in nomine Domini. *Berenguer de Palou*:
De la iensor; Dona, la ienser. *El Monje de Montaudo*:
Fort m'enoia. *Guiraut de Borneil*: Reis glorios. *Peire
Cardenal*: Un sirventes novel. *Pons d'Ortafa*: Si ay
perdut. *Guiraut de Riquier*: Canço a la Maire de Deus
(Aisi com es sobronrada, 1 stanza abridged); Fis e
verays.

Commentary in English. No original texts: only Spanish
translations furnished. One stanza sung. Very slow
tempi. Discreet use of instruments for most songs.

835

*Jaufre Rudel, XIIe Siècle. Troubadour. Instrumental and
Vocal Music of the 12th Century*. La Compagnie Médiévale, Hervé Berteaux, director. Marc Bernard, hurdy-
gurdy, voice, percussion; Hervé Berteaux, reed and
horn flutes, shawm, capped oboe; Christian Buono,
voice; Iyad Haimour, kanun, percussion; Louis Soret,
ud, rebec, fiddle, horn flute, ney, shawm, capped oboe,
voice, percussion; Gedeon Richard, narration in Old

Provençal. CD DDD, Pierre Verany PV794022, recorded 1993, issued 1994.

Beginning and ending with a recitation of the Jaufre Rudel *vida*, the disc intersperses extracts from songs of Jaufre Rudel with music drawn from elsewhere (*Carmina Burana*, Saint Martial repertory, Andalousian melody, crusading song) to describe musically the itinerary of the *vida*. Songs of Jaufre Rudel represented: Belhs m'es l'estius (borrowed melody); Quan lo rossinhols; Quan lo riu de la fontana; Qui no sap (source of melody unclear); Non sap chantar; Lan quan li jorn. Other songs: En un vergier sotz fuelha (3 stanzas); Chevaliers, mult estes guaritz (4 stanzas).

The songs are chopped up in such a manner as to render the disc useless for serious study. Original languages with translations into modern French and English. Generous use of instruments.

836
Kalenda maya: Songs and Dances from 1200 to 1550; Spain, Italy, France and Germany. <u>Kalenda Maya</u>, Hans Frederick Jacobsen, director. Tone Hulbaekmo, song, harp, percussion; Henrik Sinding-Larsen, percussion, rebab, oval fiddle; Sverre Jensen, psaltery, mandora, arab lute, long-necked lute, portative organ, harp, percussion; Knut Erik Aagaard, Arab lute, Renaissance lute, guitarra latina, bass viol; Sidsel Brevig, guitar-fiddle; 8-shaped fiddle, violin, rebec; Hans Fredrick Jacobsen, recorders, percussion, Arab lute. LP, Simax PS 1017, recorded 1984, issued 1985.

Gillebert de Berneville: De moi doleros vos chant.

Introduction in English with summaries of songs. No original texts. Instruments used.

837
The Last of the Troubadours: The Art and Times of Guiraut Riquier 1230-1292. <u>Martin Best Medieval Ensemble</u>: Jeremy Barlow, recorders, pipes; David Corkhill, nakers, hammer dulcimer, tabors, drums, bells,

timbrel; Alastair McLachlan, rebecs, fidele; Martin
Best, voice, lute, oud, psaltry. LP (45 rpm), Nimbus
45008, recorded 1981, issued 1981. CD ADD, NI 5261,
issued 1991.

Bertran de Born: Rassa, tan creis (melody only).
Guiraut Riquier: No·m sai d'amor (3 stanzas plus
tornada); La segonda retroencha (instrumental); Planh
for the Lord of Narbonne (Ples de tristor, 2 stanzas);
Fis e verays (3 stanzas plus tornada); La Redonda
(Voluntiers faria; 3 stanzas); La premieyra retroencha
(Pus astres; 4 stanzas); Jesus Crist (2 stanzas); Ja
mais non er (3 stanzas); Be·m degra (spoken text in
English). *Folquet de Marselha*: Si tot me sui a tart
aperceubutz (melody only).

The purpose is to connect Riquier's works to contexts
by placing them beside readings about the Albigensian
Crusade and using them to trace the troubadour's life.
Songs performed with instruments and with different
rhythmic treatment. Texts and translations provided.

838
*Le Manuscrit du Roi (vers 1250). Trouvères & Trouba-
dours.* Ensemble Perceval: Gérard Zuchetto et Katia
Caré, chant; Jean-Pierre Dubuquoy, rebec, vièle à arc;
Patrice Brient, psaltérion; Guy Robert, luth arabe,
harpe et luth médiéval, orgue portatif. CD DDD, Arion
ARN 68225, recorded 1992, issued 1993.

Raimon Jordan: Lo clar temps. *Guiot de Dijon*: Chanterai por mon corage. *Peire Vidal*: Pos vesem que
l'iverns s'irais. *Richard de Fournival*: Onques
n'amait. *Guillaume de Vinier*: Dame des ciux. *Jaufre
Rudel*: Lan que li jor (texte franco-occitan du manuscrit). *Conon de Béthune*: Tant ai amé. *Audefroi de
Bastart*: Bele Emmelos. *Anonymous*: A l'entrada del
tans florit (texte franco-occitan du manuscript);
Domna pos vos ay chausida.

Texts, translations, and notes provided. Texts often
follow the manuscript for linguistic features and
number of stanzas sung. Generous use of instruments.

839

Medieval Monodies: Martin Codax/Marcabru. La Romanesca:
Hartley Newnham, countertenor, percussion; Ruth
Wilkinson, vielle, recorder; Ros Bandt, recorders,
flute, psalter, percussion; John Griffiths, lute,
guitarra morisca. CD, Vox Australis VAST 005-2,
recorded Melbourne, Australia 1982.

Marcabru: L'autrier jost' una sebissa (9 stanzas); Bel
m'es quant son li fruit madur.

Introduction in English. Original texts with English
translation. Alternation of baritone and countertenor
vocal registers for "L'autrier." Instrumental accompaniment and rhythmical interpretations.

840

Music for the Lion-Hearted King. Gothic Voices,
Christopher Page, director. Margaret Philpot, alto;
Rogers Covey-Crump, tenor; John Mark Ainsley, tenor;
Leigh Nixon, tenor. CD DDD, Hyperion CDA66336,
recorded 1988, issued 1989.

Gace Brulé: A la douçour de la bele seson. *Blondel de
Nesle:* L'amours dont sui espris; Ma joie me semont. *Li
Chastelain de Couci:* Li nouviauz tanz. [Includes also
examples of the conductus, two of which use trouvère
melodies as one of their voices: "Purgator criminum"
(lowest voice, melody of "L'amours dont sui espris")
and "Ver pacis apperit" (one part, melody of "Ma joie
me semont").]

Elegant and carefully crafted interpretations. Scholarly introduction, original texts and English translations included. No instruments used. Introductory section on performance indicates that the trouvère songs
are performed according to isosyllabic principles,
"L'amours dont sui espris" in a reasonably strict way,
"Li noviauz tanz" more freely.

841

*Musique en Aquitaine au temps d'Aliénor (XIIe s.): Chants
de troubadours et versus aquitains.* Ensemble Diabolus

in Musica, Dominique Touron, director. Antoine
Guerber, chant, guiterne; Florence Rebeyrolle, vièle à
archet; Dominique Touron, chant, symphonie, guitare
sarrasine, luth, oud; Pierre Touron, flûte à bec,
psaltérion; with Bernard Janssens, chant. CD DDD,
Editions Plein Jeu DMP 9105 C, recorded, 1990.

Guillaume IX: Pos de chantar m'es pres talentz (6 stanzas plus tornada; melody Chigi 84). *Marcabru*: Dirai
vos senes duptansa (8 stanzas). *Bernart de Ventadorn*:
La doussa votz ai auzida (5 stanzas plus tornada).
Versus: O Maria Deu maïre. *Jaufré Rudel*: No sap
chantar qui so non di. *Bertran de Born*: Puois als
baros enoia e lor pesa (4 stanzas; borrowed melody).
Richard Coeur de Lion: Ja nuns hons pris. *Versus*: Be
deu hoi mais; In hoc anni circulo (10 stanzas).

Introduction in English; texts but no translations
(except from Latin to French). Printing of the texts
confusing; references to borrowed melodies incomplete.
Generous instrumental accompaniment with sometimes
lengthy preludes. "In hoc anni circulo" performed by
several voices with added polyphonic effects.

842
Planctus.   Studio der frühen Musik, Thomas Binkley, director.   Andrea von Ramm, sängerin; Richard Levitt,
   sänger; Sterling Jones, rabel morisco, lira, vielle;
   Thomas Binkley, laute, chitarra saracenica; Benjamin
   Bagby, sänger.   LP, Reflexe EMI Electrola 1C 063-30
   129, issued 1976.

Guiraut Riquier: Ples de tristor (4 stanzas plus torna-
das). *Gaucelm Faidit*: Fortz chausa es que tot lo major
dan (3 stanzas plus tornada).

Introduction in English. Original texts with translation into German only. Very generous use of instruments.

843
Proensa.   Theatre of Voices, Paul Hillier, director.
   Stephen Stubbs, lute, psaltery; Andrew Lawrence-King,

harp, psaltery; Erin Headley, vielle; Paul Hillier,
voice. CD DDD, ECM 1368 (837 360-2[Y]), recorded 1988,
issued 1989.

Guilhelm IX: Farai un vers (recited in Old Occitan).
Guiraut de Borneil: Reis Glorios. *Raimon de Miraval*:
Aissi cum es genser pascors. *Marcabru*: L'autrier
jost'una sebissa. *Bernart de Ventadorn*: Be m'an
perdut; Can vei la lauzeta. *Peire Vidal*: Pos tornatz
sui. *Guiraut Riquier*: Be·m degra de chantar (recited
in Old Occitan).

Although instruments are used, the voice and the projection of the songs are featured, with elegant diction
and interpretations. Original texts and English translations provided.

844
Songs of Chivalry. Martin Best Mediaeval Ensemble:
Martin Best, Jeremy Barlow, David Corkhill, Alastair
McLachlan, with Rosemary Thorndycraft. LP (45 rpm),
Nimbus 45023, recorded 1983, issued 1983. CD DDD, NIM
5006, issued 1983.

Guilhelm IX: Farai un vers de dreyt nien (recited in
English translation). *Huon D'oisy*: En l'an que cheva-
lier sont, from Le Tournoiement des Dames. *Thibaut de
Navarre*: Tant ai amors. *Marcabru*: Pax in Nomine Domini. *Blondel de Nesle*: L'amour dont sui espris. *Moniot
d'Arras*: Ce fu en mai. *Bernard de Ventadorn*: La dousa
votz. Chansons de toile (instrumental fantasy).
Anonymous, late 12th century: Chevaliers, mult estes
guariz. *Jaufre Rudel de Blaye*: Non sap chantar.
Beatriz de Dia: A chantar m'er (instruments only).
Raimbaut d'Aurenga: Pois tals sabers. *Peire Cardenal*:
"Now I can delight in love," recitation of "Ar mi
posc."

1-2 stanzas usually performed. English commentary and
translations. Original texts provided for the LP but
not for the CD, which has only English. Generous use
of instruments; sprightly rhythms.

845
"The sweet look and the loving manner." Trobairitz Love
Lyrics and Chansons de Femme from Medieval France.
Sinfonye, Stevie Wishart, director. Vivien Ellis
voice; Stevie Wishart, medieval fiddle, sinfonye,
voice; Paula Chateauneuf, oud; Jim Denley, bendir,
pandeiro. CD DDD, Hyperion CDA66625, recorded 1992,
issued 1993.

Carenza, Alais, Iselda: Na Carenza. Iseut de Capio
and Almuc de Castelnau: Domna N'Almucs, si-us plages.
Beatritz de Romancs: Na Maria. Anonymous: Soufrés,
maris; Toute seule, passerai; Por coi me bait mes
maris?; C'est la gieus en mi les prez; C'est desoz
l'olive en mi les prez; La jus desouz l'olive; Et une
chambre cointe et grant/ET GAUDEBIT (instrumental realisation); Main s'est levee Aëlis/NE (instrumental realisation); Tout leis en mi les prez/DOMINUS (instrumental realisation); Bele Doette as fenestres se siet;
Avant hier en un vert pre (instrumental realisation);
Li debonnaires Dieus (instrumental realisation). Anonymous Trobairitz and Pistoleta: Bona domna, un conseil
vos deman (5 stanzas). Bernart de Ventadorn: Non es
meraveilla s'eu chan (instrumental realisation). Comtessa de Dia: Estat ai en greu cossirier; Estampie on
'A chantar m'er' (instrumental realisation). Marie de
Dregnau de Lille: Mout m'abelist quant le voi (instrumental realisation). Audefroi le Bastart: Bele Emmelos
(instrumental realisation).

Introduction in English. Original texts with English
translations. Generous use of borrowed melodies for
songs of the trobairitz. Generous use of instruments
and experimental instrumental renderings of song melodies not necessarily intended to be for instruments
alone.

846
The Testament of Tristan: Songs of Bernart de Bentadorn
(1125-1195). Martin Best. LP, Hyperion A66211,
recorded 1986, issued 1986. CD DDD, CDA66211, issued
1987.

Bernart de Ventadorn: Pois preyatz me, senhor; Non es meravelha s'eu chan (5 stanzas plus tornada); Can par la flors (5 stanzas plus tornada); Can l'erba fresch' e·lh folha; Can vei la flor (2 stanzas); La dousa votz ai auzida (4 stanzas plus tornada); Lancan vei la folha (5 stanzas plus tornadas); Ara no vei luzir solelh; Ab joi moi lo vers e·l comens (3 stanzas plus tornada); Tant ai mo cor ple de joya; Amors, e que·us es vejaire? (2 stanzas); Be m'an perdut lai enves Ventadorn (5 stanzas plus tornada).

Original texts and English translations included. Discreet use of instruments with two songs unaccompanied: "Can vei la flor" and "Ara no vei luzir solelh."

847
Thibaut de Navarre. Atrium Musicae de Madrid, Gregorio Paniagua, director. LP, Harmonia Mundi France, HM 1016, recorded 1978, issued 1979.

Thirty-three melodies of Thibaut, all instrumental, no texts.

848
Tristan & Iseult. The Boston Camerata, Joël Cohen, director. Henri Ledroit, countertenor; Anne Azéma, soprano; Ellen Hargis, soprano; Richard Morisson, baritone; William Hite, tenor; Joël Cohen, lutes, percussion; Cheryl Ann Fulton, medieval harp; David Douglass, rebec, vielle; Carol Lewis, rebec, vielle; Jesse Lepkoff, transverse flute, recorder; with Steven Lundahl, slide trumpet and recorder; Dan Stillman, shawm; Andrea von Ramm, narration. CD DDD, Erato 2292-45348-2, recorded 1987, issued 1989.

Anonymous: Le lai du chèvrefeuille (instrumental); Lai mortel. *Jean Bodel*: Les un pin verdoyant. *Anonymous*: La u jou fui dedans la mer. *Contessa de Dia*: Estat ai en greu cossirer; *Guiraut de Borneilh*: Reis Glorios. *Conon de Béthune*: Se rage et derverie. *Guiraut Riquier*: Jhesu Crist. *Anonymous*: D'une fausse ypocrisie/Lux magna; Gaite de la Tor; Lonc tans a que; A vous, Tristan, amis verai; Ja fis canchonnetes

et lais; Li solaus luist. Arranged segments of *Marie
de France*: Le lai du chèvrefeuille, and of *Thomas*:
Tristan are recited or performed with borrowed melodies.

Troubadour and trouvère songs, some of them reconstructed, are used as part of a narration of the story
of *Tristan and Iseult*. Normally only selected stanzas
of the songs are performed. A booklet furnishes texts
and translations into English with all pertinent
information.

849
*Trobadors, Trouvères, Minnesänger. Lieder und Tänze des
Mittelalters. Songs and Dances of the Middle Ages.*
Ensemble für frühe Musik Augsburg: Wolfgang Zahn, bass
shawm, percussion; Hans Ganser, Singer 1, recorders,
percussion; Sabine Lutzenberger, singer, recorders;
Heinz Schwamm, vielle, lira, recorder, dulcimer,
hurdy-gurdy; Rainer Herpichböhm, singer 2, chitarra
sarazenica, medieval lute, Arabic ud. CD DDD,
Christophorus CD74519, recorded 1984, issued 1986.

Anonymous: A l'entrada del temps clar; En mai au douz
tens nouvel; Parti de mal. *Bernart de Ventadorn*: Can
vei la lauzeta (6 stanzas plus tornada).

Original texts furnished, without translations. Manuscript sources indicated. All songs accompanied.

850
A Troubadour in Hungary: Peire Vidal. Fraternitas
Musicorum, Gergely Sárközy, director and fiddle, rebec, psaltery, long-necked lute, gusla, double pipes,
ud, gemshorn, bass drum. Dániel Gryllus, shepherd's
pipe, short shepherd's pipe, panpipe, gemshorn, jingle,
percussion; András L. Kecskés, long-necked lute, kobsa,
rebec, bass rebec, gusla, Jew's harp; Béla Zsoldos,
cymbal, jingle, drum, side drum, gobelet drum, bass
drum; Éva Maros, harp; Márta Sebestyén, voice, hurdy-
gurdy; András Laczó, voice, triangle, cymbal, jingle;
Ferenc Sebö, voice, hurdy-gurdy; Zoltán Falvy, rattle,
bass rebec. LP, Hungaroton SLPX 12102, issued 1981.

CD ADD, HCD 12102-2.

Peire Vidal: Anc no mori; Baros de mon; Be·m pac
d'ivern; Ges pel temps; Neus ni glatz; Nulhs hom no·s;
Plus que·l paubres; Pois tornaz; Quant hom es en au-
trui; Quant hom honraz; S'ieu fos en cort; Tart mi
veiran; Pos vezem.

Introduction in English; original texts with French
translation only. 2 stanzas of each song performed;
the point is to give an idea of the melodies.

851
Troubadour Songs and Medieval Lyrics. Paul Hillier,
baritone, medieval harp; Stephen Stubbs, medieval
lute; Lena-Liis Kiesel, portative organ. LP, Hyperion
A66094, recorded 1982, issued 1984. CD, Hyperion
CDA66094, issued 1990.

Guiraut de Borneil: Reis glorios, verais lums e
clartatz. *Bernart de Ventadorn*: Can l'erba
fresch'e·lh folha par (6 stanzas and tornada; second
time instrumental); Be m'an perdut lai enves Ventadorn
(2 stanzas and tornada); Can vei la lauzeta mover (6
stanzas and tornada).

Introduction and notes in English. Original texts with
English translations. Instrumental accompaniments are
sometimes substantial, but projection of textual subtleties within carefully crafted melodic lines is
emphasized.

852
Troubadours. 3 volumes. Clemencic Consort, René
Clemencic, director. René Zosso, chant et vielle à
roue (vols. 1 & 3); Pilar Figueras, soprano (vol. 2);
Frederick Urrey, ténor (vols. 1 & 3); Michael Dittrich,
vièles; Andras Kecskes, rubebe, chitarra saracenica;
Anne Osnowycz, bûche, tintinnabulum (vol. 1); Frantisek
Pok, cornemuse, tambour à grelots (vols. 1 & 3); Esmail
Vasseghi, tympanon, tambour-calice, tambour; Yves
Rouquette, récitant; René Clemencic, flûte de berger,
galoubet, flûte à bec. LP, Harmonia Mundi HM 396,

recorded 1977, issued 1977 (vol. 3, 1978). CD ADD,
HMC 90396 (HM 90), abridged version containing Vol. 1
and the first part of Vol. 2.

Volume I: *Anonymous*: A l'entrada del temps clar.
Peirol: Quant Amors trobet partit. *Peire Vidal*: Vida
et Razos (recited); Barons de mon dan convit. *Bernart
de Ventadorn*: Quand vei la lauzeta mover. *Raimbaut de
Vaqueiras*: Vida (recited); Calenda maia.
Volume II: *La Comtessa de Dia*: Vida (recited); A chanter. *Azalais de Porcairagues*: Vida (recited); Ar em al
freg temps vengut (source of borrowed melody not giv-
en). *Bernart de Ventadorn*: Vida (recited); Can l'erba.
Folquet de Marselha: Vida (recited); Sitot me soi.
Guilhem de Cabestanh: Vida (recited).
Volume III: *Marcabrun*: Vida (recited); L'autrier jost'
una sebissa. *Raimon de Miraval*: Selh que non vol (instrumental). *Jaufre Rudel*: Vida (recited); Lanquan li
jorn.

The originality of this collection is to offer some
vidas recited in modern Occitan by Yves Rouquette. Pronunciation of the song texts also leans toward modern
Occitan. Texts with translation into French are provided for the LP volumes; texts only accompany the CD, and
the Comtessa de Dia texts are missing. Instruments are
used with all songs and recitations.

853
Troubadours. Louis-Jaques Rondeleux, baryton; Roger
Lepauw, vièle; Serge Depannemaker, tambourin; Jose-Luis
Ochoa, baryton. LP, Harmonia Mundi HMU 566 (no date
given).

Raimon de Miraval: Selh que no vol auzir cansos.
Guiraut Riquier: Jhesu Crist, filh de Diu viu.
Bernart de Ventadorn: Quan vei la laudeta mover.
Folquet de Marselha: En cantan m'aven a membrar.
Marcabru: L'autrier jost'una sebissa. *Gaucelm Faidit*:
Fort chausa aujatz, que tot lo major dan. *Peire
Vidal*: Pois tornatz sui en Proensa. *Jaufre Rudel*:
Lancan li jorn. *Guilhem Augier Novella*: Bella domna
cara. *Lo Monge de Montaudon*: Mout m'enoja s'o auzes
dire.

Commentary by Jean Maillard in French. No texts given. 2 stanzas of each song performed, frequently but not always with instrumental accompaniment and usually with regular rhythms.

854

Troubadours and Trouvères. Russell Oberlin, counter-tenor; Seymour Barab, viol. LP, Expériences Anonymes EA-0012, c.1958. [Also Vol. I of *Music of the Middle Ages*]. Reissued, CD, Lyrichord Early Music Series LEMS 8001, 1994.

Guiraut de Borneil: Reis glorios. *Guiraut Riquier*: Ples de tristor. *Arnaut Daniel*: Chanson do·ill mot. *Bernard de Ventadorn*: Can vei la lauzeta mover. *Gautier d'Epinal*: Commencemens de dolce saison bele. *Gace Brulé*: Cil qui d'amor me conseille.

Although it is now entirely out-of-date, for a number of years, this was the "reference" recording for trou-badours and trouvères because entire songs were in-cluded, performed in accordance with the theories of the time: melodies transcribed in modal rhythm; texts drawn from modern editions; discreet instrumental ac-companiment on the viol. Original texts and English translation for all songs provided.

855

Troubadours & Trouvères. Gérard Le Vot. CD AAD Studio SM 12 21.75 [SM 62], issued 1993. Includes all trou-badour pieces from LP 30 1043, SM 37 (D820) except Bertran de Born, "Raissa, tan creis," and all trouvère pieces from LP 3011.51, SM 37 (D821), except the anony-mous, "Bien m'ont amours entrepris" and "Molt ai esté long tens en esperance" by Joffroi de Chastillon. The CD has a new introduction in French, original texts for stanzas sung with French translations.

856

Trouvères, Troubadours, et Grégorien. L'Arche: Chanter-elle del Vasto, voice; Yves Tessier, voice; Mildred Clary, lute. LP, SM 30M - 419T, recorded c.1956.

Guiraut de Bornelh: Reis glorios. *Bernard de Ventadour*: Can vei la lauzeta. *Marcabru*: Pax in nomine
Domini; L'autrier jost'una sebissa. *Jaufré Rudel*:
Lanquan li jorn; Quan lo rossinhols. *Guillaume le
Viniers*: Vierge, pucele roiauz. *Anonymous*: C'est
là-bas; Ma vielle vieller veut un beau son; A la
clarté. *Guiraut Riquier*: Jésus-Christ; Aisi com es;
Humilz forfaitz. *Attribué au roi Saint-Louis*: Chanson
de mai.

2 or 3 stanzas of each song, performed in the original,
but only modern French translations given. No instrumental accompaniments used except, on occasion, a lute.
The interpretations of Chanterelle del Vasto are of
particular interest. Recently available as a cassette,
K438 SM35 (1987).

857
*I Trovatori nei castelli e nelle corti d'Europa dal
canzoniere provenzale Ambrosiano R71*. I Madrigalisti
di Genova, Leopoldo Gamberini, director. Grazielle
Benini, voce; Walter Benvenuti, liuto. 3 LPs, Ars
Nova C5S/155, issued 1979. Records listed separately
as VST 6190; 6191; 6192.

Record 1 (VST 6190). *Folquet de Marseilha*: Tan
m'abelis; En chantan; Ja nos cuich hom. *Bernart de
Ventadorn*: Non es meraveilla; Cant par la flor; Ben
m'an perdut; En consirer. *Gaucelm Faidit*: Lo gens cor.
Record 2 (VST 6191). *Gaucelm Faidit*: Lo roseignolet;
Jamais nulz tems; Chant e deport; Fort chausa ojatz.
Guiraudo Lo Ros: En greu pantais. *Peire Vidal*: Bem
pac d'invern; Anc no mori; Pos tornaz sui.
Record 3 (VST 6192). *Peirol*: D'un sonet vau pensan;
Per dan; Ab joi; Quan amor trobet partit. *Raimon de
Tolosa*: Atressi com la chandella. *Perdigon*: Trop ai
estat. *Raimon de Miraval*: Apena sai.

2 stanzas of each song performed. Emphasis is placed
on interpretations of the melodies. Introduction in
English with original texts and translations into
English. The lute is discreetly used to enhance the
melodic line.

858

Ultreia! sur la route de Saint-Jacques-de-Compostelle. A Pilgrimage to St. James of Compostella. Ensemble de Musique Ancienne Polyphonia Antiqua: Yves Esquieu, director. Yves Esquieu (un jongleur), chalemie, psaltérion, flûte à bec, carillon; Guy Laurent (un jongleur), chant (baryton), bombarde, flûte à bec, percussions; Marie-Hélène Coulomb (châtelaine, une villageoise, une Galicienne), chant, flûte à bec; Yves-Marie Deshays (un pèlerin), récitant, chant, orgue positif; Gilles Schneider (un pèlerin), récitant, chant (baryton), percussions; Magalie Bruzel (une villageoise, une Galicienne), chant, guitare sarrasine; Nicole Esquieu (une villageoise, une Galicienne), chant; with Frank Royon Le Mee (un pèlerin, un Galicien); chant (baryton et contre-ténor), vièle à archet, percussions. CD ADD, Pierre Verany PV.790042, recorded 1983, issued 1990.

Anonymous: Amour ou trop tard me suis pris; Chevaliers mult estes guariz (1 stanza). *Conon de Béthune*: Ahi amours, com dure departie (3 stanzas). *Colin Muset*: Sire cuens j'ai vielle.

This recording attempts to evoke the trip to Compostella. A kind of scenario is given in the introduction, in both French and English. Texts sung are provided in modern French only (no original language). Generous use of instruments.

THIRTEENTH-CENTURY INTERACTIONS: MONOPHONIC AND POLYPHONIC STYLES

859

Adam de la Halle, 13 rondeaux; 17 danses du 13e et 14e siècle. The Archiv History of European Music, The Central Middle Ages (1100-1350). Series C: Early Polyphony before 1300 and Series B: Music of the Minstrels. Pro Musica Antiqua (Brussels), Safford Cape, director. LP, Archiv Production ARC 3002, issued 1956.

Adam de la Halle: Li dous regars; Je muir; A jointes mains; Dieus soit en cheste maison; Hé Diex; Or est Baiars; A Dieu coman amouretes; Bonne amourete; Dame or suis trais; Fi maris; Dieux comment porroie; Fines amouretes; Trop desir. *Anonymous*: C'est là-gieus; C'est desoz l'olive; A l'entrada del tens clar (3 stanzas); Ainsi doit entrer en ville; Main se levoit Aëlis. *Raimbaut de Vaqueiras*: Kalenda maya (3 stanzas). *Guillaume d'Amiens*: Prendés-y garde.

Notes in English. Original texts but no translations. Performances illustrate styles prevalent in the 1950s.

860

Adam de la Halle and the 13th Century. Schola Cantorum of London, Edgar Fleet, director. LP, Harmonia Mundi HM 443, issued c.1975. [Also listed as *A Dictionary of Medieval Music*, Vol. 3 Harmonia Mundi HMF 440 (3), and as Vol. 3 of the Musical Heritage Society *History of European Music*, OR-351.]

Adam de la Halle: Li maus d'amer; Tant con je vivrai; Diex soit en cheste maison. *Petrus de Cruce*: Aucun ont trouve/Lonc tans; Je cuidoie bien metre/Si j'ai folement. *Anonymous*: Quant revient/L'autre jour; Huic main au doz mois en mai; Quant voi revenir; Trop souvent me deuille/Brunette a qui; On parole de batre/A Paris/Frese nouvele.

This is part of a series of recordings based on Archibald T. Davison and Willi Apel, *Historical Anthology of Music* (Cambridge, MA, 1946), where texts and transcriptions may be found.

861

Ars Antiqua Polyphony. Medieval Music--The Oxford Anthology of Music. Pro Cantione Antiqua, Edgar Fleet, director. LP, Peters PLE 115, issued 1978. [Further volumes projected but never issued.]

Anonymous: Quant florist/Non orphanum or El mois de mai/Et gaudebit; Cil s'entremet/Nus hom porroit/Victimae paschali. *Adam de la Halle*: Hé Diex! quant verrai.

These recordings accompany the *Oxford Anthology of Music: Medieval Music*, ed. W. Thomas Marrocco and Nicholas Sandon (Oxford University Press, 1977).

862
Chansons et Motets du 13e siècle. The Archiv History of European Music, The Central Middle Ages (1100-1350). Series A: Troubadours, Trouvères and Minnesingers. Pro Musica Antiqua (Brussels), Safford Cape, director. LP, Archiv Production ARC 3051, issued 1956.

Anonymous: L'autre jour/Au tens pascour/In saeculum; Chevauchoie lez un bruel; Chançonnète/A la cheminée/ Veritatem; Gaite de la tor; En un vergier; Prendés-y-garde/Hé mi enfant; Volez-vous que je vos chant; Dieus! je suis ja près de joïr/Et vide; Main se leva la bien faite Aelis. *Guiraut Riquier*: Pus sabers nom val ni sens. *Bernart de Ventadorn*: Lancan vei la folha. *Jaufré Rudel*: Lanquand li jorn.

Information and sources furnished with comments in English. Texts but no translations. Songs frequently performed without instruments. Performances illustrate styles prevalent in the 1950s.

863
The French Ars Antiqua. Music of the Middle Ages, Vol. VII. Saville Clark, musical director. Russell Oberlin, countertenor; Charles Bressler, Robert Price, tenors; Gordon Myers, baritone; Martha Blackman, vielle. LP, Expériences Anonymes EA-0035, issued 1960. Reissued 1994, CD, Lyrichord Early Music Series LEMS 8007.

Desconfortés ai esté/Amors qui m'a; Ne m'a pas oublié; Blanchete comme fleur/Quant je pens; J'ai si bien/ Aucun m'ont par; Qui amours/Li dous pensers/Cis a cui; Li doz/ Trop ai lonc/Ma loiauté; Ja n'amerai/Sire Dieus; J'ai mis/Je n'en puis; Povre secors/Gaude; Quant voi l'erbe/Salve, Virgo; Flor de lis/Je n'en puis/ Douce Dame; On parole/A Paris/Frese nouvelle; Dame, qui j'aim/Amors vaint/Au tans d'esté; Cest quadruble/ Voz n'i dormirés/Biaus cuers.

Motets from Mo H 196 transcribed by William Waite.

864

Frese Nouvele! Motetten in ars antiqua und ars nova: Vielfältigste Kunstform Gotischer Polyphonie. Musica Mensurata, Egbert Schimmelpfennig, director. Anita Weltzien, Gesang; Lucia Laake, Gesang; Werner Marschall, Gesang; Kai Roterberg, Gesang, Organistrum; Wilfried Staufenbiel, Gesang, Drehleier; Hans Martin Meckel, Blockflöten, Schalmei, Krummhorn; Egbert Schimmelpfennig, Fiedeln, Portativ, Krummhorn; Curt Lommatzsch, Posaunen alterMensur, Glockenspiel; with Irena Troupová, Gesang; Astrid von Brück, Schoßharfe; Stephan Maaß, Handtrommel. CD FSM, FCD 97736, tvd 9002.6, recorded 1990, issued 1990.

Anonymous: Quant voi revenir/Virgo virginum; Prennes i garde/S'on me regarde; A Paris/On parole; Ja n'amerai; Chançonete/Ainc voir d'amor/A la cheminee; L'autrier m'esbatoie/Demenant grant joie; Quant che vient en mai/Mout ai este (instrumental); Que ferai/Ne puet faillir; Je cuidoie/Se j'ai folement ame; Trois serors/Trois serors/Trois serors. *Petrus de Cruce*: Aucun ont trouve/Lonc tans me sui tenu. *Adam de la Hale*: Aucun se sont loe d'amour/A Dieu; Entre Adan/ Chief bien seantz (instrumental); Dame bele/Fi, mari (rondeau and motet attributable to Adam de la Halle). *Guillaume de Machaut*: De bon espoir/Puis que la douce.

Introduction in German only. No original texts or translations. Generous use of instruments.

865

Hare hare hye: Motetten des 13. Jahrhunderts. Schola vocalis. CD DDD, MDL Erika-Musikverlag CD1914, recorded 1991.

A collection of motets and conductus; texts in German translation only. The recording was not obtainable for review, but see John Caldwell, *Early Music* 21 (1993): 490.

866

The Marriage of Heaven and Hell. Motets and Songs from Thirteenth-Century France. Gothic Voices, Christopher Page, director. Margaret Philpot, alto; Rogers Covey-Crump, tenor; Rufus Müller, tenor; Leigh Nixon, tenor; Stephen Charlesworth, baritone; Christopher Page, medieval harp. CD DDD, Hyperion CDA66423, recorded 1990, issued 1990.

Anonymous: Je ne chant pas/Talens m'est pris/APTATUR/ OMNES; Trois sereurs/Trois sereurs/Trois sereurs/ PERLUSTRAVIT; Plus bele que flors/Quant revient/ L'autrier jouer/FLOS FILIUS EIUS; Par un matinet/Hé, sire!/Hé, bergier!/EIUS; De la virge Katerine/Quant froidure/Agmina milicie/AGMINA; A vous douce debonnaire; Mout souvent/Mout ai esté en dolour/MULIERUM; Quant voi l'aloete/Diex! je ne m'en partiré ja/NUEMA; En non Dieu/Quant voi la rose/NOBIS. Je m'en vois/Tels a mout/OMNES. *Blondel de Nesle*: En tous tans que vente bise. *Colin Muset*: Trop volentiers chanteroie. *Bernart de Ventadorn*: Can vei la lauzeta mover. *Gautier de Dargies*: Autres que je ne sueill fas.

This is a recording that both pleases and instructs. An introduction (in English) briefly describes the 13th-century motet and its social context. Original texts are provided with English translations. The performances emphasize voices alone. The high quality of these performances, and of the informative material in the booklet, the juxtaposition of troubadour and trouvère songs to related motets, all make of this CD an excellent resource for motet research.

867

Paris Médiéval: Musique de la Cité (XIIIe). Praetorius Consort, Christopher Ball, director. Nel Romano, Paul Arden Taylor, Nigel North, Alison Crum, Peter Vel. Purcell Consort of Voices, Grayston Burgess, director. Eileen Poulter, Elaine Barry, Martyn Hill, Ian Partridge, Ian Thompson, Geoffrey Shaw, Christopher Keyte. LP, Vox 36030, recorded 1973, issued 1974.

Adam de la Halle: De cuer pensieu (instrumental); En

mai, quant rosier. *Jehannot de l'Escurel*: Amours, cent
mille merciz. *Colin Muset*: Quant je voi yver retorner.
Pierre de la Croix: S'amours eust point de poer. *Anonyme*: Chançonnette; Dieus! qui porroit; Quant voi
l'aloete (instrumental); Amours dont je suis espris.

Introduction in English. Texts of stanzas sung given
in modern French only. Most songs accompanied by a
variety of instruments.

868
*Trouvères: Höfische Liebeslieder aus Nordfrankreich um
1175-1300. Courtly Love Songs from Northern France
c.1175-1300*. Sequentia: Barbara Thornton, voice,
symphonia; Benjamin Bagby, voice, harp, organetto;
Margriet Tindemans, fiddle, psalterium; with Jill
Feldman, voice; Guillemette Laurens, voice; Candace
Smith, voice; Josep Benet, voice; Wendy Gillespie,
fiddle, lute. LP (3 disks), Harmonia Mundi 1695013
(1C 3LP 157), issued 1984. CD DDD, 77155-2-RC, 2
disks, issued 1990. CD abridged as indicated below.

Conon de Béthune: Tant ai amé c'or me convient haïr.
Gace Brulé: Li consirrers de mon païs. *Blondel de
Nesle*: Onques maiz nus hom ne chanta. *Adam de la
Hale*: Bonne amourete me tient gai; Dame, or sui traïs;
Avoir cuidai engané le marchié; Se li maus c'amours
envoie; Diex, comment porroie; Tant con je vivrai;
Aucun se sont loé d'amours/A Dieu comment amouretes/
Super te (motet); A Dieu commant amouretes (rondeau);
On demande mout souvent qu'est amours (not on CD);
Hareu! li maus d'amer m'ochist; Dieux soit en cheste
maison; Amours m'ont si douchement (not on CD); J'ai
adès d'amours chanté et servi/Omnes (not on CD); Adan,
vous devés savoir (not on CD); De ma dame vient/Diex,
comment porroie/Omnes; En mai, quant rosier sont
flouri/L'autre jour, par un matin/Hé! resvelle toi
Robin; Merveille est quel talent j'ai (not on CD); Qui
a droit veut amours servir; Or est Baiars en la pas-
ture. *Jehannot de Lescurel*: Abundance de felonnie;
Dame, par vo dous regart (instrumental); Biétris est
mes delis; Gracieusette; Dame, par vo dous regart; Fi,
mesdisans esragié; Amours trop vous doi cherir; De la

grant joie d'amours; Amour, voulés vous accorder;
Belle, com loiaus amans (instrumental); A vous, douce
debonnaire; Comment que, pour l'éloignance; Dame vo
regars m'ont mis en la voie (not on CD); Diex, quant
la verrai; Bonnement m'agrée; Douce dame, je vous pri;
Guilleurs me font mout souvent. *Petrus de Cruce*:
S'Amours eust point de poer/Au renoveler du joli
tans/Ecce (not on CD); Je cuidoie bien metre jus/Se
j'ai folement amé/Solem; Aucun ont trouvé chant par
usage/Lonc tans me sui tenu de chanter/Annuntiantes.
Anonymous: Bele Doette as fenestres se siet; S'on me
regarde/Prennés i garde/Hé mi enfant; Bele Yolanz en
ses chambres seoit; Entre Copin et Bourgeois/Je me
cuidoie tenir/Bele Ysabelos. *French motets*: On the
tenor *Tanquam*: Tant grate chievre, que maugist; Qui
voudroit femme esprover/Tanquam agnus ductus/Tanquam
suscipit, vellus pluviam; On the tenor *Flos filius*:
Trois serors sor rive mer; Bele Aelis par matin se
leva/Haro, haro, je la voi la; Plus bele que flor
est/Quant revient et fuelle et flor/L'autrier joer
m'en alai.

The carefully studied performances and useful information provided in the booklet make this collection a
helpful introduction to trouvère song. Introduction
in English. Original texts with English translation.
Some pieces are performed with voices alone; for most,
instruments are generously used.

869
Weltliche Music um 1300. Secular Music circa 1300.
Studio der frühen Musik, Thomas Binkley, director.
LP, Telefunken SAWT 9504-A, issued c.1975.

Pierekins de la Coupele: Chançon faz non pas vilainne.
Moniot d'Arras: Ce fut en mai. *Anonymous*: Souvent
souspire (instruments only); La chasse/Se je chant; He
Marotele/En la praerie/Aptatur; El mois d'avril/O quam
sanctus/Et gaudebit; L'autre jour/Au tens pascour/In
seculum; Mout me fu grief/Robins m'aime/Portare.

870
The World of Adam de la Halle: Minstrel Music of the 12th

and 13th centuries. The Cambridge Consort, Joel Cohen, director. Sandra Stuart, soprano; Gian Lyman, viola da gamba; Alexander Silbiger, recorders, psaltery, percussion; Friedrich von Huene, flutes, recorders, rauschpfeif; Joel Cohen, lute, recorders, percussion; Daniel Collins, countertenor; Charles Fassett, tenor; Stephen Dinmock, bass; Frank Hoffmeister, tenor; Mark Baker, baritone. LP, TV-S 34439, issued 1972.

Guillaume d'Amiens: Prendes i garde; C'est la fins. *Adam de la Halle*: Le Jeu de Robin et Marion (sung portions); Je muir d'amouretes; Dieu soit en cheste maison; A dieu commant amouretes; Amours et ma dame; Bonne amourete; Li dous regars; Trop desir; Fines amouretes; Dame or suis trais; Dieus comment porroie; Tant can je vivrai; Fi maris; Or est Baiars. *Colin Muset*: En mai quant li rossignolet. *Bernard de Ventadorn*: Eram cosselhatz, senhor. *Gillebert de Berneville*: De moi dolereus. *Moniot d'Arras*: Ce fu en mai. *Anonymous*: En ma forest; S'on me regarde/Prenez i garde/He mi enfant; Volez-vous que je vous chant; Li jalous partout/Tuit cil qui sunt/Veritatem; Mout me fu grief/Robin m'aime/Portare.

No texts are furnished. Stanzaic songs are abridged. Most songs are accompanied by instruments.

FOURTEENTH CENTURY

871

Ars Magis Subtiliter. Secular Music of the Chantilly Codex. Ensemble Project Ars Nova: Michael Collver, countertenor, corno muto; Shira Kammen, vieille; Laurie Monahan, mezzosoprano; Crawford Young, lute; with Peter Becker, tenor; Randall Cook, vieille. CD DDD, New Albion NA 021, recorded 1987, issued 1989.

Johannes Symonis: Puisque je suis fumeux. *Jehan Suzay*: Pictagoras, Jabol et Orpheus. *Pierre des Molins*: De ce que foul pense (vocal and instrumental versions).

Anonymous: A mon pouir (instrumental); Medee fu en aimer veritable; Ha, fortune (instrumental). *Goscalch*: En nul estate (instrumental). *Solage*: Fumeux Fume par fumee. *Baude Cordier*: Tout par compas; Belle, bonne, sage (instrumental). *Grimace*: A l'arme, a l'arme. *Guillaume de Machaut*: Quant Theseus/Ne quier veoir. *Jean Vaillant*: Par maintes foys. *Fransiscus Andrieu*: Armes, Amours/O flour.

Introduction in English. Original texts of pieces sung with English translation. Complex repertory performed with aplomb and imagination.

872
Ars Nova, Le XIVᵉ siècle. Messe de Barcelone. Atrium Musicae de Madrid, Gregorio Paniagua, director. LP, Harmonia Mundi (France) HM 10/033, Musique d'abord (no date given).

From the Chantilly Codex:
Trébor: Quant joyne cuer; Se Alexandre et Hector (instrumental). *Borlet*: Ma trédol rossignol joly (instrumental); Hé, tres doulz roussignol joly. *Jacob de Senleches*: Fuions de ci; En ce gracieux tamps joli (instrumental).

Introduction and notes in French only. No original texts.

873
The Ars Nova. Music of the Middle Ages, Vol. IX. Capella Cordina: Alejandro Planchart, director. LP, Expériences Anonymous EAS 83. [1968] [Also issued as Musical Heritage Society MHS 899.]

Roman de Fauvel: Je voi douleur/Fauvel nous a fait présent/Autant m'est. *Philippe de Vitry*: Douce playsence/Garison selon nature/Neuma. *Guillaume de Machaut*: S'il estoit nulz/S'amour/Et Gaudebit; Se quanque amours. *Jacob de Senleches*: En ce gracieux temps. *Solage*: Fumeux fume par fumee. *Matteo de Perugia*: Le greygnour bien.

Notes in English on the cover. Original texts with English translations.

874

L'Art des Jongleurs. 2 vols. <u>Ensemble TRE FONTANE</u>: Maurice Moncozet, flûtes, chalemie, bombarde, bendir; Pascal Lefeuvre, vielle à roue, tambourin; Jacky Détraz, derbouka, tablas, bendir, saz, tambourin, tambour à anneaux. CD DDD, Vol. 1, TRFC 0187, Vol. 2, SCA 470 / TRFC 0389, recorded 1989.

14th-century French and Italian music, including several pieces of Machaut, *all* performed instrumentally.

875

L'Art musical et poétique de Guillaume de Machaut: Motets, Ballades, Virelays; Le Remede de Fortune; Le Veoir Dit. <u>Ensemble Guillaume de Machaut de Paris</u>, Guy Robert, director. Jean Belliard, countertenor; Bernard Huneau, recorders, crumhorns; Elisabeth Robert, lutes; Julien Skowron, fiddles; with Armie Bartelloni, contralto; Alain Zaepffel, countertenor; Jean-Claude Veilhan, recorders, crumhorns. LP, Adès 7079/80 (3 LPS), issued 1977; CD ADD, Adès 13.294-2, 13.295-2 [ACD 14077-2], issued 1991. 2 discs.

Disc 1. Comment qu'a moy lointeinne; Bone pastor Guillerme; Ma fin est mon commencement. *Le Remede de Fortune:* Qui n'auroit (lai); Tels rit au main (complainte); Joie, plaisence (chanson roiale); Dame de qui (ballade); Dame a vous (virelai); En amer (baladelle); Dame mon cuer (rondelet).
Disc 2. Pour quoy me bat mes maris; Honte, paour, doubtance (instrumental); Sanz cuer/Amis dolens/Dame par vous; Quant je sui mis au retour; Quant en moy/ Amour et Biaute; Double Ballade D'Andrieu (poème de E. Deschamps): Deploration sur la mort de Machaut. *Le Veoir Dit:* Douce dame jolie; Récitation: Lors pour alleger; Ploures dames; Recitation: Je vous envoie une ballade; Se medisants; Je ne cui pas; Nes que on porroit les estoiles nombrer; Quant Theseus/Ne quier veoir; Lay de Bonne Esperance; Recitation; Dix et Sept, Cinc; Recitation: J'ai veu le rondel; Moult sui de

bonne heure nee.

Originally published as an LP set of three records and
a booklet. For the CD, both the contents of the booklet
and the recordings have been shortened. The introduction to the CD, extracted from the original booklet, is
in French only. No original texts or translations are
furnished for the CD; texts but no translations are in
LP booklet. All pieces include instruments, and instrumental preludes and pieces performed instrumentally
are interspersed. The order of pieces for the *Remede*
does not follow the work. Some pieces taken from elsewhere have been added to the *Veoir Dit*. Includes some
recitation.

876
*The Art of Courtly Love. Machaut and His Age. Late 14th-
Century Avant Garde. The Court of Burgundy. 3 vols.*
Early Music Consort of London, David Munrow, director.
LP, EMI Seraphim SIC 6092 (3), issued 1973.

Volume I: Machaut and His Age.
F. Andrieu: Armes, amours/O flour des flours. *Jehan
de Lescurel*: A vous douce debonnaire. *Guillaume de
Machaut*: Hareu! hareu/Hélas! ou sera pris confors;
Amours me fait desirer; Trop plus est belle/Biauté
paree/Je ne sui (voices only); Se je souspir; Dame se
vous m'estes (instruments only); Quant je suis mis;
Mes esperis se combat; Ma fin est mon commencement
(instruments only); Douce dame jolie; De bon espoir/
Puis que la douce; De toutes flours (instruments only);
Quant Theseus/Ne quier veoir; Quant j'ay l'espart;
Phyton, le merveilleux serpent. *Pierre des Moulins*:
Amis tous deux (instruments only).
Volume II: Late Fourteenth Century Avant Garde.
Grimace: A l'arme a l'arme. *Franciscus*: Phiton,
Phiton. *Borlet*: Hé, très doulz rosignol; Ma tredol
rosignol (attributed to Borlet). *Solage*: Fumeux fume;
Hélas! je voy mon cuer. *Johannes de Meruco*: De home
vray. *Johannes Vaillant*: Tres doulz amis/Ma dame/Cent
mille fois (voices only). *Pykini*: Plasanche or tost.
Anthonello de Caserta: Amour m'a le cuer mis. *Matheus
de Perusio*: Andray soulet (instruments only); Le

greygnour bien (instruments only). *Johannes Simon
Hasprois*: Ma douce amour. *Anonymous*: Contre le temps;
Restoés, restoés.

Introduction in English. Original texts with English
translations. Instruments used for all songs, except
as noted.

877

*Ce diabolic chant. Ballades, Rondeaus and Virelais of the
late 14th century.* The Medieval Ensemble of London,
directed by Peter Davies and Timothy Davies. Margaret
Philpot, alto; Rogers Covey-Crump, tenor; Paul Elliott,
tenor; Michael George, baritone; Geoffrey Shaw, baritone; Robert Cooper, rebec, fiddle; Peter Davies,
douçaine, harp; Timothy Davies, gittern, lute. LP,
L'Oiseau-Lyre DSDL 704, issued 1983.

Suzoy: Prophilias; A l'arbre sec; Pictagoras, Jabol.
Jacob Senleches: Je me merveil/J'ay pluseurs fois; En
ce gracieux tamps; Fuions de ci; La harpe de melodie;
En attendant esperance; Tel me voit. *Guido*: Dieux
gart; Or voit tout. *Johannes Olivier*: Si con cy gist.
Johannes Galiot: Le sault perilleux; En atendant
d'avoir. *Anonymous*: En albion; Se j'ay perdu.

Brief introduction in English. Original texts sung (for
the ballades, one stanza) are provided, with English
translations.

878

Codex Chantilly: Airs de Cour du XIVe siècle. Ensemble
Organum, Marcel Pérès, director. Gérard Lesne, haute-
contre; Josep Benet, ténor; Josep Cabré, baryton;
François Fauché, basse; Nanneke Schapp, vièle; Marcel
Pérès, clavicythéirum Emil Jobin. LP, Harmonia Mundi
HMC 1252 [HM59], recorded 1986, issued 1987. CD HMC
901252.

Cunelier: Se Galaas et le puissant Artus. *Guido*:
Dieux gart; Or voit tout. *Baude Cordier*: Tout par
compas; Belle, bonne, sage. *Goscalch*: En nul estat.
Senleches: La harpe de mellodie (instrumental).

Solage: Fumeux fume par fumée. *F. Andrieu*: Armes, amours. *Anonymous*: Sans joie avoir (instrumental); Toute clerté; Adieu vous di.

Introduction in English. No original texts, only modern French translations. Songs are abridged.

879
Codex Faenza, Italie, XVe siècle. Ensemble Organum, Marcel Pérès, director. Gérard Lesne, haute-contre; Josep Benet, ténor; Josep Cabré, baryton; Malcolm Bothwell, basse. CD DDD, Harmonia Mundi HMC 901354, recorded 1990, issued 1991.

Vocal works. *Guillaume de Machaut*: De toutes flours; Honte, paour, doubtance. *Anonymous*: J'ay grant désespoir de ma vie.
Instrumental works based on the vocal works. Le ior; De toutes flours; Honte, paour, doubtance; J'ay grant désespoir de ma vie.

The two parts of this disc present 14th-century songs and then keyboard pieces based on them. Introduction in English. Original texts with English translations.

880
Douce Dame: Music of Courtly Love from Medieval France and Italy. Waverly Consort, Michael Jaffe, director. LP, Vanguard VSD 71179, issued 1974.

Guillaume de Machaut: Douce dame jolie; Comment qu'a moy; Foy porter; Je suis aussi; Rose, liz, printemps. *Vaillant*: Par maintes foys; Or sus, vous dormez trop.

Brief notes on the record jacket. Texts not included.

881
Febus Avant! Music at the Court of Gaston Febus (1331-1391). Huelgas Ensemble, Paul Van Nevel, director. Irène Heuvelmans, Cantus; Cecile Roovers, Cantus; Carol Schlaikjer, Cantus; Marie-Claude Vallin, Cantus; Godfried Van de Vyvere, Cantus; Katelijne Van Laethem, Cantus; Marius Van Altena, Baritone, Tenor; Harry Van

der Kamp, Bassus; Kees-Jan de Koning, Bassus; with Wim
Becu, Trumpet; Bart Coen, Alto Recorder, Tenor Record-
er, Bass Recorder; Peter de Clercq, Basset Recorder,
Double Bass Recorder, Tenor Recorder; Baldrick
Deerenberg, Tenor Recorder, Bass Recorder; Simen Van
Mechelen, Alto Sackbut; Harry Ries, Alto Sackbut,
Tenor Sackbut; An Van Laethem, Fiddle. CD DDD, Sony
Vivarte SK 48195, recorded 1991, issued 1992.

Anonymous: Le Mont Aon de Thrace; Tres dous compains.
Trebor: En seumeillant. *Solage*: Fumeux fume. *Johannes
Cuvelier*: Se Galaas.

Introduction in English. Original texts with English
translations. Detailed notes on performance.

882
*The Garden of Zephirus: Courtly Songs of the Early Fif-
teenth Century*. Gothic Voices, Christopher Page,
director. Gill Ross, soprano; Margaret Philpot,
contralto; Rogers Covey-Crump, tenor; Andrew King,
tenor; John Mark Ainsley, tenor; Leigh Nixon, tenor;
with Imogen Barford, medieval harp. LP, Hyperion
A66144, recorded 1984, issued 1985. CD DAD, CDA66144,
issued 1986.

From the Chantilly Codex:
Gacien Reyneau: Va t'en, mon cuer, avant mes yeux.
Matheus de Sancto Johanne: Fortune, faulce, parverse.

Introduction in English situates the 14th-century
styles in relation to the 15th-century works to which
the disc is chiefly devoted. Original texts with English translations.

883
Guillaume de Machaut: Chansons. 2 vols. Studio der
frühen Musik, Thomas Binkley, director. Andrea von
Ramm, mezzo-soprano, harp, organetto (vol. 2); Richard
Levitt, countertenor, glockenspeil (vol. 2); Sterling
Jones, fiddle, lyre, organetto, rebec (vol. 2); Thomas
Binkley, lute, tambourine, guittern (vol. 2), recorder
(vol. 2), douçaine (vol. 2); with, for Vol. 1,

Dominique Bello, Patricia Calamaro, Marie-Paule
Canonia, Jacqueline Grieb, Tania Kestinsky, Jacqueline
Magro, Said Saida, Denise Vial, chorus. LP, Reflexe
EM1 Electrola, 1 C 063-30 106, recorded in Marseille
1971, issued 1972; 1 C 063-30-109, recorded 1972,
issued 1973. CD ADD, CDM 7 63142 2, digital
remastering, 1989; CD ADD, CDM 7 63424 2, digital
remastering, 1990.

Volume I: Ay mi!; Loyauté, que point ne delay (a-
bridged); Comment qu'a moy lonteinne; Quand je sui;
Joie, plaisence; Tels rit au main (abridged); Dame, a
vous; Le lay de la fonteinne.
Volume II: Moult sui de bonne heure nee; Quand
Theseus, Hercules et Jason; Doulz viaire gracieus;
Honte, paour, douptance (two versions, one instrumental); De toutes fleurs (two versions, one instrumental); Quant en moy/Amour et biauté parfaite;
Comment puet on mieus ses maus dire; Dame je suis
cilz/Fins cuers dousz.

Volume I contains monophonic songs performed with
voices (including chorus of women's voices from
Marseille for "Quant je sui," "Dame, a vous" and the
"Lay de la fonteinne") and generous use of instruments. Pieces from the *Remede de Fortune* are framed by
brief Old French readings. Introduction in English.
Original texts of stanzas sung and recited passages
furnished with German translation only. Volume II is
devoted to polyphonic works, performed with combinations of voices and instruments. Introduction in English. Original texts provided with German translation
only.

884
*Guillaume de Machaut: La Messe Nostre-Dame; L'Amour
Courtois.* Ars Antiqua de Paris, Michel Sanvoisin,
director. Joseph Sage, countertenor; Hugues Primard,
tenor; Pierre Eyssartier, tenor; Marc Guillard, baritone; Michel Sanvoisin, recorders; Philippe Matharel,
cornet; Raymond Cousté, guitar; Colette Lequien, viele;
Marie Jeanne Serero, organ. CD DDD, Edelweiss (Nimbus)
ED 1021, recorded 1990, issued 1990.

Trop plus/Biauté parée/Je ne sui; Dame, ne regardés
pas (instrumental); Dame, se vous m'estes lonteinne;
De toutes flours (instrumental); Ma chiere dame; Quant
Theseus/Ne quier veoir; Ce qui soutient moy (instrumental); Ma fin est mon commencement; Rose, liz; Douce
dame jolie; Plus dure que un dyamant (instrumental).

Considerable use of instruments. Disc not available
for review.

885
*Guillaume de Machaut. La Messe de Nostre Dame; 9 secular
works.* Schola Cantorum Basiliensis, August Wenzinger,
director. LP, Archiv Production 2533 054, recorded
1969, issued 1970.

Guillaume de Machaut: De petit po; Doulz viaire
gracieus; Donnez, signeurs; De toutes flours (organ
only); Rose, lis, printemps; Mes esperis se combat;
Dame, vostre doulz viaire; Dame, comment; Quant je ne
voy ma dame.

Notes in English. Original texts with English translations. Instruments used with all pieces. [Inside the
cover, this record is connected to Archiv's *History of
European Music, The Central Middle Ages*, Series D: The
Ars Nova in France, below.]

886
*Guillaume de Machaut: La Messe de Nostre Dame; 10 Secular
Works. The Archiv History of European Music, The Central Middle Ages (1100-1350).* Series D: The Ars Nova
in France. Pro Musica Antiqua (Brussels), Safford
Cape, director. LP, Archiv Production ARC 3032, issued 1956.

Secular Works: Sans cuer/Amor doleur/Dame par vous; Je
puis trop bien; Qui est promesses/Ha! Fortune/Et non
est qui adjuvet; Puis qu'en oubli; De tout sui si
confortée; Nes que porroit les estoilles nombrer; De
triste cuer/Certes je di/Quant vrais amans; Se je
souspir; Tels rit au main (abridged); Quant Théséus/ne
quier véoir.

Introduction and information about sources in English. Original texts but no translations.

887
Guillaume de Machaut: Messe de Notre Dame; Le Lai de la Fonteinne; Ma fin est mon commencement. The Hilliard Ensemble, Paul Hillier, director. David James, Ashley Stafford, countertenors; Rogers Covey-Crump, John Potter, Mark Padmore, Leigh Nixon, tenors; Paul Hillier, Michael George, basses. CD DDD, Hyperion CDA66358, recorded 1987 and 1989, issued 1989.

Introduction in English. Original texts with English translations. Excellent performances (one of the best available for the Mass).

888
Guillaume de Machaut: 2 Polyphonic Lais. The Medieval Ensemble of London, Peter Davies and Timothy Davies, directors. Rogers Covey-Crump, tenor; Paul Elliot, tenor; Andrew King, tenor; Robert Cooper, fiddle and rebec; Peter Davies, psaltery and harp; Timothy Davies, gittern and lute. LP, L'Oiseau-Lyre DSDL 705, issued 1983.

Le lay de la fonteinne; Un lay de consolation.

Introduction in English. Original texts with English translations.

889
Homage to Johannes Ciconia. Secular Music of Johannes Ciconia, ca. 1370-1412. Ensemble Project Ars Nova: Michael Collver, countertenor, corno muto; John Fleagle, tenor, harp; Shira Kammen, vielle; Laurie Monahan, mezzosoprano; Crawford Young, lute; with Steven Lundahl, slide trumpet. CD DDD, New Albion NA 048, recorded and issued 1992.

Aler m'en veus; Poy che morir; Le ray au soleyl (vocal and instrumental versions); Sus une fontayne.

French, Italian, and non-liturgical Latin works of

Ciconia. Introduction in English. Original texts sung
are provided, with English translations.

890
The Island of St. Hylarion, Music of Cyprus 1413-1422.
Ensemble Project Ars Nova: Michael Collver, counter-
tenor, corno muto; John Fleagle, tenor, harp; Shira
Kammen, vielle; Laurie Monahan, mezzosoprano; Crawford
Young, lute; with Peter Becker, tenor; Karen Clark-
Young, mezzosoprano; Randall Cook, vielle; Steven
Lundahl, slide trumpet; Margaret Raines, mezzoso-
prano. CD DDD, New Albion NA 038, issued 1991.

Contre dolour; Tousjours (instrumental); Aspre
Fortune; Qui de Fortune (instrumental); Je prens
d'amour; Bonne e belle (instrumental); Qui n'a le
cuer; J'ai mon cuer (instrumental); J'ai maintes fois
(instrumental); Moult fort me plaist; Pymalion qui
moult subtilz estoit; Si doucement (instrumental).

Introduction in English. Original texts with English
translations (two stanzas for all ballades).

891
J'ai pris amours. Isaak Ensemble Heidelberg, Michael
Valentin, director. Eva Lebherz-Valentin, sopran;
Bethli Dürr, gamben; Martin Hinrichs, laute; Eva
Schildknecht, cembalo, virginal, orgelpositiv. CD
DDD, Bayer Records BR 100 164, recorded 1990, issued
1991.

Guillaume de Machaut: Loyauté, que point de ne delay.

Introduction in German. Original texts with German
translations. The first two strophes of the lai are
performed with voice alone.

892
Johannes Ciconia. Studio der frühen Musik, Thomas
Binkley, director. LP, Reflexe EM1 Electrola 1C
063-30 102, issued 1972.

Le ray au soleyl; Sus un'fontayne; Aler m'en veus.

Introduction in English. Original texts with German translation only. "Aler m'en veus" with voices only. Instruments used elsewhere.

893
Johannes Ciconia. 14th-Century Motets, Virelais, Ballate, Madrigals. Alla Francesca & Alta. CD DDD, Opus 111 OPS30-101, recorded 1993, issued 1994.

Sus une fontayne; Poy che morir; Aler m'en veus. Disc not available for review.

894
Johannes Ciconia & His Time. Little Consort: Lucia Meeuwsen, mezzo-soprano; Walter van Hauwe, flustes, traverseinne; Toyohiko Satoh, mediaeval lute, lute, cetra, viella; Kees Boeke, viella, flustes. CD DDD, Channel Classics CCS 0290, issued 1990.

Johannes Ciconia: Sus une Fontayne. *Phillipot de Caserta*: En remirant. *Solage*: Hélas, je voy mon cuer.

Includes also a number of Italian songs by Ciconia. Introduction in English. Original texts but no translations. Notes on performance and text underlay.

895
Lancaster and Valois. French and English music, 1350-1420. Gothic Voices, Christopher Page, director. Margaret Philpot, alto; Rogers Covey-Crump, tenor; Andrew Tusa, tenor; Charles Daniels, tenor; Leigh Nixon, tenor; Stephen Charlesworth, baritone; Dongald Greig, baritone; Andrew Lawrence-King, medieval harp; Christopher Page, medieval lute. CD DDD, Hyperion CDA66588, recorded 1992, issued 1992.

Guillaume de Machaut: Donnez, signeurs; Quand je ne voy; Riches d'amour; Pas de tor en thies pais. *Anonymous*: Puis qu'autrement ne puis avoir; Soit tart, tempre, main ou soir; Le ior (harp only); Avrai je ja de ma dame confort?; Je vueil vivre au plaisir d'amours. *Cesaris*: Mon seul voloir/Certes m'amour; Se vous scaviez, ma tres douce maistresse. *Solage*: Tres gentil cuer. *Baude Cordier*: Ce jour de l'an.

Excellent introduction (in English) on musical styles
and performance practices. Original texts sung with
English translations.

896
*Little Consort & Frans Brüggen, Guillaume de Machault,
Le Lay de Confort.* Frans Brüggen, fluste; Walter van
Hauwe, fluste; Kees Boeke, fluste, vielle, psalterium;
Lucia Meeuwsen, soprano; Toyohiko Satoh, mediaeval
lute, cistre. CD DDD, Channel Classics CCS 0390,
recorded 1988, issued 1990.

Anon: Très doulx compains (instrumental). *Guillaume
de Machault*: Le Lay de Confort.

Introduction in English. Original text with English
summary given in the introduction. "Speculative" (it
is so announced) performance of the "Lay": everything
is performed twice, with voice and recorders, stretching the piece out to a very long forty minutes.

897
*The Medieval Romantics. French Songs and Motets, 1340-
1440.* Gothic Voices, Christopher Page, director.
Margaret Philpot, alto; Rogers Covey-Crump, tenor;
Andrew Tusa, tenor; Charles Daniels, tenor; Leigh
Nixon, tenor: Stephen Charlesworth, baritone; Donald
Greig, baritone; Andrew Lawrence-King, medieval harp,
Christopher Page, medieval lute. CD DDD, Hyperion
CDA66463, recorded 1990, issued 1991.

Anonymous: Quiconques veut d'amors joïr; Je languis
d'amere mort; Quant voi le douz tans/En mai/
[Immo]LATUS; Plus bele que flors/Quant revient/L'autrier jouer/FLOS FILIEU EIUS; Mais qu'il vous viengne
a plaisance. *Guillaume de Machaut*: C'est force, faire
le weil; Tant doucement me sens emprisonnes; Comment
qu'a moy lonteinne. *Paolo Tenorista*: Sofrir m'estuet
et plus non puis durer. *Jacob de Senleches*: En ce
gracieux tamps joli. *Solage*: Joieux de cuer en
seumellant estoye.

Introduction in English comparing the musical styles of the 14th and early 15th centuries represented on the recording. Performance notes call attention to practices of vocalising textless lines and *a cappella* renditions. Original texts with English translations.

898

The Mirror of Narcissus: Songs by Guillaume de Machaut (1300-1377). Gothic Voices, Christopher Page, director. Emily van Evera, soprano; Margaret Philpot, contralto; Rogers Covey-Crump, tenor; Andrew King, tenor; Colin Scott Mason, baritone; Peter McCrae, baritone; Emma Kirkby, soprano. LP, Hyperion A66087, recorded 1983, issued 1983. CD DDD, CDA66087, issued 1987.

Guillaume de Machaut: Dame, de qui toute ma joie vient; Foy porter; Dame, je suis cilz/Fins cuers doulz; Tuit mi penser; Dame, mon cuer en vous remaint; Dame, a qui; Biauté qui toutes autres pere; Je vivroie liement; Rose, liz, printemps, verdure; Dame, a vous sans retollir; Amours me fait desirer; Douce dame jolie.

Because this was the first recording to advocate exclusively vocal performances for 14th-century music, it presents important evidence for study of text/music relationships. Brief introduction in English. Original texts with English translations.

899

Music of the Late Middle Ages and Early Renaissance, History of European Music (D795), Vol. IV. London Ambrosian Singers, Trinity Boys Choir, David Squibb, chorus master, Denis Stevens, Musical Director. LP, Musical Heritage Society OR 437 [1970?].

Guillaume de Machaut: S'il estoit nulz/S'amours tous amans joir/ET GAUDEBIT; Je puis trop bien; Comment qu'a moy; Plus dure que un dyamant. *Jacopin Selesses*: En attendant. *Baude Cordier*: Amans ames; Belle bonne.

Texts are published in the *Historical Anthology of Music* by Archibald T. Davison and Willi Apel

(Cambridge, MA, 1946).

900
Philippe de Vitry and the Ars Nova. 14th-Century Motets.
The Orlando Consort: Robert Harre-Jones, countertenor;
Charles Daniels, tenor; Angus Smith, tenor; Donald
Greig, baritone. CD DDD, Amon Ra CD-Sar 49, recorded
1990, issued 1991.

Se je chant. Douce playsence/Garison selon nature.

This disc contains most of the motets now attributed
to Vitry. Only one of these, "Douce/Garison," is in
the vernacular, taking love as its subject. "Se je
chant" is a canon. Introduction in English. Original
texts with English translations.

901
Philippe de Vitry, Motets and Chansons. Sequentia,
Benjamin Bagby and Barbara Thornton, directors.
Benjamin Bagby, voice, harp; Barbara Thornton, voice;
Patricia Neely, fiddle; with Edmund Brownless, voice;
Michael Collver, voice; David Cordier, voice; Stephen
Grant, voice, organ; Eric Mentzel, voice. CD ADD,
Deutsche Harmonia Mundi 77095-2-RC, recorded 1988,
issued 1991.

Philippe de Vitry: Je qui paoir seule ai de conforter;
Ay, amours! tant me dure; Providence la senee; Talant
j'ai que d'obeir; Se j'onques a mon vivant; Douce
playsance est d'amer loyament/Garison selon nature.

Introduction in English. Original texts with English
translations. Contains a wide selection of pieces
attributed to Vitry, of which only those in the
vernacular are listed here.

902
*Pour l'amour. Liebeslieder des 14. und 15. Jahrhunderts.
Love Songs from the 14th and 15th Century.* Almut
Teichert-Hailperin, sopran; Kevin Smith, countertenor;
Wilfried Jochens und Martin Nitz, tenors; Instrumental-
kreis Helga Weber. CD ADD, Christophorous CHE 0042-2,

recorded 1980, issued 1993.

Guillaume de Machaut: Biaute qui toutes (instrumental);
Quant Theseus/Ne quier veoir (1 double stanza).

Brief introduction in English. Original text of stanza
performed is provided, with German translation only.
"Quand Theseus" is performed with two tenors, two recorders, and two gambas.

903
Le Roman de Fauvel. Clemencic Consort, René Clemencic,
director. René Zosso, récitant et vielle à roue;
Zeger Vandersteene, contre-ténor; Mieczyslaw Antoniak,
contre-ténor; Pedro Liendo, baryton-basse; René
Clemencic, flûte de corne, flûte à bec, flûte de berger, peigne musical; Andràs Kécskès, luth, psaltérion,
rubebe, guimbarde; Wolfgang Reithofer, percussions,
tympanon, jeu de clochettes, tintinabulum; Michael
Dittrich, vièle, rebec; Renate Hildebrand, bombarde;
Frantisek Pok, cornet à bouquin, cornemuse, trompette
marine. CD ADD, Harmonia Mundi France HMC 90994,
recorded 1975, issued 1976 (first as LP), reissued
Musique d'abord 190994, 1992.

Favellandi vicium. Porchier miex estre, Vers 1-48.
Mundus a mundicia. Quare fremuerunt. Vers 49-62;
69-96. Veritas arpie. Vers 97-116; 123-148. In mari
miserie. Vers 149-168. Ad solitum vomitum. Vers
229-258. Porchier miex estre, Vers 259-280. Virtus
moritur. Vers 301-318; 395-398; 1126-1135. Fauvel
nous a fait présent; Vers 317-324. Porchier mieux
estre ameroie. Vers 1219-1240. Ade costa
dormientis. J'ai fait nouveletement. Douce dame.
Gaude Favellus. Charivari (sottes chansons). Vers
5815-5842; 5849, 5850. Quoniam secta latronum. Vers
5905-5926; Mario, virgo virginum. Vers 6023-6060.
Omnipotens domine. Vers 6051-6056; Jhesu, du dator
venie. Vers 6065-6074; Bon vin.

A mixture of singing, half-chanted recitation and
simple recitation (in modernized Old French), with
instrumental accompaniments and interludes.

Introduction in English. Original texts; no translations.

904

Roman de Fauvel. Studio der frühen Musik, Thomas
Binkley, director. Jean Bollery, sprecher; Andrea von
Ramm, mezzosopran und harfe; Willard Cobb, tenor;
Richard Levitt, altus; Lucy Craig, soprano; Sterling
Jones, lira und fidel; Thomas Binkley, laute; Karl-
Heinz Klein, bariton; Robert Eliscu, schalmei; Caroline
Bergins, schalmei. LP, Reflexe EMI Electrola 1C 063-30
103, issued 1972.

Extracts spoken and sung, from the *Roman de Fauvel.*
Introduction in English. Original texts given as
performed, with translation into German only. Side 1
draws material from Gervais du Bus; side 2 from
Chaillou's revisions.

905

Sacred and Secular Music from six centuries. The
Hilliard Ensemble, Paul Hillier, director. David
James, countertenor; Rogers Covey-Crump, tenor; John
Potter, tenor; Paul Hillier, baritone; Michael George,
bass. CD DDD, Hyperion CDA66370, recorded 1987-89,
issued 1990.

Guillaume de Machaut: Quant je suis mis.

Original text, English translation.

906

*The Service of Venus and Mars: Music for the Knights of
the Garter, 1340-1440.* Gothic Voices, Christopher
Page, director. Margaret Philpot, alto; Rogers
Covey-Crump, tenor; John Mark Ainsley, tenor; Leigh
Nixon, tenor; Peter Harvey, baritone; Colin Mason,
baritone; with Andrew Lawrence-King, medieval harp.
LP, Hyperion A66238, recorded 1986, issued 1987. CD,
CDA66238, 1987.

Pierre des Molins: De ce que fol pense. *Anonymous:* De
ce fol penser (after Pierre des Molins: instrumental).

Franchois Lebertoul: Las, que me demanderoye. *Richard Loqueville*: Je vous pri que j'aye un baysier (instrumental). *Anonymous*: Le gay playsir (instrumental); Le grant pleysir (instrumental).

Introduction delineates the French influences on music in England to which this disc is chiefly devoted. Original texts sung are provided, with English translations.

907
A Song for Francesca, Music in Italy, 1330-1430. Gothic Voices, Christopher Page, director. Margaret Philpot, contralto; Caroline Trevor, alto; Rogers Covey-Crump, tenor; John Mark Ainsley, tenor; Leigh Nixon, tenor; Christopher Page, medieval harp; Andrew Lawrence-King, medieval harp. CD DDD, Hyperion CDA66286, recorded 1987, issued 1988.

Richard Loqueville: Puisque je suy amoureux (harp); Pour mesdisans ne pour leur faulx parler (harp); Qui ne veroit que vos deulx yeulx (harp). *Hugo de Lantins*: Plaindre m'estuet. *Jean Haucourt*: Je demande ma bienvenue. *Estienne Grossin*: Va t'ent souspir. *Anonymous*: Confort d'amours.

Compares Italian and French repertories cultivated in Italy around 1400. Introduction in English. Original texts with English translations.

908
The Study of Love. French Songs and Motets of the 14th century. Gothic Voices, Christopher Page, director. Margaret Philpot, alto; Rogers Covey-Crump, tenor; Andrew Tusa, tenor; Julian Podger, tenor; Leigh Nixon, tenor; Stephen Charlesworth, baritone; Donald Greig, baritone; Andrew Lawrence-King, harp. Christopher Page, lute. CD DDD, Hyperion CDA66619, recorded and issued 1992.

Machaut: Dame, je suis cilz/Fins cuers; Trop plus/ Biauté paree/Je ne suis; Tres bonne et belle; Se mesdisans; Dame, je vueil endurer. *Anonymous*: Pour

vous servir; Puis que l'aloe ne fine; Jour a jour la
vie; Combien que j'aye (with voice and instruments, and
with harp alone); Marticius qui fu; Renouvele me feïst;
Fist on dame; Il me convient guerpir; Le ior (Faenza
codex; instrumental); En la maison Dedalus; La grant
biauté; En esperant; Ay las! quant je pans. *Solage*:
Le basile.

Informative introduction in English. Original texts
with English translations. Excellent interpretations.

909
*Le vray remède d'amour. Ballades, Rondeaux, Virelais,
Motets et Textes dits de Guillaume de Machaut.*
Ensemble Gilles Binchois, Dominique Vellard, director. Anne-Marie Lablaude, vocalist; Brigitte Lesne,
vocalist, harp, tabor; Dominique Vellard, vocalist,
lute; Emmanuel Bonnardot, vocalist, medieval fiddle;
Jean-Paul Raccodon, narrator; Pierre Hamon, recorders,
bagpipe, medieval transverse flute; Randall Cook,
medieval fiddle. CD DDD, Harmonic Records H/CD 8825,
recorded 1988, issued 1988.

Je, Guillaumes (text read: Le Jugement du Roy de
Navarre); Dame, vostre doulz viaire; Amours qui ha le
pouoir/Faus samblant m'a deceu; Je vivroie liement
(instrumental); Ce qui soustient moy; La, firent mains
divers acors (text read: Le Remède de Fortune); Dame
se vous m'estes lonteinne (instrumental); Je ne cuit
pas; Doulz viaire gracieus; Qui des couleurs (text
read: La louange des dames); Puisqu'en oubli; Dame ne
regardes pas (instrumental); Doulz amis; Long sont mi
jour (text read: Le livre du Voir-dit); Tels rit au
main (instrumental); Liement me deport; Dès quon
porroit (text read: Le livre du Voir-dit); De toutes
flours; Mon cuer, ma suer (text read: Le livre du
Voir-dit).

English translation of introduction appended. Original
texts, no translations.

REFERENCE

910
Barker, John W. *The Use of Music and Recordings For Teaching About the Middle Ages: A Practical Guide, With Comprehensive Discography and Selective Bibliography.* Kalamazoo: Medieval Institute Publications, 1988.
Comprehensive survey of recordings with a particularly useful Discographic Register organized alphabetically by label including almost all medieval recordings from the 1950s to the late 1980s.

911
Coucher, Trevor. *Early Music Discography From Plainsong to the Sons of Bach.* 2 vols. Phoenix, AZ: The Oryx Press, 1981.
Vol. 1 is a Record Index. Vol. 2 contains Composer, Plainsong, Anonymous, and Performer Indexes. Discs indexed are not numerous, but contents are given.

912
Crist, Larry S. and Roger J. Steiner. "*Musica Verbis Concordet*: Medieval French Lyric Poems with their Music: A Discography." *Mediaevalia* I (1975): 35-51.
Listings of LP albums and of author/composers with song titles to show where songs can be found.

913
Maillard, Jean. "Troubadours et trouvères: Pour une approche discographique." *Revue internationale de musique française* 1 (1980): 403-23.
Critical discussion of recording styles and techniques, followed by lists of composers, song titles, and discs.

914
Milsom, John. "Recordings: Recent Releases of Medieval Monody and Polyphony." *Plainsong and Medieval Music* 1 (1992): 111-21.
Review article followed by a listing of 34 discs. Such review articles with listings are scheduled to appear each year in this journal.

See also B28.

SUPPLEMENT TO RECORDINGS

915

Ars Subtilis Ytalica: Polyphonie pseudo française en Italie, 1380-1410. Mala Punica: Pedro Memelsdorff, flauto; Kees Boeke, flauto, viella; Christophe Deslignes, organetto; Karl-Ernst Schröder, liuto; Jill Feldman, canto; Héctor Rodriguez, canto. CD DDD, Arcana A21, recorded 1993, issued 1994.

Anthonello de Caserta: Dame d'onour (instrumental); Amour m'a le cuer mis; Beauté parfaite (instrumental); Dame zentil. *Matteo de Perusio*: Le greygnour bien. *Magister Zacharias*: Sumite karissimi.

Songs are taken from the Modena manuscript. Introduction and original texts with English translations. Instrumental and vocal effects are exploited to create a sonorous atmosphere that one could almost term decadent.

916

Le Chant des Troubadours, Vol. 1: *Les Troubadours Aquitains*. Tre Fontane: Jean Luc Madier, chant, tambourin à cordes, mandole; Hervé Berteaux, flûtes, cromorne, chalémie; Thomas Bienabe, oud; Pascal Lefeuvre, vielle à roue; Maurice Moncozet, flûtes, chalémie; Jacques Detraz, tablas, tambour à anneaux, bendhir, derbouka. CD ADD, ADDA 590128, recorded 1991.

Guillaume de Poitiers: Companho, faray un vers descovinen; Pos de chantar. *Marcabru*: Lo vers commenssa (instrumental); L'autrier, a l'essida d'abriu; Bel m'es quan son li fruch madur; L'autrier jost'una sebissa and Pax in nomine Domini (presented as part of a "suite instrumentale"); Dirai vos senes duptansa; Lo vers comens quan vei del fau. *Jaufré Rudel*: Lanquan li jorn son long en mai (instrumental); No sap chantar; Quan lo riu (presented as part of a "suite instrumental"); Quan lo rossinhols. *Anonymous*: Ven, aura douça; S'anc vos amei. *Guilhem de Figuiera*: No·m laissarai per paor. *Gausbert Ameil*: Breu vers per tal.

Most melodies are freely invented (where none exist)
or varied (where we have melodies). Excessive use of
instrumental "arrangements." The disc is useless for
scholarly research. Original texts with translation
into French only.

917
Le Chant des Troubadours, Vol. 2: *Les Troubadours du
Périgord*. Ensemble Tre Fontane: Jean Luc Madier,
chant; Hervé Berteaux, flûtes, cornamuses; Maurice
Moncozet, flûtes, chalémie; Pascal Lefeuvre, vielle à
roue; Thomas Bienabe, oud; Jacques Détraz, tambour à
anneaux, daf, bendhir, derbouka. CD ADD, Alba musica
ADDA 590 130 [WMD 872 596], recorded 1993.

Arnaud de Mareuil: La grands beutats e·l fins
ensenhaments; L'ensenhaments e·l prètz e la valors.
Bertrand de Born: Rassa, tan creis; Ai! Lemosin;
Chasuts sui de mal en pena. *Arnaud Daniel*: Sestina
(Lo ferm voler); Chançon do·lh mot son plan e prim.
Guiraud de Bornelh: Reis gloriós; Non puèsc sofrir
qu'a la dolor; Lèu chançoneta e vil.

Introduction and translations of original texts in
French only. Many of the songs are "arranged" in one
way or another: texts abridged, melodies adapted (for
Bertran de Born) where none has been preserved,
instruments freely added. Songs are interpreted by
Jean Luc Madier whose native Occitan pronunciation
provides the main interest of the disc.

918
*Les Escholiers de Paris: Motets, Chansons et Estampies
du XIIIe siècle*. Ensemble Gilles Binchois, Dominique
Vellard, director. Anne-Marie Lablaude, chant,
percussions; Brigitte Lesne, chant, harpe, percussions; Susanne Norin, chant; Dominique Vellard, chant,
guiterne; Emmanuel Bonnardot, chant, rebec, vièle;
Willem de Waal, chant, flûte; Pierre Hamon, flûtes,
flûte traverseine, cornemuses, percussions; Randall
Cook, vièle, chalemie, flûte. CD DDD, Harmonic

Records H/CD9245, recorded 1992, issued 1992.

Anonymous: Cele m'a tolu la vie/Lonc tens a que ne vi
m'amie/Et sperabit; Ave deitatis templum mirabile/Cele
m'a tolu la vie/Lonc tens a que ne vi m'amie/Et
sperabit; Cil qui aime et n'est a soi/Quant chantent
oisiaus tant seri/Portare; Puisque bele dame
m'eime/Flos filius eius; Par un matinet l'autrier/Hé,
sire! qui vos vantez/Hé, bergier! si grant envie/
Eius; N'en puis ma grant joie celer; Viderunt/Viderunt
omnes; Trois serors sor rive mer; J'ai les maus
d'amours/Que ferai biau sire Diex/In seculum; Que
ferai biaus sire Dieus/Ne puet faillir a honour/
Descendentibus; Endurez, endurez les dous maus
d'amer/Alleluia;Onques n'amai tant com je fui
amee/Sancte Germane; Hélas! tant vi de male eure.
Thibault de Champagne: De ma dame souvenir fait amors
lie mon coraige; Dou tres douz non a la virge Marie.
Gillebert de Berneville: Haute chose a en amour. *Gace
Brulé*: Douce dame, grez et graces vos rent; Biaus
m'est esté quant retentit la bruille.

Excellent presentation of motets and songs. With *The
Mariage of Heaven and Hell* (D866), offers a rich
conspectus of the 13th-century motet (only two pieces
are on both discs). The considerable but usually
judicious use of instruments is the chief stylistic
difference between this recording and the work of
Gothic Voices with Christopher Page. Informative
introduction with English translation. Original texts
with French translation only.

919
*Gérard Zuchetto chante les troubadours XIIe et XIIIe
siècles*, vol. 3: *Tensons e partimens de Trobairitz*.
Gérard Zuchetto, Katia Caré, Gisela Bellsolà, chant;
Patrice Brient, psaltérion, chiffonie, rebec; Guy
Robert, luth médiéval, oud, harpe. CD DDD, Gallo
CD-769, recorded 1993, issued 1993.

Domna H.: Rosin, digatz. *Na Lombarda*: Lombards
volgr'eu esser per na Lombarda. *Anonymous* [attributed
to Raimbaut d'Aurenga]: Amics, en gran cossirier.

Supplement / 391

Maria de Ventadorn: Gui d'Ussel, be·m pesa de vos.
Isabella: N'Elias Cairel, de l'amor. *Guillelma de
Rosers*: Na Guillelma, man cavalier arratge.

Modern musical settings with considerable emphasis on
"improvisation." The disc is useless for scholarly
research.

920
*Love's Illusion. Music from the Montpellier Codex,
13th-Century.* Anonymous 4: Ruth Cunningham; Marsha
Genensky; Susan Hellauer; Johanna Rose. CD DDD,
Harmonia Mundi HMU 907109, recorded 1993-4, issued
1994.

Plus bele que flor/Quant revient/L'autrier joer/FLOS
FILIUS; Puisque bele dame m'eime/FLOS FILIUS; Amours
mi font souffrir/En Mai/FLOS FILIUS; Ne sai, que je
die/IOHANNE; Se je chante/Bien doi amer/ET SPERABIT;
Or ne sai je que devenir/Puisque d'amer/KYRIELEYSON;
Hé Dieus, de si haut si bas/Maubatus/CUMQUE; Celui en
qui/La bele estoile/La bele, en qui/IOHANNE; Qui
d'amours se plaint/LUX MAGNA; Amours, dont je
sui/L'autrier, au douz mois/Chose Tassin; Au cuer ai
un mal/Ja ne m'en repentirai/Jolietement; Quant voi la
fleur/ET TENUERUNT; Quant se depart/Onques ne sai
amer/DOCEBIT OMNEM; Joliement/Quant voi la florete/Je
sui joliete/APTATUR; Ce que je tieng/Certes mout/Bone
compaignie/MANERE; J'ai si bien mon cuer assiz/Aucun
m'ont/ANGELUS; Ne m'oubliez mie/DOMINO; J'ai mis toute
ma pensee/Je n'en puis/PUERORUM; Blanchete/Quant je
pens/VALARE; Dame, que je n'os noumer/Amis donc
est/Lonc tans a; Li savours de mon desir/Li grant
desir/Non veul mari; Entre Copin/Je me cuidoie/Bele
Ysabelos; S'on me regarde/Prennés i garde/Hé, mi
enfant; Quant yver la bise ameine/IN SECULUM; Ne m'a
pas oublié/IN SECULUM; On doit fin[e] Amor/La
biauté/IN SECULUM; Ja n'amerai autre que cele/IN
SECULUM; Quant je parti de m'amie/TUO.

A separate booklet provides an introduction in English
and original texts with English translations. This
introduction has a number of errors and misleading

statements. Performances are purely vocal raising the issue of how these pieces sound sung by women. Some pieces are sung more than once: the motetus part of the first motet, for example, is heard alone, then the full motet is heard twice but this performance order is not specified for the listener. Drones and doublings are occasionally added. Performances display the ensemble qualities for which the group is noted.

921
Musique Médiévale du Bassin Meditérrannéen. Duo Wayal: Hayet Ayad, chant, percussions; Nannette van Zanten, vièle, flûte, harpe, viole de gambe. CD, WA 001, recorded (in concert), 1991.

Raimbaut de Vaqueiras: Kalenda maya. *Cadenet*: S'anc fuy belha ni prezada.

Neither introduction nor texts provided. Complete songs performed.

922
Remede de Fortune, Guillaume de Machaut (1300-1377). Ensemble Project Ars Nova: Michael Collver, alto, symphonia; John Fleagle, tenor, harp; Shira Kammen, vielle; Laurie Monahan, mezzosoprano; Crawford Young, lute; with Robert Mealy, vielle. CD DDD, New Albion NA068CD, recorded 1993, issued 1994.

Music from the *Remede de fortune* and other works of Guillaume de Machaut. Biaute paree de valour (instrumental); Lai: Qui n'aroit autre deport; Liement me deport (instrumental); Complainte: Tels rit; Chant royal: Joie, plaisance; Baladelle: En amer a douce vie; Toute Flour (instrumental); Ballade: Dame, de qui toute; Danse balladée (instrumental); Chanson balladée: Dame a vous; Rondelet: Dame mon cuer en vous remaint; Rondeau: Rose Liz.

Introduction in English. Original texts with English translations. The rondelet is performed without instruments. Interpretations combine some artistic license with respect to the music and thoughtful renditions of the texts.

923

*The Spirits of England and France-I: Music of the later
Middle Ages for Court and Church.* <u>Gothic Voices</u>,
Christopher Page, director. Rogers Covey-Crump,
tenor; Paul Agnew, tenor; Julian Podger, tenor; Andrew
Tusa, tenor; Leigh Nixon, tenor; Stephen Charlesworth,
bass; Henry Wickham, bass; with Pavlo Beznosiuk,
medieval fiddle. CD DDD, Hyperion CDA66739, recorded
1994, issued 1994.

Part I The Fourteenth and Fifteenth Centuries.
Anonymous: Quant la douce jouvencelle; En cest mois de
May; *Matteo da Perugia*: Belle sans per. *Guillaume de
Machaut*: Ay mi! dame de valour. *Pykini*: Plaisance, Or
tost.
Part II The Twelfth and Thirteenth Centuries.
Anonymous: Je ne puis/Par un matin/Le premier
jor/JUSTUS.

This is the first of a series of recordings that will
explore French and English music between the 12th and
15th centuries. Each recording will cover the entire
period. This disc includes Latin as well as vernacular
songs. [It was not yet available for review.]

924

The Unicorn: Anne Azéma. Medieval French Songs. Anne
Azéma, voice; Cheryl Ann Fulton, harps; Shira Kammen,
vielle, rebec, harp; Jesse Lepkoff, flute. CD DDD,
Erato 4509-94830-2, recorded 1993, issued 1994.

Gautier de Coinci: Miracles de Notre Dame (Le Cycle de
Sainte Leochade). *Moniot de Paris*: Je chevauchoie.
Thibaut de Champagne: Aussi come unicorne. *Anonymous*:
En mai au douz tens nouvel; Ensement com la panthere;
Belle Doette.

Original and beautifully executed recording. Contains
also some readings from Marie de France and Philippe
de Thaon with music adapted by Joel Cohen.

INDEX OF INDIVIDUAL POET/COMPOSERS, MEDIEVAL THEORISTS, TITLES OF SONGS AND OTHER WORKS

References to all medieval writers/composers and their works are included here.

Song titles are normally complete or abbreviated first lines. Spellings are regularized where necessary.

Medieval names are listed under the first name, unless the last name is more commonly recorded (e.g., Bernart de Ventadorn or Guillaume de Machaut, but Ciconia, Johannes). Language-specific spellings are observed (e.g., "Guillaume" for Old French, "Guilhem" for Old Occitan).

Alphabetization follows the letter-by-letter method. Capitals are used for names, italics for works, ordinary roman for song titles.

Main entries for songs and works are placed under the title. Where there is an author/composer, that name appears in parentheses following the title; a cross-reference is also placed under the name.

References to Bibliography or Discography are to item numbers. The following conventions are used:
1) Page numbers alone refer to the Introduction
2) Item numbers with "B" refer to the Bibliography
3) Item numbers with "D" refer to the Discography.

Ab greu cossire (Bernart Sicart de Marjevols), D811
Ab joi et ab joven m'apais (Beatritz de Dia), D815, D829
Ab joi mou lo vers (Bernart de Ventadorn), 96, B500, B510, D814, D846
Ab la dolchor (Guilhem de Peitieu), D829
Ab la genser que sia, B595

GENERAL INDEX

In cross-references, IPC means Index of Individual Poet/Composers.
Page numbers refer to the Introduction; item numbers preceded by B to
the Bibliography; item numbers preceded by D to the Discography.

AARSLEFF, HANS, 157n.66
ABBATE, CAROLYN, B405
ABRAMOWICZ, MACIEJ, B447
Académie Royale des In-
   scriptions, 27-8
accent, 85-93, 97, B388,
   B588, B589. See also
   rhythm; versification;
   Leys d'amors
actio, 140
ADLER, GUIDO, 61-2, 104,
   105
AGUSTIN, JAVIER DE, B448
AKEHURST, F.R.P., B83
alba, 124, B593, B594,
   B595, B596
ALEMBERT, JEAN LE ROND DE,
   36, 155n.36
ALEXANDRESCU, SORIN, B701
allegory, B533, B534
ALLEN, JUDSON BOYCE, B377
ALTENBURG, DETLEF, B611
ALTON, JEANNINE, B444
ALZA, JOSÉ-LUI OCHOA DE,
   D834
AMBROS, AUGUST WILHELM, 49,
   52
analysis, 60-1, 67, 68,
   110, 111, 114, 135-7,
   138, 142, B90, B391,
   B410, B640, B641, B709,

B710, B712, B731, B732,
   B735, B752, B784. See
   also composition, tech-
   niques of; language and
   music
Ancients and Moderns, Quar-
   rel of the, 23, 27, 36,
   37, 40
ANDERSON, GORDON A., B308,
   B309, B656, B771
ANDRIEUX-REIX, NELLY, B33,
   B34
ANGLADE, JOSEPH, B35, B36,
   B182, B256
ANGLÉS, HIGINIO, B245, B269,
   B305
Antiquity, influence of Re-
   naissance revival of, 23,
   30
APEL, WILLI, 80, 153n.9,
   B329, B330
APPEL, CARL, 52, 54, 85,
   B229, B230, B236
Arabic influence, B496
ARENS, ARNOLD, B449
ARIZCUREN, FRANCISCO J.
   OROZ, B449
ARLT, WULF, 76, 77, 107,
   113, 115, 116, 117, 125,
   151, B68, B360, B368,
   B378, B379, B380, B381,

frühe Musik, D786; Florilegium Musicum of Paris, D799; Folger Consort, D807; Fraternitas Musicorum, D850; Gothic Voices, D840, D866, D882, D895, D897, D898, D906, D907, D908, D923; Hespèrion XX, D815; Hilliard Ensemble, D808, D887, D905; Huelgas Ensemble, D881; Isaak Ensemble Heidelberg, D891; Kalenda Maya, D836; Kecskés Ensemble, D830; Little Consort, D894, D896; London Ambrosian Singers, D899; I Madrigalisti di Genova, D857; Mala Punica, D915; Martin Best Mediaeval Ensemble, D826, D837, D844, D846; La Maurache, D822; Medieval Ensemble of London, D877, D888; Musica Mensurata, D864; Musica Reservata, D797; Orlando Consort, D900; Praetorius Consort, D867; Pro Cantione Antiqua, D861; Pro Musica Antiqua (Brussels), D787, D803, D859, D862, D886; La Romanesca, D839; Schola Cantorum Basiliensis, D885; Schola Cantorum of London, D793, D798, D860; Schola vocalis, D865; Sequentia, D810, D868, D901; Sinfonye, D813, D824, D845; Sonus, D804; Studio der frühen Musik, D806, D809, D811, D814, D818, D819, D842, D869, D883, D892,

D904; Studio für alte Musik, Düsseldorf, D791; Theatre of Voices, D843; Tre Fontane, D916, D917; *See also* Ensemble Tre Fontane; Trinity Boys Choir, D899; University of Chicago Collegium Musicum, D794; Waverly Consort, D880; Western Wind, D808
ensenhamen, B453
ERICKSON, RAYMOND, B170
ESQUIEU, YVES, D858
estampie, 124, 126, B469, B487. See also *Kalenda maya* (IPC)
EUSEBI, MARIO, B128, B223
EVANS, BEVERLY, 98, 126, 168n.211, B667, B668
EVERIST, MARK, xx, 127, 130, 138, 154n.15, 159n.105, 162n.134, B90, B116, B129, B413, B669, B670, B671, B672
EWERT, ALFRED, B40

FALLOWS, DAVID, B76, B106
FALVY, ZOLTÁN, B493, B494
FARAL, EDMOND, B174
FASSLER, MARGOT E., 153n.5, B388
fatras, B779
FAUCHET, CLAUDE, 25
FAUCON, JEAN-CLAUDE, B328
FAULHABER, CHARLES, 81
feminism, 147, B505, B511. *See also* gender
FENLON, IAIN, B122
FENOALTEA, DORANNE, B714
FERNANDEZ DE LA CUESTA, ISMAEL, B217
FERNANDEZ, MARIE-HENRIETTE, 107, B389, B495, B496

PRESSOUYRE, LÉON, B197, B399
PRÉVOST, PAUL, B768
printing: and authenticity, 21; and author's original, 21, 56; and editing, 69-70; and historicism, 21, 22, 25; music, 25-7; and reproducibility, 21; and standardization, 21-2, 56, 73. See also authenticity; author
pronuntiatio, 140, 141
PROUT, EBENEZER, 62
Provençal. See Occitan
psychoanalysis (critical approaches), 62, B461, B481
PULEGA, ANDREA, B604
PULIDO, ALEJANDRO, 102, 169n.219, B766

QUÉRUEL, DANIELLE, B72
QUEUX DE SAINT-HILAIRE, A., B176
Quintillian, 121

RAHN, JOHN, B687
RAJNA, PIO, 42
RÄKEL, HANS-HERBERT, 107, B605, B606, B607
RANAWAKE, SILVIA, B606, B608
RANDEL, DON MICHAEL, 117, 167n.200, B26, B767
RASTALL, RICHARD, B442
RAUGEI, ANNA-MARIA, B288
RAYNAUD, GASTON, 44, 45, B28, B107, B115, B176, B295, B313
RAYNAUD DE LAGE, GUY, B8, B48
RAYNOUARD, FRANÇOIS-JUST-

MARIE, 29, 39-40, B52, B60
razo, 17-18, 144, B195, B453, B566, B592
REA, JOHN A., B609
reader (reading), 64, B612, B614
reader-response criticism, 62, 145
REANEY, GILBERT, B106, B108, B109, B158, B171, B768
reception of troubadour song in Italy, 18, 19-20
reception theory, 65, 67, 121, 144, 162n.144, B512, B566, B585, B612, B614, B774
REESE, GUSTAVE, 53, 54
refrain, 125, 130-1, 132, 143, B30, B490, B523, B658, B661, B676, B678, B683, B692, B695, B724, B725, B742. See also
formes fixes, romances with lyric insertions
refrain cento, 127, B667, B670, B672
REGALADO, NANCY FREEMAN, 100, 101, 166n.191, B98, B118, B769
register, 106, 107, 108, 122
RÉGNIER, CLAUDE, B38
REID, T.B.W., B562
RELIHAN, JOEL C., B316
REMY, PAUL, B99
reproducibility (of sound), 152; electronic edition, 70, 81-2; mechanical reproduction, 64; mechanical vs. electronic reproduction, 67, 171n.245. See also printing
RESTANI, DONATELLA, B706, B708